{ THE GREAT MOVIES }
II

OTHER BOOKS BY ROGER EBERT

An Illini Century

A Kiss Is Still a Kiss

Roger Ebert's Movie Home Companion (1986–1993)

A Perfect London Walk *(with Daniel Curley)*

Two Weeks in the Midday Sun: A Cannes Notebook

Behind the Phantom's Mask: A Serial

Roger Ebert's Video Companion (1994–1998)

Ebert's Little Movie Glossary

Roger Ebert's Book of Film: A Norton Anthology

Questions for the Movie Answer Man

Roger Ebert's Movie Yearbook (1999–)

Ebert's Bigger Little Movie Glossary

I Hated, Hated, Hated This Movie

The Great Movies

DVD COMMENTARY TRACKS

Beyond the Valley of the Dolls

Dark City

Casablanca

Citizen Kane

Floating Weeds

THE
{ GREAT MOVIES }
II

ROGER EBERT

Photo Stills Selected by Mary Corliss,
Former Assistant Film Curator, Museum of Modern Art

Broadway Books

New York

Film stills appear courtesy of Photofest.
Photo still from *Sunrise* courtesy of Springer/Photofest.

PRINTED IN THE UNITED STATES OF AMERICA

Visit our website at www.broadwaybooks.com
Visit Roger Ebert's website at www.suntimes.com/ebert

Previous versions of these essays have appeared in the *Chicago Sun-Times*, 2001–2004.

First edition published 2005

Book design by Maria Carella

Library of Congress Cataloging-in-Publication Data

Ebert, Roger.
  The great movies II / Roger Ebert; photo stills by Mary Corliss.—1st ed.
    p. cm.
  1. Motion pictures. I. Title: Great movies 2. II. Title: Great movies two.
III. Corliss, Mary. IT. Title.
PN1994.E232 2005
791.43'75—dc22   2004054574

ISBN 0-7679-1950-5

10 9 8 7 6 5 4 3 2 1

For Chaz

My love for you is immeasurable
My respect for you immense
You're ageless, timeless, lace, and fineness
You're beauty and elegance

CONTENTS

Contents

Contents

INTRODUCTION

This is the second *Great Movies* book, but the titles in it are not the second team. I do not believe in rankings and lists and refuse all invitations to reveal my "ten all-time favorite musicals," etc., on the grounds that such lists are meaningless and might well change between Tuesday and Thursday. I make only two exceptions to this policy: I compile an annual list of the year's best films, because it is graven in stone that movie critics must do so, and I participate every ten years in the *Sight & Sound* poll of the world's directors and critics.

As I made clear in the introduction to the first *Great Movies* book, it was *not* a list of "the" 100 greatest movies but simply a collection of 100 great movies—unranked, selected because of my love for them and for their artistry, historical role, influence, and so on. I wrote the essays in no particular order, inspired sometimes by the availability of a newly restored print or DVD.

To be sure, the first book includes such obviously first-team titles as *Citizen Kane, Singin' in the Rain, The General, Ikiru, Vertigo,* the Apu trilogy, *Persona, 2001: A Space Odyssey, Battleship Potemkin, Raging Bull,* and *La Dolce Vita.* But because I was not writing in any order, this second volume contains titles of fully equal stature, including *The Rules of the Game, Children of Paradise, The Leopard, Au Hasard, Balthazar, The Birth of a Nation, Sunrise, Ugetsu, Kieslowski's* Three Colors Trilogy, *Tokyo Story, The*

Searchers, and *Rashomon*. In the case of the first two titles, I delayed a *Great Movie* review until new DVDs were available and felt with both *The Rules of the Game* and *Children of Paradise* that the prints had been so wonderfully restored that I was essentially seeing the movies for the first time.

I have cited before the British critic Derek Malcolm's definition of a great movie: any movie he could not bear the thought of never seeing again. During the course of a year I review about 250 films and see perhaps 200 more and could very easily bear the thought of not seeing many of them again, or even for the first time. What a pleasure it is to step aside from the production line and look closely and with love at films that vindicate the art form.

The DVD has been of incalculable value to those who love films, producing prints of such quality that the film can breathe before our eyes instead of merely surviving there. The supplementary material on some of them is so useful and detailed that today's audiences can know more about a title than, in some cases, their directors knew when they were made. Of all directors, Martin Scorsese has been the leader in assembling commentary tracks and supplementary materials, not only for his own films but for others he loves; consider his contribution to the DVDs of the films of Michael Powell, notably in this book *The Life and Death of Colonel Blimp*. To listen to Powell and Scorsese as they watch the film together is a rare privilege.

I have seen these movies in various times and places and ways, many of them three or four times, some a dozen or twenty-five times. I've been through sixteen of them a shot at a time, in sessions I conduct annually at the universities of Colorado, Virginia, and Hawaii and at film festivals. The Colorado screenings, part of the Conference on World Affairs, have been an annual event for going on thirty-five years. We sit in the dark in Macky Auditorium, sometimes as many as a thousand of us, and take ten or twelve hours over five days to go through a film with a stop-action analysis. Remarkable what you can see with all of those eyes.

Consider my experience in 2003 with Ozu's masterpiece *Floating Weeds*, which was included in the first book and which I once went through shot by shot at the side of the great critic Donald Richie at the Hawaii Film Festival. In 2003 Criterion invited me to contribute a commentary track to their DVD of the film; Richie would do the commentary on Ozu's earlier silent version. I asked myself frankly whether I could talk for two hours about a film in which the director never once moves his camera; with Ozu it is all placement, composition, acting, and editing. I suggested to Kim Hendrickson of Criterion that we take *Floating Weeds* to Boulder as a sort of dress rehearsal. Some of the audience members were less than thrilled by my choice, but then a wonderful thing happened: Ozu's aura enveloped the audience, his genius drew them into his work, and his style was seen not as "difficult" but as obviously the right way to deal with his material and sensibility. At the end of the week, the watchers in that room loved Ozu, some of them for the first time; sooner or later, if you care for the movies enough, you get to Ozu and Bresson and Renoir and stand among the saints.

In 2004 I proposed Renoir's *Rules of the Game* at Boulder, and again the greatness of the film persuaded the reluctant ones in the audience (they had hoped for *Kill Bill*—which would, for that matter, also have been a good choice). The more closely you look at Renoir's film, the better it becomes. There are intricate movements of camera and actors that reveal astonishing depths of beauty. The scene in the upstairs corridor when everybody turns in for the night took us more than an hour to deal with, and even then we could have continued. At the end of the week, I wrote about *The Rules of the Game* for this book.

I look over the titles and my memory stirs. I saw *Kind Hearts and Coronets* in London, during a revival of Ealing comedies. A restored print of *The Leopard* was playing in London at the beloved Curzon Cinema. *The Man Who Laughs* played at the Telluride Film Festival, with a live score by Philip Glass. *My Dinner with Andre* was also at Telluride, and when the lights went up I found myself sitting right in front of Andre Gregory and Wallace Shawn, whom I wouldn't have recognized two hours earlier. I saw *Patton* on a giant screen in the seventy-millimeter Dimension 150 projection system at my own Overlooked Film Festival at the University of Illinois, and after the screening Dr. Richard Vetter, the inventor of the system, joined me onstage and said he had never seen it better projected. *Romeo and Juliet* brought back memories of my night on the Italian location for the filming of the balcony scene.

Touchez Pas au Grisbi was in revival in Seattle in December 2003, when I spent a month in the city for medical treatment, and it and many other movies lifted me far above my problems. I arrived at the film via *Bob le Flambeur*, which is also in this book; anyone who knows both films will understand how and why. *Breathless* seemed as fresh to me in 2003 as it did when I saw it the first time forty years earlier. Viewing *Bring Me the Head of Alfredo Garcia* for the first time since I put it on my annual best-ten list in 1974, I was relieved to discover that I was absolutely correct about its greatness.

The most difficult film to deal with was Griffith's *The Birth of a Nation*. It contains such racism that it's difficult to press ahead with the undoubted fact of its artistry and influence. I sidestepped it for the earlier book; having taught it in my University of Chicago class, I dreaded dealing with it again. In the event, I wrote a two-part consideration of it, the first part essentially an apologia. For this book I have combined and rewritten that material. It is the only film in this book that doesn't, for me, pass the Derek Malcolm test.

One of my delights in these books, on the other hand, has been to include movies not often cited as "great"—some because they are dismissed as merely popular (*Jaws, Raiders of the Lost Ark*), some because they are frankly entertainments (*Planes, Trains and Automobiles, Rififi*), some because they are too obscure (*The Fall of the House of Usher, Stroszek*). We go to different movies for different reasons, and greatness comes in many forms.

Of course there is no accounting for taste, and you may believe some of these titles don't belong in the book. The reviewer of the first volume for the *New York Times Book Review* ignored the introduction and the book jacket and persisted in the erroneous belief that it was a list of "*the*" 100 greatest movies. He felt such a listing was fatally compromised by my inclusion of Jacques Tati's *Mr. Hulot's Holiday*—which was not, he declared, a great film. Criticism is all opinion, so there is no such thing as right and wrong—except in the case of his opinion of *Mr. Hulot's Holiday*, which is wrong.

My gratitude to my friend of many years, Mary Corliss, who once again drew on her unequaled archival knowledge in selecting still photographs to reflect the essence of the 100 films. Mary, her husband, Richard, my wife, Chaz, and I have had countless and endless movie conversations at Cannes, where we always stay right down the hall from each other at Madame Cagnet's legendary Hotel Splendid.

Thanks also to Gerald Howard, my editor, who inspired the Norton anthology *Roger Ebert's Book of Film* and at Broadway Books has been the steadying hand for the *Great Movies* books. His knowledge of film is encyclopedic, his taste is sure. When I hesitated to include *A Christmas Story*, despite my boundless affection for it, he assured me he could not imagine the book without it.

ROGER EBERT

THE FIGHT

FOR PRESERVATION

I live in the past." With these words I began my essay in the first volume of *The Great Movies*. I was describing my job as assistant curator of the Museum of Modern Art's Film Stills Archive, where since 1968 I had organized and expanded the museum's collection of movie photographs. It was in the Stills Archive that I learned to appreciate these frozen testaments to a film's ravishing visual style and to an actor's ephemeral beauty, though each might be generations old. As stills preserved those qualities on paper and saved them for generations to come, so my colleague Terry Geesken and I worked lovingly to care for those images and make them available to the public. Working in the Stills Archive was an open invitation to informed nostalgia.

Today I feel nostalgic for a more recent past—three years ago. When I wrote that plangent declaration of love for my job, I did not know that I would soon lose it—even worse that the Film Stills Archive would, without warning, be closed down on January 11, 2002. The world's most comprehensive trove of movie stills would be accessible neither to the researchers, writers, scholars, and editors who used it nor to the people whose vocation it had been to nurture it. As I write in July 2004, the archive remains closed in cold storage.

The inaccessibility of MoMA's Stills Archive had several practical consequences. One is that people had to go elsewhere for pictures of deceased film artists. My sadness on hearing of the passing of Marlon Brando, Katharine Hepburn, Gregory Peck, Chuck Jones, Elia Kazan, and so many other luminaries was deepened by my knowledge of the glorious and pertinent visual documentation of their careers locked away in the MoMA vaults.

Another effect of the closing is that the pictures for this book had to be obtained somewhere else. Fortunately for me, New York City has a wonderful photographic service called Photofest, created in 1982 by Carlos Clarens and Howard Mandelbaum. Howard, who operates the business with his brother Ron, is not just a superb archivist but also a generous, spirited soul. He graciously allowed me to plunder Photofest's capacious collection for my selection of stills to accompany Roger's probing prose.

Roger may have achieved fame as a critic of new movies, but his lasting legacy, I believe, will be as a proselytizer and educator for grand and challenging movies of all eras, through his columns, his frame-by-frame analyses at film festivals, his rediscoveries of forgotten or buried treasures in his Overlooked Film Festival, and in books like this one—for grand and challenging movies of all eras. He has expanded the vision of moviegoers, widened the aperture of their film appreciation, and introduced the finest works from many countries to an audience that might otherwise be wary of innovation. By promoting great films, he plants them in moviegoers' minds and encourages video and DVD companies to release more challenging fare. Progress begets progress; student becomes teacher. The young person inspired by a Kurosawa or Renoir film today may be the Roger Ebert of tomorrow.

Obviously, I wish I could still be in the MoMA archive, foraging for the perfect photo for each film Roger has chosen. But there is something sweetly appropriate in Photofest's involvement in this book. And that is because, of all the arts, cinema is the one that has benefited the most from the curatorship of obsessive amateurs. Amateurs in the full French meaning of the word: movie lovers who become movie experts.

Discoveries in literature, art history, and archaeology are typically made by professionals, accredited scholars. Film archaeologists are a different breed. Often they began, like the rest of us, as starstruck fans. They may never have taken a graduate degree or even a film course. Instead, they schooled themselves in the unofficial university of midnight matinees and movie magazines. They scoured the dusty stacks of libraries and the corners of their relatives' attics. Garage sales were their field trips. From youth, an ad hoc scholar is blessed with the impulse to collect, the intelligence to collate, the devotion to turn a fan's fancy into a heroic mission. That mission is to preserve film, film stills, and film posters by any means necessary and to share them with the world. They are the savers and saviors of cinema's legacy.

We would not have such a desperate need for these ad hoc scholars if the studios that made and owned old films had recognized their financial and ethical obligation to preserve them. But Hollywood had no more interest in preserving what it produced than Procter & Gamble had in storing stale cans of Pringles. Few of the studios bothered to save their films and other priceless artifacts. And if valuable material was saved, it was often uncared for. In 1977 Carlos and I went to Los Angeles to prepare a MoMA exhibition on the art of the Hollywood art director. Entering the David O. Selznick Collection in search of sketches from *Gone With the Wind* and *Rebecca*, we found the place littered with art that should have been on a museum wall, not a warehouse floor.

If the studio executives didn't realize the value of the gems they had mined, the collectors did. Our understanding of this wondrous medium would be far narrower if it were not for the likes of William K. Everson and Kevin Brownlow, David Shepard and John Kobal, Carlos and Howard and Ron. They are the conscience and the memory of the film industry.

At times, they had to employ guerrilla tactics to rescue film history from the dumpster. In the 1960s someone in the New York office of Paramount Pictures ordered that the studio's cache of movie stills be thrown out. Fortunately, a young Canadian named John Kobal was there to save these treasures. Alerted by William Kenly, a Paramount staffer who shared Kobal's love of film, John was in the back alley, carting away in the nick of time a half century of indelible images. From this and other righteous raids, John built the renowned Kobal Collection, which remains, thirteen years after its founder's death, a superb photographic resource.

Everson was a London boy who was stricken with movie-love as a kid. As an adult in New York, he shared with cinema lovers in the prevideo days the sixteen-millimeter prints he had acquired of rare old movies with screenings at his home and at the New School. He later used his enormous collection as a basis for the film history courses he taught at New York University. Brownlow, also raised in London, began collecting films at eleven and acquired two reels of Abel Gance's *Napoleon* when he was fifteen. He came to America to meet silent-film artists and from his interviews assembled a fascinating history, *The Parade's Gone By*. Kevin has restored many silent classics and produced a half dozen superb documentaries on the movies' first golden age. Shepard, a native New Yorker, bought a used sixteen-millimeter projector for his twelfth birthday and began buying old films. At Blackhawk Films and the American Film Institute, he helped save and restore silent and early sound films, which he now markets through his own company, Film Preservation Associates.

Carlos, a globe-trotting Cuban who radiated sexual glamour, was also a meticulous film researcher; his books *An Illustrated History of the Horror Film* and *Crime Movies* are classics. Howard, from Queens, New York, began collecting film stills as a teenager; for a few years he worked at Movie Star News, the New York photo memorabilia shop where Irving Klaw also sold his notorious bondage shots of the '50s model Bettie Page. When Carlos died in 1987, Howard drafted his brother Ron to help manage Photofest, which has a staff of twenty-five and is the premier commerical agency for movie photographs. So it was that in New York and London, in Canada and Cuba, the benign passion to preserve films and film stills blossomed in this hardy breed of home-schooled scholars.

I do not elect myself to the film savers' pantheon, but for more than thirty-four years I did my best to nurture and preserve a corner of movie history. In addition to organizing forty-one exhibitions on subjects ranging from Alfred Hitchcock to Pier Paolo Pasolini, from Yiddish films to Disney cartoons, I helped make the Stills Archive's holdings available to thousands of students, authors, and filmmakers. Countless film books and numerous documentary films on the art and business of movies acknowledge gratitude by citing the archive's name (and mine) in their small print.

In 2001 the Museum started clearing out its Fifty-third Street headquarters in preparation for a three-year expansion project. Most of the staff and galleries were moved to the borough of Queens. The only public archive to be shut down was the Film Stills Archive. The day after our lay-off, the *New York Times* ran a story about the closing of the archive; sympathetic articles were published in the *Los Angeles Times, Newsday*, the *New York Observer*, the *Village Voice*, and other papers. Roger, a friend in need, wrote an outraged letter to the *New York Times*.

Terry and I believed that the closing of the archive was retaliation for our union participation and activities during a strike of the MoMA staff in the spring and summer of 2000. Our parent union, the United Auto Workers, pursued a grievance with the National Labor Relations Board. After completing its investigation, the NLRB charged the museum with discrimination and began preparing its case in our defense. The case was presented in court to an administrative law judge on September 29, 2003, and ended on January 30, 2004. We now await the judge's verdict.

By the time you read this, a decision will have been made and a collection of unrivaled breadth and beauty will have been declared either reopened or indefinitely, perhaps permanently, out of reach. For the past two and a half years I have been encouraged by the kindness of strangers and friends in our fight to preserve the Stills Archive. I am told I live by my family's dour Ukrainian motto, "Expect the worst and you'll never be disappointed." But I dare to hope.

Even someone who lives in the past can believe in the future.

MARY CORLISS

{ 12 ANGRY MEN }

In form, *12 Angry Men* is a courtroom drama. In purpose, it's a crash course in those passages of the Constitution that promise defendants a fair trial and the presumption of innocence. It has a kind of stark simplicity: Apart from a brief setup and a briefer epilogue, the entire film takes place within a small New York City jury room, on "the hottest day of the year," as twelve men debate the fate of a young defendant charged with murdering his father. The film shows us nothing of the trial itself except for the judge's perfunctory, almost bored, charge to the jury. His tone of voice indicates that the verdict is a foregone conclusion. We hear neither prosecutor nor defense attorney, and learn of the evidence only secondhand, as the jurors debate it. Most courtroom movies feel it necessary to end with a clear-cut verdict. But *12 Angry Men* never states whether the defendant is innocent or guilty. It is about whether the jury has a reasonable doubt about his guilt.

The principle of reasonable doubt, the belief that a defendant is innocent until proven guilty, is one of the most enlightened elements of our Constitution, although many Americans have had difficulty in accepting it. "It's an open-and-shut case," snaps Juror No. 3 (Lee J. Cobb) as the jury first gathers in their claustrophobic little room. When the first ballot is taken, ten of his fellow jurors agree, and there is only one holdout—Juror No. 8 (Henry Fonda).

This is a film where tension comes from personality conflict, dialogue, and body language, not action; where the defendant has been glimpsed only in a single brief shot; where logic, emotion, and prejudice struggle to control the field. It is a masterpiece of stylized realism—the style coming in the way the photography and editing comment on the bare bones of the content. Released in 1957, when Technicolor and lush production values were common, *12 Angry Men* was lean and mean. It got ecstatic reviews and a spread in *Life* magazine but was a disappointment at the box office. Over the years it has found a constituency, however, and in a 2002 Internet Movie Database poll it was listed twenty-third among the best films of all time.

The story, based on a television play by Reginald Rose, was made into a movie by Sidney Lumet, with Rose and Henry Fonda acting as coproducers and putting up their own money to finance it. It was Lumet's first feature, although he was much experienced in TV drama, and the cinematography was by the veteran Boris Kaufman, whose credits (*On the Waterfront, Long Day's Journey into Night*) show a skill for tightening the tension in dialogue exchanges. The cast included only one bankable star, Fonda, but the other eleven actors were among the best then working in New York, including Martin Balsam, Lee J. Cobb, E. G. Marshall, Jack Klugman, Jack Warden, Ed Begley, and Robert Webber. They smoke, they sweat, they swear, they sprawl, they stalk, they get angry.

In a length of only ninety-five minutes (it sometimes feels as if the movie is shot in real time), the jurors are all defined in terms of their personalities, backgrounds, occupations, prejudices, and emotional tilts. Evidence is debated so completely that we feel we know as much as the jury does, especially about the old man who says he heard the murder and saw the defendant fleeing, and the lady across the street who says she saw it happen through the windows of a moving El train. We see the murder weapon, a switchblade knife, and hear the jurors debate the angle of the knife wound. We watch as Fonda imitates the shuffling step of the old man, a stroke victim, to see if he could have gotten to the door in time to see the murderer fleeing. In its ingenuity, in the way it balances one piece of evidence against another that seems contradictory, *12 Angry Men* is as meticulous as the summation of an Agatha Christie thriller.

But it is not about solving the crime. It is about sending a young

man to die. The movie is timely in view of recent revelations that many death row convictions are based on contaminated evidence. "We're talking about somebody's life here," the Fonda character says. "We can't decide in five minutes. Supposing we're wrong?"

The defendant, when we glimpse him, looks "ethnic" but of no specific group. He could be Italian, Turkish, Indian, Jewish, Arabic, Mexican. His eyes are ringed with dark circles, and he appears exhausted and frightened. In the jury room, some jurors make veiled references to "these people." Finally Juror No. 10 (Ed Begley) begins a racist rant: "You know how these people lie. It's born in them. They don't know what the truth is. And let me tell you, they don't need any real big reason to kill someone, either . . ." As he continues, one juror after another stands up from the jury table and walks away, turning his back. Even those who think the defendant is guilty can't sit and listen to Begley's prejudice. The scene is one of the most powerful in the movie.

The vote, which begins as eleven to one, shifts gradually. Although the movie is clearly in favor of the Fonda position, not all of those voting "guilty" are portrayed negatively. One of the key characters is Juror No. 4 (E. G. Marshall), a stockbroker wearing rimless glasses, who depends on pure logic and tries to avoid emotion altogether. Another juror, No. 7 (Jack Warden), who has tickets to a baseball game, grows impatient and changes his vote just to hurry things along. Juror No. 11 (George Voskovec), an immigrant who speaks with an accent, criticizes him: "Who tells you that you have the right to play like this with a man's life?" Earlier, No. 11 was attacked as a foreigner: "They come over and in no time at all they're telling us how to run the show."

The visual strategy of the movie is discussed by Lumet in his *Making Movies,* one of the most intelligent and informative books ever written about the cinema. In planning the movie, he says, a "lens plot" occurred to him: To make the room seem smaller as the story continued, he gradually changed to lenses of longer focal lengths, so that the backgrounds seemed to close in on the characters. "In addition," he writes, "I shot the first third of the movie above eye level, shot the second third at eye level and the last third from below eye level. In that way, toward the end the ceiling began to appear. Not only were the walls closing in, the ceiling was as well.

The sense of increasing claustrophobia did a lot to raise the tension of the last part of the movie." In the film's last shot, he observes, he used a wide-angle lens "to let us finally breathe."

The movie plays like a textbook for directors interested in how lens choices affect mood. By gradually lowering his camera, Lumet illustrates another principle of composition: A higher camera tends to dominate; a lower camera tends to be dominated. As the film begins we look down on the characters, and the angle suggests they can be comprehended and mastered. By the end, they loom over us, and we feel overwhelmed by the force of their passion. Lumet uses close-ups rarely, but effectively: One man in particular—Juror No. 9 (Joseph Sweeney, the oldest man on the jury)—is often seen in full frame, because he has a way of cutting to the crucial point and stating the obvious after it has eluded the others.

For Sidney Lumet, born in 1924, *12 Angry Men* was the beginning of a film career that has often sought controversial issues. Consider these titles from among his forty-three films: *The Pawnbroker* (the Holocaust), *Fail-Safe* (accidental nuclear war), *Serpico* (police corruption), *Dog Day Afternoon* (homosexuality), *Network* (the decay of TV news), *The Verdict* (alcoholism and malpractice), *Daniel* (a son punished for the sins of his parents), *Running on Empty* (radical fugitives), and *Critical Care* (health care). There are also comedies and a musical (*The Wiz*). If Lumet is not among the most famous of American directors, that is only because he ranges so widely he cannot be categorized. Few filmmakers have been so consistently respectful of the audience's intelligence.

THE ADVENTURES OF ROBIN HOOD

The *Adventures of Robin Hood* was made with sublime innocence and breathtaking artistry, at a time when its simple values rang true. In these cynical days when swashbucklers cannot be presented without an ironic subtext, this great 1938 film exists in an eternal summer of bravery and romance. We require no Freudian subtext, no revisionist analysis; it is enough that Robin wants to rob the rich, give to the poor, and defend the Saxons—not against all Normans but only the bad ones: "It's injustice I hate, not the Normans."

The movie involved some milestones: It was the third Warner Bros. film shot in the three-strip Technicolor process, the fifth of twelve times Flynn would be directed by Michael Curtiz, and the third of nine films that Errol Flynn and Olivia de Havilland would make together.

And it is a triumph of the studio system. The producer, Hal B. Wallis, was the most creative executive on the Warners lot, and when the studio's biggest star, James Cagney, walked off the set in anger and left *Robin Hood* without a leading man, Wallis immediately cast Flynn—the rising star from the Australian island of Tasmania, who had starred for him in *Captain Blood* (1935) and *Charge of the Light Brigade* (1936). It was Wallis who decided to use the new and expensive Technicolor process, Wallis who fired an early writer who wanted to dispense with Maid Marian, Wallis who was powerful enough to replace the original director, William Keighley,

with Curtiz—because Keighley fell ill, according to one story, or because Wallis wanted Curtiz to pump up the action scenes, according to another. Keighley did most of the outdoor scenes; Curtiz did most of the studio shooting.

The result is a film that justifies the trademark Glorious Technicolor. "They just don't make movies with this level of tonal saturation anymore," writes the British critic Damian Cannon. Consider the opulent tapestries of the castle interiors, and reds and golds and grays and greens of Milo Anderson's costumes, the lush greens of Sherwood Forest (actually Bidwell Park at Chico, California). The cinematographers, Sol Polito and Tony Gaudio, were using the original three-strip Technicolor process, which involved cumbersome cameras and a lot of extra lighting but produced a richness of color that modern color films cannot rival.

For all of its technical splendor, however, the film would not be a masterpiece without the casting—not just of Flynn and de Havilland, who are indispensable, but also of such dependable Warners supporting stars as Claude Rains, as the effete Prince John; Basil Rathbone, as the snaky Sir Guy of Gisbourne; and Patric Knowles, Eugene Pallette, and Alan Hale as Will Scarlett, Friar Tuck, and Little John, the fearless Merry Men. Unlike modern films where superstars dominate every scene, the Hollywood films of the golden era have depth in writing and casting, so the story can resonate with more than one tone.

Because in later life Errol Flynn became a caricature of himself and a rather nasty man, it's exhilarating to see him here at the dawn of his career. He was improbably handsome, but that wasn't really the point: What made him a star was his lighthearted exuberance, the good cheer with which he embodies a role like Robin Hood. When George C. Scott was asked what he looked for in an actor, he mentioned "joy of performance," and Flynn embodies that with a careless rapture. Watch his swagger as he enters John's banqueting hall and throws a deer down before the prince, knowing full well that the punishment for poaching a deer is death. Surrounded by his enemies, he fearlessly accuses John of treason against his brother Richard the Lion-Hearted, then fights his way out of the castle again. Another actor might have wanted to project a sense of uncertainty, or resolve, or danger; Flynn shows us a Robin Hood so supremely alive that the whole adventure is a lark. Yes, his eyes shift to note that the exit is being barred and guards are readying their swords; he observes, however, not in fear but in anticipation.

This is the scene at which Maid Marian first sees Robin, and we first see her. That Olivia de Havilland was a great beauty goes without saying, but as I watched the new DVD of *The Adventures of Robin Hood* I found myself more than once pausing the film to simply look at de Havilland in close-up, her cheeks rosy in Technicolor, her features fine and resolute. The shift in her feelings about Sir Robin is measured out scene by scene. It is not a sudden transition but a gradual dawning upon her that this is the man she loves, and that she must escape her arranged marriage to Gisbourne.

Their love scenes, so simple and direct, made me reflect that modern love scenes in action movies are somehow too realistic; they draw too much on psychology and not enough on romance and fable. It is touching and revealing to see the lovers in middle age in *Robin and Marian* (1976), with Sean Connery and Audrey Hepburn bridging the poignancy of their long separation, but how much more satisfying on an elementary level to see Flynn and de Havilland playing their characters as the instruments of fate; they come together not simply because of love or desire but because they are so destined. Their union suggests the medieval ideal of chivalric love, in which marriage is a form of God's will.

The swashbuckling in the movie is thrilling precisely because it is mostly real. The weakness of modern special effects pictures is that much of the action is obviously impossible, and some of the computer animation defies the laws of gravity and physics. It is no more possible to be thrilled by Spider-Man's actions than by the Road Runner's. It is more exciting to see the real Jackie Chan scampering up a wall than to see the computer-assisted Jackie Chan flying.

Stuntmen were used in some shots in *The Adventures of Robin Hood*. But many daring scenes obviously use the real Flynn, who, like Douglas Fairbanks Sr. in the 1922 *Robin Hood*, wanted it known he took his chances. Some stunts are the same in both pictures, as when Robin cuts the rope holding a gate and then rides the rope up as the gate comes down. Others include carefree leaps from ankle-breaking heights, and of course the swordfights. The new Warners DVD assembles the historians Rudy Behlmer, Paula Sigman, Leonard Maltin, Bob Thomas, and Robert Osborne for a documentary about the making of the film, and from them I learned that it was fencing master Fred Cavens who was primarily responsible for the modern movie swordfight; he believed "it should look like a fight, not like a fencing match," and Flynn, coached by Cavens, hurls himself into the sword scenes with a robust glee.

Seeing Flynn in the swordfights, I tried to imagine the studio's first choice, James Cagney, in the role. "It's an interesting concept to think of James Cagney in his little green outfit," muses Robert Osborne. "This little short fellow running around Sherwood Forest." Cagney was a fearless physical actor, and as a dancer he would have had the footwork for the fencing; the casting is not unthinkable, but many scenes show bodies full-figure, which would have emphasized the difference in height between Cagney and Rathbone (but not Rains); cast changes might have been necessary. As Cagney watched this film even he must have conceded that Flynn was perfect for the role.

There are moments in *Robin Hood* as playful as a child's game, as when Robin and his men rise to the bait of Prince John's archery tournament. Are we to believe that the most wanted men in the kingdom could disguise themselves simply by pulling their hats low over their faces? And there are moments a little too obvious, as when Robin takes Marian to a part of Sherwood Forest occupied by some of the Saxons he has helped, who skulk about like an engraving of tired and huddled masses, rousing themselves to express gratitude to him. We knew that Robin Hood took from the rich to give to the poor, but we didn't know he ran his own refugee camp.

There are also moments of bravado, as when an arrow extinguishes a candle on its way to killing a Norman. And when Robin's arrow splits his opponent's in the archery tourney. And the great swordfight between Robin and Sir Guy that cuts between the men and their shadows. And Technicolor is never more glorious than in the big outdoor scenes of pageantry, such as the assembling of the court for the tournament.

The intimate scenes have a directness that is almost bold. When Robin and Marian look into each other's eyes and confess their love, they do it without edge, without spin, without arch poetry. The movie knows when to be simple. And it is the bond between Robin and Marian, after all, that stands at the heart of the movie. The ideal hero must do good, defeat evil, have a good time, and win the girl. *The Adventures of Robin Hood* is like a textbook on how to get that right.

{ ALIEN }

At its most fundamental level *Alien* is a movie about things that can jump out of the dark and kill you. It shares a kinship with the shark in *Jaws,* Michael Myers in *Halloween,* and assorted spiders, snakes, tarantulas, and stalkers. Its most obvious influence is Howard Hawks's *The Thing* (1951), which was also about the members of a team in an isolated outpost who discover a long-dormant alien, bring it inside, and are picked off one by one as it haunts the corridors. Look at that movie, and you see *Alien* in embryo.

In another way, Ridley Scott's 1979 movie is a great original. It builds on the seminal opening shot of *Star Wars* (1977), with its vast ship in lonely interstellar space, and sidesteps Lucas's space opera to tell a story in the genre of traditional "hard" science fiction; with its tough-talking crew members and their mercenary motives, the story would have found a home in John W. Campbell's *Astounding Science Fiction* during its nuts-and-bolts period in the 1940s. Campbell loved stories in which engineers and scientists, not space jockeys and ray-gun blasters, dealt with outer space in logical ways. And, in fact, there is a connection that circles back to Campbell: His short story "Who Goes There?" was adapted as Howard Hawks's production of *The Thing,* which obviously inspired *Alien.* (Then came John Carpenter's 1982 *Thing,* even closer to Campbell.)

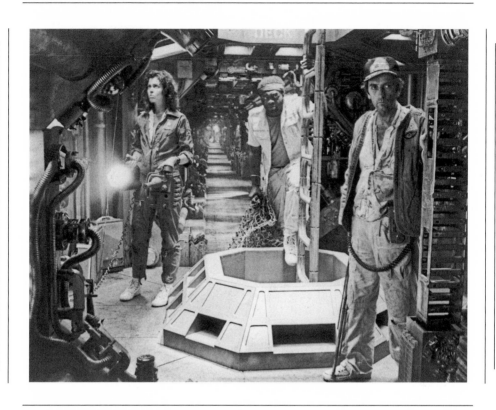

Certainly the character of Ripley, played by Sigourney Weaver, would have appealed to readers in the golden age of science fiction. She has little interest in the romance of finding the alien, and still less in her employer's orders that it be brought back home as a potential weapon. After she sees what it can do, her response to "Special Order 24" ("Return alien life form, all other priorities rescinded") is succinct: "How do we kill it?" Her implacable hatred for the alien is the common thread running through all three *Alien* sequels, which have gradually descended in quality but retained their motivating obsession.

One of the great strengths of *Alien* is its pacing. It takes its time. It waits. It allows silences (the majestic opening shots are underscored by Jerry Goldsmith with scarcely audible far-off metallic chatterings). It suggests the enormity of the crew's discovery by building up to it with small steps: The interception of a signal (is it a warning or an SOS?). The descent to the extraterrestrial surface. The bitching by Brett and Parker, who are concerned only about collecting their shares. The masterstroke of the surface murk through which the crew members move, their helmet lights hardly penetrating the soup. The shadowy outline of the alien ship. The sight of the alien pilot, frozen in his command chair. The shock of the discovery inside the ship ("It's full of . . . leathery eggs . . .").

A recent version of this story would have hurtled toward the part where the alien jumps on the crew members. Today's slasher movies, in the sci-fi genre and elsewhere, are all payoff and no buildup. Consider the wretched 2003 remake of *Texas Chainsaw Massacre* (1992), which cheats its audience out of an explanation, an introduction of the chainsaw family, and even a proper ending. It isn't the slashing that we enjoy. It's the waiting for the slashing. M. Night Shyamalan's *Signs* knows that, and hardly bothers with its aliens at all. And the best scenes in Hawks's *The Thing* involve the empty corridors of the Antarctic station where the Thing might be lurking.

Alien uses a tricky device to keep the alien fresh throughout the movie: It evolves the nature and appearance of the creature, so we never know quite what it looks like or what it can do. We assume at first that the eggs will produce a humanoid, because that's the form of the petrified pilot on the long-lost alien ship. But of course we don't even know if the pilot is of the same race as his cargo of leathery eggs. Maybe he also considered using them as a weapon. The first time we get a good look at the alien, it bursts from the chest of poor Kane (John Hurt). It is unmistakably phallic in shape, and the critic Tim Dirks mentions its "open, dripping vaginal mouth."

Yes, but later, as we glimpse it during a series of attacks, it no longer assumes this shape at all; it looks octopod, reptilian, or arachnoid. And then it uncorks another secret: The fluid dripping from its body is a "universal solvent," and there is a sequence both frightening and delightful as it eats its way through one deck of the ship after another. As the sequels (*Aliens, Alien 3, Alien Resurrection*) will make all too abundantly clear, the alien is capable of being just about any monster the story requires. Because it doesn't play by any rules of appearance or behavior, it becomes an amorphous menace, haunting the ship with the specter of shape-shifting evil. Ash (Ian Holm), the science officer, calls it a "perfect organism. Its structural perfection is matched only by its hostility," and admits, "I admire its purity, its sense of survival; unclouded by conscience, remorse, or delusions of morality."

Sigourney Weaver, whose career would be linked for years to this strange creature, is of course the only survivor of this original crew, except for the . . . cat. The producers must have hoped for a sequel, and by killing everyone except a woman they cast their lot with a female lead for their series. *Variety* noted a few years later that Weaver remained the only actress who could "open" an action movie, and it was a tribute to her versatility that she could play the hard, competent, ruthless Ripley and then double back for so many other kinds of roles. One of the reasons she works so well in the role is that she comes across as smart; the 1979 *Alien* is a much more cerebral movie than its sequels, with the characters (and the audience) genuinely engaged in curiosity about this weirdest of life forms.

A peculiarity of the rest of the actors is that none of them were particularly young. Tom Skerritt, the captain, was forty-six, Hurt was thirty-nine but looked older, Holm was forty-eight, Harry Dean Stanton was fifty-three, Yaphet Kotto was forty-two, and only Veronica Cartwright at twenty-nine and Weaver at thirty were in the age range of the usual thriller cast. Many recent action pictures have improbably young actors cast as key roles or sidekicks, but by skewing older, *Alien* achieves a certain texture without even making a point of it: These are not adventurers but workers, hired by a company to return twenty million tons of ore to earth (the vast size of the ship is indicated in a deleted scene, included on the DVD, which takes nearly a minute just to show it passing).

The screenplay by Dan O'Bannon, based on a story he wrote with Ronald Shusett, allows these characters to speak in distinctive voices. Parker and Brett (Kotto and Stanton), who work in the engine room, complain about delays and worry about their cut of the profits. But listen to Ash: "I'm still collating it, actually, but I have confirmed that he's got an outer layer of protein polysaccharides. He has a funny habit of shedding his cells and replacing them with polarized silicon, which gives him a prolonged resistance to adverse environmental conditions." And then there is Ripley's direct way of cutting to the bottom line.

The result is a film that absorbs us in a mission before it involves us in an adventure, and that consistently engages the alien with curiosity and logic, instead of simply firing at it. Contrast this movie with a latter-day space opera like *Armageddon,* with its average shot a few seconds long and its dialogue reduced to terse statements telegraphing the plot. Much of the credit for *Alien* must go to director Ridley Scott, who had made only one major film before this, the cerebral, elegant *The Duelists* (1977). His next film would be another intelligent, visionary sci-fi epic, *Blade Runner* (1982). And although his career has included some inexplicable clinkers (*Someone to Watch Over Me*) it has also included *Thelma & Louise, G.I. Jane, Gladiator* (unloved by me, but not by audiences), *Black Hawk Down,* and *Matchstick Men.* These are simultaneously commercial and intelligent projects, made by a director who wants to attract a large audience but doesn't care to insult it.

Alien has been called the most influential of modern action pictures, and so it is, although *Halloween* also belongs on the list. Unfortunately, the films it influenced studied its thrills but not its thinking. We have now descended into a bog of Gotcha! movies in which various horrible beings spring on a series of victims, usually teenagers. The ultimate extension of the genre is the geek movie, illustrated by the remake of *Texas Chainsaw Massacre,* which essentially sets the audience the same test as an old-time carnival geek show: Now that you've paid your money, can you keep your eyes open while we disgust you? A few more ambitious and serious sci-fi films have also followed in *Alien*'s footsteps, notably the well-made *Aliens* (1986) and *Dark City* (1998). But the original still vibrates with a dark and frightening intensity.

{ AMADEUS }

Happy people are pleased by the happiness of others. The miserable are poisoned by envy. They vote with Gore Vidal and David Merrick, both credited with saying, "It is not enough that I succeed. Others must fail." Miloš Forman's *Amadeus* is not about the genius of Mozart but about the envy of his rival Salieri, whose curse was to have the talent of a third-rate composer but the ear of a first-rate music lover, so that he knew how bad he was, and how good Mozart was.

The most moving scene in the movie takes place at Mozart's deathbed, where the great composer, only thirty-five, dictates the final pages of his great *Requiem* to Salieri, sitting at the foot of the bed with quill and manuscript, dragging the notes from Mozart's fevered brain. This scene is moving not because Mozart is dying but because Salieri, his lifelong rival, is striving to extract from the dying man yet another masterpiece that will illuminate how shabby Salieri's work is. Salieri hates Mozart but loves music more, and cannot live without one more work that he can resent for its perfection. True, Salieri plans to claim the work as his own—but for a man like him, that will be just another turn of the screw. (The real Salieri was a good composer who was not present at Mozart's death, but the movie prefers it otherwise.)

Amadeus (1984) swept the Academy Awards and had considerable popular success. When you consider that 98 percent of the American pub-

lic never listens to a classical music station, it is astonishing that Mozart became for a time a best-seller, and not only to women assured by talk-show gurus that his music boosted the IQs of embryos. The movie's success is partly explained, I think, by its strategy of portraying Mozart not as a paragon whose greatness is a burden to us all but as a goofy proto-hippie with a high-pitched giggle, an overfondness for drink, and a buxom wife who liked to chase him on all fours.

This is not a vulgarization of Mozart but a way of dramatizing that true geniuses rarely take their own work seriously, because it comes so easily for them. Great writers (Nabokov, Dickens, Wodehouse) make it look like play. Almost-great writers (Mann, Galsworthy, Wolfe) make it look like Herculean triumph. It is as true in every field; compare Shakespeare to Shaw, Jordan to Barkley, Picasso to Rothko, Kennedy to Nixon. Salieri could strain and moan and bring forth tinkling jingles; Mozart could compose so joyously that he seemed, Salieri complained, to be "taking dictation from God."

Amadeus was brought forth by the independent producer Saul Zaentz (*One Flew over the Cuckoo's Nest, Unbearable Lightness of Being, The English Patient*), who bought Peter Shaffer's play and assigned the playwright to adapt it with the director Miloš Forman. Zaentz's pattern, as you can see, is to take literary successes that seem unfilmable—too ambitious, too specialized—and film them. Forman, a Czech filmmaker who turned his back on the Russians and came to work in America but not exactly in Hollywood, had directed *Cuckoo's Nest* (1975), *Hair* (1979), and *Ragtime* (1981)—and while still in Czechoslovakia, *The Firemen's Ball* (1968), which, with *Cuckoo's Nest*, is also in this book.

The key precursor is *Hair*. He sees Wolfgang Amadeus Mozart as a spiritual brother of the hippies who thumbed their noses at convention, muddled their senses with intoxicants, and delighted in lecturing their elders. In a film where everybody wears wigs, Mozart's wigs (as I noted in my original review) do not look like everybody else's. They have just the slightest suggestion of punk, just the smallest shading of pink. There is something about Mozart's Vienna apartment, especially toward the end, that reminds you of the pad of a newly rich rock musician: The rent is sky-high, the furnishings are sparse and haphazard, work is scattered everywhere, housekeeping has been neglected, there are empty bottles in the corners, and the bed is the center of life.

The flower child Mozart tries to govern his life, unsuccessfully, by the lights of three older men. His father Leopold (Roy Dotrice) trained the child genius to amaze the courts of Europe but now stands aside, disapproving, at the untidy mess Mozart has made of his adulthood. His patron, Emperor Joseph II (Jeffrey Jones) passes strict rules (no ballet in operas!) but cannot enforce them because, God love him, he enjoys what he would forbid. Then there is Salieri (F. Murray Abraham), who poses as Mozart's friend while plotting against him, sabotaging productions, blocking appointments. The irony (not least to Salieri) is that Salieri is honored and admired while Mozart is so new and unfamiliar that no one knows how good he is, except Salieri. Even the emperor, who indulges him, is as amused by Mozart's insolence as by his art. Mozart's role in the court of Joseph II is as the fool, saying truth wrapped in giggles. Mozart's ally in his struggles with authority is his wife, Constanze (Elizabeth Berridge), who seems a child, stays too late in bed, calls him "Wolfie," yet has a good head for business and a sharp eye for treachery.

The film is told in flashback by Salieri at the end of his life. Confined in a madhouse, he confides to a young priest; he thinks perhaps he killed Mozart. It is more likely that Mozart killed himself, with some deadly cocktail of tuberculosis and cirrhosis, but Salieri seems to have killed Mozart's art, and for that he feels remorse. It is all there in Mozart's deathbed scene: the agony of the older rival who hates to lose, who would lie and betray, and yet who cannot deny that the young man's music is sublime.

The movie was shot on location in Forman's native Prague, one of a handful of European cities still in large parts unchanged since the eighteenth century. The film is a visual feast of palaces, costumes, wigs, feasts, opening nights, champagne, and mountains of debt. Mozart never had enough money, or much cared; Salieri had money, but look at his face when people snicker behind his back while he plays one of his compositions, and you will see what small consolation it was.

"Director's cuts" are a mixed blessing in this age of the DVD. Many of them seem inspired entirely by the desire to sell another video. Forman says his new version of *Amadeus*, which runs 188 minutes, or thirty minutes longer than the 1984 version, is in fact the original cut: Afraid that a historical biopic about Mozart would find tough sailing at the box office, Forman and Zaentz trimmed half an hour for pragmatic reasons.

The major addition to the film is a scene explaining more fully why Constanze has such contempt for Salieri. Salieri, the court composer, has in his gift a lucrative appointment that, he explains to Mozart's young bride, will be her husband's—if she will grant Salieri her favors. Since there is little indication that Salieri has any great interest in women (or in anything, other than Mozart), this favor seems motivated not by sexual desire but by the need to humiliate Mozart. Constanze, desperate to help her Wolfie, does indeed visit Salieri at his apartments, and bares her breasts before having second thoughts.

In a film of grand gestures, some of the finest moments are very subtle. Notice the way Jeffrey Jones, as the emperor, balances his duty to appear serious and his delight in Mozart's impudence. Watch Jones's face as he decides he may have been wrong to ban ballet from opera. And watch Abraham's face as he internalizes envy, resentment, and rage. What a smile he puts on the face of his misery! Then watch his face again at Mozart's deathbed, as he takes the final dictation. He knows how good it is. And he knows at that moment there is only one thing he loves more than himself, and that is Mozart's music.

{ AMARCORD }

If ever there was a movie made entirely out of nostalgia and joy, by a filmmaker at the heedless height of his powers, that movie is Federico Fellini's *Amarcord*. The title means "I remember" in the dialect of Rimini, the seaside town of his youth, but these are *memories* of memories, transformed by affection and fantasy and much improved in the telling. Here he gathers the legends of his youth, where all of the characters are at once larger and smaller than life—flamboyant players on their own stages.

At the center is an overgrown young adolescent, the son of a large, loud family, who is dizzied by the life churning all around him: the girls he idealizes, the tarts he lusts for, the rituals of the village year, the practical jokes he likes to play, the meals that always end in drama, the church's thrilling opportunities for sin and redemption, and the vaudeville of Italy itself—the transient glories of grand hotels and great ocean liners, the play-acting of Mussolini's Fascist costume party.

Sometimes from this tumult an image of perfect beauty will emerge, as when in the midst of a rare snowfall, the count's peacock escapes and spreads its dazzling tail feathers in the blizzard. Such an image is so inexplicable and irreproducible that all the heart can do is ache with gratitude, and all the young man can know is that he will live forever, love all the women, drink all the wine, make all the movies, and become Fellini.

Amarcord (1973) is Fellini's final great film. The other masterpieces are *La Strada, Nights of Cabiria, La Dolce Vita, 8½,* and *Juliet of the Spirits.* He made other films of consequence, including *Il Bidone, Fellini's Roma, Fellini Satyricon, Casanova,* and *The Clowns,* but those six titles show him in the full flood of his talent. All of his films are autobiographical in one way or another—feeding off his life, his fantasies, his earlier films—and from them a composite figure takes shape, of a hustler on the make, with a rakish hat and a victorious grin, spinning delight out of thin air, entranced by dreams of voluptuous temptresses, restrained by Catholic guilt—a ringmaster in love with the swing dance tempos of the 1940s and '50s who liked to organize his characters into processions and parades.

Fellini was more in love with breasts than Russ Meyer, more wracked with guilt than Ingmar Bergman, more of a flamboyant showman than Busby Berkeley. He danced so instinctively to his inner rhythms that he didn't even realize he was a stylistic original; did he ever devote a moment's organized thought to the style that become known as "Felliniesque," or was he simply following the melody that always played when he was working?

The melody was literal most of the time. Like his Italian contemporaries he postsynched most of his dialogue, so it didn't matter so much how his actors read their lines, and he often had a small orchestra or a phonograph to supply music while a scene was being filmed. That's why so often in a Fellini film the actors seem not to be simply walking but moving subtly to an unheard melody. They seem to be able to hear the soundtrack.

Amarcord is like a long dance number, interrupted by dialogue, public events, and meals. It is constructed like a guided tour through a year in the life of the town, from one spring to the next. There are several narrators, including an old rummy-dummy who visibly forgets his lines and a professor who lectures us learnedly on the town's historical precedents. Other narrators include the singing voices of the children, heralding the arrival of the first dandelion balls of spring, and a confiding voice on the sound track that is Fellini himself.

The film is set during the stage-opera phase of Italian fascism, which it sees as a delusion of foolish people—and yet the father in the family, a Communist who plays the "Internationale" from a phonograph in the church tower to protest the visit of a Fascist leader, is no less foolish. Politics

in *Amarcord* are on the level of the endless battle between the parish priest and the Communist mayor in *The Little World of Don Camillo*, Giovanni Guareschi's best-seller of a half century ago: Both sides are so Italian they prefer the fun of their public drama to winning or losing. Fascism was no fun in real life, but for that you have to see De Sica's *The Garden of the Finzi-Continis*, because in Fellini's garden only characters grow.

The town itself is a character. We meet the buxom Gradisca (Magali Noel), who runs a beauty parlor and parades her innocent carnality and her red fur hat past the inflamed local men as if she had been elected to a public office; young Titta (Bruno Zamin), who finds Gradisca beyond his reach but boldly offers to show the voluptuous proprietor of the tobacco shop that he is such a man he can lift her off her feet; "Ronald Colman," who runs the local cinema; Titta's father (Armando Brancia), who rules the family table with what is intended to be an iron hand; Titta's mother (Pupella Maggio), who offers to kill herself more or less daily because of her husband's idiocy; her brother, who vainly trains his hair beneath a net and focuses on his meals with a hypnotic concentration; the local priest, obsessed with whether the boys touch themselves; and all of Titta's playmates, who gather for enthusiastic mutual touchings of self.

Every day brings a drama. Every summer the family liberates Uncle Teo from the local asylum for a picnic in the country, and this year while they are distracted he climbs a tree and refuses to come down, moaning, "I want a woman!" like a lovesick bull. He throws apples at those who try to climb up to him, and finally the family sends to the asylum for help, and a midget nun arrives to order Teo down. This nun wears a headdress so exaggerated we never see her face, and we form an instant opinion that she is, in fact, a man.

The arrival of a provincial Fascist leads to an absurd public ceremony, all of the Fascists trotting from the train station to the public square, where a papier-mâché Mussolini looks like a comic bulldog. The local youth go through gymnastics exercises no doubt connected to national security. We also glimpse their education, in a hilarious montage of classes in the local school, one interrupted by the most novel and ingenious delivery of urine that can possibly be imagined.

There is a poetic and melancholy side, too, as when fog blankets the town and the characters seek softly for their bearings, and when the great liner *Rex* passes offshore and the townspeople all row out in their boats to watch it pass (it is as artificial as the "waves" the boats ride on, suggesting how much the national image depends on illusion). Local imaginations are inflamed by what must go on at the Grand Hotel, which none of the locals can afford to step foot in, although Gradisca, their heroine, figures in a popular legend there—and so does the rummy-dummy, when the women in a sultan's harem let down their rope ladders for him. Gradisca is their carnal fantasy, their symbol of hope, their good-hearted friend. She also supplies an example of the way Fellini's films become his parallel autobiography; Gradisca is virtually the same character, in appearance and behavior, as Carla (Sandra Milo), Marcello's mistress in *8½*.

The film's most beautiful scene involves the snowfall and the peacock feathers. The snow is plowed into impossibly tall walls to make a maze within which the boys and Gradisca have a snowball fight. The saddest scene, at the beach, is Gradisca's wedding to a slick Fascist leader; the marriage is of their hopes and their doom. She pulls away from her husband to throw her bride's bouquet, but there is no one to catch it.

The film is saturated with Fellini's affection for these people, whose hopes are so transparent they can see through their own into another's. All of the Fellini visual trademarks are here, including the half-finished scaffold that mediates between heaven and earth, and the grotesque faces of the extras, and the parades and processions, and, always, the Nino Rota music (and his arrangements of standards, especially "Stormy Weather"). Fellini shoots in color and makes special use of the reds and whites of Gradisca's outfits. He is careful to stay mostly in mid- and long-shot, the correct distance for comedy, and he uses close-ups mostly for intense longing.

His film seems almost to flow from the camera, as anecdotes will flow from one who has told them often and knows they work. If there is a bittersweet undertone, perhaps it is because Fellini suspected that the film business was changing and his funding and access would never again be the same; this was the last of his films made for no better reason than that Fellini wanted to make it.

{ ANNIE HALL }

Annie Hall contains more intellectual wit and cultural references than any other movie ever to win the Oscar for best picture, and in winning the award for 1978 it edged out *Star Wars*, an outcome unthinkable today. The victory marked the beginning of Woody Allen's career as an important film-maker (his earlier work was funny but slight), and it signaled the end of the 1970s golden age of American movies. With *Star Wars* the age of the block-buster was upon us, and movies this quirky and idiosyncratic would find themselves shouldered aside by Hollywood's greed for megahits. *Annie Hall* grossed about $40 million—less than any other modern best picture winner, and less than the budgets of many of them.

Watching it again, twenty-five years after its April 1977 premiere, I am astonished by how scene after scene has an instant familiarity. Some of its lines have seeped into the general consciousness; they're known by countless people who never saw the movie, like Jack Nicholson's chicken salad speech from *Five Easy Pieces*. For years I've invariably described spiders as being "as big as a Buick," and this movie may be where most people first heard Groucho Marx's comment that he would not want to belong to any club that would have him as a member.

Alvy Singer, the gag writer and stand-up comic played by Allen in the movie, is the template for many of his other roles—neurotic, wisecrack-ing, kvetching, a romantic who is not insecure about sex so much as dubi-

ous about all the trouble it takes. Annie Hall, played by Diane Keaton, sets the form for many of Allen's on-screen girlfriends: pretty, smart, scatterbrained, younger, with affection gradually fading into exasperation. Women put up with a lot in Allen's movies, but at a certain point they draw the line.

Alvy Singer, like so many other Allen characters and Allen himself, accompanies every experience in life with a running commentary. He lives in order to talk about living. And his interior monologues provide not merely the analysis but the alternative. After making love with Annie for the first time, Alvy rolls over, exhausted and depleted, and observes, "As Balzac said, 'There goes another novel.' "

Alvy is smarter than the ground rules of Hollywood currently allow. Watching even the more creative recent movies, one becomes aware of a subtle censorship being imposed, in which the characters cannot talk about anything the audience might not be familiar with. This generates characters driven by plot and emotion rather than by ideas; they use catchphrases rather than witticisms. Consider the famous sequence where Annie and Alvy are standing in line for the movies and the blowhard behind them pontificates loudly about Fellini. When the pest switches over to McLuhan, Alvy loses patience, confronts him, and then triumphantly produces Marshall McLuhan himself from behind a movie poster to inform him, "You know nothing of my work!" This scene would be penciled out today on the presumption that no one in the audience would have heard of Fellini or McLuhan.

Annie Hall is built on such dialogue, and centers on conversation and monologue. Because it is just about everyone's favorite Woody Allen movie, because it won the Oscar, because it is a romantic comedy, few viewers probably notice how much of it consists of people talking, simply talking. They walk and talk, sit and talk, go to shrinks, go to lunch, make love and talk, talk to the camera, or launch into inspired monologues like Annie's free association as she describes her family to Alvy. This speech by Diane Keaton is as close to perfect as such a speech can likely be, climaxing with the memory of her narcoleptic Uncle George falling asleep and dying while waiting in line for a free turkey. It is all done in one take of brilliant brinksmanship, with Keaton (or Annie) right on the edge of losing it.

Because *Annie Hall* moves so quickly, is so fresh and alive, we may not notice how long some of Allen's takes are. He famously likes to shoot most scenes in master shots with all of the actors on-screen all of the time, instead of cutting on every line of dialogue. The critic David Bordwell has an illuminating article in the Spring 2002 issue of *Film Quarterly* that points out that Allen's average shot length (ASL) ranges high: 22 seconds for *Manhattan* and 35.5 seconds for *Mighty Aphrodite*. Bordwell tells me *Annie Hall* has an ASL of 14.5 seconds (he says other 1977 films he clocked had an ASL of from 4 to 7 seconds). By comparison, the recent film *Armageddon* has an ASL of 2.3 seconds, a velocity that arguably makes intelligent dialogue impossible.

Alvy and Annie take a sly delight in their conversational skill; they're attracted to each other not by pheromones but by pacing. In the first conversation they have, after meeting as tennis partners, they fall naturally into verbal tennis:

> *Alvy:* You want a lift?
>
> *Annie:* Oh, why? Uh, you got a car?
>
> *Alvy:* No, I was going to take a cab.
>
> *Annie:* Oh, no. I have a car.
>
> *Alvy:* You have a car? I don't understand. If you have a car, so then why did you say, "Do you have a car?" like you wanted a lift?
>
> *Annie:* I don't, I don't, geez, I don't know. I wasn't. . . . I got this VW out there. (*To herself:*) "What a jerk, yeah. Would you like a lift?"
>
> *Alvy:* Sure. Which way you goin'?
>
> *Annie:* Me? Oh, downtown.
>
> *Alvy:* Down . . . I'm going uptown.
>
> *Annie:* Oh well, you know I'm going uptown too.
>
> *Alvy:* You just said you were going downtown.
>
> *Annie:* Yeah, well, but I could . . .

This is not merely dialogue, it is a double act in the process of discovering itself. The more we listen to Annie and Alvy talk, the more we doubt they meet many people who can keep up with them. When Alvy expresses reluctance to let Annie move in with him, and she complains that her apartment is too small and has bad plumbing and bugs, who but Alvy could take "bugs" as his cue and observe, "Entomology is a rapidly growing field." And only Annie could interpret this as "You don't want me to live with you."

> *Alvy:* I don't want you to live with me?! Whose idea was it?
> *Annie:* Mine.
> *Alvy:* Yeah, it was yours, actually, but I approved it immediately.

There are, of course, other women in Alvy's life, including the *Rolling Stone* correspondent (Shelley Duvall) who is a Rosicrucian (Alvy: "I can't get with any religion that advertises in *Popular Mechanics*"). And the liberal Democrat (Carol Kane) who Alvy marries but later splits up with because of their disagreements about the second-gun theory of the Kennedy assassination. That Annie Hall is the great love of his life is immediately clear, and the movie is a flashback from the opening monologue in which he sadly notes that a year earlier they were in love; the film is his analysis of what went wrong, and his answer is that he found happiness but couldn't accept it. Groucho's line, he says, "is the key joke of my adult life, in terms of my relationships with women."

Lore about *Annie Hall* on IMDb.com includes the revealing detail that Diane Keaton, who lived with Allen at the time, was born as Diane Hall, and her nickname was Annie. The movie originally contained a murder subplot, entirely dropped; a 140-minute rough cut became a 94-minute film in a process described in editor Ron Rosenblum's book *When the Shooting Stops, the Cutting Begins.*

Viewing the final cut, I sensed not only how well the remains hold together but how miraculously, since the parts would seem to be an ungainly fit. Consider Allen's astonishing range of visual tactics, including split screens in which the characters on either side directly address each other; a bedroom scene where Annie's spirit gets up during sex to sit, bored, in a chair by the bed; autobiographical flashbacks; subtitles that reveal what characters are really thinking; children who address us as if they were adults ("I'm into leather"); an animated sequence pairing Alvy with Snow White's wicked witch; and the way Alvy speaks directly out of the screen to the audience.

This is a movie that establishes its tone by constantly switching between tones: The switches reflect the restless mind of the filmmaker, turning away from the apparent subject of a scene to find the angle that reveals the joke. *Annie Hall* is a movie about a man who is always looking for the loopholes in perfection. Who can turn everything into a joke, and wishes he couldn't.

AU HASARD, BALTHAZAR

Robert Bresson is one of the saints of the cinema, and *Au Hasard, Balthazar* (1966) is his most heartbreaking prayer. The film follows the life of a donkey from birth to death, while all the time giving it the dignity of being itself—a dumb beast, noble in its acceptance of a life over which it has no control. Balthazar is not one of those cartoon animals that can talk and sing and is a human with four legs. Balthazar is a donkey, and it is as simple as that.

We first see Balthazar as a newborn, taking its first unsteady steps, and there is a scene that provides a clue to the rest of the film: Three children sprinkle water on its head and baptize it. What Bresson may be suggesting is that although the church teaches that only humans can enter into heaven, surely there is a place at God's side for all of his creatures.

Balthazar's early life is spent on a farm in the rural French district where all the action takes place; the donkey will be owned by many of the locals, and will return to some of them more than once. A few of them are good, but all of them are flawed, although there is a local drunk who is not cruel or thoughtless to the animal, despite his other crimes.

Balthazar's first owner is Marie (Anne Wiazemsky), who gives the donkey its name. Her father is the local schoolmaster, and her playmate is Jacques (Walter Green), who agrees with her that they will marry someday. Jacques's mother dies, and his grief-stricken father leaves the district, en-

trusting his farm to Marie's father (Philippe Asselin), in whom he has perfect trust. Marie loves Balthazar and delights in decorating the donkey's bridle with wildflowers, but she does nothing to protect the beast when local boys torment it. The leader of this gang is Gérard (François Lafarge), and when Marie glances up to the church choir during Mass as Gerard sings, he brings an evil even to the holy words.

Marie's father is a victim of the sin of pride. Although he has managed the farm with perfect honesty, after rumors are spread by jealous neighbors that he is stealing from the owner, he refuses to produce records or receipts to prove himself. To the despair of Marie's mother (Nathalie Joyaut), he follows his stubbornness straight into bankruptcy. Balthazar becomes the possession of the local baker and is used by the baker's boy (none other than Gérard) to deliver bread. Gérard mistreats and abuses Balthazar, who eventually simply refuses to move. Gérard responds by tying a newspaper to Balthazar's tail and setting it on fire. Eventually, under Gérard's mistreatment, the donkey collapses, and there is talk of putting it down.

But the town drunk, Arnold (Jean-Claude Guilbert), saves the animal and brings it back to life, and Balthazar enjoys a brief moment of glory when he is hired out as a circus animal—the Mathematical Donkey, who can solve multiplication tables. This life is soon brought to an end, as Balthazar becomes the property of a recluse, then finally wanders back on its own to the stable where it began its life, and where it finds Marie's father and even Marie.

But this is not a sentimental ending. Marie is a weak girl; when the sincere Jacques returns as a young man to say he still loves her, she rejects him. She prefers Gérard, who mistreats her but seems glamorous, with his leather jacket and motorbike. What we see through Balthazar's eyes is a village filled with small, flawed, weak people, in a world where sweetness is uncommon and cruelty comes easily. That is what we see—but what does Balthazar see? The genius of Bresson's approach is that he never gives us a single moment that could be described as one of Balthazar's "reaction shots." Other movie animals may roll their eyes or stomp their hooves, but Balthazar simply walks or waits, regarding everything with the clarity of a donkey who knows it is a beast of burden, and that its life consists of either bearing or not bearing, of feeling pain or not feeling pain, or even feeling pleasure. All of these things are equally beyond its control.

There is, however, Balthazar's bray. It is not a beautiful sound, but it is the sound a donkey can make; when Balthazar brays it might sound to some like a harsh complaint, but to me it sounds like a beast who has been given one noise to make in the world, and gains some satisfaction by making it. It is important to note that Balthazar never brays on cue to react to specific events; that would turn it into a cartoon animal.

Although the donkey has no way of revealing its thoughts, that doesn't prevent us from supplying them; we regard that white-spotted furry face and those big eyes, and we feel sympathy with every experience the donkey undergoes. That is Bresson's civilizing and even spiritual purpose in most of his films; we must go to the characters instead of passively letting them come to us. In the vast majority of movies, everything is done for the audience. We are cued to laugh or cry, be frightened or relieved; Hitchcock called the movies a machine for causing emotions in the audience. Bresson (and Ozu) take a different approach. They regard, and ask us to regard along with them, and to arrive at conclusions about their characters that are our own. This is the cinema of empathy. It is worth noting that both Ozu and Bresson use severe stylistic limitations to avoid coaching our emotions. In his sound films, Ozu almost never moves his camera; every shot is framed and held, and frequently it begins before the characters enter the scene and continues after they leave.

Bresson's most intriguing limitation is to forbid his actors to act. He was known to shoot the same shot ten, twenty, even fifty times, until all "acting" was drained from it and the actors were simply performing the physical actions and speaking the words. There was no room in his cinema for De Niro or Penn. It might seem that the result would be a movie filled with zombies, but quite the contrary: By simplifying performance to the action and the word without permitting inflection or style, Bresson achieves a kind of purity that makes his movies remarkably emotional. The actors portray lives without informing us how to feel about them; forced to decide for ourselves how to feel, forced to empathize, we often have stronger feelings than if the actors were providing them for us.

Given this philosophy, a donkey becomes the perfect Bresson character. Balthazar makes no attempt to communicate its emotions to us, and it communicates its physical feelings only in universal terms: Covered with snow, it is cold. Its tail set afire, it is frightened. Eating its dinner, it is content. Overworked, it is exhausted. Returning home, it is relieved to find a familiar place. Although some humans are kind to it and others are cruel, the motives of humans are beyond its understanding, and it accepts what they do because it must.

Now, here is the essential part: Bresson suggests that we are all Balthazars. Despite our dreams, hopes, and best plans, the world will eventually do with us whatever it does. Because we can think and reason, we believe we can figure a way out, find a solution, get the answer. But intelligence gives us the ability to comprehend our fate without the power to control it. Still, Bresson does not leave us empty-handed. He offers us the suggestion of empathy. If we will extend ourselves to sympathize with how others feel, we can find the consolation of sharing human experience, instead of the loneliness of enduring it alone.

The final scene of *Au Hasard, Balthazar* makes that argument in a beautiful way. The donkey, old and near death, wanders into a herd of sheep—as, indeed, it began its life in such a herd. The other animals come and go, sometimes nuzzling up against it, taking little notice, accepting this fellow animal, sharing the meadow and the sunshine. Balthazar lies down and eventually dies, as the sheep continue about their business. The donkey has at last found a place where the other creatures think as it does.

{ THE BANK DICK }

You mustn't make fun of the gentleman, Clifford.
You'd like to have a nose like that full of nickels, wouldn't you?
MOTHER TO SON ABOUT EGBERT SOUSE

W. C. Fields is the most improbable star in the first century of the movies, a man widely (and accurately) thought to be drunk during most of his adult life, who created a screen character that hated women, children, and dogs and could not be redeemed even by the requirements of the Hollywood censors. During Fields's career, industry standards required good to be rewarded and evildoing punished, but in *The Bank Dick* Fields plays an alcoholic misanthrope who lies, cheats, and steals and is rewarded with wealth and fame.

The Bank Dick (1940) is probably Fields's best film, but his career resides not so much in individual films as in scenes and moments scattered here and there between his first short subject, in 1915, and his last films in the mid-1940s. He recycled material tirelessly. Bits from his vaudeville act were being dusted off forty years later, and he always played more or less the same character. Even as Mr. Micawber in *David Copperfield* (1935), his most disciplined and polished performance, he was recognizably himself in costume (or, it could be argued, Micawber was simply an earlier fictional version of Fields).

Today Fields (1880–1946) is not as well known as he once was. Even his revival in the 1960s has been forgotten. No doubt the wheel of memory will revolve to bring him back into fashion, because his appeal is timeless: It is the appeal of the man who cheerfully embraces a life of antisocial hedonism, basking in serene contentment with his own flaws. He is self-contained.

Fields was an accomplished juggler as a youth on the vaudeville stage and seems to have come into his screen persona gradually, helped by the introduction of sound, which permitted audiences to hear his peculiar nasal twang. As a comedian, he had unusual timing: His dialogue does not end in punch lines that invite laughter, but trails off into implications and insinuations of things better left unsaid. Audiences suspected he was sneaking double meanings past the censors, and they were right.

Legend has it he wanted his tombstone to read "On the whole, I'd rather be in Philadelphia." During his lifetime, on the whole, he'd rather be in a bar. He was a serious drinker who was often under a doctor's care, checked into sanitoriums between movies, and died a horrible alcoholic's death. David Thomson has written of "the mottling of his sad face." That he nevertheless brought exquisite timing to his performances and joy to his audiences exhibits a species of courage, and of course on the days when the booze was working he could be playful and entertaining; his Hollywood parties were eagerly attended even if the host was seldom conscious at their conclusion.

"I knew Fields well," Groucho Marx told me in 1972. "He used to sit in the bushes in front of his house with a BB gun and shoot at people. Today, he'd probably be arrested. He invited me over to his house. He had a girlfriend there. I think her name was Carlotta Monti. *Car-lot-ta MON-ti!* That's the kind of a name a girl of Fields would have. He had a ladder leading up to his attic. Without exaggeration, there was fifty thousand dollars in liquor up there. Crated up like a wharf. I'm standing there and Fields is standing there, and nobody says anything. The silence is oppressive. Finally he speaks: *This will carry me twenty-five years.*"

Stories like that were well known to Fields's fans and contributed to the legend that drew crowds to his movies. He also became famous for a long-running feud with Charlie McCarthy, the dummy of the ventriloquist

Edgar Bergen, and for on-screen hostility to small children, who were hostile right back at him. "Shall I bounce a rock off his head?" asks Elsie, his daughter in *The Bank Dick,* and her mother tells her, "Respect your father, darling. What kind of a rock?"

Fields was paid $125,000 a picture in his later years, a good salary, and insisted on another $15,000 for his "screenplays," which consisted of mental notes and scrawlings on the backs of envelopes. The synopsis of any of his films is hallucinatory. My source is his biographer, Robert Lewis Taylor, who writes that *My Little Chickadee* (1940) and *Never Give a Sucker an Even Break* (1941), two of his best-known films, "will probably stand up among the worst movies ever made," but tellingly adds, "This scarcely detracts from their overall worth." You didn't go for a good movie. You went for Fields, and for the surrealism of his plots. Consider *The Bank Dick*, in which he plays a man named Egbert Souse ("accent grave upon the *e*")—an unhappily married drunk who accidentally catches a thief, is rewarded with a job at the bank, and falls in with a con man.

At one point he wanders into his favorite bar, the Black Pussy Cat (bartender: Shemp Howard), and meets a movie producer, who hires him on the spot to fill in for A. Pismo Clam, the director of a movie being made in town. Fields arrives on the set, announces that the story will switch from an English drawing room drama to a circus picture, and begins to instruct the actors for a football scrimmage. The male lead is very tall, the female lead very short. ("Is she standing in a hole?" he asks.) After several funny minutes Fields simply walks off the set, and the directing job is never referred to again until a chase scene at the end of the film.

This kind of abrupt disconnect is common in Fields movies. Even a Marx Brothers plot was a masterpiece of construction by comparison. One sketch segues into another one, not seamlessly, and no effort is made at realism. (In his famous short *The Fatal Glass of Beer,* he repeatedly looks out a cabin door, intones, "It's not a fit night out for man nor beast," and is hit in the face with what is obviously a handful of soap flakes hurled from just out of sight.)

Assimilating the unique fact of W. C. Fields is a lifelong occupation for any filmgoer, conducted from time to time according to no particular plan. There is not a single Fields film that you "must" see in order to qualify as a literate movie lover, and yet if you are not eventually familiar with Fields you are not a movie lover at all. What is amazing about him is that he exists. He is not lovely, and although he is graceful it is a lugubrious grace, a kind of precarious balance in a high psychic wind. All of his scenes depend, in one way or another, on sharing his private state: He is unloved, he detests life, he is hungover, he wants a drink, he is startled by sudden movements and loud noises, he has no patience for fools, everyone is a fool, and middle-class morality is a conspiracy against the man who wants to find surcease in alcoholic bliss. These are not the feelings of his characters; they are his own feelings.

Fields met his match in *My Little Chickadee* when he costarred with Mae West, another Hollywood force of nature. They wrote their scenes separately, we learn. She could not stand his drinking, Taylor reports, and although Fields at sixty was far from West's usual muscle-builder type, he grew boozily enamored of her, at one point fondly referring to her off-camera as "my little brood mare." Pauline Kael finds *Chickadee* "a classic among bad movies," observing that it never really gets off the ground "but the ground is such an honest mixture of dirt, manure, and corn that at times it is fairly aromatic." Only Fields would compliment a woman, after kissing her hand, by observing, "What symmetrical digits!" Only West would have been able to look complimented.

{ BEAT THE DEVIL }

As the village band pounds out an oom-pah-pah tune, policemen march four disreputable characters across the square. Already we're smiling. One is tall and round, one is tall and cadaverous, one is short and round, and the fourth is a little ratface with a bristling mustache. On the sound track, Humphrey Bogart tells us they are all criminals, but we know that; they were born looking guilty.

John Huston's *Beat the Devil* (1953) shows how much Hollywood has lost by devaluing its character actors. In an age when a $20 million star must be on the screen every second, this picture could not be made. Huston has stars, too: Bogart, Jennifer Jones, Gina Lollobrigida, but his movie is so funny because he throws them into the pot with a seedy gang of charlatans. "We have to beware of them," the Jones character warns her husband. "They're desperate characters. Not one of them looked at my legs."

Beat the Devil went straight from box office flop to cult classic and has been called the first camp movie, although Bogart, who sank his own money into it, said, "Only phonies like it." It's a movie that was made up on the spot; Huston tore up the original screenplay on the first day of filming, flew the young Truman Capote to Ravello, Italy, to crank out new scenes against a daily deadline, and allowed his supporting stars, especially Robert Morley and Peter Lorre, to create dialogue for their own characters. (Capote spoke daily by telephone with his pet raven, and one day when the raven re-

fused to answer he flew to Rome to console it, further delaying the production.)

The story involves a crowd of raffish misfits killing time in the little Italian seaport until repairs are completed on the rust-bucket ship that will take them to British East Africa. They all have secret schemes to stake a claim to a uranium find. Bogart and Lollobrigida play Billy and Maria Dannreuther; he once owned a local villa but has been reduced to having his hotel bills paid by Peterson (Robert Morley), a crook in a magnificent ice-cream suit, his tie laid out like a Dover sole on the upper reaches of his belly. Peterson's other associates include a man named O'Hara (Peter Lorre) who has a German accent and says, suspiciously, that there are a lot of O'Haras in Chile; the rat-faced little Major Ross (Ivor Barnard), who observes approvingly, "Hitler knew how to put women in their place," and the gaunt, mournful hawk-nosed Ravello (Marco Tulli). Also waiting for the boat to sail are Gwendolen and Harry Chelm (Jennifer Jones and Edward Underdown), who claim to be from the landed gentry of Gloucestershire.

These characters are imported, more or less, from an original novel by "James Helvick," actually the left-wing British critic Claud Cockburn (whose son Alexander named his column in *Nation* magazine after the movie). The film was originally set in a French town, and intended to be a halfway serious thriller about the evils of colonial exploitation. When Bogart signed aboard, that's what he thought it would be, but at some point in the transfer to Italian locations John Huston decided to make it a comedy, and hired the twenty-eight-year-old Capote on the advice of Jones's husband, the tireless memo writer David O. Selznick.

There are times during the movie when you can sense Capote chuckling to himself as he supplies improbable dialogue for his characters. Lollobrigida, the Italian sex star, was making her first English-language movie, but Capote has her explain, "Emotionally, I am English." She claims to take tea and crumpets every afternoon, and quotes the writer George Moore, who, I believe, has not been quoted before or since in any movie. Bogart describes his early upbringing: "I was an orphan until I was twenty. Then a rich and beautiful lady adopted me." And Peter Lorre, of course, has his famous lines about time, which deserves comparison with Orson

Welles's "cuckoo clock" speech in *The Third Man.* "Time . . . time," Lorre says. "What is time? Swiss manufacture it. French hoard it. Italians squander it. Americans say it is money. Hindus say it does not exist. Do you know what I say? I say time is a crook."

The plot is an afterthought. This is a movie about eccentric behavior. Edward Underdown, as Jones's husband, affects British upper-class manners, travels with his hot-water bottle, takes to his bed with "a shocking chill on my liver," and seems not to notice that his wife has fallen in love with the Bogart character. For that matter, Bogart's wife (Lollobrigida) has fallen in love with Chelm, and he seems oblivious to that as well. It is a measure of the movie that we are never quite sure if the Dannreuthers are both committing adultery or simply trying to discover the Chelms' secret plans for the uranium; when Hollywood censors questioned the adultery in the original story, Huston and Capote simply made it enigmatic.

Much of the humor is generated by the two women. Jones plays a busybody, one of those women who accidentally blurts out exactly what she intends to say. Lollobrigida wears a series of similarly low-cut, cinched-waist evening dresses at all times of the day. And Morley's gang turns up inappropriately dressed for the hot weather, sweating and squirming, all except for the imperturbable Lorre, who has died his hair platinum and sucks continuously on a cigarette in a holder that he holds like a flute.

Even the third-team supporting characters are entertaining. When the two couples drive out for dinner, Bogart hires an antique open-topped Hispano-Suiza automobile he claims to have gotten from a bullfighter and given to the driver (Juan de Landa). Later, when the car is lost through hilarious miscalculation, the driver wants compensation. "Why, you thief, I *gave* you that car!" Bogart roars. "How I came into possession of it is beside the point," the driver insists.

Other bit players include the ship's purser (Mario Perrone), who has the knack of materializing instantly when anything goes wrong and knowing exactly what has happened. And the captain (Saro Urzì), continuously drunk. And Ahmed (Manuel Serano), the Arab leader who arrests them after they're shipwrecked in Africa, and pumps Bogart for details about Rita Hayworth. When Ahmed asks Bogart to betray Morley, Bogart wants to be paid. "Your demands are very great, under the circumstances," the official tells him. "Why shouldn't they be?" says Bogart. "Fat Gut's my best friend, and I will not betray him cheaply."

One of Huston's running jokes through the film involves the composition of his shots of Morley and his three associates. They are so different in appearance, height, and manner that they hardly seem able to fit into the same frame, and Huston uses a system of rotation to bring each one forward as he speaks, mournfully framed by the others. Despite their differences, they form a unit, and when it appears that Morley may have been killed in the auto mishap, the rat-faced major is distraught: "Mussolini, Hitler—and now, Peterson!"

If *Beat the Devil* puzzled audiences on its first release, it has charmed them since. Jennifer Jones told the critic Charles Champlin that Huston promised her, "Jennifer, they'll remember you longer for *Beat the Devil* than for *The Song of Bernadette*." True, but could Huston have guessed that they would remember him more for *Beat the Devil* than for the picture he made next, *Moby Dick*?

The movie has, above all, effortless charm. Once we catch on that nothing much is going to happen, we can relax and share the amusement of the actors, who are essentially being asked to share their playfulness. There is a scene on a veranda overlooking the sea, where Bogart and Jones play out their first flirtation, and by the end of their dialogue you can see they're all but cracking up; Bogart grins during the dissolve. The whole movie feels that way. Now that movies have become fearsome engines designed to hammer us with entertainment, it is nice to recall those that simply wanted to be witty company.

{ BEING THERE }

On the day that Kasparov was defeated by Deep Blue, I found myself thinking of the film *Being There* (1979). The chess champion said there was something about the computer he did not understand, and it frightened him. There were moments when the computer seemed to be . . . thinking. Of course, chess is not a game of thought but of mathematical strategy; Deep Blue has demonstrated that it is possible to be very good at it without possessing consciousness.

The classic test of artificial intelligence has been: Can a computer be programmed to conduct a conversation that seems human to another human? *Being There* is a film about a man whose mind works like a rudimentary A.I. program. It has been supplied with a fund of simplistic generalizations about the world, phrased in terms of the garden where he has worked all his adult life. But because he presents himself as a man of good breeding (he walks and talks like the wealthy older man whose house he lived in, and wears the man's tailored suits) his simplicity is mistaken for profundity, and soon he is advising presidents and befriending millionaires.

The man's name is Chance. We gather he has lived all of his life inside the town house and walled garden of a rich recluse (perhaps he is his son). He knows what he needs to know for his daily routine: where his bedroom and bathroom are, and how to tend the plants of the garden. His meals are produced by Louise, the cook. The movie provides no diagnosis of his condition. He is able to respond to given cues and can, within limits, adapt and learn. Early in the film he introduces himself as "Chance . . . the gardener" and is misunderstood as having said "Chauncey Gardiner." Just the sort of WASP name that matches his clothing and demeanor, and soon he is telling the president, "Spring, summer, autumn, winter . . . then spring again." Indeed.

Chance is played by Peter Sellers, an actor who once told me he had "absolutely no personality at all. I am a chameleon. When I am not playing a role, I am nobody." Of course he thought himself ideal for this role, which comes from a novel by Jerzy Kosinski. Sellers plays Chance as a man at peace with himself. After the old man dies, the household is broken up, and Chance is evicted, there is a famous scene where he is confronted by possible muggers; he simply points a channel changer at them and clicks. He is surprised when they do not go away.

Sellers plays Chance at exactly the same note for the entire film. He is detached, calm, secure in his own knowledge, unaware of his limitations. Through a series of happy chances, he is taken into the home of a dying millionaire named Benjamin Rand (Melvyn Douglas). The millionaire's wife, Eve (Shirley MacLaine), establishes Chance in a guest suite, where he is happy to find a television. (His most famous line is "I like to watch.") Soon the rich man grows to treasure his reassuring friend. The family doctor (Richard Dysart) is perceptive and begins to have doubts about Chance's authenticity, but silences himself when his patient says Chauncey "has made the thought of dying much easier." Chauncey is introduced by Ben to the president (Jack Warden), becomes an unofficial adviser, and soon is being interviewed on television, where his insights fit nicely into the limited space available for sound bites.

Satire is a threatened species in American film, and when it does occur, it's usually broad and slapstick, as in the Mel Brooks films. *Being There*, directed by Hal Ashby, is a rare and subtle bird that finds its tone and stays with it. It has the appeal of an ingenious intellectual game in which the hero survives a series of challenges he doesn't understand, using words that are both universal and meaningless. But are Chance's sayings noticeably less useful than when the president tells us about "staying the course"? Sensible public speech in our time is limited by 1) the need to stay within

the confines of the ten-second TV sound bite, 2) the desire to avoid being pinned down to specific claims or promises, and 3) the abbreviated attention span of the audience, which, like Chance, likes to watch but always has a channel-changer poised.

If Chance's little slogans reveal how superficial public utterance can be, his reception reveals still more. Because he is WASP, middle-aged, well-groomed, dressed in tailored suits, and speaks like an educated man, he is automatically presumed to be a person of substance. He is, in fact, socially naive ("You're always going to be a little boy," Louise tells him). But this leads to a directness that can be mistaken for confidence, as when he addresses the president by his first name or enfolds his hand in both of his own. The movie argues that if you look right, sound right, speak in platitudes, and have powerful friends, you can go far in our society. By the end of the film, Chance is being seriously proposed as a presidential candidate. Well, why not? I once watched Lamar Alexander for forty-five minutes on C-SPAN, as he made small talk in a New Hampshire diner, and heard nothing that Chance could not have said. And many of George W. Bush's utterances are Chance-speak.

The film is not flawless. There are two sex-oriented subplots, and neither one is necessary. The story of the president's impotence could have been completely dispensed with. And the seduction attempt by Shirley MacLaine, as the millionaire's wife, requires her to act in a less intelligent way than she should. MacLaine projects brains; she, like the doctor, should have caught on, and that would have created more intriguing scenes than her embarrassing poses on a bear rug.

In the much-discussed final sequence of *Being There*, Chance casually walks onto the surface of a lake. We can see that he is really walking on the water, because he leans over curiously and sticks his umbrella down into it. When I taught the film I had endless discussions with my students over this scene. Many insisted on explaining it: He is walking on a hidden sandbar, the water is only half an inch deep, there is a submerged pier, and so on. "Not valid!" I thundered. "The movie presents us with an image, and while you may discuss the meaning of the image, it is not permitted to devise explanations for it. Since Ashby does not show a pier, there is no pier—a movie is exactly what it shows us, and nothing more."

So what does it show us? It shows us Chance doing something that is primarily associated with only one other figure in human history. What are we to assume? That Chance is a Christ figure? That the wisdom of great leaders only has the appearance of meaning? That we find in politics and religion whatever we seek? That like the Road Runner (who also defies gravity), he will not sink until he understands his dilemma? The implications are alarming. Is it possible that we are all just clever versions of Chance the gardener? That we are trained from an early age to respond automatically to given words and concepts? That we never really think out much of anything for ourselves but are content to repeat what works for others in the same situation?

The last words in the movie are "Life is a state of mind." So no computer will ever be alive. But to the degree that we are limited by our programming, neither will we. The question is not whether a computer will ever think like a human but whether we choose to free ourselves from thinking like computers.

THE BIG HEAT

Glenn Ford plays a straight-arrow police detective named Bannion in Fritz Lang's *The Big Heat* (1953)—unbending, courageous, fearless. He takes on the criminals who control the politics in his town, and defeats them. One of his motives is revenge for the murder of his wife, but even before that happens he has an implacable hatred for the gang headed by Mike Lagana (Alexander Scourby) and his right-hand man, Vince Stone (Lee Marvin). "Thieves," he calls them, preferably to their faces. He is the good cop in a bad town.

That, at least, is the surface reality of the film. But there is another level coiling away underneath, a subversive level in which Lang questions the human cost of Bannion's ethical stand. Two women lose their lives because they trust Bannion, and a third is sent to her death because of information Bannion gives her. That may not have been his conscious intention, but a cop as clever as Bannion should know when to keep his trap shut.

The film is as deceptive and two-faced as anything Lang ever made, with its sunny domestic tranquillity precariously separated from a world of violence. Bannion thinks he can draw a line between his loving wife and adorable child, and the villains he deals with at work. But he invites evil into the lives of his wife and two other women by his self-righteous heroism. Does it ever occur to him that he is at least partly responsible for their deaths? No, apparently it doesn't, and that's one reason the film is so insid-

iously chilling; he continues on his mission oblivious to its cost. Oh, he's right, of course, that Lagana and Stone are vermin. But tell that to the women he obliviously sends into harm's way.

He's working on a case that begins with the suicide of a cop who was sick of being on the mob's payroll. He questions Bertha, the cop's widow (Jeanette Nolan), who says her husband killed himself because he was sick. Bannion doesn't think her story smells right, and then is approached by Lucy (Dorothy Green), the cop's mistress, who tells him the cop was in perfect health. Bannion unwisely tells Bertha what Lucy told him, she tells Lagana, and Lucy is dumped dead on a county road. If he suspects Bertha and half-believes Lucy, and Bertha is still alive, then she must be talking to the mob. Why didn't Bannion suspect that? How naive can he be?

Bannion is told by his boss to lay off the case: "I got a call from upstairs." That night his wife (Jocelyn Brando, Marlon's sister) gets a threatening telephone call, and Bannion is enraged. He walks into Lagana's house, threatens him, and beats up his bodyguard. Does he think this might put his own family in danger? Apparently not, until a bomb goes off when his wife starts the car.

Within a few days he threatens Vince Stone and orders him out of the bar where the mob hangs out. Stone's girl, Debby (Gloria Grahame), fed up with Stone, follows Bannion onto the street. He takes her to his hotel room, where they drink and he pumps her for information, and there is just a moment when he almost forgets he is a recent widower.

Debby was followed to the hotel, and when she returns to Stone he throws a pot of boiling coffee at her face, in one of the most famous scenes in noir history. Her face half-covered by bandages, she escapes from the hospital and asks Bannion to protect her. He tells her that Bertha the widow has the goods on the mob, is being paid off by the week, and has arranged for the information to go to the papers if she dies. Does he tell Debby this because he wants her to kill the widow? Does it even occur to him that she might, as a way of avenging the scars to her face? Does he expect that will lead to her own death? Of course not. In a passive-aggressive way he blandly sets these women up for death. When the elderly, lame bookkeeper at a junkyard risks her life to give him information about his wife's killer, he even persuades her to knock on the killer's door so she can identify him. Dangerous? Yes, but, to Bannion, an acceptable risk—for her.

Fritz Lang (1890–1976) was one of the cinema's great architects of evil. His *Metropolis* (1926) is one of the best of all silent films, but it was with *M* (1931), and Peter Lorre's eerie performance as a child murderer, that he stared unblinking at pure malevolence. He fled Hitler and Germany and became a prolific director of Hollywood genre pictures—some competent, some masterpieces of film noir, the greatest *The Big Heat.* There is a kind of ironic pessimism in his work, undermining the apparent bravery of his heroes.

Glenn Ford plays a perfectly acceptable honest cop in *The Big Heat.* He can be quiet and contained and implacable, but that Bannion is for surface and show. When he gets angry he's capable of sudden violence—as when he nearly strangles two characters. *The Big Heat* advances dutifully with Bannion like a conventional police procedural until about the halfway point, when it takes fire with the performances of Lee Marvin and Gloria Grahame.

This is one of the inspired performances of Grahame, a legendary character who became known as the "Can't Say No Girl," and not just because she sang the song in *Oklahoma!* Her untidy personal life led to four marriages and many affairs; one of her husbands was the director Nicholas Ray, after she worked for him in *In a Lonely Place* (1950), and another was Ray's son Anthony. She won an Oscar for best supporting actress for *The Bad and the Beautiful* (1952) and should have won again the next year for *The Big Heat,* where her energy is the best reason to see the film. There was something fresh and modern about Grahame; she's always a little ditzy, as if nodding to an unheard melody. She was pretty but not beautiful, sassy but in a tired and knowing way, and she had a way of holding her face and her mouth relatively immobile while she talked, as if she was pretending to be well behaved. "It wasn't the way I looked at a man," she said, "it was the thought behind it."

She always seems a little unstrung in *The Big Heat,* as if she knows she's in danger and is trying to kid herself that she isn't. The Marvin character can be brutal to women; he hits one in a nightclub, and she tells Bannion that he hit her, too, "but most times, it's a lot of fun. Expensive fun." Intriguing, how she half-tries to seduce him in his fleabag hotel room: "You're about as romantic as a pair of handcuffs. Didn't you ever tell a girl pretty things? You know, she's got hair like the west wind, eyes like limpid pools, and skin like velvet?"

Lee Marvin made a scary foil for her, with his long, lean face and his ugly-handsome scowl. If Alexander Scourby's mob boss seems like a writer's conceit, Marvin's character brings real menace into the picture, coldly and without remorse. The scene with the scalding coffee has become so famous that you forget it happens off-screen. Afterward, when the bandaged Debby turns to Bannion for protection, she bravely still tries to keep up her act: "I guess the scar isn't so bad—not if it's only on one side. I can always go through life sideways."

On the surface, *The Big Heat* is about Bannion's fearless one-man struggle against a mob so entrenched that the police commissioner is a regular at Marvin's poker game. But if that were its real subject, it would be long and flat and dry. The women bring the life into it, along with Lee Marvin. We add up the toll: Lucy Chapman, the B-girl who loved the suicidal cop and is betrayed by Bannion. Bannion's wife, who trusted him to protect her. And Debby, who likes him and maybe feels sorry for him, and gets her face scarred as a result, and then is sent to do his errand for him. After he explains to her how the widow's death will destroy the mob, he quietly mentions that he himself almost killed Bertha an hour ago, planting the seed. (Before she kills the widow, Debby stays in character: "We should use first names, Bertha. We're sisters under the mink.")

When Bannion returns to his job, reclaims his old desk, is greeted by his fellow cops, and goes out on another case, he lets the guys know it's still business as usual; as he leaves the office he calls back over his shoulder, "Keep the coffee hot." Not, under the circumstances, very tactful. Bannion's buried agenda is to set up the women, allow their deaths to confirm his hatred of the Lagana-Stone crew, and then wade in to get revenge. Of course, he doesn't understand this himself, and it is perfectly possible for us to watch the movie and never have it occur to us. That's the beauty of Lang's moral ambidexterity. He tells the story of a heroic cop while using it to mask another story, so much darker, beneath.

THE BIRTH
OF A NATION

*He achieved what no other known man has achieved. To watch his
work is like being witness to the beginning of melody, or the first
conscious use of the lever or the wheel; the emergence, coordination and
first eloquence of language; the birth of an art: and to realize that this is
all the work of one man.*

These words by James Agee about D. W. Griffith are almost by definition
the highest praise any film director has ever received from a great film critic.
On the other hand, the equally distinguished critic Andrew Sarris wrote
about Griffith's masterpiece, "Classic or not, *Birth of a Nation* has long been
one of the embarrassments of film scholarship. It can't be ignored . . . and
yet it was regarded as outrageously racist even at a time when racism was
hardly a household word."

Here are two more quotations about the film:

It is like writing history with Lightning. And my only regret is that it is
all so terribly true.—President Woodrow Wilson, allegedly after seeing it
at a White House screening. The words are quoted on-screen at the beginning of most prints of the film.

The President was entirely unaware of the nature of the play before it was presented and at no time has expressed his approbation of it.—Letter from J. M. Tumulty, secretary to President Wilson, to the Boston branch of the NAACP, which protested against the film's blackface villains and heroic Ku Klux Klanners.

Nobody seems to know the source of the Wilson quote, which is cited in every discussion of the film. Not dear Lillian Gish, whose *The Movies, Mr. Griffith, and Me* is a touchingly affectionate and yet clear-eyed memoir of a man she always called "Mr. Griffith" and clearly loved. And not Richard Schickel, whose *D. W. Griffith: An American Life* is a great biography. Certainly the quote is suspiciously similar to Coleridge's famous comment about the acting of Edmund Kean: "like reading Shakespeare by flashes of lightning."

My guess is that Wilson said something like it in private, then found it prudent to deny the comment when progressive editorialists attacked the film. Certainly *The Birth of a Nation* (1915) presents a challenge for modern audiences. Unaccustomed to silent films and uninterested in film history, they find it quaint and not to their taste. Those evolved enough to understand what they are looking at find the early and wartime scenes brilliant but cringe during the postwar and Reconstruction scenes, which are racist in the ham-handed way of an old minstrel show or a vile comic pamphlet.

Cited until the 1960s as the greatest American film, *Birth* is still praised as influential, groundbreaking, and historically important, yes—but is it actually seen? Despite the release of an excellent DVD restoration from Kino, it is all but unwatched. More people may have seen Griffith's *Intolerance* (1916), made in atonement after the protests against *Birth*. It says something about my own conflicted state of mind that I included Griffith's *Broken Blossoms* (1919) in the first *Great Movies* collection but have only now arrived at *Birth of a Nation*. I was avoiding it.

Yet the film is an unavoidable fact of American movie history, and must be dealt with, so allow me to rewind to a different quote from James Agee: "The most beautiful single shot I have seen in any movie is the battle charge in *The Birth of a Nation*. I have heard it praised for its realism, but

it is also far beyond realism. It seems to me to be a realization of a collective dream of what the Civil War was like."

I have just looked at the battle charge again, having recently endured the pallid pieties of the pedestrian Civil War epic *Gods and Generals,* and I agree with Agee. Griffith demonstrated to every filmmaker and moviegoer who followed him what a movie was, and what a movie could be. That this achievement was made in a film marred by racism should not be surprising. As a nation once able to reconcile democracy with slavery, America has a stain on its soul; to understand our history we must begin with the contradiction that the Founding Fathers believed that all men (except black men) were created equal.

Griffith will probably never lose his place in the pantheon, but there will always be the blot of the later scenes of *The Birth of a Nation.* It is a stark history lesson to realize that this film, for many years the most popular ever made, expressed widely held and generally acceptable white views. Miss Gish reveals more than she realizes when she quotes Griffith's paternalistic reply to accusations that he was anti-Negro: "To say that is like saying I am against children, as they were our children, whom we loved and cared for all of our lives."

Griffith and *The Birth of a Nation* were no more enlightened than the America that produced them. The film represents how racist a white American could be in 1915 without realizing he was racist at all. That is worth knowing. Blacks already knew that, had known it for a long time, witnessed it painfully again every day, but *The Birth of a Nation* demonstrated it in clear view, and the importance of the film includes the clarity of its demonstration. That it is a mirror of its time is, sadly, one of its values.

To understand *The Birth of a Nation* we must first understand the difference between what we bring to the film and what the film brings to us. All serious moviegoers must sooner or later arrive at a point where they see a film for what it is, and not simply for what they feel about it. *The Birth of a Nation* is not a bad film because it argues for evil. Like Riefenstahl's *The Triumph of the Will,* it is a great film that argues for evil. To understand how it does so is to learn a great deal about film, and even something about evil.

But is it possible to separate the content from the craft? Garry Wills observes that Griffith's film "raises the same questions that Leni

Riefenstahl's films do, or Ezra Pound's poems. If art should serve beauty and truth, how can great art be in the thrall of hateful ideologies?" The crucial assumption here is that art should serve beauty and truth. I would like to think it should, but there is art that serves neither, and yet provides an insight into human nature, helping us understand good and evil. In that case, *The Birth of a Nation* is worth considering, if only for the inescapable fact that it did more than any other work of art to dramatize and encourage racist attitudes in America. (The contemporary works that made the most useful statements against racism were *Uncle Tom's Cabin* and *Huckleberry Finn.*)

Racism of the sort seen in *The Birth of a Nation* has not been acceptable for decades in American popular culture. Modern films make racism invisible, curable, an attribute of villains, or the occasion for optimistic morality plays. *The Birth of a Nation* is unapologetic about its attitudes, which are those of a white southerner raised in the nineteenth century, unable to see African Americans as fellow beings of worth and rights. It is based in part on Thomas Dixon's racist play *The Clansman,* and the fact that Griffith wanted to adapt it reveals his own prejudices.

Griffith, for example, was criticized for using white actors in blackface to portray his black villains. There are bizarre shots where a blackface character acts in the foreground while real African Americans labor in the fields behind him. His excuse, as relayed by Miss Gish: "There were scarcely any Negro actors on the Coast" and "Mr. Griffith was accustomed to working with actors he had trained." But of course there were no black actors, because blackface whites were always used, and that also explains why he did not need to train any.

Griffith's blindness to the paradox in his own statement is illuminating. His blackface actors tell us more about his attitude toward those characters than black actors ever could have. Consider the fact that the blackface is obvious; the makeup is not as good as it could have been. That makes its own point: Black actors could not have been used in such sexually charged scenes, even if Griffith had wanted to, because white audiences would not have accepted them. Griffith wanted his audience to notice the blackface.

Some of the film's most objectionable scenes show the Ku Klux

Klan riding to the rescue of a white family trapped in a cabin by sexually predatory blacks and their white manipulators. These scenes are credited with the revival of the popularity of the Klan, which was all but extinct when the movie appeared. Watching them today, we are appalled. But audiences in 1915 were witnessing *the invention of intercutting in a chase scene.* Nothing like it had ever been seen before: parallel action building to a suspense climax. Do you think they were thinking about blackface? They were thrilled out of their minds.

Today, what they saw for the first time, we cannot see at all. Griffith assembled and perfected the early discoveries of film language, and his cinematic techniques have influenced the visual strategies of virtually every film made since; they have become so familiar we are not even aware of them. We, on the other hand, are astonished by racist attitudes that were equally invisible to most white audiences in 1915.

What are those techniques? They start at the level of film grammar. Silent films began with crude constructions designed to simply look at a story as it happened before the camera. Griffith, in his short films and features, invented or incorporated anything that seemed to work to expand that vision. He did not create the language of cinema so much as codify and demonstrate it, so that after him it became conventional for directors to tell a scene by cutting between wide (or "establishing") shots and various medium shots, close-ups, and inserts of details. The first close-up must have come as an alarming surprise for its audiences; Griffith made them and other kinds of shots indispensable for telling a story.

In his valuable book *On the History of Film Style,* David Bordwell observes that Griffith "is usually credited with perfecting the enduring artistic resources of the story film." Bordwell has some quarrels with that widely accepted basic version of film history, but he lists Griffith's innovations and observes that the film "is often considered cinema's first masterpiece."

One of Griffith's key contributions was his pioneering use of crosscutting to follow parallel lines of action. A naive audience might have been baffled by a film that showed first one group of characters, then another, then the first again. From Griffith's success in using this technique comes the chase scene and many other modern narrative approaches. The critic Tim Dirks adds to crosscutting no less than sixteen other ways in which

Griffith was an innovator, ranging from his night photography to his use of the iris shot and color tinting.

Certainly *The Birth of a Nation* is a film of great visual beauty and narrative power. It tells the story of the Civil War through the experiences of families from both North and South, shows the flowing of their friendship, shows them made enemies as the nation was divided, and in a battlefield scene has the sons of both families dying almost simultaneously. It is unparalleled in its re-creations of actual battles on realistic locations; the action in some scenes extends for miles. For audiences at the time there would have been great interest in Griffith's attempts to reproduce historic incidents, such as the assassination of Lincoln, with exacting accuracy. His re-creation of Sherman's march through Georgia is so bloody and merciless that it awakened southern passions all over again.

The human stories of the leading characters have the sentiment and human detail we would expect of a leading silent filmmaker, and the action scenes are filmed with a fluid ease that seems astonishing compared to other films of the time. Griffith uses elevated shots to provide a high-angle view of the battlefields, and cuts between parallel actions to make the battles comprehensible; they are not simply big tableaux of action.

Yet when it comes to his version of the Reconstruction era, he tells the story of the liberation of the slaves and its aftermath through the eyes of a southerner who cannot view African Americans as possible partners in American civilization. In the first half of the film the black characters are mostly ignored in the background. In the second half, Griffith dramatizes material in which white women are seen as the prey of lustful freed slaves, often urged on by evil white northern carpetbaggers whose goal is to destroy and loot the South. The most exciting and technically accomplished sequence in the second half of the film is also the most disturbing: A white family is under siege in a log cabin, attacked by blacks and their white exploiters, while the Ku Klux Klan rides to the rescue.

Meanwhile, Elsie (Lillian Gish), the daughter of the abolitionist Senator Stoneman, fights off a sexual assault by Stoneman's mulatto servant, Lynch. Stoneman has earlier told Lynch, "You are the equal of any man here." Returning home, he is told by Lynch, "I want to marry a white woman," and pats him approvingly on the shoulder. But when he is told that his daughter Elsie is the woman Lynch has in mind, Stoneman turns violent toward him—Griffith's way of showing that the abolitionists and carpetbaggers lied to the freed slaves, to manipulate them for greed and gain.

The long third act of the film is where the most offensive racism resides. There is no denying the effectiveness of the first two acts. The first establishes a bucolic, idealistic view of America before the Civil War, with the implication that the North should have left well enough alone. The second involves unparalleled scenes of the war itself, which seem informed by the photographs of Matthew Brady and have a powerful realism and conviction.

Griffith has a sure hand in the way he cuts from epic shots of enormous scope to small human vignettes. He was the first director to understand instinctively how a movie could mimic the human ability to scan an event quickly, noting details in the midst of the larger picture. Many silent films moved slowly, as if afraid to get ahead of their audiences; Griffith springs forward eagerly, and the impact on his audiences was unprecedented—they were learning for the first time what a movie was capable of.

As slavery is the great sin of America, so *The Birth of a Nation* is Griffith's sin, for which he tried to atone all the rest of his life. So instinctive were the prejudices he was raised with as a nineteenth-century southerner that the offenses in his film actually had to be explained to him. To his credit, his next film, *Intolerance,* was an attempt at apology. He also once edited a version of the film that cut out all of the Klan material, but that is not the answer. If we are to see this film, we must see it all, and deal with it all.

{ THE BLUE KITE }

In a small room on a courtyard off Dry Well Lane in Beijing, a marriage is celebrated and a child is born. The people of the courtyard all know one another, and share joys and sorrows and food. They are ordinary, unsophisticated citizens; when a loudspeaker announces the death of Stalin, one of them asks, "Who is this Stalin person?" Into their lives during the next twenty-five years will come wave after wave of political hysteria, rendering all of their hopes and plans meaningless. *The Blue Kite* (1993) is nothing less than the attempt to show what it was like to live in times of ideological madness.

The boy is called Tietou. The name translates as "Iron Head." His mother is a teacher, his father is a librarian, and his childhood memories include playmates and family gatherings and the portentous comings and goings of an uncle and his girlfriend who have both joined the army. He treasures a blue kite, and when it is caught in a tree, his father promises to give him a new one. The kite becomes an emblem of loss.

In the early days of the film, China still lives under an informal capitalism, but changes are in the wind. A neighborhood committee comes to question the landlady about her holdings, but is mollified to learn that the courtyard is the property of the state, and she has lowered the rents. These good citizens understand that the nation must change after the revolution. They do their best to go along, but what they do not understand is that no rational national plan exists. The political winds, which change direction from season to season, function only to bring an end to dissent and individuality—to create a climate of fear within which the country can be controlled.

Eventually one of those winds blows Tietou's father away forever. Shalong (Pu Quanxin) is a good librarian, a faithful employee who is one day called to a meeting as part of the Rectification Movement, in which those with right-wing tendencies must be identified. There is a quota, and the library has not met it. Shalong unwisely leaves the meeting to go to the toilet, and when he returns, all of the eyes in the room are turned to him. He pauses in the doorway and in a chilling instant realizes he chose the wrong time to leave the room.

His father has been sent "far, far away," Tietou learns from his mother Shujuan (Lu Liping). Shalong goes to a labor camp and eventually is killed in an accident. Now *The Blue Kite* will be the story of this strong mother trying to raise her child in a society where disruption seems to exist for its own sake. Together they will live through the Great Leap Forward and the insanity of the Cultural Revolution, through poverty and famine, through two more marriages, all the time hoping to spend ordinary lives in ordinary ways.

The Blue Kite was directed by Tian Zhuangzhuang, a member of the Fifth Generation of Chinese filmmakers, which also includes Zhang Yimou and Chen Kaige. He had a hard time of it. In a statement about the film, he says he finished filming in 1992. "But while I was involved in post-production, several official organizations involved with China's film industry screened the film. They decided that it had a problem concerning its political 'leanings,' and prevented its completion. The fact that it can appear today seems like a miracle."

His contemporaries had similar problems with films critical of recent history. Chen Kaige's *Farewell My Concubine* (1993) and Zhang Yimou's *To Live* (1994) were scarcely seen within China, which was happy to share in the money they earned overseas but was not eager to dramatize those hard times for the people who had lived through them. The Communist Party that rules China today is directly descended from the

party that went haywire during the Cultural Revolution, even if it rules a nation racing headlong toward capitalism.

The Blue Kite gains much of its power by being about everyday, unexceptional lives. There are no villains. We never see a major party leader. Even the mobs that roam through the streets, plastering posters and shouting slogans, are neighbors who at some level are simply trying to do the right thing. A teacher is denounced and her hair is cut, but the mob seems young and jolly, and Tietou cheerfully tells his mother, "Mom, today we struggled our principal and wrote posters against her and cut her hair. She's such a bad person. She scolds and punishes us. Everybody spat at her." ("Struggle" is used throughout the film as a word for political correction.)

His mother marries a family friend who adores her and her boy, and who sees their room as his home. But one night, carrying dumplings to the table, he collapses, and two weeks later he is dead; the enigmatic diagnosis is "liver, underworked, malnourished." Eventually she marries again, this time to a minor party official, and they live in his house and are comfortable for a time, but then one night he sits them down, gives them money, and suggests a divorce: He has been denounced at work and it will be best for them not to be identified with him. The saddest line in this scene comes as he touches Tietou, now a young teenager, and says, "I really am fond of this kid. Even if he's never liked me. Kids are like that."

The official, ill from heart disease, is carried from his house on a stretcher by a shouting mob. We see that there is no right or wrong in this mad society, only degrees of immunity from the mob. And yet Tian Zhuangzhuang never blames or names. The mobs never seem to come from outside; they consist of ordinary people trying to be good citizens. They have been betrayed by their leaders and insanity is abroad in the land, so they embrace political zealotry as a patriotic duty. "The stories in the film are real, and they are related with total sincerity," the director said at the time. Some of them were based on his own experiences. "What worries me is that it is precisely a fear of reality and sincerity that has led to the ban on such stories being told."

The power of his film comes from its resolutely human focus; we get a palpable sense of what it was like to live on Dry Well Lane in those days, to share food and fuel, to play gladly in the school yard, to know by looking out the window who was coming or going. The Beijing in the film is balanced between the China of time immemorial and the emerging new world. Motor vehicles are seen in the army scenes, but there are hardly any in the streets of the city, where people hurry by bicycle and foot. The neighborhood is so much the focus of life that we never really sense the great metropolis. The film is photographed with remarkable gracefulness, colors and compositions finding beauty in the lives of these people, and especially in their faces.

Is it wrong, is it bourgeois reactionary thinking, to desire a safe and happy life for your family? To want to do a job well and be rewarded for it? Not at all. These are universal hopes, and throughout *The Blue Kite* we can see characters seeking them. An old mother sips her tea and states that she is beyond politics—"too old for it." And there is a poignant scene when the army brother, who has left the service because of bad eyes, goes for a last visit to his girlfriend, who is still in uniform. She advises him to forget her, because she will be where she is for a long, long time. (There is an echo here of Ha Jin's stories about romance and marriage put on hold for long years by duties to the state.)

The Blue Kite is a profoundly political film, but it achieves its purpose by indirection. It is not so much about China as about human nature. To read about the Cultural Revolution is to wonder how such madness swept a nation. To see this film is to understand that unthinking patriotism gone wrong can lead to great mischief. It is appropriate that the film is, in a sense, left unfinished.

BOB LE FLAMBEUR

Flamber *(verb, French): to wager not only the money you have but the money you don't have.*

I was born with an ace in my palm.
BOB

Before the New Wave, before Godard and Truffaut and Chabrol, before Belmondo flicked the cigarette into his mouth in one smooth motion and walked the streets of Paris like a Hollywood gangster, there was Bob. *Bob le Flambeur*, Bob the high roller, Bob the Montmartre legend whose style was so cool, whose honor was so strong, whose gambling was so hopeless that even the cops liked him. Bob with his white hair slicked back, with his black suit and tie, his trench coat, his Packard convertible, and his penthouse apartment with the slot machine in the closet. Bob, who on the first day of this movie wins big at the races and then loses it all at roulette, and is cleaned out. Broke again.

Jean-Pierre Melville's *Bob le Flambeur* has a good claim to be the first film of the French New Wave. Daniel Cauchy, who stars in it as Paolo, Bob's callow young friend, remembered that Melville would shoot scenes on location using a handheld camera on a delivery bike, "which Godard did in *Breathless*, but this was years before Godard." Melville worked on poverty

row, and told his actors there was no money to pay them but that they would have to stand by to shoot on a moment's notice. "Right now I have money for three or four days," he told Cauchy, "and after that we'll shoot when we can."

This film was legendary but unseen for years, and Melville's career is only now coming into focus. He shot gangster movies, he worked in genres, but he had such a precise, elegant simplicity of style that his films play like the chamber music of crime. He was cool in the 1950s sense of that word. His characters in *Bob* glide through gambling dens and nightclubs "in those moments," Melville tells us in the narration, "between night and day . . . between heaven and hell."

His story involves a gambler named Bob Montagne (Roger Duchesne), who is known to everybody in Montmartre. Yvonne (Simone Paris), who owns the corner bar, bought it with a loan from Bob. A local police inspector (Guy Decomble) had his life saved when Bob pushed a killer's arm aside. Paolo (Cauchy) is under Bob's wing because his father was Bob's old friend. As the movie opens, Bob sees a young streetwalker named Anne (Isabelle Corey) eat some French fries and then accept a ride from a client on a scooter. Later, when Anne seems about to fall into the power of the pimp Marc (Gérard Buhr), Bob orders Marc away and brings Anne home to his apartment—not to sleep with her, because that would not be cool, but as a favor to Paolo.

It is 1955. Bob has gone straight for twenty years. Before that, we understand, there was a bank job that led to some time in prison. Bob was a gangster in prewar Paris; "it's not the same anymore," he observes. Cauchy, whose memories are included in a filmed monologue on the DVD, explains that the war brought an end to the old criminal way of life: "These days, gangsters are pathetic delinquents. Gangsters back then, there was more to them." Everybody understands that Bob belongs to the old school.

Melville (1917–1973) was born Grumberg. He changed his name in admiration for the author of *Moby-Dick*. He was a lover of all things American. He went endlessly to American movies, he visited America, he shot a film in New York (*Two Men in Manhattan*), and Cauchy remembers, "He drove an American car and wore an American hat and Ray-Bans, and he always had the Armed Forces Network on his car radio, listening to

Glenn Miller." He inhaled American gangster films, although when he made his own they were not copies of Hollywood but were infused by understatement, a sense of cool; his characters need few words because so much goes without saying, especially when it comes to what must be done, and how it must be done, and why it must be done that way.

Bob le Flambeur opens by establishing the milieu. We see water trucks washing the streets at dawn. We follow Bob to the track, to the casino, and finally back to the neighborhood to lose his final two hundred francs. He hears an amazing thing: The safe of the casino at Deauville sometimes contains eight hundred million francs. He determines to assemble a gang of friends and experts and crack it. Melville is well aware of the convention where a mastermind uses a chart so his confederates (and the audience) can understand the logistics of a heist, but *Bob le Flambeur* surprises us: First, Bob walks everyone through their paces inside a large chalk outline of the casino, painted on the grass of an empty field. "Here's how Bob pictured the heist," the narrator tells us, and we see the gang moving through a casino that, in this fantasy, is entirely empty of customers or employees. The scheme is fairly simple, involving gunmen who hold everyone at bay while an expert cracks the safe. As the expert practices on a duplicate safe, he uses earphones and finally an oscilloscope to hear what the tumblers are doing, and Melville punctuates the intense silence of this rehearsal with shots of the safecracker's dog, a German shepherd who pants cheerfully and seems encouraged by his progress.

The safecracker is played by René Salgue, who was, Cauchy says, a real gangster. It was not easy for Melville to find successful actors who would agree to work for nothing and drop everything when he had raised more money. Duchesne, who plays Bob, was considered a risk because of a drinking problem. And as for Isabelle Corey, whose performance as Anne is one of the best elements of the movie, Melville picked her up off the street. Offered her a ride in his American car. Found out she was almost sixteen. Partially as a result of the legend of *Bob*, famous actors came around later. Melville's *Le Cercle Rouge* (1970), which his admirer John Woo restored for a 2003 release, starred Alain Delon and Yves Montand. Delon also worked for him in *Le Samourai* (1967), and Delon and Deneuve starred in his *Un Flic* (1972).

The actors are not required to do much. Like actors in a Bresson film, they embody more than they evoke. Most of what we think about Bob is inspired by what people say about him and how they treat him. Duchesne plays the character as poker-faced; he narrows his eyes but never widens them, and after Paolo blabs in bed to Anne about the plan and she blabs in bed to Marc, who is a police informer, Bob slaps her and walks out without betraying any emotion. Oh, first he leaves the key to his apartment with Yvonne, "for the kid," because he knows Anne will need a place to stay now that Bob knows about Paolo and Paolo knows about Marc.

Women are the source of most of the trouble in Bob's world. Anne's imprudence is repaired in the film, but there is also betrayal from the wife of a casino employee, who finds out about the plot from her husband. Melville liked women, Cauchy tells us, but he preferred to hang out with his pals, talking about the movies. Bob gets Anne a job as a bar girl in a night-club, notes her quick advancement to cigarette girl and then to "hostess," and tries his best to prevent Marc from becoming her pimp. One night, per-haps because despite her coldness she feels a certain gratitude, she hands Bob a flower. The gesture must have meant something to Melville, whose *Le Cercle Rouge* also has a man being offered a flower by a cigarette girl.

The climax of *Bob le Flambeur* involves surprising developments that approach cosmic irony. How strange, that a man's incorrigible nature would lead him both into and through temptation. The twist is so inspired many other directors have borrowed it, including Paul Thomas Anderson in *Hard Eight,* Neil Jordan in *The Good Thief,* and Lewis Milestone and Steven Soderbergh, the directors of the *Ocean's Eleven* movies. But *Bob* is not about the twist. It is about Bob being true to his essential nature. He is a gambler.

{ BREATHLESS }

When we talked, I talked about me, you talked about you,
when we should have talked about each other.
MICHEL TO PATRICIA

Modern movies begin here, with Jean-Luc Godard's *Breathless* in 1959. No debut film since *Citizen Kane* in 1941 has been as influential. It is dutifully repeated that Godard's technique of "jump cuts" is the great breakthrough, but, startling as they were, they were actually an afterthought, and what is most revolutionary about the movie is its headlong pacing, its cool detachment, its dismissal of authority, and the way its narcissistic young heroes are obsessed with themselves and oblivious to the larger society. There is a direct line through *Breathless* to *Bonnie and Clyde, Badlands,* and the youth upheaval of the late 1960s. The movie was a crucial influence during Hollywood's 1967–74 golden age. You cannot even begin to count the characters played by Pacino, Beatty, Nicholson, Penn, who are directly descended from Jean-Paul Belmondo's insouciant killer, Michel.

Breathless remains a living movie that still has the power to surprise and involve us after all these years. What fascinates above all is the naïveté and amorality of these two young characters: Michel, a car thief who pretends to be tougher than he is, and Patricia (Jean Seberg), an American who peddles the Paris edition of the *New York Herald Tribune* while waiting to enroll at the Sorbonne. Do they know what they're doing? Both of the important killings in the movie occur because Michel accidentally comes into possession of someone else's gun; Patricia's involvement with him seems inspired in equal parts by affection, sex, and fascination with his gangster persona.

Michel wants to be as tough as the stars in the movies he loves, and he idolizes Bogart. He practices facial expressions in the mirror, wears a fedora, and is never, ever seen without a cigarette, removing one from his mouth only to insert another. So omnipresent is this cigarette that Godard is only kidding us a little when Michel's dying breath is smoky. But Belmondo at twenty-six still had a little of the adolescent in him, and the first time we see him, his hat and even his cigarette seem too big for his face. He was "hypnotically ugly," Bosley Crowther wrote in his agitated *New York Times* review, but that did not prevent him from becoming the biggest French star between Jean Gabin and Gérard Depardieu.

Seberg was restarting her career after its disastrous launch in America. Otto Preminger staged a famous talent search for the star of his *Saint Joan* (1957) and cast an inexperienced eighteen-year-old Marshalltown, Iowa, girl; Seberg received terrible reviews, not entirely deserved, and more bad notices for *Bonjour Tristesse* (1958), which Preminger made next to prove himself right. She fled to Europe and was only twenty-one when Godard cast her for *Breathless*.

Her Patricia is the great enigma of the movie. Michel we can more or less read at sight: He postures as a gangster, maintains a cool facade, is frightened underneath. His persona is a performance that functions to conceal his desperation. But what about Patricia? Somehow it is never as important as it should be that she thinks she is pregnant, and that Michel is the father. She receives startling items of information about Michel (that he is a killer, that he is married, that he has more than one name) with such apparent detachment that we study that perfectly molded gamine face and wonder what she can possibly be thinking. Even her betrayal of him turns out to be not about Michel, and not about right and wrong, but only a test she sets for herself to determine if she loves him or not. It is remarkable that the reviews of this movie do not describe her as a monster—more evil, because less deluded, than Michel.

The filming of *Breathless* has gathered about it a body of legend. It was one of the key films of the French New Wave, which rejected the well-made traditional French cinema and embraced a rougher, more experimental personal style. Many of the New Wave directors began as critics for the antiestablishment magazine *Cahiers du Cinema*. The credits for *Breathless* are a New Wave roll call, including not only Godard's direction but an original story by François Truffaut (Godard famously wrote each day's shooting script in the morning). Claude Chabrol is production designer and technical adviser, the writer Daniel Boulanger plays the police inspector, and there are small roles for Truffaut and Godard himself (as the informer). Everyone was at the party; the assistant director was Pierre Rissient, who wears so many hats he is most simply described as knowing more people in the cinema than any other single person.

Jean-Pierre Melville, whose own crime movies in the 1950s pointed the way to the New Wave, plays the writer interviewed by Patricia at Orly, where he expounds on life and sex: "Two things are important in life. For men, women. For women, money." Melville's *Bob le Flambeur* (1955) is referenced when we meet the man who informed on Bob, and when Michel tells a friend, "Bob the gambler would have cashed my check." One inside joke in the film is always mentioned but is not really there. Michel's alias is "Laszlo Kovacs," and countless writers inform us that this is a reference to the legendary Hungarian cinematographer. In fact, Godard had not met Kovacs at the time, and the reference is to the character Belmondo played in Chabrol's *À Double Tour* (1959). In a film with so many references to the past of the cinema, it is amusing to find a coincidental reference to its future.

Godard's key collaborator on the film was the cinematographer Raoul Coutard, who worked with him many times, notably on *Weekend* (1967). It was only Coutard's fourth film, and his methods became legend: How when they could not afford tracks for a tracking shot, he held the camera and had himself pushed in a wheelchair. How he achieved a grainy look that influenced many other fiction films that wanted to seem realistic. How he scorned fancy lighting. How he used handheld techniques even before lightweight cameras were available. How he timed one shot of Belmondo so that the streetlights on the Champs-Élysées came on behind him. There is a lovely backlit shot of Belmondo in bed and Seberg sitting beside the bed, both smoking, the light from the window enveloping them in a cloud.

That's from a long scene that's alive with freshness and spontaneity. Patricia returns home to find Michel in her bed, and they talk, flirt, smoke, fight, finally make love. She quotes Faulkner: "Between grief and nothing, I will take grief." Michel says he would choose nothing; "grief is a compromise." She poses in front of a Renoir poster of a young girl, and asks who is prettier. Michel sits below a Picasso poster of a man holding a mask. Throughout this long scene, perplexingly, they both throw their discarded cigarettes out the window.

In this scene and throughout the film, Godard uses jump cuts—cuts within continuous movement or dialogue, with no attempt made to make them match. The technique "was a little more accidental than political," writes the Australian critic Jonathan Dawson. The finished film was thirty minutes too long, and "rather than cut out whole scenes or sequences, Godard elected to trim within the scene, creating the jagged cutting style still so beloved of action filmmakers. Godard just went at the film with the scissors, cutting out anything he thought boring."

The technique adds charm to a scene where the two drive through Paris in a stolen convertible, and there is a series of close-up cuts over her shoulder as Michel describes her. When the two lovers, fleeing the police, sneak into a movie, it is a scene directly quoted in *Bonnie and Clyde*—which, we recall, both Godard and Truffaut were once to direct. In each case, the dialogue reflects the action; Bonnie and Clyde hear "we're in the money," and Michel and Patricia hear dialogue about a woman "covering up for a cheap parasite."

The movie had a sensational reception; it is safe to say the cinema was permanently changed. Young directors saw it and abandoned their notions of the traditional studio film before they left the theater. Crowther of the *Times,* who was later to notoriously despise its descendant *Bonnie and Clyde,* said of *Breathless* that "sordid is really a mild word for its pile-up of gross indecencies." The jump cuts to him were "pictorial cacophony." Yet Crowther conceded, "It is no cliché," and the film's bold originality in style, characters, and tone made a certain kind of genteel Hollywood movie quickly obsolete. Godard went on to become the most famous innovator of the 1960s, although he lost the way later, with increasingly mannered experiments. Here in one quick, sure move, knowing somehow just what he wanted and how to obtain it, he achieved a turning point in the cinema just as surely as Griffith did with *The Birth of a Nation* and Welles with *Citizen Kane*.

THE BRIDGE
ON THE RIVER KWAI

The last words in David Lean's *The Bridge on the River Kwai* are "Madness! Madness . . . madness!" Although the film's two most important characters are both mad, the hero more than the villain, we're not quite certain what is intended by that final line. Part of the puzzle is caused by the film's shifting points of view.

Seen through the eyes of Colonel Nicholson (Alec Guinness), commanding officer of a battalion of British war prisoners, the war narrows to a single task, building a bridge across the Kwai. For Shears (William Holden), an American who escapes from the camp, madness would be returning to the jungle. For Colonel Saito (Sessue Hayakawa), the Japanese commandant of the camp, madness and suicide are never far away as the British build a better bridge than his own men could. And to Clipton (James Donald), the army doctor who says the final words, they could simply mean that the final violent confusion led to unnecessary death.

Most war movies are either for or against their wars. *The Bridge on the River Kwai* is one of the few that focuses not on larger rights and wrongs but on individuals. Like Robert Graves's World War I memoir, *Goodbye to All That*, it shows men grimly hanging on to military discipline and pride in their units, as a way of clinging to sanity. By the end of *Kwai* we are less interested in who wins than in how individual characters will behave.

The film is set in 1943, in a POW camp in Burma, along the route of a rail line the Japanese were building between Malaysia and Rangoon. Shears is already in the camp; we've seen him steal a cigarette lighter from a corpse to bribe his way into the sick bay. He watches as a column of British prisoners, led by Nicholson, marches into camp whistling "The Colonel Bogey March."

Nicholson and Saito, the commandant, are quickly involved in a face-off. Saito wants all of the British to work on the bridge. Nicholson says the Geneva Convention states that officers may not be forced to perform manual labor. He even produces a copy of the document, which Saito uses to whip him across the face, drawing blood. Nicholson is prepared to die rather than bend on principle, and eventually, in one of the film's best-known sequences, he's locked inside "the Oven"—a corrugated iron hut that stands in the sun.

The film's central relationship is between Saito and Nicholson, a professional soldier approaching his twenty-eighth anniversary of army service ("I don't suppose I've been at home more than ten months in all that time"). The Japanese colonel is not a military pro; he learned English while studying in London, he tells Nicholson, and likes corned beef and Scotch whiskey. But he is a rigidly dutiful officer, and we see him weeping privately with humiliation because Nicholson is a better bridge builder; he prepares for hara-kiri if the bridge is not ready on time. The scenes in the jungle are crisply told. We see the bridge being built, and we watch the standoff between the two colonels. Hayakawa and Guinness make a good match as they create two disciplined officers who never bend but nevertheless quietly share the vision of completing the bridge.

Hayakawa was Hollywood's first important Asian star; he became famous with a brilliant silent performance in Cecil B. DeMille's *The Cheat* (1915). Although he worked on stage and screen in both Japan and the United States, he was unusual among Japanese actors of his generation in his low-key delivery; in *Kwai* he doesn't bluster, but is cool and understated—as clipped as Guinness. (Incredibly, he was sixty-eight when he played the role.)

Alec Guinness, oddly enough, was not Lean's first choice for the role, which won him an Oscar as best actor. Charles Laughton was originally cast as Colonel Nicholson, but "could not face the heat of the Ceylon

location, the ants, and being cramped in a cage," his wife, Elsa Lanchester, wrote in her autobiography. The contrasts between Laughton and Guinness are so extreme that one wonders how Lean could see both men playing the same part. Surely Laughton would have been juicier and more demonstrative. Guinness, who says in *his* autobiography that Lean "didn't particularly want me" for the role, played Nicholson as dry, reserved, yet burning with an intense obsession.

That obsession is with building a better bridge, and finishing it on time. The story's great irony is that once Nicholson successfully stands up to Saito, he immediately devotes himself to Saito's project as if it is his own. He suggests a better site for the bridge, he offers blueprints and timetables, and he even enters Clipton's hospital hut in search of more workers and marches out at the head of a column of the sick and the lame. On the night before the first train crossing, he hammers into place a plaque boasting that the bridge was "designed and built by soldiers of the British Army."

It is Clipton who asks him, diffidently, if they might not be accused of aiding the enemy. Not at all, Guinness replies: War prisoners must work when ordered, and besides, they are setting an example of British efficiency. "One day," he says, "the war will be over, and I hope the people who use this bridge in years to come will remember how it was built, and who built it." A pleasant sentiment, but in the meantime the bridge will be used to advance the war against the Allies. Nicholson is so proud of the bridge that he essentially forgets about the war.

The story in the jungle moves ahead neatly, economically, powerfully. There is a parallel story involving Shears that is not as successful. Shears escapes, is taken to a hospital in British-occupied Ceylon, drinks martinis and frolics with a nurse, and then is asked by Major Warden (Jack Hawkins) to return as part of a plan to blow up the bridge. "Are you crazy?" Shears cries, but he is blackmailed by Warden's threat to tell the Americans he has been impersonating an officer. Holden's character, up until the time their guerrilla mission begins, seems fabricated; he's unconvincing playing a shirker, and his heroism at the end seems more plausible.

Lean handles the climax with precision and suspense. There's a nice use of the boots of a sentry on the bridge, sending hollow reverberations down to the men wiring the bridge with plastic explosives. Meanwhile, the

British celebrate completion of the bridge with an improbable musical re-vue that doesn't reflect what is known about the brutal conditions of the POW camps. The next morning brings an elaborate interplay of characters and motives, as the sound of the approaching train creates suspense, while Nicholson, incredibly, seems ready to expose the sabotage rather than see his beloved bridge go down. (The shot of the explosion and the train tumbling into the river uncannily mirrors a similar scene in Buster Keaton's silent classic *The General,* in which the train looks more convincing.)

Although Sir David Lean (1908–1991) won his reputation and perhaps even his knighthood on the basis of the epic films he directed, start-ing with *The Bridge on the River Kwai* in 1957, there's a contrarian argument that his best work was done before the Oscars started to pile up. After *Kwai* came *Lawrence of Arabia, Dr. Zhivago, Ryan's Daughter,* and *A Passage to India;* all but *Ryan* were nominated for best picture, and the first two won. Before *Kwai* he made smaller, more tightly wound films, including *Brief Encounter, Oliver Twist,* and *Great Expectations.* There is a majesty in the later films (except for *Ryan's Daughter*) that compensates for the loss of hu-man detail, but in *Kwai* he still has an eye for the personal touch, as in Saito's private moments, and Nicholson's smug inspection of the finished bridge. There is something almost Lear-like in his final flash of sanity: "What have I done!"

BRING ME THE HEAD OF ALFREDO GARCIA

I think I can feel Sam Peckinpah's heart beating and head pounding in every frame in *Bring Me the Head of Alfredo Garcia* (1974), a film he made during a period of alcoholic fear and trembling. I believe its hero, Bennie, completes his task with the same dogged courage as Peckinpah used to complete the movie, and that Bennie's exhaustion, disgust, and despair at the end might mirror Peckinpah's own. I sense that the emotional weather on the set seeped onto the screen, haunting it with a buried level of passion. If there is anything to the auteur theory, then *Alfredo Garcia* is the most autobiographical film Peckinpah ever made.

The film was reviled when it was released. The reviews went beyond hatred into horror. It was grotesque, sadistic, irrational, obscene, and incompetent, wrote Joy Gould Boyum in the *Wall Street Journal.* It was a catastrophe, said Michael Sragow in *New York* magazine. "Turgid melodrama at its worst," said *Variety.* Martin Baum, the producer, recalled a sneak preview with only ten people left in the theater at the end: "They hated it! Hated it!"

I gave it four stars and called it "some kind of bizarre masterpiece." Now I approach it again, after twenty-seven years, and find it extraordinary, a true and heartfelt work by a great director who endured despite, or perhaps because of, the demons that haunted him. Courage usually feels good in the movies, but it comes in many moods, and here it feels bad but neces-

sary, giving us a hero who is heartbreakingly human—a little man determined to accomplish his mission in memory of a woman he loved, and in truth to his own defiant code.

The film stars Warren Oates (1928–1982), that sad-faced, gritty actor with the crinkled eyes, as Bennie, a forlorn piano player in a Mexican brothel—an American at a dead end. When a powerful Mexican named El Jefe (Emilio Fernández) discovers that his daughter is pregnant, he commands, "Bring me the head of Alfredo Garcia," and so large is the reward he offers that two bounty hunters (Gig Young and Robert Webber) come into the brothel looking for Alfredo, and that is how Bennie finds out about the head. He knows that a prostitute named Elita (Isela Vega) was once sweet on Alfredo, and he discovers that the man is already dead. He and Elita love each other, in the desperate fashion of two people who see no other chance of survival. He needs money to escape from the trap he is in. He will dig up the body, steal the head, deliver it to El Jefe, and then he and Elita will live happily ever after—a prospect they honor but do not believe in. During Bennie's odyssey across the dusty roads of Mexico, many will die, and the head, carried in a gunnysack, will develop a stink and attract a blanket of flies. But it represents Bennie's fortune, and he will die to defend it.

The parallels with *Treasure of the Sierra Madre* are obvious, starting with a broken-down barfly down on his luck, and when Gig Young's character says his name is "Fred C. Dobbs," the name of Bogart's character in *Treasure,* it's a wink from Peckinpah. Dobbs is finally defeated, and so is Bennie, but Bennie at least goes out on his own terms—even though his life spirals down into proof that the world is a rotten place and has no joy for Bennie.

Alfredo Garcia is a mirror-image of formula movies, where the hero goes on the road on a personal mission. The very reason for wanting Alfredo Garcia's head—revenge—is moot because Garcia is already dead. By the end, Bennie identifies with the head, talks to "Al," acknowledges that Al was the true love of Elita's life, and puts the stinking head under a shower where he once sat on the floor and watched Elita. He tells it, "A friend of ours tried to take a shower in there."

The sequences do not flow together; they bang together, daily trials under the scorching sun. Of all the extraordinary scenes in the film, the best is the one where Bennie and Elita pull off the road for a picnic and talk long and softly, tenderly, to each other. Kris Kristofferson, who plays a biker who interrupts this scene, recalled years later that it was supposed to end with Bennie confessing he had never thought of asking Elita to marry him. "But the scene didn't stop there," he told Garner Simmons, author of *Peckinpah: A Portrait in Montage*. "She [Vega] didn't stop. She says, 'Well, ask me.' And he says, 'What?' And she says, 'To marry you.' And I swear to God, Warren just looked like every other guy who's ever been confronted like that. But he didn't break character. He says, 'Will you marry me?' And then she starts crying. And every time I saw it, it broke me up. Warren said to me: 'I just knew there was no place to hide in that scene. She had me, and I was cryin', too.'"

Then the two bikers appear, and the one played by Kristofferson intends to rape Elita. She knows Bennie has a concealed gun, but the bikers are dangerous and she tells the man who has just proposed to her not to risk his life, because, as a prostitute, "I been here before and you don't know the way." It is the sad poetry of that line that expresses Peckinpah's vision, in which people find the courage to do what they must do in a world with no choices.

The film's screenplay and story, by Peckinpah, Gordon T. Dawson, and Frank Kowalski, has other dialogue as simple, direct, and sad. When Elita questions the decision to cut off Garcia's head, Bennie tells her, "There's nothing sacred about a hole in the ground or the man that's in it— or you, or me." Then he says, "The church cuts off the toes and fingers and every other damn thing—they're saints. Well, Alfredo is our saint." Later, there is a hint of Shakespeare, even, in Bennie's remark to the sack: "You got jewels in your ears, diamonds up your nose."

The thing is, Oates and Vega are so tired and sweet and utterly without movie-actor affect in this film. They seem worn out and hopeless. These are holy performances. Maybe the conditions of the shoot and the director's daily personal ordeal wore them down, and that informed their work. David Weddle, who wrote a book on Peckinpah titled *If They Move . . . Kill 'Em!*, quotes Gordon Dawson as a daily witness on the location. Dawson had worked with Peckinpah many times before but refused to ever work with him again: "He really lost it on *Alfredo*. It tore my heart right out."

Peckinpah was a tragic drunk, and booze killed him in 1984, at age fifty-nine. When I visited the Durango, Mexico, set of his *Pat Garrett and Billy the Kid* (1973), he sat in a chair under an umbrella, his drink in his hand, and murmured his instructions to an assistant. "The studio screwed him so thoroughly on that picture that he got sick," Kristofferson told me. "There were days when he couldn't raise himself up from his chair." When Peckinpah visited Chicago to promote *Alfredo Garcia,* he sat in a darkened hotel room, wearing dark glasses, hungover, whispering, and I remembered that in the movie Bennie even wears his dark glasses to bed.

Booze destroyed Peckinpah's life, but in this film, I believe, it allowed him, or forced him, to escape from the mindless upbeat formulas of the male action picture, and to send Bennie down a road on which, no matter how bad a man feels, he finishes his job. Some days on the set there must not have been a dime's worth of difference between Peckinpah and Bennie.

Sam Peckinpah directed *The Wild Bunch* (1969), the best Western I have seen, and he brought in a lot of box office money in a career that included *Straw Dogs* and *The Getaway.* He came up as a writer on TV Westerns, starting with *Gunsmoke* in 1955, and in his earliest Western as a director, *Ride the High Country* (1962) he featured the old-timers Randolph Scott and Joel McCrea in a story of two professionals hired to do a job. *The Wild Bunch* was also about aging men whose loyalty was to one another and not to society.

A real director is at his best when he works with material that reflects his own life patterns. At a film festival, after *Pat Garrett* had become the latest of his films to be emasculated by a studio, he was asked if he would ever make a "pure Peckinpah." He replied, "I did *Alfredo Garcia* and I did it exactly the way I wanted to. Good or bad, like it or not, that was my film."

BUSTER KEATON

The greatest of the silent clowns is Buster Keaton, not only because of what he did but because of how he did it. Harold Lloyd made us laugh as much, Charlie Chaplin moved us more deeply, but no one had more courage than Buster. I define courage as Hemingway did: "grace under pressure." In films that combined comedy with extraordinary physical risks, Buster Keaton played a brave spirit who took the universe on its own terms, and gave no quarter.

I'm immersed in his career right now, viewing all of the silent features and many of the shorts with students at the University of Chicago. Having already written about Keaton's *The General* in the previous volume, I thought to choose another title. *The Navigator,* perhaps, or *Steamboat Bill, Jr.,* or *Our Hospitality.* But they are all of a piece; in an extraordinary period from 1920 to 1929, he worked without interruption on a series of films that make him, arguably, the greatest actor-director in the history of the movies.

Some of these movies were thought to be lost. *The General,* with Buster as a train engineer in the Civil War, was always available, hailed as one of the supreme masterpieces of silent filmmaking. But other features and shorts existed in shabby, incomplete prints, if at all, and it was only in the 1960s that film historians began to assemble and restore Keaton's life-work. Now almost everything has been recovered, restored, and made available on DVDs and tapes that range from watchable to sparkling.

It's said that Chaplin wanted you to like him, but Keaton didn't care. I think he cared but was too proud to ask. His films avoid the pathos and sentiment of the Chaplin pictures, and usually feature a jaunty young man who sees an objective and goes after it in the face of the most daunting obstacles. Buster survives tornadoes, waterfalls, avalanches of boulders, and falls from great heights, and never pauses to take a bow: He has his eye on his goal. And his movies, seen as a group, are like a sustained act of optimism in the face of adversity; surprising, how without asking, he earns our admiration and tenderness.

Because he was funny, because he wore that porkpie hat, Keaton's physical skills are often undervalued. We hear about the stunts of Douglas Fairbanks Sr., but no silent star did more dangerous stunts than Buster Keaton. Instead of using doubles, he himself doubled for some of his actors, doing their stunts as well as his own. He said he learned to "take a fall" as a child, when he toured in vaudeville with his parents, Joe and Myra. By the time he was three, he was being thrown around the stage and into the orchestra pit, and his little suits even had a handle concealed at the waist, so Joe could sling him like luggage. Today this would be child abuse; then it was showbiz. "It was the roughest knockabout act that was ever in the history of the theatre," Keaton told the historian Kevin Brownlow. He claimed that Harry Houdini dubbed him "Buster" because of those falls; Houdini was a friend, but the nickname came before the Keatons met him.

Buster and Joe discovered that when he was hurled through the bass drum and emerged waving and smiling, the audience didn't see the joke in treating a kid that way. But when Buster emerged with a solemn expression on his face, for some reason the audience loved it. For the rest of his career, Keaton was "the great stone face," with an expression that ranged from the impassive to the slightly quizzical.

He falls and falls and falls in his movies: from second-story windows, cliffs, trees, trains, motorcycles, balconies. The falls are usually not faked: He lands, gets up, keeps going. He was one of the most gifted stuntmen in the movies. Even when there is fakery, the result is daring; in *Go West* he seems to fall from a high suspension bridge but actually drops only fifty feet or so before landing in a net; there's a cut to another shot showing him falling the last twenty feet. Both halves of this "faked" stunt are dangerous.

And in *Our Hospitality*, where he was almost killed when a safety wire snapped and he was swept toward a waterfall, he finished the sequence with a fake waterfall—but even it was twenty-five feet high.

Keaton is famous for a shot in *Steamboat Bill, Jr.* where he stands in front of a house during a cyclone and a wall falls on top of him; he is saved because he happens to be exactly where the open window is. There was scant clearance on either side, and you can see his shoulders tighten a little just as the wall lands. He refused to rehearse the stunt because, he explained, he trusted his setup, so why waste a wall?

In film after film, Keaton does difficult and dangerous things and keeps the poker face. His philosophy is embodied in his body language: The world throws its worst at him, but he is plucky and determined, ingenious and stubborn, and will do his best. Walter Kerr, in his definitive book *The Silent Clowns*, writes of Keaton's "stillness of emotion as well as body, a universal stillness that comes of things functioning well, of having achieved harmony." When Harold Lloyd dangled from a clock face far above the street, he intended to terrify his audience. When Keaton sat on the front of a moving locomotive in *The General* and attempted to knock one railroad tie off the tracks with another, he could have been crushed beneath the train, but he presents the action as a strategy, not a stunt.

Kerr talks of the "Keaton Curve," the way an action ends up where it began. There's a shot in the early short *Neighbors* where Keaton escapes a house via a clothesline, swings safely across to his own house—then finds that the clothesline keeps rotating, depositing him right back in trouble. In *The General*, there are innumerable examples of the Curve, for example a scene where the train goes around a bend so that a cannon now points at Buster instead of the enemy. You can also see the Curve in many of those scenes where he invents ingenious "labor-saving" devices—to serve breakfast, for example. One of his funniest shorts is *The Scarecrow*, which includes a house where everything—table, bed, stove—has more than one function, so that a meal consists of a tour through the parabola of the house's gadgets.

Another of Keaton's strategies was to avoid anticipation. Instead of showing you what was about to happen, he showed you what was happening; the surprise and the response are both unexpected, and funnier. He also gets laughs by the application of perfect logic. In *Our Hospitality*, he discovers he is in the house of a family sworn to kill him. But southern hospitality insists that they cannot shoot a visitor in their own house. So Buster invites himself to spend the night.

In the last decade of silent film, Keaton worked as an independent auteur. He generally used the same crew, worked with trusted riggers who understood his thinking, conceived his screenplays mostly by himself. He had backing from the mogul Joe Schenck (they were brothers-in-law, both married to Talmadge girls), but Schenck sometimes missed the point. He was outraged that Buster spent $25,000 to buy the ship used in *The Navigator*, but then, without consulting Keaton, he spent $25,000 to buy the rights to a third-rate Broadway farce that Buster somehow transformed into *Seven Chances*.

Like Chaplin and Lloyd, Keaton was a perfectionist who would reshoot sequences until the laughs worked, would take as long as necessary on a single shot, would supervise every element of his films. No filmmaker has ever had a better run of genius than Keaton during that decade. But then talkies came in, and he made what he calls "the biggest mistake of my life," signing on with MGM for a series of sound comedies that mostly made money but were not under his personal control. He didn't like them.

By the late 1930s, Buster Keaton (1895–1966) was out of business as a self-starting auteur. He continued to work all his life, doing innumerable TV appearances and turning up in movies like Chaplin's *Limelight*, Wilder's *Sunset Boulevard*, and even *Film*, an original screenplay by Samuel Beckett. He lived in the San Fernando Valley, raised chickens, and thought his work had been forgotten. Then came a 1962 retrospective at the Cinémathèque Française in Paris, and a tribute at the 1965 Venice Film Festival. He was relieved to see that his films were not, after all, lost, but he observed, no doubt with a stone face, "The applause is nice, but too late."

CHILDREN
OF PARADISE

All discussions of Marcel Carné's *Children of Paradise* begin with the miracle of its making. Named at Cannes as the greatest French film of all time, costing more than any French film before it, *Les Enfants du Paradis* was shot in Paris and Nice during the Nazi occupation and released in 1945. Its sets sometimes had to be transported between the two cities. Its designer and composer, both Jews sought by the Nazis, worked from hiding. Carné was forced to hire pro-Nazi collaborators as extras; they did not suspect they were working next to resistance fighters. The Nazis banned all films over about ninety minutes in length, so Carné simply made two films, confident he could show them together after the war was over. The film opened in Paris right after the liberation and ran for fifty-four weeks. It is said to play somewhere in Paris every day.

That this film, wicked, worldly, flamboyant, set in Paris in 1828, could have been imagined under those circumstances is astonishing. That the production, with all of its costumes, carriages, theaters, mansions, crowded streets, and rude rooming houses, could have been mounted at that time seems logistically impossible. ("It is said," wrote Pauline Kael, "that the starving extras made away with some of the banquets before they could be photographed.") Carné was the leading French director of the decade 1935–45, but to make this ambitious costume film during wartime required more than clout; it required reckless courage.

Despite the fame of *Children of Paradise*, most of the available prints are worn and dim. It used to play every New Year's Day at Chicago's beloved Clark Theater, and that's where I first saw it, in 1967, but the 1991 laser disc was of disappointing quality, and videotapes even worse. Now the film has been released in sparkling clarity on a Criterion DVD that begins with a restored Pathé thirty-five-millimeter print and employs digital technology to make the blips, dirt, and scratches disappear. It is likely the film has not looked better since its premiere. There are formidably informative commentary tracks by Brian Stonehill and Charles Affron.

The film's original trailer (on the disc) calls *Children of Paradise* the French answer to *Gone With the Wind*. Although in its scope and its heedless heroine, there is a similarity, the movie is not a historical epic but a sophisticated, cynical portrait of actors, murderers, swindlers, pickpockets, prostitutes, impresarios, and the decadent rich. Many of the characters are based on real people, as is its milieu of nightclubs, dives, and dens, theaters high and low, and the hiding places of the unsavory.

Carné plunges us directly into this world with his famous opening shot on the "Boulevard of Crime," which rivals the "street of dying men" scene in *Gone With the Wind*, reaching seemingly to infinity, alive with activity, jammed with countless extras. This was a set designed by the great art director Alexandre Trauner, working secretly; the credits list his contribution as "clandestine." To force the perspective and fool the eye, he used buildings that fell off rapidly in height, and miniature carriages driven by dwarfs. The street is a riot of lowlifes. Mimes, jugglers, animal acts, and dancers provide previews outside their theaters, to lure crowds inside. One of the first attractions we see is advertised as "Truth." This is the elegant courtesan Garance, who revolves slowly in a tub of water, regarding herself naked in a mirror. The water conceals her body, so that she supplies "truth, but only from the neck up." This is also what she supplies in life.

Garance is played by Arletty (1898–1992), born as Léonie Bathiat, who became a star in the 1930s and was, truth to tell, a little old to play a sexual temptress who mesmerizes men. Like Marlene Dietrich, to whom she was often compared, Arletty's appeal was based not on fresh ripeness but on a tantalizing sophistication. What fascinates men is that she has seen it all, done it all, admits it, takes their measure, and yet flatters them that she adores them. Even cutthroats fall under her spell; when the criminal Lacenaire tells her, "I'd spill torrents of blood to give you rivers of diamonds," she looks him in the eye and replies, "I'd settle for less."

Around Arletty circle many of the movie's most important characters. The mime Baptiste (Jean-Louis Barrault) sees her from her stage, defends her in pantomime against a pickpocket charge, is rewarded by a rose, and falls for her. So does Frederick Lemaître (Pierre Brasseur), as an actor who dreams of doing something good—perhaps Shakespeare. And Lacenaire (Marcel Herrand), who, with his ruffled shirt, curly hair, villain's mustache, and cold speech is the Rhett Butler of the piece. And the Count Edward de Monteray (Louis Salou), who thinks he has bought her but discovers he was only renting.

It is possible that Arletty truly loves the innocent Baptiste, who triumphs in a bar brawl and brings her home to his rude rooming house, where he rents her a room of her own and retires chastely for the night. But Frederick, who lives in the rooming house, has no such scruples—and, for that matter, Baptiste is no saint. He marries the theater manager's daughter, sires "an abominable offspring" (as Kael puts it), and cheats on his wife by still loving Garance. Lacenaire, who strides through the underworld like a king, basking in his reputation for ruthlessness, thinks he can have Arletty for the asking ("You are the only woman for whom I do not have contempt"), but it is the count whose money makes her his mistress. When Lacenaire pulls back a drapery so that the count can see Garance in the arms of Baptiste, so many men think they have the right to her that the actor observes, "Jealousy belongs to all if a woman belongs to none."

Most of the movie is frankly shot on sets, including exteriors. A misty dawn scene involving a duel provides a rare excursion outside Paris. Carné had "an eye for the sad romance of fog-laden streets and squalid lodging houses," David Thomson writes. His characters live artificially in the demimonde, actors who are always onstage; if we meet a street beggar, like the blind man Fil de Soie (Gaston Modot), we are not much surprised to find he can see well enough indoors.

Carné's screenplay was by his usual collaborator, Jacques Prévert; they not only set their story in a theatrical world but divert from the action to show the actors at work. Kael counts "five kinds of theatrical performances," and they would include Baptiste's miming and a scene from *Othello* that provides oblique reflections on the plot. It is Baptiste whose art leaves the greatest impression. Jean-Louis Barrault (1910–1994), then a star at the Comédies-Française, is first seen in clown makeup, glumly surveying the Boulevard of Crime, brought to life only by his mimed defense of Garance. Later, he stages his own extended mime performance—only to see, from the stage, Garance flirting in the wings. No one's trust is repaid in this movie.

If Carné was France's leading director, Prévert was the leading screenwriter, at a time when writers were given equal billing with directors. They both continued to work for decades—Prévert into the 1960s, Carné into the 1980s—but never surpassed *Children of Paradise*. Indeed, it was precisely this kind of well-mounted, witty film that was attacked by the young French critics of the 1950s who later became known as the New Wave. They wanted a rougher, more direct, more improvisational feel—theater not on a stage but in your face.

If the Cannes festival were to attempt again today to choose the best French film ever made, would *Children of Paradise* win? Perhaps. Perhaps not. Just as American audiences prefer *Gone With the Wind* or *Casablanca* while the critics always choose *Citizen Kane*, at Cannes the palm might go to Godard or Truffaut, or Jean Vigo's *L'Atalante*. But *Children of Paradise*, now finally available in a high-quality print and ready to win new admirers, might have a chance. Few achievements in the world of cinema can equal it.

{ A Christmas Story }

One of the details that *A Christmas Story* gets right is the threat of having your mouth washed out with Lifebuoy soap. Not any soap. Lifebuoy. Never Ivory or Palmolive. Lifebuoy, which apparently contained an ingredient able to nullify bad language. The only other soap ever mentioned for this task was Lava, but that was the nuclear weapon of mouth-washing soaps, so powerful it was used for words we still didn't even know.

There are many small but perfect moments in *A Christmas Story*, and one of the best comes after the Lifebuoy is finally removed from Ralphie's mouth and he is sent off to bed. His mother studies the bar, thinks for a moment, and then sticks it in her own mouth, just to see what it tastes like. Moments like that are why some people watch *A Christmas Story* every holiday season. There is a real knowledge of human nature beneath the comedy.

The movie is based on the memoirs of Jean Shepherd, the humorist whose radio programs and books remembered growing up in Indiana in the 1940s. It is Shepherd's voice on the sound track, remembering one Christmas season in particular, and the young hero's passionate desire to get a Daisy Red Ryder two-hundred-shot carbine-action BB gun for Christmas—the one with the compass in the stock, "as cool and deadly a piece of weaponry as I had ever laid eyes on."

I owned such a weapon. I recall everything about it at this moment with a tactile memory so vivid I could have just put the carbine down before writing these words. How you stuffed newspapers into the carton it came in to use it for target practice. How the BBs came in a cardboard tube with a slide-off top. How they rattled when you poured them into the gun. And, of course, how everybody warned that you would shoot your eye out.

Ralphie's life is made a misery by that danger. He finds that nobody in northern Indiana (not his mother, not his teacher, not even Santa Claus) is able to even *think* about a BB gun without using the words "shoot your eye out." At one point in the movie, in a revenge daydream, he knocks on his parents' door with dark glasses, a blind man's cane, and a beggar's tin cup. They are shocked, and ask him tearfully what caused his blindness. He replies coolly, "Soap poisoning."

The movie is not only about Christmas and BB guns. It is about childhood, and one detail after another rings true. The school bully, who when he runs out of victims beats up on his own loyal sidekick. The little brother who has outgrown his snowsuit, which is so tight that he walks around looking like the Michelin man; when he falls down he can't get up. The aunt who thinks Ralphie is a four-year-old girl, and sends him a pink bunny suit. Other problems of life belong to that long-ago age and not this one: clinkers in the basement coal furnace, for example, or the blowout of a tire. Everybody knows what a flat tire is, but many now alive have never experienced a genuine terrifying loud instantaneous *blowout*.

A Christmas Story was released in the Christmas season of 1983 and did modest business at first. (People don't often go to movies with specific holiday themes.) It got warm reviews and two Genie awards (the Canadian Oscars), for Bob Clark's direction and for the screenplay. And then it moved on to home video and has been a stealth hit season after season, finding a loyal audience. "Bams," for example, one of the critics at the hip Three Black Chicks movie-review Web site, confesses that she loves it: "How does one describe, in short form, the smiles and shrieks of laughter one has experienced over more than fifteen years of seeing the same great movie over and over, without sounding like a babbling, fanboyish fool who talks too much?"

The movie is set in Indiana but was filmed mostly around Toronto, with some downtown shots from Cleveland, by Clark, whose other big hits were *Porky's* and *Baby Geniuses*. It is pitch-perfect, telling the story through

the enthusiastic and single-minded vision of its hero, Ralphie, and finding in young Peter Billingsley a sly combination of innocence and calculation.

Ralphie's parents, Mr. and Mrs. Parker, are played by Darren McGavin and Melinda Dillon, and they exude warmth, zest, and love; they are about the nicest parents I can remember in a nonsmarmy movie. Notice the scene where Mrs. Parker gets her younger son, Randy, to eat his food by pretending he is "Mommy's little piggie." Watch the delight in their laughter together. And the enthusiasm with which the Old Man (as he is always called) attacks the (unseen) basement furnace, battles with the evil neighbor dogs, and promises to change a tire in "four minutes flat—time me!" And the lovely closing moment as the parents tenderly put their arms around each other on Christmas night.

Some of the movie's sequences stand as classic. The whole business, for example, of the Old Man winning the "major award" of a garish lamp in the shape of a woman's leg (watch Mrs. Parker hiding her giggles in the background as he tries to glue it together after it is "accidentally" broken). Or the visit by Ralphie and Randy to a department-store Santa Claus, whose helpers spin the terrified kids around to bang them down on Santa's lap, and afterward kick them down a slide to floor level. Or the sequence where a kid is not merely dared but triple-dog-dared to stick his tongue onto a frozen lamppost, and the fire department has to be called. And the deep disillusionment with which Ralphie finally gets his Little Orphan Annie Secret Decoder Ring in the mail, when Annie's secret message turns out to be nothing but a crummy commercial.

There is also the matter of Scott Farkus (Zack Ward), the bully, who Ralphie assures us has yellow eyes. Every school has a kid like this, who picks on smaller kids but is a coward at heart. He makes Ralphie's life a misery. How Farkus gets his comeuppance makes for a deeply satisfying scene, and notice the perfect tact with which Ralphie's mom handles the situation. (Do you agree with me that Dad already knows the whole story when he sits down at the kitchen table?)

In a poignant way, *A Christmas Story* records a world that no longer quite exists in America. Kids are no longer left unattended in the line for Santa. The innocence of kids' radio programs has been replaced by slick, ironic children's programming on TV. The new Daisy BB guns have a muzzle velocity higher than that of some police revolvers, and are not to be sold to anyone under sixteen. Nobody knows who Red Ryder was, let alone that his sidekick was Little Beaver.

So much has been forgotten. There is a moment when the Old Man needs an answer for the contest he is entering. The theme of the contest is "Characters in American Literature," and the question is, "What was the name of the Lone Ranger's nephew's horse?"

Victor, of course. Everybody knows that.

THE COLOR PURPLE

Returning to *The Color Purple* after almost twenty years, I can see its flaws more easily than when I named it the best film of 1985, but I can also understand why it moved me so deeply, and why the greatness of some films depends not on their perfection or logic but on their heart. The movie may have inconsistencies, confusions, and improbabilities, but there is one perfect thing at its center, and that is the character of Celie, as played by Whoopi Goldberg. "Here is this year's winner for best actress," I wrote in my original review, and that should have been true, but although *The Color Purple* had eleven nominations, it won not a single Oscar.

Celie is a woman cruelly treated by the world, a shy, frightened little creature whose life consists mostly of eluding the men who want to rape and beat her. Her eventual flowering provides one of the most joyous experiences I have had at the movies; the scene where she is coaxed and persuaded and finally teased into smiling is the turning point of the story, and one of those moments when we see humanity shining out of the screen upon us.

Steven Spielberg's movie is based on a novel by Alice Walker, darker and more complex than the movie, although Celie's life could hardly be more painful. As a young teenager she is raped by the man she takes to be her father, and both of her babies are taken away from her. Told she cannot have more children, she is given to a brutal farmer she calls Mister

(Danny Glover), who beats her, uses her as a servant and a receptacle for his lust, and convinces her she is ugly. There is one beautiful thing in her life: her sister, Nettie (Akosua Busia). When their father tries to assault her, she flees to Celie for safety, but then Mister comes after her, and when she fights him off he throws her off the land. Thus begins a long separation between the two sisters; Nettie, through a rather improbable coincidence, goes to Africa with the missionary couple who adopted Celie's children.

The movie takes place in a landscape that seems more inspired by set decoration than real life—more *Green Pastures* than *Grapes of Wrath*. Although there are whites in the nearby town and they are racist to one degree or another, they and their racism have only walk-on roles, and the greater part of the story takes place in a bucolic farm landscape populated by African Americans. Mister lives in a handsome two-story house with a broad porch and a deep lawn. Nearby is a church that could pose for a greeting card. There is a stream, and winding dusty lanes, and although farmwork apparently gets done, Mister is seen only once on a tractor and spends most of his time playing the villain in Celie's life. The biggest local crop seems to be fields of purple flowers.

Mister has a son, Harpo (Willard Pugh) by his first marriage, and one day the misery is shaken up when Harpo brings home Sofia (Oprah Winfrey), the woman he loves, who is unapologetically great with child. Sofia will not allow herself to be addressed in the way Mister is accustomed to speaking to women and gives Harpo a choice between his father and herself. Harpo cannot choose and spends most of his life trying to keep everyone happy. That makes him the ideal proprietor for a "jook joint" down by the river, within shouting distance of the church.

There is one person Mister cherishes in his miserable life, and that is Shug Avery (Margaret Avery), a jazz singer who remains his one and only true love. When she arrives at their home one rainy night, sick and in need of care, her first words to Celie are, "You sho is ugly!" But Shug is able to see the beauty beneath Celie's fear, and there is a delicate and hushed scene where she teaches her for the first time what it feels like to be kissed with love. She is the transformative power in Celie's life, the prime mover in Celie's eventual triumph and Mister's defeat.

When I first saw the movie, I focused on Celie with such care and concern that the whole movie became her story. This time, I was uneasily aware that the movie is single-minded in its conviction that African-American women are strong, brave, true, and will endure, but African-American men are weak, cruel, or comic caricatures. Harpo falls through so many roofs while trying to build them that he could be in a Keaton movie; he means well, but is comic relief. Shug's father, the preacher, repeats truisms from his Bible but is not a forgiving man. Mister is a monster, and his father, Old Mister (Adolph Caesar), is a vile and nasty little man who makes selfish comments from behind his cigarette.

If Shug was born with nobility and Celie slowly absorbs it, Winfrey's Sofia is the life force, telling the town's white mayor to go to hell, getting in a fight, and paying for it with a blind eye and years in jail. She emerges broken and confused, in a daze, to find herself the maid of the very mayor's wife whose original job offer led to her trouble. There is a scene where the wife, who has been taking driving lessons from Sofia, grandly offers to drive her home to spend Christmas with her children. This could have been a deeply emotional reunion, but Spielberg misses it by making the mayor's wife a lousy driver, creating a slapstick scene in which the car bucks and stalls and the wife thinks she is being attacked by the black men trying to help her. She insists that Sofia drive her back home, after only fifteen minutes with the children who barely remember her. It should have been Sofia's scene, quiet and sad and joyous, not easy laughs followed by facile cruelty. That Sofia eventually recovers her pride and spirit is a triumph, and leads to a passionate angry speech, but the movie sidesteps her great scene.

There is also some confusing intercutting between the rural South and Africa, where Celie's children inexplicably grow up speaking only a local language, even though they are being raised by English-speaking missionaries and Nettie. Because Mister hid all of Nettie's letters over the years, it is only because of Shug that Celie discovers that Nettie is alive, and that so are her children. "I have children!" Celie says proudly and defiantly. "I have two children!" A bolt of emotion shot through me. Her eventual reunion with them is one of the great heartrending moments in the movies.

Celie's rebirth is the spiritual center of the film, even if one detail (she opens a shop selling one-size-fits-all pants) seems unlikely. It is enough for her to find self-respect, love, and joy; she need not succeed in retail. This was Whoopi Goldberg's first major performance, and it remains her best, because she was allowed to draw from her inner truth and not required to play a sappy or comic role. She has had other true moments, including a scene of personal revelation in *Fatal Beauty* (1987) and a role in *The Long Walk Home* (1990) where she is a maid who supports the 1955 Montgomery bus boycott at great personal cost. Those movies, and a few others, show that we lost a serious actress when Goldberg started playing nuns and *Star Trek* characters.

There is a tendency to demand perfection even at the cost of effect. *The Color Purple* was rightly criticized for Spielberg's postcard landscapes, his broad characterizations, and the convolutions of his plot. But what he made was a movie of great mass appeal with a powerful truth at its center. When a movie character is really working, we become that character. That's what the movies offer: escapism into lives other than our own. I am not female, I am not black, I am not Celie, but for a time during *The Color Purple* my mind deceives me that I am all of those things, and as I empathize with her struggle and victory I learn something about what it must have been like to be her. Celie is a great, powerful movie character, played with astonishing grace and tenderness, and to feel her story is to be blessed with her humanity. Have we all felt ugly? Have we all been afraid to smile? Have we all lost precious things in our lives? Have we dared to dream? Celie endures and prevails, and so hope lives. If it touches you deeply enough, it's not just a movie.

{ THE CONVERSATION }

His colleagues in the surveillance industry think Harry Caul is such a genius that we realize with a little shock how bad he is at his job. Here is a man who is paid to eavesdrop on a conversation in a public place. He succeeds, but then allows the tapes to be stolen. His triple-locked apartment is so insecure that the landlord is able to enter it and leave a birthday present. His mail is opened and read. He thinks his phone number is unlisted, but both the landlord and a client have it. At a trade show, he allows his chief competitor to fool him with a mike hidden in a freebie ballpoint. His mistress tells him, "Once I saw you up by the staircase, hiding and watching for a whole hour."

Harry, the subject of Francis Ford Coppola's *The Conversation* (1974), is not only bad at his job but deeply unhappy about it. Once his snooping may have led to the deaths of a woman and child. Now he fears that his new tapes will lead to another murder. In the confessional, he warms up by telling the priest that he has taken the Lord's name in vain and stolen some newspapers from a rack. Then he says, "I've been involved in some work that I think will be used to hurt these two young people. It's happened to me before. People were hurt because of my work and I'm afraid it could happen again and I'm . . . I was in no way responsible. I'm not responsible. For these and all my sins of my past life, I am heartily sorry."

If he's not responsible, why is he sorry? Harry, played by Gene

Hackman in one of the key performances of a great career, tries to distance himself from his work. But even Meredith (Elizabeth MacRae), the hooker he brings home from a convention, can see how worried he is. "Forget it, Harry. It's only a trick—a job. You're not supposed to think anything about it. Just supposed to do it." She's talking for herself as well. When he wakes, it's to discover that she has taken her own advice and stolen the tapes.

Coppola, who wrote and directed, considers this film his most personal project. He was working two years after the Watergate break-in, amid the ruins of the Vietnam effort, telling the story of a man who places too much reliance on high technology and has nightmares about his personal responsibility. Harry Caul is a microcosm of America at that time: not a bad man, trying to do his job, haunted by a guilty conscience, feeling tarnished by his work.

The movie works on that moral level, and also as a taut, intelligent thriller. It opens with a virtuoso telephoto shot, showing a San Francisco plaza filled with people. Faraway music mixes with electronic sounds. There is a slow zoom in to the back of Caul's head, and then the camera follows him. Other shots show a man with a shotgun microphone, on top of a nearby building, holding in his cross hairs a young couple (Cindy Williams and Fredric Forrest) who are the subject of the investigation. Eventually we go inside a van packed with electronic gear, where Stan (John Cazale), Harry's assistant, is waiting.

"Who's interested in these people, anyway?" asks Cazale. One of Harry's crosses is that Stan is irreverent about their work, which to Harry is a sacred calling. Later we find out who's interested: Harry has been hired by the director of a large corporation (Robert Duvall), although at first he deals only with the man's assistant (Harrison Ford). It becomes clear that Ann, the young woman, is the director's wife, and Mark, the young man, is her lover. But what will happen next? "He'd kill us if he had the chance," says Mark. Will he? Harry plays the tapes back and forth, juggling a bank of three tape recorders, in a scene Coppola says was partly inspired by the photographer trying to coax the truth out of his prints in Antonioni's *Blow-Up*. Snatches of conversation advance and recede, maddeningly mixed with a band in the plaza that's playing "Red, Red Robin."

Harry is impatient with Stan, impatient with everyone. At home,

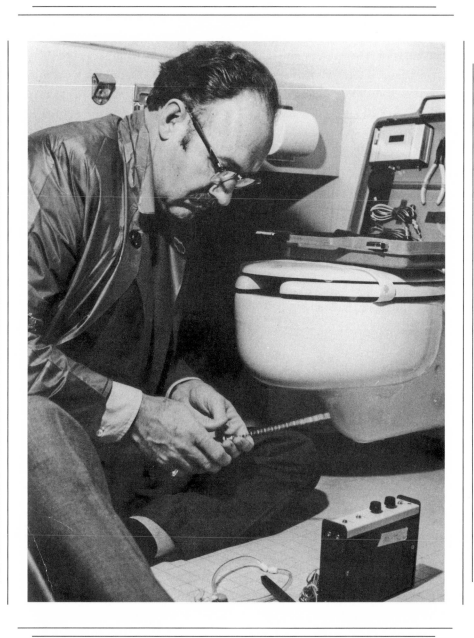

he's shocked to find that his landlord entered his apartment, knows it is his birthday, and knows how old he is. On the phone, the landlord explains he needs his own key for an emergency. "I'd be perfectly happy if all my personal things burnt up in a fire," Harry tells him, "because I don't have anything personal. Nothing of value—*only my key*." He visits his mistress, Amy (Teri Garr). She knows it's him from the way he thinks he comes quietly through the door. She asks him to share something personal with her.

"I don't have any secrets," he says.

"I'm a secret," she says.

The best supporting performance is by Allen Garfield, as Moran, Harry's successful competitor. At a trade show, Harry discovers Stan has left him and gone to work for Moran. Yet he recklessly invites Moran, Stan, and a crowd back to his office, an area behind steel mesh in an otherwise empty warehouse. He is humiliated to discover that Moran bugged him, and of course later that night he is betrayed by the hooker. A nightmare gives key information: As a child, Harry was paralyzed on one side, and nearly drowned during a bath. The word "Caul" has two meanings, both relevant: It is a spider's web, and the membrane that encloses a fetus. If it is found on a child's head after birth, we learn, "it is supposed to protect against drowning."

From his troubled childhood, Harry has grown up into a lonely man. He lives alone and has no entertainment except playing his saxophone with jazz records (again trying to make a recording more complete). No woman has any influence over him, that's for sure, or he wouldn't be seen in that crappy plastic raincoat, the kind that folds up into a travel pouch. His Catholicism is rooted not in faith and hope but in shame. Searching his apartment for a hidden bug, he rips everything apart, but hesitates at a statue of the Virgin Mary.

As pure thriller, the movie works best during a scene where Harry checks into a hotel room next door to a rendezvous between Mark and Ann. Listening through the wall, he hears a struggle and perhaps a murder. His reaction is to hide in terror under the covers. Much later, when he enters the room, it's spick-and-span. But when he flushes the toilet it overflows with bright red blood.

Much has been written about that scene. Is it real or imagined? The new DVD of *The Conversation* has commentary tracks by both Coppola and Walter Murch, the editor and sound wizard, but neither addresses that question. Coppola says the scene was suggested by the shower scene in *Psycho,* and for Murch, the guilty evidence welling up reminds him of his adolescent shame when he tried to flush some porno magazines and they came floating back at just the wrong time. I think the scene is meant to be real. Later, the quick cuts of what might have happened in the room are, I think, Harry's speculations.

The Conversation comes from another time and place than today's thrillers, which are so often simpleminded. This movie is a sadly observant character study of a man who has removed himself from life, thinks he can observe it dispassionately at an electronic remove, and finds that all of his barriers are worthless. The cinematography (opening scene by Haskell Wexler, the rest by Bill Butler) is deliberately planned from a voyeuristic point of view; we are always looking but imperfectly seeing. Here is a man who seeks the truth, and it always remains hidden. He plays the conversation over and over, but does Mark say "He'd *kill* us if he had the chance" or "He'd kill *us* if he had the chance"?

{ CRIES AND WHISPERS }

Cries and Whispers envelops us in a tomb of dread, pain, and hate, and to counter these powerful feelings it summons selfless love. It is, I think, Ingmar Bergman's way of treating his own self-disgust, and his envy of those who have faith. His story, which takes place inside a Swedish manor house on the grounds of a large estate, shows us a dying woman named Agnes and those who have come to wait with her: her sisters Maria and Karin, her servant Anna. Three men drift through, two husbands and a doctor, and there is a small role at the end for the pastor, but this is essentially a story of women who are bound together by a painful history.

This is a monstrous family. Maria (Liv Ullmann) is flighty and shallow, cheats on her husband, and refuses to come to his aid when he stabs himself after learning of her infidelity. Karin (Ingrid Thulin) is cold and hostile, hates her husband, cuts herself with a shard of glass in an intimate place and then smiles triumphantly as she smears the blood on her face. In one of the film's most devastating scenes, Karin tells Maria how much she had always hated her.

Agnes (Harriet Andersson), the dying sister, has been caught in a crucible of pain. Sometimes she screams, wounded animal sounds, and then Anna (Kari Sylwan) comes to her, holds her head to her breasts, and tries to comfort her. Anna is the wholly good person in the movie; she prays to God for the soul of her dead daughter and moves silently in the background

119

as the family eats at its own soul. She loves Agnes and would love the others if they could be loved.

Bergman never made another film this painful. To see it is to touch the extremes of human feeling. It is so personal, so penetrating of privacy, we almost want to look away. *Persona* (1966) points to it, especially with its use of close-ups to show the mystery of the personality; no other director has done more with the human face. It's as if *Cries and Whispers,* made in 1972, brought him to the end of his attempts to lance the wound of his suffering; his later films draw back into more realism, more sensible memories of his life and failings (for no director is more consistently autobiographical). And near the end there is *Faithless* (2000), directed by Ullmann from his screenplay, in which an old man summons actors (or ghosts) to help him deal with his regret for having hurt others.

Cries and Whispers was photographed by Sven Nykvist, his longtime cinematographer, in a house where the wallpaper, rugs, and curtains are all a deep blood-red. "I think of the inside of the human soul," Bergman writes in his screenplay, "as a membranous red." The women are all dressed in old-fashioned floor-length white dresses or bedclothes, except after Agnes dies, when Karin and Maria change to black. In an essay with the DVD, the critic Peter Cowie quotes the director: "All of my films can be thought of in terms of black and white, except *Cries and Whispers.*" Yes, because the colors represent their fundamental emotional associations, with blood, death, and spirituality. There are only a few respites. An opening shot looks out on the estate grounds, and there are brief sequences in the middle and at the end when the family strolls through the green park. These moments release us briefly from the claustrophobic arena of pain and death.

Bergman uses flashbacks into the lives of the women, beginning and ending them with full frames of deep red, then fading into or out of close-ups where their faces are half-illuminated. These flashbacks are intended not to explain biographical details but to capture moments of extreme emotion, as when Maria wantonly seduces the doctor who has come to care for Anna's child, or when Karin triumphantly wounds herself to wound her husband even more.

One flashback involves both surviving sisters and their husbands, who coldheartedly decide to reward Anna's twelve years of faithful service with only "a small payment and a keepsake of Agnes." Another scene shows Maria asking Karin if they cannot be friends and Karin rebuffing her venomously, only to allow her sister, moments later, to caress her face. And then, in a scene where we see them talking but do not hear their words, the two women pet each other like friendly kittens, while expressing what look like words of endearment. When Karin later recalls this moment, Maria coldly rejects the memory.

Some deep wound has scarred this family. Agnes and Anna, never marrying, living together (possibly as lovers) in the family home, seem to have escaped it. Toward the end of the film there is an extraordinary dream sequence in which the dead Agnes asks first one sister and then another to hold her and comfort her. They reject her. Then Anna (whose dream it is) comforts her, in a composition that mirrors the *Pietà*. In this scene there seem to be shots indicating that Agnes has come back to life; they are ambiguous, until her hand clearly moves; but remember, it is a dream.

When *Cries and Whispers* was released, it had an impact greater than any other Bergman film except for *The Seventh Seal* and *Persona*. In an extraordinary achievement for a foreign film, it won Academy nominations for best picture, director, screenplay, and cinematography. Oddly, it did not inspire a lot of complex interpretations, of the sort that have showered on puzzling recent films like *Memento, Mulholland Drive,* and *Fight Club*. Perhaps that's because it did not much appeal to young male viewers, who are the most enthusiastic theory weavers, or perhaps it's because the movie is simply beyond explanation: The emotions it portrays and evokes speak for themselves. It would be hard to say that any of the sisters, or any of their actions, "stand" for anything except the inexplicable way that life can bless and punish us.

Bergman, born in 1918, the son of a Lutheran minister, was a lifelong agnostic (although in a conversation with Erland Josephson included on the new DVD, he says he hopes to see his wife in the next life). Spirituality is often at the center of his films, and usually involves the silence of God in a world of horror. The knight plays a chess game with Death in *The Seventh Seal,* and a Lutheran minister has a crisis of faith in *Winter Light* when he reflects on the possibility of nuclear holocaust.

In *Cries and Whispers,* Anna's faith is simple and direct. She lights a candle, kneels before a photo of her dead girl, and asks God to love her. Then she blows out the candle and takes a healthy bite out of an apple (with perfect timing, intercepting some juice before it can fall). When Agnes dies, the scenes of the preparation of her body remind us of the biblical account of the women who took Christ down from the cross, and her cries of pain seem to ask the Father why he has forsaken her.

The ending of the film is overwhelming in its emotional strategy. Anna is called before the heartless family, given her pittance, and told to be on her way. Offered a "keepsake," she raises her voice for the only time in the movie: "I want nothing." But later we find she has kept something. From a drawer she takes a parcel and unwraps it to reveal Agnes's journal, and she reads as Agnes recalls a perfect day in the autumn, when the pain was not so bad, and the four women took up their parasols and walked in the garden. "This is happiness. I cannot wish for anything better," she writes. "I feel profoundly grateful to my life, which gives me so much."

Anna's keepsake is Agnes's gratitude in the face of pain and death. When Karin and Maria come to the point of their deaths, we feel, they will be without resources, empty-handed in the face of oblivion. Bergman has made it clear from his other films that he feels imperfect, sometimes cruel, a sinner. Anna's faith is the faith of a child, perfect, without questions, and he envies it. It may be true, it may be futile, but it is better to feel it than to die in despair.

THE DISCREET CHARM
OF THE BOURGEOISIE

All movies toy with us, but the best ones have the nerve to admit it. Most movies pretend their stories are real, and that we must take them seriously. Comedies are allowed to break the rules. Most of the films of Luis Buñuel are comedies in one way or another, but he doesn't go for gags and punch lines; his comedy is more like a dig in the ribs, sly and painful.

Consider two of his best films side by side. *The Exterminating Angel* (1962) is about a group of guests who arrive for dinner, enjoy it, and then cannot leave. They're mysteriously compelled to spend days and weeks squatting in the house of their host. Civilized behavior erodes, as the press and the police gather helplessly outside. Now look at *The Discreet Charm of the Bourgeoisie* (1972), about people who are trapped on the other side of the mirror: They constantly arrive for dinner, and sometimes even sit down for it, but are never able to eat. They arrive on the wrong night, or are alarmed to find the corpse of the restaurant owner in the next room, or are interrupted by military maneuvers.

Dinner is the central social ritual of the middle classes, a way of displaying wealth and good manners. It also offers the convenience of something to do (eat) and something to talk about (the food), and that is a great relief, since so many of the bourgeoisie have nothing much to talk about and a great many things they hope will not be mentioned. The joke in *The Discreet Charm of the Bourgeoisie* is the way Buñuel interrupts the meals with the secrets that lurk beneath the surface of his decaying European aristocracy: witlessness, adultery, drug dealing, cheating, military coups, perversion, and the paralysis of boredom. His central characters are politicians, the military, and the rich, but in a generous mood he throws in a supporting character to make fun of the church—a bishop whose fetish is to dress up as a gardener and work as a servant in the gardens of the wealthy.

The Discreet Charm of the Bourgeoisie was Buñuel's most successful film; it made more money even than his famous *Belle de Jour* (1967), won the Oscar as best foreign film, and was named the year's best by the National Society of Film Critics. It was released in a year when social unrest was at its height, the Vietnam War was in full flower, and the upper middle class was a fashionable target of disdain. How different to see it again at a time when affluence is once again praised and envied. The primary audience for the film in 1972 saw it as attacking others; the primary audience today will, if it is perceptive, see it as an attack on itself.

Buñuel (1900–1983), a Spaniard who worked in Mexico and Hollywood before returning at last to his homeland, was a surrealist in the 1920s (he collaborated with Salvador Dalí on *Un Chien Andalou*, probably the most famous short film ever made). He spent years in political, financial, and artistic exile, and many of his Mexican films were done for hire, but he always managed to make them his own, with his anarchic disrespect for authority and his jaundiced view of human nature. His characters are often selfish and self-centered, willing to compromise any principle in order to find gratification. Even when he makes a movie like *Simon of the Desert* (1965), about the saint who lived for thirty-seven years atop a pillar, Buñuel finds him motivated by his ego; Simon likes the crowds he draws.

From the first shots of *Discreet Charm,* we are aware of the way his characters carry themselves. They exude their status; they are sure of who they are, and wear their position in society like a costume. Fernando Rey's little peacock of an ambassador, Stéphane Audran's rich hostess, Bulle Ogier's bored daughter—all act as if they're playing roles. And consider the bishop (Julien Bertheau), who appears at the door in gardener's clothes and is scornfully turned away, only to reappear in his clerical garb to "explain himself" and be embraced. In Buñuel the clothes not only make the man

but are the man (especially true for a director with lifelong fetishes involving clothes and shoes).

The movie is broken into self-contained sequences, showing the bland surface of polite society and the lusts that lurk beneath. A couple expects guests for dinner. In the bedroom, they are overcome by lust. The guests arrive. Now they cannot make love in the bedroom, because the wife "makes too much noise," the husband complains, so they sneak out a window and passionately have sex in the woods. Then they sneak back into the house, leaves and grass in their hair. Bourgeois manners, Buñuel believes, are the flimsiest facade for our animal natures. Another example: After soldiers open fire on the dinner guests, a man escapes death by hiding under a table, then betrays himself by greedily reaching up for the meat still on his plate.

The film's narrative flow is cheerfully shattered by Buñuel's devices. As women have drinks in a garden café, a lieutenant walks over and begins a harrowing tale of childhood. We see his story in flashback. He finishes, bids them good day, and leaves. A dinner party develops strangely when the roast chickens dropped by the servant turn out to be stage props—and then the curtain goes up and the guests find themselves onstage before an audience. Dreams fold within dreams, not because the characters are confused but because Buñuel is amusing himself by using such obvious tricks.

The movie is not savage or angry, but bemused and cynical. Buñuel was seventy-two when he directed it. "It belongs both to his old age and to his second childhood," says A. O. Scott. Backed by the French producer Serge Silberman, he was free at last to indulge his fancies, and *Discreet Charm* is liberated from any commercial or narrative requirements. A few years later, with *That Obscure Object of Desire*, he actually had two actresses play the same role, without any explanation. All of these later films were written by Jean-Claude Carrière, who also helped on Buñuel's autobiography, and who shared the master's conviction that hypocrisy was the most entertaining target.

The year 2000 was Buñuel's centenary. Rialto Pictures marked the milestone with releases of restored prints not only of *Discreet Charm* but also *Diary of a Chambermaid* (1964), with Jeanne Moreau; *The Milky Way* (1968), with its pilgrims on a perplexing spiritual odyssey; *That Obscure*

Object of Desire (1977); and *The Phantom of Liberty* (1974), with its famous scene where dinner guests defecate in public but sneak off alone in order to eat; Buñuel wickedly suggests that the two activities are, in some fundamental way, equivalent.

Of all the things he found hilarious, Buñuel was perhaps most amused by fetishes. To him, sex was something we take seriously when it involves ourselves and consider ribald when it involves others. What's funnier than someone saddled with a fetish that is absurd, inconvenient, or not respectable? Consider the situation in *Tristana,* where the woman with one leg (Catherine Deneuve) cruelly and knowledgeably toys with the servant boy who is fascinated by her disability.

Buñuel's films constitute one of the most distinctive bodies of work in the first century of films. He was cynical, but not depressed. We say one thing and do another, yes, but that doesn't make us evil—only human and, from his point of view, funny. He has been called a cruel filmmaker, but the more I look at his films the more wisdom and acceptance I find. He sees that we are hypocrites, admits to being one himself, and believes we were probably made that way.

{ DON'T LOOK NOW }

The hero of *Don't Look Now* is a rational man who does not believe in psychics, omens, or the afterlife. The film hammers down his skepticism and destroys him. It involves women who have an intuitive connection with the supernatural, and men who with their analytical minds are trapped in denial—men like the architect, the bishop, and the policeman, who try to puzzle out the events of the story. The architect's wife, the blind woman, and her sister try to warn them, but cannot.

Nicolas Roeg's 1973 film remains one of the great horror masterpieces, working not with fright, which is easy, but with dread, grief, and apprehension. Few films so successfully put us inside the mind of a man who is trying to reason his way free from mounting terror. Roeg and his editor, Graeme Clifford, cut from one unsettling image to another. The film is fragmented in its visual style, accumulating images that add up to a final bloody moment of truth.

The movie takes place entirely on late-autumn days when everything is gray and damp and on the edge of frost. It opens in the country cottage of John and Laura Baxter (Donald Sutherland and Julie Christie), who are curled up before the fire, working, while their children play outside. There is never a moment when this scene in the British countryside seems safe or serene. The little girl Christine, wearing a shiny red raincoat, plays near a pond. Inside, her father studies slides of Venetian churches. Her

brother runs his bicycle over a pane of glass, breaking it. Her father looks up sharply, as if sensing the sound. Christine throws her ball into the pond. Her father spills a glass, and a bloodlike stain spreads across the surface of a slide—a slide showing the red hood of a raincoat in a Venetian church. Shots show Christine's raincoat reflected upside down in the pond. Something causes John to look up, run from the house, and then find his daughter's body beneath the water and lift it up with an animal cry of grief.

This sequence not only establishes the loss that devastates the Baxters but sets the visual themes of the movie. There will be shots that occur out of time, as characters anticipate future events or impose past events on the present. There will be sharp intakes of psychic foresight. Christine's death by water will lead in an obscure way to Venice, where John Baxter is restoring an old church, where a killer is loose, where the police pull a body from a canal, where a child's doll lies drowned at the water's edge.

The shiny red raincoat will be a connector all the way through. In Venice, Baxter will get glimpses of a little figure in red running away from him or hiding from him, and may wonder if this is the ghost of his daughter. We will see the red figure more often than he does, glimpsing it on a distant bridge, or as a boat passes behind two arches. And the precise tone of red will be a marker through the movie; Roeg's palate is entirely in dark earth tones, except when he introduces bright red splashes—with a shawl, a scarf, a poster on a wall, a house front painted with startling brilliance. The color is a link between death past and future.

The marriage of John and Laura seems real and constant in the film, not just a convenience of the plot. The death of their daughter devastates them, and when we see them in Venice (an undetermined time later, but again in very late autumn), there is a sadness between them. Then in the restroom of a restaurant Laura meets two English sisters, Heather (Hilary Mason) and Wendy (Clelia Matania). Heather, who is blind, tells Laura she "saw" little Christine sitting with her parents at lunch, laughing and smiling: "She's happy now!"

Laura at first doubts, then joyously believes. She collapses at the restaurant, but that night, probably for the first time since Christine's death, the Baxters make love. This scene is celebrated for its passion and truthfulness, but its full emotional impact comes through the editing: The lovemaking is intercut with shots of John and Laura dressing afterward, so that they are at once together and apart, now and later, passionate and preoccupied. There is a poignancy here beyond all reason; in a movie concerned with time, this is the sequence that insists that our future is contained in our present—that everything passes, even ecstasy.

Venice, that haunted city, has never been more melancholy than in *Don't Look Now*. It is like a vast necropolis, its stones damp and crumbling, its canals alive with rats. The cinematography, by Anthony B. Richmond and an uncredited Roeg, drains it of people. There are a few shots, on busy streets or near the Grand Canal, when we see residents and tourists, but during the two sustained scenes where John and Laura are lost (first together, later separately) there is no one else about, and the streets, bridges, canals, dead ends, and wrong turns fold in upon themselves. Walking in Venice, especially on a foggy winter night, is like walking in a dream.

The city is old and ominous. John struggles to raise a statue to its perch on a church wall, then uncovers it to reveal a hideous gargoyle, sticking its tongue out at him. A church scaffold collapses beneath him. The hotel where the Baxters are staying is eager to close at the end of season; the lobby furniture is already shrouded. The canals yield drowned bodies. And John's concern mounts as his wife listens to the two strange sisters, and becomes convinced that their daughter is sending them messages. "She's dead, Laura," John says. "Our daughter is dead. Dead, dead, dead, dead, dead."

But it is John who has second sight. "He has the gift, even if he doesn't know it, even if he's resisting it," the sisters tell each other. After Laura is called home to be with their son, who has had a minor accident at boarding school, John sees her and the sisters standing at the front of a motorboat passing him on the Grand Canal. How can she be here and there? Those who have been to Venice will recognize it as a funeral boat.

The plot of *Don't Look Now*, if it were summarized in a realistic way, would be fairly standard horror stuff. The identification of the red-hooded figure is arbitrary and perhaps even unnecessary. It is the film's visual style, acting, and mood that evoke its uncanny power. Like the films of M. Night Shyamalan, it works through apprehension, not plot or action. The "explanation" is perfunctory but the dread is palpable.

The movie is based on a novel by Daphne du Maurier. "Romantic sludge," Michael Dempsey calls it in his *Film Quarterly* review, explaining how the screenplay extends and deepens it but does not improve on the device of the hooded red figure. Dempsey makes a key point about the film's use of montage: Unlike Eisenstein, who suggests that shots are linked, he says, Roeg and Clifford put together shots that *might* be linked. We are always as uncertain as John Baxter about the connections between what he sees, what exists, what will exist, and what does not exist.

Roeg, born in 1928, used a similar freedom of movement through time in his first two films, *Performance* (1970) and *Walkabout* (1971), and has continued to play with chronology. He doesn't always enter his stories at the beginning and leave at the end but rummages around in them, as if separated moments can shed light on one another.

I've been through the film with students a shot at a time, paying close attention to the use of red as a marker in the visual scheme. It is a masterpiece of physical filmmaking, in the way the photography evokes mood and the editing underlines it with uncertainty. The admitted weakness of the denouement is beside the point, and I have come to an accommodation with the revelations about the figure in the red raincoat. That figure need not be who and what it seems to be, or anything at all—except for the gargoyle that awaits us all at the end of time, sticking out its tongue.

THE EARRINGS
OF MADAME DE...

Unhappiness is an invented thing.

So the General tells his wife. He is convinced she wants to be unhappy. She places herself willfully in the way of sadness. It is her choice. There was a time when Louise would have agreed with him, when their views on society matched perfectly. But now she is truly unhappy, and it is beyond her choice. The General will never understand that. Neither, probably, will her lover the Baron. It is the gift these men have given her: the ability to mourn what she has lost or never found. It is the one gift they cannot take back. Without it, she would have been unable to understand happiness. Certainly the men cannot.

The Earrings of Madame de . . . , directed in 1953 by Max Ophuls, is one of the most mannered and contrived love movies ever filmed. It glitters and dazzles, and beneath the artifice it creates a heart, and breaks it. The film is famous for its elaborate camera movements, its graceful style, its sets, its costumes, and, of course, its jewelry. It stars Danielle Darrieux, Charles Boyer, and Vittorio De Sica, who effortlessly embody elegance. It could have been a mannered trifle. We sit in admiration of Ophuls's visual display, so fluid and intricate. Then, to our surprise, we find ourselves caring.

The story takes place in Vienna a century or so ago. The General (Boyer) has married late, and well, to Louise (Darrieux), a great beauty. He gives her expensive diamond earrings as a wedding present. As the film opens, Madame is desperately in debt, and rummaging among her possessions for something to sell. The camera follows her in an unbroken shot as she looks through dresses, furs, jewelry, and finally settles on the earrings, which she never liked anyway. "What will you tell your husband?" asks her servant. She will tell him that she lost them.

She trusts the discretion of Rémy, the jeweler. She should not. Rémy, who originally sold the earrings to the General, tells him the whole story. The General buys back the earrings as a farewell present to his mistress, who is leaving him and going to Constantinople. Certainly the wife will never see them again, and there is poetic justice involved.

The mistress sells the earrings to finance her gambling. The Baron Donati (De Sica) buys them. In his travels he encounters the Countess Louise, falls in love, courts her, and gives her the earrings. She is startled to see them but intuits how they came into the Baron's hands. How to explain their reappearance to the General? In his presence, she goes through the motions of "finding" them. The General knows this is a falsehood, and the whole tissue of deceptions dissolves, even though the jewels are bought and sold two more times. (There is always a laugh when the jeweler turns up in the General's office for "our usual transaction.")

Standing back a little from the comings and goings of the earrings, which is the stuff of farce, the movie begins to look more closely at Louise (whose husband's name is never given, so that she is always vaguely the "Countess de . . ."). She and her husband live in a society where love affairs are more or less expected; "your suitors get on my nerves," the General fusses as they leave a party. If they do not know specifically who their spouse is flirting with, they know generally. There is, however, a code in such affairs, and the code permits sex but not love. The General confronts the Baron with his knowledge of the earrings. ("Constantinople?" "Yes.") The General tells him, "It is incompatible with your dignity, and mine, for my wife to accept a gift of such value from you."

The General's instinct is sound. The Countess has indeed fallen in love. The Baron thought that he had, too. Their tragedy is that the intensity of her love carries her outside the rules, while the Baron remains safely in bounds.

The scene where they fall in love shows Ophuls's mastery. He likes to show his characters surrounded by, even drowning in, their milieu. Interior spaces are crowded with possessions. Their bodies are adorned with gowns, uniforms, jewelry, decorations. Ophuls likes to shoot past foreground objects, or through windows, to show the characters contained by possessions. But in the key love scene, a montage involving several nights of dancing, the circling couple is gradually left all alone.

The Baron and the Countess are at a resort. On the dance floor, they observe that it has been three weeks since they danced together—two days—one day—and then they are dancing still and no time has passed. The dialogue and costumes indicate the time transitions, but the music plays without interruption, as do their unbroken movements. They dance and dance, in love. An admiral's wife whispers, "They're seen everywhere—because they can't meet anywhere." On the last night, one orchestra member after another packs up and goes home. A servant extinguished the candles. Finally a black drop cloth is thrown over the harp, and the camera moves in until the screen is black and the dance is over. The economy of storytelling here—a courtship all told in a dance—resembles the famous montage in *Citizen Kane* where a marriage dissolves in a series of breakfasts.

The discovery of a possession in the wrong place at the wrong time is an ancient trick in fiction, from Desdemona's handkerchief to Henry James's golden bowl to the brooch that should not be around Judy's neck in *Vertigo*. What is interesting in *Madame de . . .* is the way the value of the earrings changes in relationship to their meaning. At the start Madame Louise wants only to sell them. Then, when they are a gift from her lover, they become invaluable. The General wants to buy them back once, twice, but finally is reduced to telling the jeweler, "Stay away from me with those infernal earrings!" An expensive bauble, intended to symbolize love, becomes an annoyance and a danger when it finally *does* represent it.

For Louise, the earrings teach a lesson. She is no more morally to blame than her husband or her lover, if only adultery is at stake. But if the General's honor is the question—if being gossiped about by the silly admiral's wife is the result—then she is to blame. Certainly the Baron understands this, and withdraws, his love suddenly upstaged by his regard for his own reputation. The final meeting between the two men is brought about, curiously, by the General's discovery that he *does* have real feelings for his wife.

Max Ophuls (1902–1957) was a German who made films in Germany, Hollywood, and France. His career was used by the critic Andrew Sarris as a foundation-stone of his auteur theory. Sarris famously advised moviegoers to value the *how* of a movie more than the *what*. The story and message are not as important, he said, as the style and art. In Ophuls, he had a good test case, because Ophuls is seemingly the director most obsessed with surfaces, with the visual look, with elaborate camera movements. He was dismissed by many as nothing more than a fancy stylist, and it took Sarris (and the French auteurists) to show what a master he was.

His films are one of the great pleasures of the cinema. *Madame de . . .* is equaled by *La Ronde* (1950) and *Lola Montès* (1955) as movies whose surfaces are a voluptuous pleasure to watch, regardless of whether you choose to plunge into their depths. The long, impossibly complex opening shot of *La Ronde,* with the narrator introducing us to the story and even singing a little song, is one of the treasures of the movies. And who else has such romantic boldness that he will show Louise writing her Baron day after day, with no letter back, and then have him tell her when they finally meet, "I always answered your letters, my love—but I lacked the courage to mail them." And then to show his unmailed letters torn into bits and flung into the air to become snow.

THE FALL OF
THE HOUSE OF USHER

The great hall in Jean Epstein's *The Fall of the House of Usher* is one of the most haunting spaces in the movies. Its floor is a vast marble expanse, interrupted here and there by an item of furniture that seems dwarfed by the surrounding emptiness. An odd staircase rises from one distant corner. It is not impossible that this vision, in one of the best-known French surrealist films, inspired the designers of the great hall of Xanadu in *Citizen Kane*. In both films, shadows are made to substitute for details that are not really there, and a man and a woman, their lives ruled by his obsession with her, move like wraiths through the haunted space.

The hall is not simply cold, enormous, and forbidding but has surrealistic details. "Leaves blow ominously across the floor," writes the critic Gary Morris, and the long white curtains "flutter menacingly, as if the house is under constant, quiet, insidious siege by a vengeful nature." This is not a room for human habitation but a set for a surrealist opera.

The occupants of the house are Roderick Usher and his young wife, Madeline. In the original story by Edgar Allan Poe, they were brother and sister, but the implication of incest has been removed by Epstein, who explains with a title card that the men of the house of Usher have all been obsessed with painting their wives. Roderick is consumed with fear that his wife will die, and no less fearful that she will be buried alive. Does he hope that his portrait will transfer her essence to a form that will live forever?

To the house an unnamed friend is summoned. There are echoes of the Dracula films and of the silent classic *Nosferatu* (1922) in the way the locals refuse to convey the visitor to the house, even though poor Roderick Usher is merely demented, not vampirish. The friend's arrival is curiously staged, with Roderick standing at the top of a flight of steps and leaning far forward to extend his hand to the other man, but apparently not daring to take even one actual step down to approach him. An umbilical seems to tie him to the interior.

The exterior of the house, seen in the midst of the obligatory blasted heath, is obviously a drawn miniature, and critics point out the unconvincing stars in the sky, proudly fake. This kind of obvious artifice, which hardly even attempts to fool the eye, owes something to the German expressionist tradition in films like *The Cabinet of Dr. Caligari*. Although the interior of the house looks more real, or at least more physically present, its nightmare details and vistas are also less concerned with realism than with effect.

Epstein's assistant director on the film was young Luis Buñuel, who had just finished his notorious collaboration with Salvador Dalí on *Un Chien Andalou*, a boldly surrealist film. Did he contribute to this film's weirdness? No doubt, although Epstein was a surrealist himself and the underlying story itself is less interested in psychological plausibility than in the creepiness and oddness of its immediate impression. (Buñuel eventually quit after a quarrel with Epstein.)

Roderick is played by Jean Debucourt, more convincing than many silent stars, who goes less for the demented madman effect and more for the aura of a man consumed by his fears. Madeline is played by Marguerite Gance, wife of the French director Abel Gance (*Napoleon*). Her task is to be an object. All attention and animation is concentrated in the two men, while Madeline poses for her painting and slowly sinks toward the grave. The visitor and narrator is Charles Lamy.

There is an amusing ambiguity about the painting, which we see at regular intervals throughout the film. In some shots it is a real canvas, which Roderick daubs at. In others it is the real Marguerite Gance standing within the frame and pretending to the camera she is the painting. "In a motif lifted from Wilde's 'Picture of Dorian Gray,' " writes the critic Mark

Zimmer, "her life and vitality pours into the painting, such that it begins to blink and move, as she dies." Perhaps, but not according to the critic Glenn Erickson, who writes, "Roderick's portraits are represented by having Madeline sit very still behind the frame and pretend to be a painted image. Unfortunately, she blinks in almost every take, ruining the illusion."

Both critics are seeing exactly the same thing. Which critic is correct? The surrealists would have been delighted by the confusion.

Jean Epstein (1897–1953), born in Poland, studied medicine before falling into the Parisian orbit of the surrealists in the 1920s. He directed films throughout the 1920s, finding as others did that silent films gave themselves naturally to fantasy and impressionism; the talkies would discover that dialogue tended to tilt stories toward realism. *The Fall of the House of Usher*, made in 1928, the last great year of silent films, was based on a Poe story that is more atmosphere than plot anyway. There have been many versions of *Usher*, from another 1928 silent film through to Roger Corman's excellent 1960 version with Vincent Price. Epstein seems to focus less on the mechanics of the situation than on its very oddness: the man and woman both trapped by his mad obsession with death, the woman almost helpfully fading away.

I was struck, watching the film recently on a new DVD, by how completely it engaged me. Some silent films hold you outside: You admire them but are aware of them as a phenomenon. With *The Fall of the House of Usher*, I barely stirred during the film's sixty-six-minute running time. A tone, an atmosphere, was created that actually worked. As with *Nosferatu*, the film seemed less a fiction than the realization of some phantasmagoric alternative reality. Epstein's openness to the grand gesture is helpful, as when Madeline is in her coffin and her white bridal veil spills outside and blows in the wind.

Two modern additions to the film also enhance it. Instead of replacing the original French titles and their boldly stylized calligraphy, this version uses the voice of actor Jean-Pierre Aumont to read them in English. The effect is that the titles are as real as the film, and Aumont is standing outside of it, next to us, confiding the horror they contain.

The other addition is the score for a revival of the film in 1960, by Rolande de Cande. Based on medieval music, composed for woodwinds and strings, it is an extraordinary piece of work. It feels as if it emerges from the images themselves, odd, sad, and vaguely liturgical.

Characters in horror films tend to pose. They are presented not in terms of complex human nature but within the narrow definition of their obsession, or weakness, or limitation. Stories often involve an outside visitor whose function is to provide an audience and, later, a report. The story of Roderick and Madeline would be less dramatic if there was no one there to witness it and provide the reaction of a normal person. Yet more than many horror characters, Roderick and Madeline seem complete in their drama, as if they do not need the observer. Roderick thinks only of death, decay, and Poe's beloved dread of being buried alive. And Madeline—well, why did she marry him? What was their courtship like? Has it ever occurred to her to simply walk away? One does not ask such practical questions about a horror film, I know, but Marguerite Gance succeeds in suggesting that Madeline has fallen under the spell, whether willingly or not, and is also caught up in the obsession.

There are times when I think that of all the genres, the horror film most misses silence. The Western benefited from dialogue, and musicals and film noir are unthinkable without words. But in a classic horror film, almost anything you can say will be superfluous or ridiculous. Notice how carefully the Draculas of talkies have to choose their words to avoid bad laughs. The perfect horror situation is such that there is nothing you can say about it. What words are necessary in *The Pit and the Pendulum*? *The Fall of the House of Usher* resides within its sealed world, as if—yes, as if buried alive.

{ THE FIREMEN'S BALL }

Miloš Forman's *The Firemen's Ball* was banned "permanently and forever" by the Communist regime in Czechoslovakia in 1968, as Soviet troops marched in to suppress a popular uprising. It was said to be a veiled attack on the Soviet system and its bureaucracy, a charge Forman prudently denied at the time but now happily agrees with. Telling a seductively mild and humorous story about a retirement fete for an elderly fireman, the movie pokes fun at citizens' committees, the culture of thievery, and solutions that surrender to problems.

Forman and his writer, Ivan Passer, found the inspiration for their film while writing another one. They'd just had an international success with *Loves of a Blonde* (a 1966 Oscar nominee). That one told the story of a young woman in a factory town where the women vastly outnumber the men; she unwisely falls in love with a musician who is not serious about her. Working on a new idea, Forman and Passer moved to a small town to get away from the pressures of Prague, attended the local firemen's ball, and realized they had the premise for their next picture.

The film follows a pattern common enough in Eastern Europe at the time, where small human stories seemed to be a slice of life but might actually be subtle parables about the restrictive Soviet system. Screenplays had to be approved by censors, but many a change took place between approval and premiere, and in the case of *The Firemen's Ball* that was almost fatal. The movie was cofinanced by the Italian producer Carlo Ponti, but after the Czech authorities withdrew their approval, Ponti pulled out, and only the intervention of French director François Truffaut saved the film and found it international distribution.

The movie takes place during about twenty-four hours, as the firemen prepare for their event, attend it, and survive it. They're planning a tribute to their former chief, although it may be coming too late: "We should have given it to him last year, when he was eighty-five," one observes, "instead of now when he's about to die." The ancient fireman, diagnosed with cancer, will be presented with a handsome miniature fire ax in a velvet-lined box.

Some feel the old fireman represents the almost forgotten values and traditions of the pre-Soviet years. The film's climactic scene could easily be seen as a perfect symbol for the paradoxes of Soviet communism: During the ball, a local barn catches fire, and the firemen race to the scene. But their truck gets stuck in the snow, the barn is engulfed by flames by the time they get there, and when the farmer complains that he is cold, the firemen do what they can: They move his chair closer to the flames.

The buildup to that wonderful scene is in a series of vignettes that have the savor of real life, perhaps because Forman cast all local people—no professional actors—in his roles. We see the committee meeting at which the miniature fire ax is admired and plans are made. At the local hall, a fireman teeters atop a tall ladder to scorch the sides of a paper banner; his ladder slips, he is left dangling from a beam, and the poster goes up in flames.

The firemen plan to have a beauty pageant, with the queen delegated to present the fire ax. They fill a table with raffle prizes—cheeses, hams, cakes, and chocolates—that are precious at a time when consumer goods are in short supply. But "he who does not steal, steals from his family," according to a saying Forman quotes in an interview on the DVD. The prizes disappear prematurely from the table; even the respectable couple assigned as guards are guilty.

The beauty pageant is a disaster, not least because few of the local girls, and none of the pretty ones, have any interest in it. Eagle-eyed firemen circulate through the crowd, trying to recruit candidates, and there is a

lineup of reluctant finalists, who look like citizen volunteers who would rather be elsewhere.

Forman is making fun not of his characters but of the system they inhabit. Yet censors criticized the film because it painted a "negative portrait" of Czech society. That is often the tactic in a system that fears criticism; the wonderful Iranian film *Children of Heaven* was said by censors to show a society where children could not afford sneakers. That's the last thing the movie is about, but still, in Iran, some children cannot afford sneakers, and so there you are. Censors often disguise themselves as patriots, treating any criticism as unpatriotic, when in fact criticism is a patriotic duty. When, in a free society, the press is criticized for negativity, that almost always simply means it has dared to question the policies of the party in power. "Patriotism," Samuel Johnson said, "is the last refuge of a scoundrel." He could have been speaking of those who use it to shield themselves from dissent.

Visiting the Czech Republic in the summer of 2002 for the Karlovy Vary film festival, I met people who'd survived the Soviet occupation, there and elsewhere. They were still bitter; the presence of a patriotic Russian film was sharply questioned by several of my fellow jury members, who found it a holdover from the bad old days. (I found it an echo of the standard war film from every country, in which the heroes are considered to be in the right because, after all, the movie is about them.)

The Firemen's Ball was released in 1967, late in the "Prague spring" of liberalism and free expression that generated, and was nourished by, the Czech New Wave. Inspired by the New Wave of France, a generation of Czech filmmakers created, for a time, a zone of freedom. The leading names were Forman, his cowriter Ivan Passer (who directed *Intimate Lighting*, 1965), Jan Nemec (*A Report on the Party and the Guests*, 1966), Jan Kadar (*The Shop on Main Street*, the 1965 Oscar winner for best foreign film), Vera Chytilova (*Daisies*, 1966), and Jiri Menzel (*Closely Watched Trains*, winner of the 1967 Oscar). It was a period when the Czechs found much Academy favor; *Firemen's Ball* was nominated in 1969.

In 1967 there was a popular uprising against the Soviets, which was quickly crushed, and most of these films and their directors were banned. Many left the country. I remember a reception at the 1968 New York Film

Festival, with a roomful of exiled Czechs, including Forman, Passer, and Menzel, all uneasily facing the possibility of working in a new land and a new language. This period in history was written about by the Czech novelist Milan Kundera in *The Unbearable Lightness of Being,* and in Philip Kaufman's movie version one of the actors is Miloš Forman.

Many of the Czech New Wave directors found success in America, none more than Forman, who made two of the most honored films in Academy Award history (*One Flew over the Cuckoo's Nest* and *Amadeus*). His first American film was *Taking Off* (1971), a social satire that shared with *The Firemen's Ball* a rich appreciation for the everyday lives of people who do not realize how funny they are. When a hippie girl runs away, he turns a sharp satirical eye at her affluent parents, showing a sympathy for the underdog and nonconformist that would be mirrored in many of his films— not only *Cuckoo's Nest,* with the asylum standing in for all bureaucracies, but in the hippie musical *Hair* (1979), *The People vs. Larry Flynt* (1996), and *Man on the Moon* (1999), about the outsider comic Andy Kaufman.

Is *The Firemen's Ball* dated today? That's an interesting question. It no longer borrows energy from its risk taking, as so many Soviet bloc films did in the 1960s and 1970s. In those days any new film from Poland, Hungary, Yugoslavia, or Czechoslovakia, in particular, was likely to be a veiled attack, wreathed in the glamour of danger. But *The Firemen's Ball* hasn't dated as entertainment; Forman doesn't push his political points, being content to let them make themselves, unfolding gracefully from the human drama. The movie is just plain funny. And as a parable it is timeless, with relevance at many times in many lands. Remarkable, how often when I hear of a White House brainstorm I think of the firemen moving the farmer's chair closer to the flames.

{ FIVE EASY PIECES }

E*asy Rider* proved in 1969 that Jack Nicholson was a great character actor. *Five Easy Pieces* proved in 1970 that he was a great actor and a star. This is the film, more than ten years into his career, where he flowered as a screen presence, as Jack the lad, the outsider, capable of anger, sarcasm, self-pity, also capable of tenderness and grief, ready for violence but not very good at it. There were glimpses of this persona in earlier films (see his character Poet in *Hell's Angels on Wheels* in 1967), but now here was a film of uncommon depth and originality, a canvas for a man named Robert Eroica Dupea, his middle name inspired by Beethoven's Third Symphony.

It is difficult to explain today how much Bobby Dupea meant to the film's first audiences. I was at the New York Film Festival for the premiere of *Five Easy Pieces,* and I remember the explosive laughter, the deep silences, the stunned attention as the final shot seemed to continue forever, and then the ovation. We'd had a revelation. This was the direction American movies should take: into idiosyncratic characters, into dialogue with an ear for the vulgar and the literate, into a plot free to surprise us about the characters, into an existential ending not required to be happy. *Five Easy Pieces* was a fusion of the personal cinema of John Cassavetes and the new indie movement that was tentatively emerging. It was, you could say, the first Sundance film.

Nicholson was not the film's only discovery. There were quirky

supporting roles for Karen Black, Lois Smith, and Ralph Waite, all pitch-perfect, all relatively new to movies. It established Bob Rafelson, the director and cowriter, as a leader of the American New Wave. Its cinematography was by Laszlo Kovacs, a Hungarian who'd also shot *Easy Rider* and *Hell's Angels on Wheels* and became one of the best of all cameramen. The film's greatest influence came through the screenplay, by Rafelson and Carole Eastman; it allowed detours and digressions, cared more about behavior than plot, ended in a way and tone that could not have been guessed from its beginning.

And it had moments that passed permanently into the collective memory of moviegoers. The most famous of those is always referred to as the Chicken Salad Scene. Is there a movie lover who cannot quote it? That speech, and the shot of Nicholson in a football helmet on the back of a motorcycle in *Easy Rider,* are the defining moments in his sudden transition from anonymity to legend.

The movie has other memorable lines ("I faked a little Chopin, and you faked a big response"), but what it has above all is Bobby Dupea: He's a voluntary outcast who can't return to his early life yet has no plausible way to move forward. He's stranded between occupations, personas, ambitions, social classes. In 1970 (and before and since) most American movies centered on heroes who defined the plot, occupied it, made it happen. *Five Easy Pieces* is about a character who doesn't fit in the movie. There's not a scene where he's comfortable with the people around him, not a moment when he feels at home. The movie's story traces a journey back through a life where Bobby (in his own view) disappointed people, could not be counted on, misbehaved, underachieved. The only person in the movie who openly criticizes him is the one who knows him the least; his family and his waitress girlfriend overlook or forgive his flaws, but he can't forgive himself.

The first half of the film, set in the oil fields of California, gives no hint of the second. Bobby is an oil-well rigger who lives with Rayette Dipesto (Karen Black), a waitress with big hair, frosted lips, and a worship of Tammy Wynette. She's pathetic in her hunger for him, her fear of losing him. When she learns that she's pregnant, Bobby only finds out from his buddy Elton (Billy "Green" Bush), a rigger with a high laugh and downhome seriousness. When Elton lectures him on the joy of family life, we get the first glimpse of Bobby's concealed idea of himself: "It's ridiculous. I'm sitting here listening to some cracker asshole, lives in a trailer park, compare his life to mine." But at that point we think of Bobby as a cracker, too. Who is he?

The action moves easily through the blue-collar world of Bobby and Rayette. They have a fight and make up. They go bowling with Elton and his wife. Bobby gets to hold their baby, and we see his discomfort around children—he's not ready for the responsibility, or even the thought, of a child. Afraid of commitment to Rayette, Bobby has sex with Betty (Sally Struthers), a pickup. They are wild, abandoned; Betty screams in delight and Bobby loses himself in sex, carrying Betty around the room, finally ending exhausted. Then we can read the motorcycle logo on his T-shirt: TRIUMPH. That gets a laugh, to mask the sadness of the scene. Betty isn't what he's looking for, either.

Earlier, there's a preview of the hidden Bobby. Caught in a traffic jam, he sees a piano on the back of a moving truck, climbs aboard, and plays as the truck pulls away. His style is frantic, angry, loud, fast; he wants to hurt the music. We didn't even know he could play. Later, in an abrupt transition, he walks into a recording studio and we learn that the pianist is his sister Partita (Lois Smith). She loves him unconditionally, as we can tell by her smile and her manner; she tells him it's time for him to come home, that their father has had a stroke. That opens the movie's second half.

He will drive from California to an island off the Washington coast where his family lives communally. He reluctantly brings along Rayette, then dumps her in a motel and goes for the first time in years to meet his father, Nicholas (William Challee); his brother, Carl Fidelio (Ralph Waite); Carl's student and lover, Catherine (Susan Anspach); and the newest member of the household, the male nurse Spicer (John P. Ryan), who Partita has an eye for.

The father never speaks. Carl is friendly in a distant, jolly way that is critical by its very refusal to pass judgment. Bobby is attracted to Catherine, a musician of class and poise, and she has sex with him but scoffs at the notion that they have a future: "You have no love for yourself, no love for family, for friends—how can you ask for love?"

This visit produces many memorable scenes, two in particular. One involves Rayette's surprise arrival by taxi and her dumb-like-a-fox behavior as she works her redneck persona to let everyone know what she thinks of them. When an insufferable visiting mystic (Irene Dailey) tries to put her down, Rayette loudly tells Carl about a friend's kitten "that got squashed flat as a tortilla outside their mobile home," and we know exactly what she's doing. When the woman tries to put her down, Bobby rises to Rayette's defense: "You shouldn't even be in the same room with her, you pompous celibate."

Dialogue like that, and there is a lot of it, makes the movie alive with surprise and possibility. These characters are not limited to banalities that can easily be dubbed for the foreign release, but speak varieties of American vernacular from top to bottom of the social spectrum (sometimes switching their styles to fit an occasion—Bobby does a lot of that). Listen to the other great scene, as Bobby wheels his father's chair out to the shoreline and in a monologue tries to explain his life, cannot, and breaks down in tears. This scene, so wonderfully performed by Nicholson, is where the heart of the movie resides. This remorseful son, whose piano playing never pleased his father ("We both know I wasn't very good at it") is the Bobby that all the other Bobbys seek to conceal.

The last long scene, at the gas station, is the kind of ending the film deserves. It would not be allowed today, when happy endings are legislated by contract. It is true to the Bobby Dupea we have come to know. It shows him escaping from all of his lives, because he can't face any of them.

Five Easy Pieces has the complexity, the nuance, the depth of the best fiction. It involves us in *these* people, *this* time and place, and we care for them even though they don't request our affection or applause. We remember Bobby and Rayette because they are so completely themselves, so stuck, so needy, so brave in their loneliness. Once you have seen movie characters who are alive, it's harder to care about the robots in their puppet shows.

{ GOLDFINGER }

Not every man would like to be James Bond, but every boy would. In one adventure after another, he saves the world, defeats bizarre villains, gets to play with neat gadgets, and seduces, or is seduced by, stupendously sexy women (this last attribute appeals less to boys younger than twelve). He is a hero, but not a bore. Even faced with certain death, he can cheer himself by focusing instead on the possibility that first he might get lucky. He's obsessed with creature comforts, a trial to his superiors, a sophisticate in all material things, and able to parachute into enemy territory and be wearing a tuxedo five minutes later. When it comes to movie spies, Agent 007 is full-service, one-stop shopping.

James Bond is the most durable of the twentieth century's movie heroes, and the one most likely to last well into the twenty-first—although Sherlock Holmes, of course, is also immortal, and Tarzan is probably good for a retread. (The *Star Wars* and *Star Trek* movies are disqualified because they do not have a single hero or a continuous time frame.)

One of the reasons for Bond's longevity among series heroes is quality control; while almost all the Bond films have the same producing team, Tarzan has been the hero of films of wildly divergent quality. And while Holmes has inspired more revisionist interpretations than Hamlet, Bond is consistently Bond: He remains recognizably the same man he was in 1962, when *Dr. No* first brought Ian Fleming's spy to the screen. Even the crypto-Bonds, like the oddball David Niven hero of the maverick *Casino Royale*, or the spoof-Bonds, like Our Man Flint, Matt Helm, and Austin Powers, follow the general outlines of the Fleming legend. Bond is an archetype so persuasive that to change him would be sacrilegious.

Of all the Bonds, *Goldfinger* (1964) is the best, and can stand as a surrogate for the others. If it is not a great film, it is a great entertainment, and contains all the elements of the Bond formula that would work again and again. It's also interesting as the link between the more modest first two Bonds and the later big-budget extravaganzas; after this one, producers Albert "Cubby" Broccoli and Harry Saltzman could be certain that 007 was good for the long run.

At 111 minutes, *Goldfinger* ties with *Dr. No* as the shortest of the James Bond films, and yet it probably contains more durable images than any other title in the series: the young woman killed by being coated with gold paint; the steel-rimmed bowler of the mute Korean assassin Oddjob (Harold Sakata); the Aston-Martin tricked out with deadly gimmicks and an ejector seat; Bond's sexy karate match with Pussy Galore (Honor Blackman); the villain Goldfinger with his gold-plated Rolls-Royce, and, of course, the laser beam pointed at that portion of Bond's lower anatomy that he most requires if he is to continue as hero of the series.

The Broccoli-Saltzman formula found its lasting form in the making of *Goldfinger.* The outline was emerging in the first two films, and here it is complete. First, the title sequence, establishing Bond as a sex hound while linking him with a stunt sequence or a spectacular death. Then the summons by M, head of the British Secret Service, and the briefing on a villain obsessed by global domination. The flirtation with Moneypenny. The demonstration by Q of new gimmicks invented especially for his next case. Then the introduction of the villain, his murderous and bizarre sidekick, and his female assistant/accomplice/mistress. Bond's discovery of the nature of the villain's evil scheme. Bond's capture and the certainty of death. Bond's seduction of the villain's woman. And so on, leading always to a final scene in which Bond is about to enjoy his victory reward: the sensuous fruits of his latest conquest.

"About to enjoy." An essential phrase. There are no extended sex scenes in the Bond pictures, only preludes and epilogues. "Bond sex is a spe-

cial movie style," observes the critic Steve Rhodes. "It consists of a quick but intense kiss followed by a cutaway to later. The sex is hinted at with cute puns and sexual innuendo, but never discussed explicitly." Starting with the Venus-like appearance of Ursula Andress from the sea in *Dr. No,* all of the Bond movies have featured beautiful women, although in a publicity tradition, they appear nude not in the movies but in an issue of *Playboy* that hits the stands right before the premiere.

Goldfinger contains a classic example of the Talking Killer Syndrome, one of the entries in my *Little Movie Glossary.* Auric Goldfinger (Gert Frobe) has captured Bond and has him under his complete control. Indeed, all he has to do is remain silent and the laser will slice Bond from stem to sternum. But Bond dissuades him with some quick thinking, and is released to become Goldfinger's prisoner. Goldfinger, like many another Bond villain, seems to have the makings of a frustrated host: It must be galling to have the most elaborate secret hideaway on earth and no way to show off. So Goldfinger flies Bond to his horse farm in Kentucky, where Bond is able to eavesdrop on the outlines of a scheme between the Chinese and Goldfinger to assault Fort Knox—making the gold baron Goldfinger the most powerful man in the world, while the Commies benefit from world chaos. Later, in a pleasant chat, Goldfinger foolishly answers all of Bond's remaining questions, such as how he could possibly remove those tons of gold.

This stretch of the film is based on a fundamental absurdity. Goldfinger has assembled the heads of all the Mafia families of America at his Kentucky farm. He pushes buttons, and the most elaborate presentation in movie history unfolds. Screens descend from the ceiling. Film of Fort Knox is shown. The floor itself rolls back, and a vast scale model of the fort rises on hydraulic lifts (with Bond hidden inside). Goldfinger tells the mobsters what he plans to do, while Bond listens in. Then shutters fall to lock the mafiosi in the room, and they are immediately killed with poison gas. My question: Why bother to show them that expensive presentation if you're only going to kill them afterward? My best guess: Goldfinger had workmen crawling all over the place for weeks, constructing that presentation, and he wanted to show it to *somebody.*

Bond is played in these early films, of course, by Sean Connery, who took the bloom off the role for all of his successors (George Lazenby, Roger Moore, Timothy Dalton, Pierce Brosnan) while simultaneously sidetracking his own film career. For several years no one could think of Connery as anyone but Bond, and he left the series after *You Only Live Twice,* in 1967, returning for *Diamonds Are Forever* (1971) after the Lazenby fiasco, and a last time in *Never Say Never Again* (because he owned the rights to that property). The other Bonds were not wrong in the role (even Lazenby has his defenders), but they were not Connery, and that was their cross to bear.

Connery had the sleek self-assurance needed for the role, and a gift with deadpan double entendres. But he had something else that none of the others, save perhaps Dalton, could muster: steely toughness. When his eyes narrowed and his body tensed up, you knew the playing was over and the bloodshed was about to begin.

Fleming's James Bond novels took off in the States only after it became known that they were President Kennedy's favorite recreational reading. Indeed, the more we learn about JFK, the more we see how he resembled Bond, or vice versa. At a time when "swinging London" was overtaking pop culture, the Bond series was perfectly positioned (although Bond makes a rare lapse of taste in *Goldfinger* when he recommends listening to the then-new Beatles with earmuffs on). But swinging London has swung, and Bond stays on.

THE GOOD, THE BAD AND THE UGLY

A vast empty western landscape. The camera pans across it. Then the shot slides onto a sunburned, desperate face. The long shot has become a close-up without a cut, revealing that the landscape was not empty but occupied by a desperado very close to us. In these opening frames Sergio Leone establishes a rule that he follows throughout *The Good, the Bad and the Ugly*. The rule is that the ability to see is limited by the sides of the frame. At important moments in the film, what the camera cannot see, the characters cannot see, and that gives Leone the freedom to surprise us with entrances that cannot be explained by the practical geography of his shots.

There is a moment, for example, when men do not notice a vast encampment of the Union Army until they stumble upon it. And a moment in a cemetery when a man materializes out of thin air even though he should have been visible for a mile. And the way men walk down a street in full view and nobody is able to shoot them, maybe because they are not in the same frame with them.

Leone cares not at all about the practical or the plausible, and he builds his great film on the rubbish of Western movie clichés, using style to elevate dreck into art. When the movie opened in America in late 1967, not long after its predecessors *A Fistful of Dollars* (1964) and *For a Few Dollars More* (1965), audiences knew they liked it, but did they know why? I saw it sitting in the front row of the balcony of the Oriental Theater, whose vast,

159

wide screen was ideal for Leone's operatic compositions. I responded strongly, but I had been a movie critic for less than a year and did not always have the wisdom to value instinct over prudence. Looking up my old review, I see I described a four-star movie but gave it only three stars, perhaps because it was a "spaghetti Western" and so could not be art.

But art it is, summoned out of the imagination of Leone and painted on the wide screen so vividly that we forget what marginal productions these films were—that Clint Eastwood was a Hollywood reject, that budgetary restraints ($200,000 for *Fistful*) caused gaping continuity errors, that there wasn't a lot of dialogue because it was easier to shoot silent and fill the sound track with music and effects. There was even a pathetic attempt to make the films seem more American; I learn from the critic Glenn Erickson that Leone was credited as "Bob Robertson" in the early prints of *Fistful*, and composer Ennio Morricone, whose lonely, mournful scores are inseparable from the films, was "Dan Savio." Even Eastwood's character, the famous Man with No Name, was an invention of the publicists; he was called Joe in the first movie, Manco in the second, and Blondie in the third.

Perhaps it is the subtly foreign flavor of the spaghetti trilogy, and especially the masterpiece *The Good, the Bad and the Ugly*, that suggests the films come from a different universe than traditional Westerns. Instead of tame Hollywood extras from central casting, we get locals who must have been hired near the Spanish locations—men who look long-weathered by work and the sun. Consider the legless beggar who uses his arms to propel himself into a saloon, shouting, "Hand me down a whiskey!"

John Ford made Monument Valley the home turf of his western characters, and he made great films there, but there is something new and strange about Leone's menacing Spanish vistas. We haven't seen these deserts before. John Wayne has never been here. Leone's stories are a heightened dream in which everything is bigger, starker, more brutal, more dramatic, than life.

Leone tells the story more with pictures than words. Examine the masterful scene in the cemetery. A fortune in gold is said to be buried in one of the graves, and three men have assembled, all hoping to get it. The actors are Clint Eastwood (the Good), Lee Van Cleef (the Bad), and Eli Wallach (the Ugly). Each man points a pistol at another. If one shoots, they all shoot, and all die. Unless two decide to shoot the third man before he can shoot either one of them. But which two, and which third?

Leone draws this scene out beyond all reason, beginning in long shot and working in to close-ups of firearms, faces, eyes, and lots of sweat and flies. He seems to be testing himself, to see how long he can maintain the suspense. Or is it even suspense, really? It may be entirely an exercise in style, a deliberate manipulation by the director, intended to draw attention to itself. If you savor the freedom with which Leone flirts with parody, you understand his method. This is not a story but a celebration of bold gestures.

Eastwood, thirty-four when he first worked with Leone, already carried unquestioned authority. Much is made of the fact that he came from television, that he starred in *Rawhide,* that in those days it was thought that a movie audience wouldn't pay to see an actor it could watch for free. Eastwood overcame that jinx, but not any actor could have done it—and not with any director. He says he took the roles with Leone because he wanted to make movies and Hollywood wouldn't hire him. Yes, but Eastwood himself was to become an important director, and even at the time he must have sensed in Leone not just another purveyor of the Italian sword-and-sandal epics but a man with passion. Together, Leone and Eastwood made the Man with No Name not simply bigger than a television star but bigger than a movie star—a man who never needed to explain himself, a man whose boots and fingers and eyes were deemed important enough to fill the whole screen.

I wonder if Eastwood's character has a tenth as much dialogue as Tuco, the Eli Wallach character. The Man never talks, Tuco never stops. This is one of Wallach's inspired performances, as he sidesteps his character's potential to seem ridiculous and makes him a desperate, frightened presence. When he makes a clown of himself, we sense it is Tuco's strategy, not his personality. Trained in the Method, a stage veteran, Wallach took this low-rent role seriously and made something evocative out of it. Lee Van Cleef, as Angel Eyes, was New Jersey–born, already a veteran of fifty-three films and countless TV shows, many of them Westerns (his first movie credit was *High Noon,* where he played a member of the gang). In a movie with a lot of narrowed eyes, he has the narrowest, and they gleam with insane obsession.

All three men are after the fortune in Civil War gold, and the secret of its location is parceled out among them (one knows the cemetery but not the grave, the other knows the name on the tombstone but not the cemetery). So they know that they will remain alive until the grave is found, and then it is likely that each of them will try to kill the others.

In a film that runs 180 minutes in its current restored version, that is not enough plot, but Leone has no shortage of other ideas. There is the opening shoot-out, involving unrelated characters. There is the con game in which Wallach plays a wanted man, Eastwood turns him in for the reward, and then Eastwood waits until he is about to be hanged and severs the rope with a well-aimed shot. There is the magnificent desert sequence, after Eastwood abandons Wallach in the desert, and then Wallach does the same to Eastwood, and the sun burns down like a scene from *Greed.* There is the haunting runaway wagon, filled with dead and dying men. And, surprisingly, there is an ambitious Civil War sequence, almost a film within a film, featuring a touching performance by Aldo Giuffrè as a captain in the Union Army who explains his alcoholism simply: The commander who has the most booze to get his troops drunk before battle is the one who wins. His dying line: "Can you help me live a little more? I expect good news."

Sergio Leone (1929–1989), a director of boundless vision and ambition, invented himself almost as he invented the spaghetti Western. Erickson notes that Leone hyped his own career "by claiming to be the assistant director on Robert Aldrich's Italian production of *Sodom and Gomorrah* (1962), even though he was fired after only a day." Leone made a forgotten Roman Empire epic in 1961, and then based *A Fistful of Dollars* so closely on Akira Kurosawa's samurai film *Yojimbo* that perhaps Gus Van Sant's shot-by-shot remake of *Psycho* was not the first time the technique was tried.

A man with no little ideas, Leone made two other unquestioned masterpieces, *Once Upon a Time in the West* (1968), and *Once Upon a Time in America* (1984). By the end of his career Hollywood was suspicious of films with long running times, and criminally chopped *America* from 227 minutes to a sometimes incomprehensible 139. Nineteen minutes were cut from the first release of *The Good, the Bad and the Ugly*. But uncut versions of many of his films are available on DVD, and gradually it becomes clear how good he really was.

{ GOODFELLAS }

As far back as I can remember, I always wanted to be
a gangster. To me, being a gangster was better than being president
of the United States.

So says Henry Hill in the opening moments of Martin Scorsese's *Goodfellas*, a movie about the tradecraft and culture of organized crime in New York. That he narrates his own story—and is later joined by his wife, narrating hers—is crucial to the movie's success. This is not an outsider's view, but a point-of-view movie based on nostalgia for the lifestyle. "They were blue-collar guys," Hill's wife explains. "The only way they could make extra money, real extra money, was to go out and cut a few corners." Their power was intoxicating. "If we wanted something, we just took it," Henry says. "If anyone complained twice they got hit so bad, believe me, they never complained again."

At the end of the film, Henry (Ray Liotta) still misses the old days. His money is gone, most of his friends are dead, and his best friend is preparing to kill him, but after he finds safety in the federal witness protection program, he still complains. "We were treated like movie stars with muscle," he remembers. "Today, everything is different. There's no action. I have to wait around like everyone else."

The rewards of unearned privilege are at the heart of *Goodfellas*

(1990). There's an early scene introducing Henry's partner Jimmy Conway (Robert De Niro), and he enters the shot in a sort of glowing modesty; his body language says, "No applause, please." Henry's other partner is Tommy DeVito (Joe Pesci), who makes the mistake of overexercising his clout instead of letting it go without saying. In one of the great buildups and payoffs in movie history, he believes he's going to become a "made" man, realizes his mistake too late, and says, "Oh, no" before being shot in the head. He never learned to relax and enjoy his privileges. He always had to push things.

The early scenes of *Goodfellas* show young Henry Hill as a gofer for the local Brooklyn mob, which has its headquarters in a taxi garage right across the street from his house. (A shot of Henry looking out the window mirrors Scorsese's own childhood memories from Manhattan's Little Italy neighborhood, and so does a following sequence that uses subtle slow motion for close-ups of the mobster's shoes, ties, hair, rings, and cigars.) In a movie famous for violence that arrives instantly, without warning, the most shocking surprise comes when Henry is slapped by his father for missing school. He had to "take a few beatings" at home because of his teenage career choice, Henry remembers, but it was worth it. Violence is like a drumbeat under every scene.

Henry's joy in his emerging career is palpable. He sells stolen cigarettes out of car trunks, torches a car lot, has enough money at twenty-one to tip lavishly. In the most famous shot in the movie, he takes his future wife, Karen (Lorraine Bracco), to the Copacabana nightclub. There's a line in front, but he escorts her across the street, down stairs and service corridors, through the kitchen area, and out into the showroom just as their table is being placed right in front of the stage. This unbroken shot, which lasts 184 seconds, is not simply a cameraman's stunt but an inspired way to show how the whole world seems to unfold effortlessly before young Henry Hill.

There is another very protracted shot, as Henry introduces us to his fellow gangsters. Henry leads the camera through a crowded club, calling out names as the characters nod to the camera or speak to Henry. Sometimes the camera seems to follow Henry, but at other times it seems to represent his point of view; sometimes he's talking to them, sometimes to us. This strategy implicates us in the action. The cinematographer, Michael Ballhaus, did not get one of the film's six Oscar nominations, but was a key collaborator. Following Scorsese's signature style, he almost never allows his camera to be still; it is always moving, if only a little, and a moving camera makes us not passive observers but active voyeurs.

The screenplay by Nicholas Pileggi and Scorsese is based on Pileggi's book about Hill, *Wiseguy: Life in a Mafia Family*. It is equally based, probably, on Scorsese's own memories of Little Italy. It shows a mob family headed by Paul Cicero (Paul Sorvino), who never talks on the phone, dislikes group conversations, disapproves of drugs (because the sentences are too high), and sounds like a parish priest when he orders Henry to return home to his wife. That doesn't mean he has to dump his mistress; all the guys seem to have both a wife and a mistress, who are plied with stolen goods of astonishing tastelessness.

Goodfellas is unusual in giving good screen time to the women, who are generally unseen in gangster movies. Karen Hill narrates her own side of the story, confessing that she was attracted to Henry's clout and fame; after she tells Henry that the guy across the street tried to hit on her, Henry pistol-whips him and then gives her the gun to hide. She tells us, "I know there are women, like my best friends, who would have gotten out of there the minute their boyfriend gave them a gun to hide. But I didn't. I got to admit the truth. It turned me on." It is reasonable to suggest that *The Sopranos* finds its origin in the narrations in *Goodfellas*, especially Karen's.

Underlying the violence is a story of economic ambition. Henry and Karen come from backgrounds that could not easily lead to Cadillacs, vacations in Vegas, and fur coats, and she justifies what he has to do to pay for the lifestyle: "None of it seemed like crimes. It was more like Henry was enterprising and that he and the guys were making a few bucks hustling, while the other guys were sitting on their asses waiting for handouts."

The story arc follows Henry's movement up into the mob and then down into prison sentences and ultimate betrayal. At first the mob seems like an opening up of his life, but later, after he starts selling drugs, there is a claustrophobic closing in. The camera style in the earlier scenes celebrates his power and influence with expansive ease. At the end, in a frantic sequence concentrated in a single day, the style becomes hurried and choppy as he races around the neighborhood on family and criminal missions while a helicopter always seems to hover overhead.

What Scorsese does above all else is share his enthusiasm for the material. The film has the headlong momentum of a storyteller who knows he has a good one. Scorsese's camera caresses these guys, pays attention to the shines on their shoes and the cut of their clothes. And when they're planning the famous Lufthansa robbery, he has them whispering together in a tight three-shot, their heads leaning low and close with the thrill of their own audacity. You can see how much fun it is for them to steal.

The film's method is to interrupt dialogue with violence. Sometimes there are false alarms, as in Pesci's famous restaurant scene, where Tommy wants to know what Henry meant when he said Tommy was "funny." Other moments well up suddenly out of the very mob culture: the way Tommy shoots a kid in the foot, and later murders him; the way kidding around in a bar leads to a man being savagely beaten. That violence penetrates the daily lives of the characters is always insisted on. Tommy, Henry, and Jimmy, with a body in their trunk, stop at Tommy's mother's house to get a knife, and she insists that they sit down at three A.M. for a meal.

Scorsese seems so much in command of his gift in this film. It was defeated for the best picture Oscar by *Dances with Wolves*, but in November 2002 a poll by *Sight & Sound* magazine named it the fourth-best film of the past twenty-five years (after Coppola's *Apocalypse Now*, Scorsese's *Raging Bull*, and Bergman's *Fanny and Alexander*). It is an indictment of organized crime, but it doesn't stand outside in a superior, moralistic position. It explains crime's appeal for a hungry young man who has learned from childhood beatings not to hate power but to envy it. When Henry Hill talks to us at the opening of the film, he sounds like a kid in love: "To me, it meant being somebody in a neighborhood that was full of nobodies. They weren't like anybody else. I mean, they did whatever they wanted. They double-parked in front of a hydrant and nobody ever gave them a ticket. In the summer when they played cards all night, nobody ever called the cops."

THE GOSPEL ACCORDING TO MATTHEW

Pier Paolo Pasolini was stranded in St. Francis's hometown of Assisi. He had come there in 1962 to attend a seminar at a Franciscan monastery. Although it was well known that Pasolini was an atheist, a Marxist, and a homosexual, he had accepted the invitation after Pope John XXIII called for a new dialogue with non-Catholic artists. Now the streets were jammed because the pope was in town, and Pasolini waited in his hotel room. He found a copy of the Gospels and "read them straight through." The notion of basing a film on one of them, he wrote, "threw in the shade all the other ideas for work I had in my head."

The result was *The Gospel According to Matthew* (1964), which was filmed mostly in the poor, desolate Italian district of Basilicata, and its capital city, Matera. (Forty years later, Mel Gibson would film *The Passion of the Christ* on the very same locations.) Pasolini's is one of the most effective films on a religious theme I have ever seen, perhaps because it was made by a nonbeliever who did not preach, glorify, underline, sentimentalize, or romanticize his famous story but tried his best to simply record it.

I learned the story of the hotel room and found much of the other information below from Barth David Schwartz's *Pasolini Requiem*, an invaluable book about the artist, whose work ranged from the profane to the divine, and whose untidy private life ended with murder in a city wasteland. Although Pasolini directed some twenty-five films (most famously

Accatone!, Hawks and Sparrows, Salo, The Decameron, Mamma Roma, and *Teorema*) and contributed to the screenplays of Fellini's *Nights of Cabiria* and *La Dolce Vita,* he considered himself a poet before a filmmaker, and his films are built of images, impressions, and words that sometimes function more as language than as dialogue.

That is certainly the case with *The Gospel According to Matthew,* which tells the life of Christ as if a documentarian on a low budget had been following him from birth. The movie was made in the spirit of Italian neo-realism, which believed that ordinary people, not actors, could best embody characters—not every character, but the one they were born to play. His Christ is Enrique Irazouqi, a Spanish economics student who visited Pasolini one day to talk to him about his work. Irazouqi had never acted, but Schwartz quotes Pasolini: "Even before we had started talking, I said, 'Excuse me, but would you act in one of my films?'" Schwartz describes Irazouqi as the "son of a Basque father and a Jewish mother . . . thin, stoop-shouldered, heavy-browed, anything but the muscular Christ of Michelangelo." For his other roles Pasolini cast local peasants, shopkeepers, factory workers, truck drivers. For Mary at the time of the Crucifixion, he cast his own mother.

Whether these actors could handle the dialogue was beside the point. Pasolini decided to shoot without a screenplay, following Matthew page by page and compressing only as much as necessary to give the film an acceptable running time. Every word of dialogue is from Matthew, and much of it is heard during long shots, so that we need not see the lips moving.

Jesus is, however, often seen speaking, and his presence and appearance are unusual in terms of traditional depictions. Like most of the Jewish men of his time, he wears his hair short—none of the flowing locks of holy cards. Because he wears a dark, hooded robe, his face is often in shadow. He is unshaven but not bearded. His personal style is sometimes gentle, as during the Sermon on the Mount, but more often he speaks with a righteous anger, like a union organizer or a war protestor. His debating style, true to Matthew, is to answer a question with a question, a parable, or dismissive scorn. His words are clearly a radical rebuke of his society, its materialism, and the way it values the rich and powerful over the weak and poor. No one

who listens to this Jesus can confuse him for a defender of prosperity, although many of his followers have believed that he rewards them with affluence.

The film, in black and white, is told with stark simplicity. Consider the opening shots. We see Mary in close-up. We see Joseph in close-up. We see Mary in long shot, and that she is pregnant. We see Joseph regarding this fact. We see him go out of his house and fall asleep against a boulder, and then he is awakened by an angel (who looks like an ordinary peasant girl), and the angel tells him that Mary will bear the son of God. The angel later warns them to flee to Egypt before Herod orders the killing of the firstborn. The massacre of the babies is a brief scene, the more horrific because Pasolini does not use close-up details of violence. Here and later, he uses the spiritual "Sometimes I Feel Like a Motherless Child" on the sound track; the singer, I believe, is Odetta, although some sources credit Marian Anderson.

The arrival of the Three Wise Men is filmed as it might have happened, with their horses (not camels) followed by a joyous, shouting crowd of children. Indeed, curious children seem drawn to Jesus, and in the scene where he debates the elders in the temple, the little ones sit in a row at his feet and when he makes what they consider a good point, they turn around and grin triumphantly at the old men.

The miracles of the loaves and fishes and the walking on the water are treated in a low key. Christ tells his disciples to depart in their boat, "and I will follow you." No triumphant music, no waving of hands and shouts of incredulity, no sensational camera angles—just a long shot of a solitary figure walking on the water.

The trial of Jesus in this film, as in Gibson's, places much of the blame on the Jewish high priests, as Matthew does. But those who found Gibson's depiction of them anti-Semitic may appreciate Pasolini's decision to film the debates mostly in long shot, and to show the priests not as angry and spiteful but as learned and ponderous, dealing soberly with heresy. Pasolini's priests conclude, "He must die. Deliver him to Pontius Pilate." And Pilate refers to Jesus as "an innocent man." Later we hear Matthew's notorious line "May his blood be on our children," which Gibson excised from his subtitles (but not from the Aramaic dialogue).

The crucifixion is entirely lacking in the violence of the Gibson version. It is almost underplayed, and we note that for much of the way to Calvary, the cross is carried only by Simon, while Jesus walks behind it. There is a crown of thorns, but only a few drops of blood. Yet this version is not softened and dramatized in the style of Hollywood's biblical epics; in its harsh realism, it seems matter-of-fact about a cruel death.

Father Andrew Greeley, in his essay on Gibson's film, corrects Catholic-school graduates (like me) who were taught that Christ died to take away original sin. Greeley says he died to show that he felt our pain, and that he loved us. That is a Christ closer to Pasolini's version, but what Pasolini also insists is that his Christ did not love those whose kingdom was of the earth; his Christ is of the left, not the right, and would have lumped many modern Christians with the scribes and Pharisees.

The Gospel According to Matthew won the Special Jury Prize at the Venice Film Festival (the Golden Lion went to Antonioni's fiercely secular *The Red Desert*). Right-wing Catholic groups picketed it, but the film won the first prize of the International Catholic Office of the Cinema, which screened the film inside Notre Dame Cathedral in Paris; the French left was as outraged as the Italian right, and Sartre met with Pasolini, telling him somewhat obscurely, "Stalin rehabilitated Ivan the Terrible; Christ is not yet rehabilitated by Marxists."

To compare the film with Gibson's is to understand that there is no single version of Christ's story. It acts as a template into which we fit our ideas, and we see it as our lives have prepared us for it. Gibson saw Christ's suffering as the overwhelming fact of his life, and his film contains very little of Christ's teachings. Pasolini thought the teachings were the central story. If a hypothetical viewer came to *The Passion* with no previous knowledge of Jesus and wondered what all the furor was about, Pasolini's film would argue this: Jesus was a radical whose teachings, if taken seriously, contradict the values of most human societies ever since.

{ THE GRAPES OF WRATH }

John Ford's *The Grapes of Wrath* is a left-wing parable, directed by a right-wing American director, about how a sharecropper's son, a barroom brawler, is converted into a union organizer. The message is boldly displayed but told with characters of such sympathy and images of such beauty that audiences leave the theater feeling more pity than anger or resolve. It's a message movie, but not a recruiting poster.

The ideological journey of the hero, Tom Joad, can be seen by the two killings he is responsible for. The first one takes place in a saloon before the action begins, and Tom describes it to a former preacher: "We was drunk. He got a knife in me and I laid him out with a shovel. Knocked his head plumb to squash." After serving four years, Tom is paroled and returns to his family farm in Oklahoma only to learn the Joads have been "tractored off the land" and are joining the desperate migration to California. Near the end of the film, after seeing deputies and thugs beat and shoot at strikers, he is once again attacked, this time by a "tin badge" with a club. He snatches away the club, and kills him. The lesson is clear: Tom has learned who his real enemies are and is working now with more deserving targets.

The movie was based on John Steinbeck's novel, arguably the most effective social document of the 1930s, and it was directed by the filmmaker who did more than any other to document the westward movement of American settlement. John Ford was the director of *The Iron Horse* (1924),

about the dream of a railroad to the West, and made many other films about the white migration into Indian lands, including his Cavalry trilogy (*Fort Apache, She Wore a Yellow Ribbon, Rio Grande*). *The Grapes of Wrath* tells the sad end of the dream. The small shareholders who staked their claims fifty years earlier are forced off their land by bankers and big landholders. "Who's the Shawnee Land and Cattle Company?" asks Muley, a neighbor of the Joads' who refuses to sell. "It ain't anybody," says a land agent. "It's a company."

The movie finds a larger socialist lesson in this, when Tom tells Ma, "One guy with a million acres and a hundred thousand farmers starvin'." Of course Tom didn't know the end of the story, about how the Okies would go to work in war industries and their children would prosper more in California than they might have in Oklahoma, and their grandchildren would star in Beach Boys songs. It is easy to forget that for many, *The Grapes of Wrath* had a happy, unwritten, fourth act.

When Steinbeck published his novel in 1939, it was acclaimed as a masterpiece, won the Pulitzer Prize, was snatched up by Darryl F. Zanuck of Twentieth Century–Fox and assigned to his top director, John Ford. It expressed the nation's rage about the Depression in poetic, biblical terms, and its dialogue does a delicate little dance around words like "agitators" and "Reds"—terms, we are intended to understand, that the fat cats apply to anyone who stands up for the little man. With Hitler rising in Europe, communism would enjoy a brief respite from the American demonology.

The movie won Oscars for best director and best supporting actress (Jane Darwell as Ma Joad) and was nominated for five others, including best actor (Henry Fonda) and best picture (it lost to Hitchcock's *Rebecca*). In a year when there were ten best film nominees Ford had even another entry, *The Long Voyage Home*. *The Grapes of Wrath* was often named the greatest American film until it was dethroned by the re-release of *Citizen Kane* in 1958, and in the recent American Film Institute poll it finished in the top ten. But do many people watch it anymore? I have the feeling it has become an official masterpiece, honored but not seen. And that is a shame, because unlike some cause-oriented message pictures, it has life and breath and excitement.

Ford uses realistic black-and-white cinematography to temper its sentiment and provide a documentary quality to scenes like the entry into the Okie transient camp near the California border. Even though the Joad farm is a studio set, Ford liked to shoot on location, and he records a journey down Route 66 from the Dust Bowl through New Mexico and Arizona, past shabby gas stations and roadside diners. The dialogue sometimes grows a little too preachy to fit within the simple vernacular of farmers, and Tom Joad's famous farewell to Ma ("Wherever there's a fight so hungry people can eat, I'll be there. Wherever there's a cop beatin' up a guy, I'll be there . . .") always sounds to me like writing, not spontaneous expression.

But it is dialogue spoken by Henry Fonda, whose Tom Joad is one of the great American movie characters, so pure and simple and simply *there* in the role that he puts it over. Fonda was an actor with the rare ability to exist on the screen without seeming to reach or try, and he makes it clear even in his silences how he has been pondering the preacher's conversion from religion to union politics. We're not surprised when he tells Ma, "Maybe it's like Casy says. A fella ain't got a soul of his own, just a little piece of a big soul. The one big soul that belongs to everybody." Just as, in the dream of One Big Union, transcendentalism meets Marxism.

The photography is by the great innovator Gregg Toland, who also shot *The Long Voyage Home* and after those two Ford pictures and William Wyler's *The Westerner* moved on directly to his masterpiece, Orson Welles's *Citizen Kane*. In *Voyage* he experimented with the deep-focus photography that would be crucial to *Kane*. In *Grapes* he worked with astonishingly low levels of light; consider the many night scenes and the shots in the deserted Joad homestead, where Tom and the preacher seem illuminated of a single candle, Tom silhouetted, Casy side-lit.

The power of Ford (1895–1973) was rooted in strong stories, classical technique, and direct expression. Years of apprenticeship in low-budget silent films, many of them quickies shot on location, had steeled him against unnecessary setups and fancy camera work. There is a rigorous purity in his visual style that serves the subject well. *The Grapes of Wrath* contains not a single shot that seems careless or routine.

Fonda and Jane Darwell are the actors everyone remembers, although John Carradine's Casy is also instrumental. Darwell worked in the movies for fifty years, never more memorably than here, where she has the final word. ("We'll go on forever, Pa, because we're the people.") The novel, of course, ends with a famous scene that stunned its readers, as Rose of Sharon, having lost her baby, offers her milk-filled breasts to a starving man in a railroad car. Hollywood, which stretched itself in allowing Clark Gable to say "damn" a year earlier in *Gone With the Wind*, was not ready for that scene, even by implication, in 1940. The original audiences would have known it was left out; the film ended with safe sentiment instead of Steinbeck's bold, melodramatic masterstroke.

I wonder if American audiences will ever again be able to understand the original impact of this material, on the page and on the screen. The centenary of Steinbeck's birth was observed with articles sniffing that he was not, after all, all that good, that his Nobel was undeserved, that he was of his time and has dated. But one would not want *The Grapes of Wrath* written differently; irony, stylistic experimentation, and "modernism" would weaken it.

The novel and movie do last, I think, because they are founded in real experience and feeling. My parents were scarred by the Depression, it was a devastation I sensed in their very tones of voice, and *The Grapes of Wrath* shows half a nation with the economic rug pulled out from under it. The story, which seems to be about the resiliency and courage of "the people," is built on a foundation of fear: fear of losing jobs, land, self-respect. To those who had felt that fear, who had gone hungry or been homeless, it would never become dated. And its sense of injustice, I believe, is still relevant. The banks and land agents of the 1930s have been replaced by financial pyramids so huge and so chummy with the government that Enron, for example, had to tractor itself off its own land.

GRAVE OF THE FIREFLIES

In the waning days of World War II, American bombers drop napalm canisters on Japanese cities, creating firestorms. These bombs, longer than a tin can but about as big around, fall to earth trailing cloth tails that flutter behind them; they are almost a beautiful sight. After they hit, there is a moment's silence, and then they detonate, spraying their surroundings with flames. In a Japanese residential neighborhood, made of flimsy wood-and-paper houses, there is no way to fight the fires.

Grave of the Fireflies is an animated film telling the story of two children from the port city of Kobe, made homeless by the bombs. Seita is a young teenager, and his sister, Setsuko, is about five. Their father is serving in the Japanese navy, and their mother is a bomb victim; Seita kneels beside her body, which is covered with burns, in an emergency hospital. Their home, neighbors, schools are all gone. For a time an aunt takes them in, but she's cruel about the need to feed them, and eventually Seita finds a hillside cave where they can live. He does what he can to find food, and to answer Setsuko's questions about their parents. The first shot of the film shows Seita dead in a subway station, and so we can guess Setsuko's fate; we are accompanied through flashbacks by the boy's spirit.

Grave of the Fireflies is an emotional experience so powerful that it forces a rethinking of animation. Since the earliest days, most animated films have been "cartoons" for children and families. Recent animated features like *The Lion King, Princess Mononoke,* and *The Iron Giant* have touched on more serious themes, and the *Toy Story* movies and classics like *Bambi* have had moments that moved some audience members to tears. These films, however, exist within safe confines; they inspire tears but not grief. *Grave of the Fireflies* is a powerful dramatic film that happens to be animated, and I know what the critic Ernest Rister means when he compares it to *Schindler's List* and says, "It is the most profoundly human animated film I've ever seen."

It tells a simple story of survival. The boy and his sister must find a place to stay and food to eat. In wartime their relatives are not kind or generous, and after their aunt sells their mother's kimonos for rice, she keeps a lot of the rice for herself. Eventually, Seita realizes it is time to leave. He has some money and can buy food—but soon there is no food to buy. His sister grows weaker. Their story is told not as melodrama but simply, directly, in the neorealist tradition. And there is time for silence in it. One of the film's greatest gifts is its patience; shots are held so we can think about them, characters are glimpsed in private moments, atmosphere and nature are given time to establish themselves.

Japanese poets use "pillow words," which are halfway between pauses and punctuation, and the great director Ozu uses "pillow shots"—a detail from nature, say, to separate two scenes. *Grave of the Fireflies* uses them, too. Its visuals create a kind of poetry. There are moments of quick action, as when the bombs rain down and terrified people fill the streets, but this film doesn't exploit action; it meditates on its consequences.

The film was directed by Isao Takakata, who is associated with the famous Studio Ghibli, source of the greatest Japanese animation. His colleague there is Hayao Miyazaki (*Princess Mononoke, Kiki's Delivery Service, My Neighbor Totoro*). Takakata's films are not usually this serious, but *Grave of the Fireflies* is in a category by itself. It's based on a semiautobiographical novel by Akiyuki Nosaka—who was a young boy at the time of the firebombs, whose sister did die of hunger, and whose life has been shadowed by guilt.

The book is well known in Japan, and might easily have inspired a live-action film. It isn't the typical material of animation. But for *Grave of the Fireflies,* I think animation was the right choice. Live action would have

been burdened by the weight of special effects, violence, and action. Animation allows Takakata to concentrate on the essence of the story, and the lack of visual realism in his animated characters allows our imagination more play; freed from the literal fact of real actors, we can more easily merge the characters with our own associations.

Hollywood has been pursuing the ideal of "realistic animation" for decades, even though the term is an oxymoron. People who are drawn do not look like people who are photographed. They're more stylized, more obviously symbolic, and (as Disney discovered in painstaking experiments) their movements can be exaggerated to communicate mood through body language. *Grave of the Fireflies* doesn't attempt even the realism of a film like *The Lion King* or *Princess Mononoke*, but paradoxically it is the most realistic animated film I've ever seen—in feeling.

The locations and backgrounds are drawn in a style owing something to the nineteenth-century Japanese artist Hiroshige and his modern disciple Hergé (the creator of Tin Tin). There is great beauty in them—not cartoon beauty but evocative landscape drawing, put through the filter of animated style. The characters are typical of much of modern Japanese animation, with their enormous eyes, childlike bodies, and features of great plasticity (mouths are tiny when closed but enormous when opened in a child's cry—we even see Setsuko's tonsils). This film proves, if it needs proving, that animation produces emotional effects not by reproducing reality but by heightening and simplifying it, so that many of the sequences are about ideas, not experiences.

There are individual moments of great beauty. One involves a night when the children catch fireflies and use them to illuminate their cave. The next day, Seita finds his little sister carefully burying the dead insects—as she imagines her mother was buried. There is another sequence in which the girl prepares "dinner" for her brother by using mud to make "rice balls" and other imaginary delicacies. And note the timing and the use of silence in a sequence where they find a dead body on the beach, and then more bombers appear far away in the sky. Rister singles out another shot: "There's a moment where the boy Seita traps an air bubble with a wash rag, submerges it, and then releases it into his sister Setsuko's delighted face—and that's when I knew I was watching something special."

Ancient Japanese cultural currents flow beneath the surface of *Grave of the Fireflies,* and they're explained by the critic Dennis H. Fukushima Jr., who finds the story's origins in the tradition of double-suicide plays. It is not that Seita and Setsuko commit suicide overtly, but that life wears away their will to live. He also draws a parallel between their sheltering cave and hillside tombs. Fukushima cites an interview with the author, Nosaka: "Having been the sole survivor, he felt guilty for the death of his sister. While scrounging for food, he had often fed himself first, and his sister second. Her undeniable cause of death was hunger, and it was a sad fact that would haunt Nosaka for years. It prompted him to write about the experience, in hopes of purging the demons tormenting him."

Because it is animated and from Japan, *Grave of the Fireflies* has been little seen. When anime fans say how good the film is, nobody takes them seriously. Now that it's available on DVD with a choice of subtitles or English dubbing, maybe it will find the attention it deserves. Yes, it's a cartoon, and the kids have eyes like saucers, but it belongs on any list of the greatest war films ever made.

{ GREAT EXPECTATIONS }

One of the great things about Dickens is the way his people colonize your memory. I wonder if there's any writer except Shakespeare who has created more characters whose names we remember, and whose types seem so true to human nature. A director adapting a Dickens novel finds that much of his work has been done for him.

Certainly that's the case with David Lean's *Great Expectations* (1946), which has been called the greatest of all the Dickens films, and which does what few movies based on great books can do: create pictures on the screen that do not clash with the images already in our minds. Lean brings Dickens's classic set pieces to life here as if he'd been reading over our shoulder: Pip's encounter with the convict Magwitch in the churchyard, Pip's first meeting with the mad Miss Havisham, and the ghoulish atmosphere in the law offices of Mr. Jaggers, whose walls are decorated with the death masks of clients he has lost to the gallows.

The British critic Adrian Turner has observed that *Great Expectations* resembles a horror film, and certainly there is horror and the macabre in the existence of Miss Havisham, who was jilted on her wedding day and has spent the rest of her life in bitter resentment—all of the clocks in her house stopped at the moment when she discovered that her fiancé had betrayed her. Dickens (and Lean) have a chilling success with the early scene where Pip, an orphan being raised in a blacksmith's house, is sum-

moned to the Gothic mansion of a rich local woman and finds old Miss Havisham, still in her wedding dress, occupying the room where the wedding feast was to be held. She points out the "bride cake," nibbled by mice, festooned by cobwebs, and requires Pip to push her wheelchair around and around the long table where the wedding feast had been planned.

The atmosphere of the mansion and its deranged occupant no doubt inspired Billy Wilder's *Sunset Boulevard*, made four years later, with its aging movie queen in gloomy exile inside her mansion in Beverly Hills. Turner, who has written books on both Lean and Wilder, makes the comparison, and also wonders if the early graveyard scene of Magwitch jumping at Pip from outside the screen hasn't inspired countless imitations in horror films ever since.

In Miss Havisham's mansion is the young girl Estella (Jean Simmons, astonishingly beautiful at seventeen). The old woman has adopted the girl, and raised her for one purpose only: to break men's hearts. Pip falls instantly in love with her, but Estella tries to warn him away, perhaps because she really likes him. Her purpose is to cause men pain, so that Miss Havisham can somehow settle her account with an unfair world. Pip, who has been raised by his shrewish older sister (Freda Jackson) and her husband, the good-hearted blacksmith Joe Gargery (Bernard Miles), is too rough-hewn for the elegant Estella, but a mysterious benefactor finances his transformation. Pip is summoned by Jaggers, Miss Havisham's lawyer, and told his expenses will be paid while he undergoes education and training in London—not least in how to dress and speak like a gentleman. He shares rooms with elegant young Herbert Pocket (Alec Guinness), who sets a fine example.

Of course Pip assumes that Miss Havisham is his benefactor, and that he is being groomed to marry Estella (Valerie Hobson, who was then twenty-nine, played Estella at twenty). Whether he is right or wrong is one of the questions Dickens solves in his story's melodramatic conclusion. The Lean version makes minor repairs to the ending to satisfy the sentimental requirements of audiences, which means that those familiar with the novel will not necessarily know how the film ends.

Since Dickens draws his characters in bold, colorful strokes, typecasting is probably the best approach to filling the roles. Pip himself is a somewhat colorless hero; like many of Dickens's central characters, he's not the source of the action but a witness to the colorful events and people who thrust themselves into his life. It's the supporting cast that makes the story vivid.

Martita Hunt dominates the early scenes, playing Miss Havisham as a beak-nosed, shabby figure, bedecked in crumbling lace and linen, not undernourished despite her long exile; at times in profile she looks uncannily like a late bronze of Queen Victoria. Another fount of energy is the towering Francis L. Sullivan as Jaggers; his voice rolls and booms from a vast frame, and he dwarfs his eager little assistant, Wemmick (Ivor Barnard). The scene in which Wemmick brings Pip home to meet his Aged Parent is typical of the appeal Dickens makes to our imaginations; there is no reason such a peripheral character as the "Aged P" needs to be preserved in a film version—but we remember how the Aged was deaf and loved to be nodded to, and a lot of amusing nodding goes on.

The only misstep in the casting may have been the choice of John Mills as the adult Pip. Mills was thirty-eight when the film was made, and Pip is supposed to be twenty going on twenty-one. It's a jolt when the film cuts from young Pip (Anthony Wager), who is about sixteen, to the grown Pip, who is supposed to be only four years older but frankly looks middle-aged. (Alec Guinness, who plays Pip's contemporary Herbert Pocket, was thirty-two; this was his first substantial screen role.)

The movie was made by Lean at the top of his early form; his *Brief Encounter* (1945), starring Trevor Howard and Celia Johnson in the story of a sad and touching romance, remains one of the great British classics. His *Blithe Spirit* was made the same year, and he went directly from *Great Expectations* to another Dickens adaptation, *Oliver Twist* (1948). He was an editor for seven years before directing his first film, and his career stands as an argument for the theory that editors make better directors than cinematographers do; the cinematographer is seduced by the look of a film, while the editor is faced with the task of making it work as a story.

Sir David Lean (1908–1991) was considered by many the greatest British filmmaker of his time, although a better case can be made for Michael Powell, for whom he worked as an editor (*49th Parallel*, 1941). He achieved his great fame with a series of epics, beginning with *The Bridge on the River Kwai* (1957), and continuing with a series of monuments: *Lawrence of Arabia* (1962), *Doctor Zhivago* (1965), *Ryan's Daughter* (1970), and, after a long sojourn with a doomed production of *Mutiny on the Bounty*, *A Passage to India* (1984). He won Oscars for directing *Kwai* and *Lawrence* and was nominated for five other films (including *Great Expectations*). The later pictures, of course, made Lean's worldwide reputation. They show, as all of his films do, a fondness for dramatic visual compositions; he liked to arrange the elements in a frame to draw the eye to the dramatic center of the shot. What the earlier films have is greater economy, and thus greater energy, in their storytelling. The later Lean worked more like a former cinematographer than a former editor.

When the British Film Institute celebrated its fiftieth anniversary with a banquet at the Cannes Film Festival, Lean, Charles, and Diana were the guests of honor, while his rivals, including Lindsay Anderson and Alan Parker, sat in the cheap seats. But there were those who felt that his earlier, smaller films, such as *Great Expectations,* were his best, and that the later pictures were weakened by a crisp perfectionism. I visited the set of *Ryan's Daughter* on the Dingle Peninsula of Ireland in 1969, and remember a night when Robert Mitchum held court in a rain-swept cottage. "Our director has filmed for one day," he said, "and he is a week behind."

Note: Alfonso Cuaron's 1998 version of *Great Expectations* updated the story to a Florida mansion choked in vegetation and starred Ethan Hawke as Pip, Gwyneth Paltrow as Estella, and Anne Bancroft as Miss Havisham. It caught the same notes of horror and pathos but got unfavorable reviews, perhaps because it was so willing to follow the story right over the top. I liked its nerve.

{ HOUSE OF GAMES }

Almost all of David Mamet's movies involve some kind of con game. Sometimes it is a literal con, as in *House of Games,* where a character is deliberately deceived by fraudsters. Sometimes it is an inadvertent con, as in *Things Change,* where an old shoeshine man is mistaken for the head of the Chicago mob. Sometimes it is a double con, as in *Glengarry Glen Ross,* where real estate salesmen con customers while they are themselves being conned by the company they work for.

None of these cons are written or presented in simple criminal terms, as classic confidence games. They all involve an additional level of emotional conning, which make them such splendid material for drama. In *House of Games,* Mamet's first film, there is a scene where the underlying strategy of the con is explained, and the explanation fits for all of his films. "The basic idea is this," the con man (Joe Mantegna) explains to the woman who has become his student (Lindsay Crouse). "It's called a *confidence* game. Why? Because you give me your confidence? No. Because I give you *mine.*"

He demonstrates. They are in a Western Union office, pretending to wait for money to be wired to him. A man enters and asks the clerk if his money has arrived. It has not. He sits down. Mantegna gets him into conversation, finds out he is a marine who needs bus fare to get back to Camp Pendleton, and smoothly says, "You're in the Corps? *I* was in the Corps." Having established this bond, Mantegna offers to give the guy the bus fare, just as soon as Mantegna's own wire arrives. He *gives* his confidence. He shows he trusts the other guy. Of course, the other man's wire arrives first, and, of course, he offers Mantegna money. The beauty of it is that in the entire transaction, Mantegna has never asked for money—only offered it.

This fraudulent offering of trust underlies one Mamet film after another, and yet it is never repetitive, because it unlocks unlimited dramatic possibilities. There is hardly ever a slow moment in Mamet's films, because even small talk, even passing the time of day, is fraught with the hidden motives of the speakers. Even when nothing seems to be happening, our attention is held by the illusion that something *must be* happening, but we can't spot it. This is Mamet's con on us. He offers us his confidence that we can follow his plot.

Sometimes we can't. Consider the labyrinthine depths of *The Spanish Prisoner*. A man (Steve Martin) appears on a tropical island. It is assumed by his mark (Campbell Scott) that he arrived by seaplane, but actually no one has seen that happen. Scott has access to secret company information—a formula worth millions. Martin offers him his trust. He asks Scott to deliver a book to Martin's sister in New York, and indeed hints that the sister might be a romantic possibility. The book ploy looks like a devious way of seducing Scott into revealing the secret, but actually there are levels deeper than that, and at the end we are left with a truly astonishing revelation.

I left the movie convinced there was yet *another* level of deception beneath Mamet's apparent explanation. Perhaps there was not. Certainly the real con in *The Spanish Prisoner* is the one pulled on the audience by Mamet, who convinces us there is a con and that he has revealed it, when the con might not be what we think it is and the revelation may not explain anything. Wonderful. He does it by giving us his confidence.

I am particularly fond of Mamet's films. They strike some kind of responsive chord in me. I like the dry way his actors are instructed to behave—the way they don't go for effects but let the effects come to them. I like the slightly mannered style of movement, by both actors and camera. There is a hint in Mamet's stagings of the influence of Fassbinder, who liked his actors to behave as if they were posing in tableaux, and knew they were.

There is a teasing quality to Mamet's presentations, which remind

me of a skilled magician, meticulously laying out his cards while telling us a story. We know the story has nothing to do with the cards ("The Queen of Diamonds decided she would have an affair with the King of Hearts . . ."). The story is a diversion. The real story is, what's happening to the cards? What is he really doing while he's telling us he's doing something else? The magician's voice never sounds as if he really believes the Queen and King are having an affair. There is a slightly mocking, formal quality to his speech. He is going through the ritual of telling us a story, while meanwhile the trick is operating in another, hidden way. That's how a Mamet film feels: like a magician whose real cards are hidden. It makes sense that he uses the same actors over and over again, just as a magician always starts with the same fifty-two cards. (Indeed, Mamet directed the Broadway show starring Ricky Jay, the master card manipulator who appears in most of his films.)

House of Games, Mamet's first film, is my favorite, not because it is better than, say, *Things Change, Homicide, The Spanish Prisoner, Oleanna, The Winslow Boy, Spartan,* or the screenplays for *Glengarry Glen Ross, The Edge,* and *Wag the Dog,* but because it arrived with the shock of the new: I saw it, and was in the presence of a new style, a distinctive voice.

It stars Crouse as a best-selling author/therapist whose patient has been threatened with broken legs by a gambler. One night she goes to the House of Games, crossing a street that is an Edward Hopper landscape, to confront the gambler (Mantegna). Through an open doorway, she sees a card game in progress. Mantegna comes out to talk to her, and she goes through the motions of threatening him. We sense that threats have nothing to do with it—that she gets an erotic charge out of talking tough to a dangerous guy. Mantegna reads her in a second. He says there is a way to forgive the debt. It involves the woman helping him with a con. There is a rich Texan in the game (Ricky Jay). He has a "tell"—a giveaway gesture that reveals if he has a good hand. Mantegna tells Crouse he'll leave the room, and Crouse should look for the tell. Crouse looks, and sees. She grows excited. She knows they can win the hand. The Texan shoves his whole pile into the pot. Mantegna can't cover it. Crouse offers to write him a check. Beautiful. He gave her his confidence, and she gives him her money.

Oh, the movie is a lot more complicated than that. Don't think I've given away too much (I will give away nothing more). I like the way the mechanics of the con provide the surface of the story (the Kings and Queens) while the real story is about how the woman's libido is urgently aroused by the thrill of being included in a con. Later, she and Mantegna enter another man's hotel room, and walking through that forbidden door operates on her like violent foreplay. It is crucial to the mechanics of the story that every scene is observed only from her point of view.

Mamet's dialogue starts with the plain red bricks of reality, then mortars them into walls that are slightly askew. Nobody uses a word you don't know. They like vulgarities and obscenities and clichés. But the dialogue is rotated into a slightly new dimension; it is mannered a little, and somewhat self-consciously assembled, as if the speaker is dealing with a second language or an unrehearsed role. That makes us listen more carefully. There is a line near the end ("You're a bad pony. And I'm not going to bet on you") that, coming when it does and how it does (and why it does) has a kind of sublime perfection. It is the final taking back of the gift of confidence. The game is over.

{ THE HUSTLER }

Bert: You got talent.
Eddie: So I got talent? So what beat me?
Bert: Character.

There are only a handful of movie characters so real that the audience refers to them as touchstones. Fast Eddie Felson is one of them. The pool shark played by Paul Newman in *The Hustler* (1961) is indelible—given weight because the film is not about his victory in the final pool game but about his defeat by pool, by life, and by his lack of character. This is one of the few American movies in which the hero wins by surrendering, by accepting reality instead of his dreams.

Billiards is the arena for the movie's contests, but there is no attempt to follow the game shot by shot, or even to explain the rules. The players are contesting each others' inner strength. The film could be about any seedy game depending on bluff, self-confidence, money management, and psychology; it was remade as *The Cincinnati Kid,* about poker. The world of pool halls, flophouses, bars, and bus stations provides no hiding place. You will eventually reveal what you are made of, and pool is a game where skill can carry you only so far.

The film thrust Paul Newman into the first rank of Hollywood actors, but it is instructive to see how important the other actors are, how *The*

Hustler benefited by being made before the big-money star was required to appear in almost every shot. The test of Newman's character comes not so much at a pool table as in his relationship with Sarah Packard (Piper Laurie), whose story is told as fully as Felson's own; this is not one of the macho 1990s movies in which the filmmakers are unable to see a woman except in the simplest terms. The real contest in *The Hustler* is not between Fast Eddie and Minnesota Fats but between Eddie's love for Sarah and his self-destructive impulses.

George C. Scott, as the cold, vicious gambler and manager Bert Gordon, was appearing in only his third movie. He has the absolute authority we would see again and again: the air of a man serenely himself. The way he plays against Sarah, with a cruel word here and a whispered suggestion there, is as hard and painful as his order to have Eddie's thumbs broken. Bert is always calculating. When he tells Eddie he's a "loser," we know he says that to goad him to win or push him to lose; he's never just supplying his opinion.

Then there is Jackie Gleason, as the legendary pool champion Minnesota Fats—the man Eddie must beat to prove himself the best. Gleason and Scott won Oscar nominations for their supporting performances; what is interesting is that they make equally unforgettable impressions, although Scott has a lot of dialogue and Gleason has only a handful of words, apart from calling his shots. With Gleason it is all presence, body language, the sad face, the concise, intent way he works the table, the lack of wasted moves. He gives the impression of a man purified by pool, who has endured all the sad compromises and crooked bets and hustling moves and emerged as a man who simply, elegantly, plays the game. He has long ago given up hustling; unlike Eddie, he makes his living by dependably being the best, time after time, so that others can test themselves against him. He is the ruler of a shabby kingdom, and at the end of the film, as Eddie and Bert have their merciless confrontation, he sits passive in the middle of the floor, listening to what he has heard countless times before, knowing that to practice his gift he has to accept this world.

The movie was produced and directed by Robert Rossen, a writer from the 1940s who first refused to "name names" when called in the McCarthyite witch hunt, and then changed his mind, said he had been a

Communist, and named fifty-seven others. That was the price he paid to be able to work, and there must be a shadow of that price in the compromises Fast Eddie is asked to make. The movie, based on a novel by Walter Tevis, was written by Rossen and Sydney Carroll, and filmed in black-and-white CinemaScope by Eugene Shuftan, who won an Oscar. To see why black and white is the right choice, contrast it with Martin Scorsese's *The Color of Money* (1986), also starring Newman as Fast Eddie, but looking too bright and alive for the stygian gloom of the billiard parlor at midnight. (Newman won his only Oscar for *Color*—ironic, unless it was belated amends for *The Hustler*.)

Rossen's crucial decision is to allow full weight and screen time to all of his characters. Piper Laurie's Sarah is the greatest beneficiary, a lame alcoholic who sits in the bus station when she cannot sleep, who goes to college on Tuesdays and Thursdays and drinks on the other days, who turns her face away from Eddie's first kiss and says, "You're too hungry," and who wisely tells him: "Look, I've got troubles and I think maybe you've got troubles. Maybe it'd be better if we just leave each other alone."

When Bert wants to take Eddie to Louisville for a big-money match with the millionaire Findley (Murray Hamilton), Eddie caves in to Sarah's tears and takes her along. Bert sees her as a rival and expertly and mercilessly destroys her in a few days; learning that Eddie's broken thumbs have healed, he says, "I'd hate to think I was puttin' my money on a cripple"—a line aimed straight at Sarah. And when she is drunk and leaning against a wall at Findley's party, he approaches her and says something into her ear, something we cannot hear, that causes her to throw her drink at him and then collapse, and sets in motion the process of her death. That the movie attends to these two supporting actors, gives heft to their rivalry, adds depth and savor to the story. Watching it, we reflect that many modern movies are one-dimensional and linear, telling one story about one character with superficial haste.

The Hustler is one of those films where scenes have such psychic weight that they grow in our memories. That's true of the matches between Eddie and Fats. One respected critic writes of "the two climactic matches with Gleason as Minnesota Fats," when in fact the first match, by far the longest, comes at about the one-third mark, and the final showdown between the two men is not given much screen time, although it leads to the perfect coda:

> *Eddie:* Fat Man, you shoot a great game of pool.
> *Minnesota Fats:* So do you, Fast Eddie.

Remembering the movie, I thought the second match was the longer one, lasting all night and into the next day. But Minnesota Fats is such a legendary character and Eddie's need to defeat him so burning that Rossen wisely realizes he doesn't need to replay the first long match to get the effect. This was the fourth film edited by the great Dede Allen (her next would be *Bonnie and Clyde*), and she finds a rhythm in the pool games—the players circling, the cue sticks, the balls, the watching faces—that implies the trancelike rhythm of the players. Her editing "tells" the games so completely that if we don't understand pool, we forget that we don't.

The first meeting of Eddie and Fats was about pool. The second, as Bert correctly predicted, is about character. Bert's secret is that by "character" he doesn't mean goodness, honesty, or other Boy Scout virtues. He means the snakelike ability to put winning above any other consideration, and to never tempt the odds.

The film is populated with an unobtrusive gallery of bit players. Willie Mosconi, for years the U.S. billiard champion, has a walk-on as "Willie," who holds the money for an early match; he also performed some of the movie's trick shots, although legend has it that Gleason made his own shots and Newman most of his. Murray Hamilton (Mr. Findley) had a famous role six years later as Mr. Robinson in *The Graduate*. One of the bartenders is the Raging Bull, Jake La Motta. Myron McCormick, a stage actor who appeared infrequently in films, plays Eddie's first manager—battered, honest, cast aside by Eddie on the way to the top.

Among the male faces in the movie, most of them old, weathered, cold, or cruel, Paul Newman's open and handsome looks are a contrast. But the casting is correct. He isn't too handsome for this ugly world, but a hustler who trades on his boyish grin and aw-shucks way of asking if anybody feels like a game. His face has gotten Eddie almost as far as his pool skills. He doesn't look like a hustler, but then the best ones never do.

{ In Cold Blood }

Since 1966, when Truman Capote published *In Cold Blood,* the true-crime genre has expanded to fill whole sections of bookstores. Factual accounts of crime were common enough before, but Capote combined in-depth reporting with the techniques of the New Journalism, then in its golden age; his book, he said, was a "non-fiction novel." He told of the senseless 1959 killing of the four members of the Clutter family, living in a ranch home outside Holcomb, Kansas, and the patient police work that led to the arrest of two clueless ex-cons.

The newsmagazines were filled with the saga of Capote's reporting—how the effete society creature from Manhattan moved to Kansas and established first-name relationships, even friendships, with the convicted killers Dick Hickock and Perry Smith, the police investigator Alvin Dewey, and local residents. Capote claimed a photographic memory that allowed him to remember conversations verbatim, and his book's construction let him delay the description of the murder until the end, so that he could make his point that six people died in cold blood: the Clutters, and their killers. The book was intended as opposition to capital punishment, and some critics believed Capote had grown so close to Smith and Hickock that he was blinded by sympathy for their luckless lives, and lost focus on the massacre of the Clutters.

In Cold Blood was the great best-seller of its time, and a year later

Richard Brooks made a stark black-and-white film from the book, using Conrad Hall's wide-screen compositions to capture the flat, wide, windswept plains where the murders took place. He had originally hoped to use Paul Newman and Steve McQueen as the two killers, but that casting would have hopelessly skewed the film in the wrong direction, making Smith and Hickock into glamorous Dostoyevskian heroes who would have been wrong, all wrong, for this sad and shabby story. Eventually he found two newcomers, Scott Wilson and Robert Blake, who embodied the drifters and their unshaped, witless personalities.

As individuals, a psychiatrist in the film tells us, they would have been incapable of murder; together they formed a personality that took four lives. The Smith character says, "When Dick first told me the plan, it didn't even seem real. And then the closer we got, the more real it became." The plan was for him to kill the Clutters; Hickock, who knew himself incapable of murder, wanted to leave no witnesses, and so found himself a man "crazy enough" to pull the triggers. That Smith, who is the nicer of the two, the one who wants to back out, who feels pity for the Clutters, is the one who kills them is explained in the film by flashbacks to his own tortured childhood. In the most famous line from book or movie, he observes, "I thought Mr. Clutter was a very nice gentleman. I thought so right up to the time I cut his throat."

The film generated controversy from those who found it gratuitously violent (even though all the killings take place off-screen), an apology for murderers, a knee-jerk liberal attack on capital punishment. It was much more shocking in 1967 than it would be today, and it was linked with *Bonnie and Clyde,* another 1967 film, in laments about the decay of Hollywood values. But it won Oscar nominations for Brooks's direction and screenplay, Conrad Hall's cinematography, and the score by Quincy Jones (which launched his Hollywood career).

In Cold Blood achieved renewed notoriety in 2002 with the arrest of Robert Blake for the alleged murder of his wife. Conrad Hall's most famous shot began to turn up on all the newscasts: a close-up of Blake's face on the night he, as Perry Smith, is scheduled to be hanged, with light shining onto it through a rainy window so that the rain seems to be tears running down his skin.

To the degree that there's any connection between *In Cold Blood* and Blake's real-life troubles, it can be explained by typecasting: Robert Blake, in person and in many of his characters, seems born to be a victim pushed around by others, dismissed because of his short stature, carrying old grievances and wounds. For his entire professional life he was haunted by resentment about the way his family and the studios treated him as a hardworking child star. He was in the Our Gang comedies (billed as Mickey Gubitosi and later as Bobby Blake) and played Little Beaver in the Red Ryder movies; he had made nearly one hundred features and shorts by the time, at ten, he had a bit role in *Treasure of the Sierra Madre*, as the little Mexican boy who sells the lottery ticket to Humphrey Bogart.

Blake's unhappy childhood seems to find a mirror in the tortured childhood of Perry Smith, who is seen in flashbacks idolizing a glamorous Mexican mother who appears with her husband in a rodeo show before alcoholism turns her into a prostitute. The moment of Herbert Clutter's murder, in the movie, is intercut with a flashback to Perry's enraged father turning a shotgun on the boy and pulling the trigger; unloaded, that gun seemingly waited for decades for Smith to pull its trigger and shoot back at his father.

Just as Capote plundered real lives for his "non-fiction novel," so Brooks shot on real locations, using Holcomb and the actual Clutter home, and hiring local people as extras. There is creepy voodoo at work in scenes where we see actors re-creating the Clutters' happy lives in the very house where the real family lived. Was this necessary? When I interviewed Blake in 1968, he said, "If we shot it in Nebraska, people would say, 'Isn't that just like Hollywood? It happens in Kansas and they shoot it in Nebraska.' "

Brooks's great achievement in the film is to portray Smith and Hickock as the unexceptional, dim-witted, morally adrift losers they were. There is an outlaw tradition in Hollywood that tends to glamorize killers, but there is nothing attractive about Perry Smith, chewing aspirin by the handful because of the pain of legs torn apart in a motorcycle accident, or Dick Hickock, fixated on "leaving no witnesses." The film follows them on a road odyssey down long, lonely highways, shows them escaping to Mexico only to return, reduces their dreams of wealth to an extraordinary sequence where they team with a little boy and his grandfather in collecting empty soda bottles for the three-cent redemption fee.

From time to time during the film, investigator Alvin Dewey (John Forsyth) talks to a journalist (Paul Stewart) who is apparently meant to suggest Capote; in the scenes after Hickock and Smith are on death row, he steps in as a narrator and engages in fairly heavy-handed dialogue about the uselessness of capital punishment. This character and everything he says are flaws in the film, which would have been better advised to stay with the flat minimalism of the earlier scenes. Brooks is wise, for example, to shoot the killings with no musical score, simply the background sound of the wind howling outside.

The film's message goes astray for several reasons, the best being that most people will agree that Hickock and Smith deserved to die. The main body of the film generates considerable sympathy for the two killers, who were indeed warped by miserable childhoods, but essentially the film finds, as the book did, that the Clutters died for stupid, senseless reasons. The Smith character expresses this best, after it becomes clear that a safe containing $10,000 does not exist: "We're ridiculous. You tapping on the walls for a safe that isn't there, tap-tap-tap, like some nutty woodpecker. And me, crawling around on the floor with my legs on fire, and all to steal a kid's silver dollar."

{ JAWS }

We're going to need a bigger boat.

So the police chief famously informs the shark hunter, right after the first brief appearance of the man-eater in *Jaws*. It's not simply a splendid line, it's an example of Steven Spielberg's strategy all through the film, where the shark is more talked about than seen, and seen more in terms of its actions than in the flesh. There is a story that when producers Richard Zanuck and David Brown first approached Spielberg with an offer to direct the film of Peter Benchley's best-seller, he said he would do it on one condition: that the shark not be seen for the first hour. Viewing the movie's twenty-fifth anniversary DVD, I was surprised to realize how little the shark is seen at all.

In keeping the great white off-screen, Spielberg was employing a strategy used by Alfred Hitchcock throughout his career. "A bomb is under the table, and it explodes: That is surprise," said Hitchcock. "The bomb is under the table but it does not explode: That is suspense." Spielberg leaves the shark under the table for most of the movie. And many of its manifestations in the later part of the film are at second hand: We see not the shark but the results of his actions. The payoff is one of the most effective thrillers ever made.

The movie takes place over the Fourth of July weekend on Amity Island, a tourist resort that feeds off the dollars of its visitors. A famous

opening sequence establishes the presence of a man-eating shark in the coastal waters; a girl goes swimming by moonlight and is dragged under, screaming. All evidence points to a shark, but the town's Mayor Vaughn (Murray Hamilton) doesn't want to scare away tourists, and orders Brody (Roy Scheider), the police chief, to keep the beaches open. "If people can't swim here, they'll be glad to swim in the beaches of Cape Cod, the Hamptons, Long Island," the mayor tells Brody, who spits back: "That doesn't mean we have to serve them up a smorgasbord." But the mayor strides along the beach wearing a sport coat and tie, encouraging people to go into the water. They do, with predictable results.

A town meeting is interrupted by the second of the film's central characters, the rough-edged, narrow-eyed Quint (Robert Shaw). He gets attention by scraping his fingernails down a blackboard that displays a drawing of a shark, and offers his services as a bounty hunter: "You all know me. Know how I make a living." Soon after, Brody sits at home paging through books on sharks, a device that allows Spielberg to establish the killer in our minds as we look at page after page of fearsome teeth, cold little eyes, and victims with chunks taken out of their bodies. (One of the photos shows a shark with a diver's air tank in its mouth, possibly suggesting where Brody gets his bright idea for killing the creature.)

The third key character is Hooper (Richard Dreyfuss), an oceanographer, brought in as an adviser, and useful to the movie because he can voice dramatic information. ("What we're dealing with here is a perfect engine. An eating machine.") Brody is convinced that the beaches must be closed and the shark killed. The mayor stalls, and then after the shark makes the TV news a $3,000 bounty is offered, and Amity is crawling with reckless fortune hunters.

It's here that Spielberg uses one of his most inventive visuals for suggesting the shark. Three or four men gather on a wooden pier, hoping to catch the shark. One has stolen his wife's beef roast to use as bait. They put a fearsome hook through the roast, fasten the chain to the pier, and toss in the bait. The shark simply pulls the end of the pier loose from its moorings and drags it out to sea. Effective, but even more chilling is the next shot, in which we see the floating pier *turn around* and move back toward shore.

Floating objects are used all through the movie to suggest the invisible shark. After Brody, Quint, and Hooper put out to sea in Quint's leaky boat, they fire harpoons into the shark. The harpoons are roped to floating yellow kegs, designed to tire the shark with their lift and drag. In the crucial action sequences at the end, we are often looking at kegs and not at a shark, but the premise is so well established that the shark is *there*.

The screenplay, by Spielberg, Benchley, and Carl Gottlieb, with contributions by Howard Sackler and a crucial speech by Shaw, does not twist itself into parables. The characters all have straightforward motivations. A little dialogue goes a long way. Individual lines stand out for hard-edged terseness:

> I'm not gonna stand here and see that thing cut open and see that little Kintner boy spill out all over the dock.

> I pulled a tooth the size of a shot glass out of the rectal of a boat out there, and it was the tooth of a great white.

> The thing about a shark, he's got lifeless eyes, black eyes, like a doll's eyes. When he comes after you, he doesn't seem to be living until he bites you, and those black eyes roll over white . . .

After all of the shark-establishing and curtain-raising scenes, the heart of the movie is in the long passage at sea, where Hooper and Brody (who is afraid of the water) join Quint on his boat. Brody is right, and they need a bigger boat. Quint's boat is terrifyingly inadequate, leaky, with an engine that produces clouds of black smoke, a bridge that seems designed to topple a crew member overboard, and a harpooning platform jutting out from the bow so that a man standing on it looks like an appetizer on a kebab stick.

The best scene in the movie takes place at nighttime in the galley, where the men drink apricot brandy and Quint and Hooper compare scars. Finally Quint launches into a moody monologue, telling the World War II story of the sinking of the *Indianapolis*. He was one of its crew members. Of the 1,100 men who went overboard, he says, sharks ate all but 316 before rescue arrived: "They averaged six an hour."

When the shark does appear for its close-ups, it is quite satisfactorily terrifying, and most audiences are too startled to ask why the shark seems prepared to inconvenience itself so greatly, at one point even attempting to eat the boat. The shark has been so thoroughly established, through dialogue and quasi-documentary material, that its actual presence is enhanced in our imaginations by all we've seen and heard.

Spielberg's first big hit contained elements that repeat in many of his movies. A night sea hunt for the shark provides an early example of his favorite visual hallmark, a beam of light made visible by fog. He would continue to devote close attention to characters, instead of hurrying past them to the special effects as so many 1990s F/X directors did. In *Jaws* and subsequently, he prefers mood to emotional bludgeoning, and one of the remarkable things about the picture is its relatively muted tone. The familiar musical theme by John Williams is not a shrieker, but low and insinuating. It's often heard during point-of-view shots, at water level and below, which are another way Spielberg suggests the shark without showing it. The cinematography, by Bill Butler, is at pains to tell the story in the midst of middle-class America; if Spielberg's favorite location would become the suburbs, *Jaws* shows suburbanites on vacation.

Jaws was released in 1975, quickly becoming the highest-grossing picture made up to that time and forever wresting the summer releasing season away from B movies and exploitation pictures. The major Hollywood studios, which had avoided summer, now identified it as the prime releasing season, and *Jaws* inspired hundreds of summer thrillers and F/X pictures. For Spielberg, the movie was the launching pad for the most extraordinary directorial career in modern movie history. Before *Jaws,* he was known as the gifted young director of such films as *Duel* (1971) and *The Sugarland Express* (1974). After *Jaws, Close Encounters of the Third Kind* (1977), and *Raiders of the Lost Ark* (1981), he was the king.

{ JULES AND JIM }

François Truffaut's *Jules and Jim* opens with carousel music and a breathless narration that tells of two young men—one French, one Austrian—who meet in Paris in 1912 and become lifelong friends: "They taught each other their languages; they translated poetry." Jules, the Austrian, wants a girl, but those he dates are too silent or too talkative or otherwise flawed, and although he tries a professional, that's not the answer, either: Truffaut explains everything with a shot of her ankle with a wristwatch around it. This magical opening sequence reminds me of Welles's *The Magnificent Ambersons,* which also hurtles through the early lives of its characters, knowing the real story is still to come. The Welles hero eventually gets his "comeuppance," and Truffaut's heroes do too, but what heedless cheer they feel in the beginning.

The movie was released in 1962, at the time of the creative explosion of Godard, Chabrol, Rohmer, Resnais, Malle, and the other New Wave directors, and it was Truffaut's third feature (after *The 400 Blows* in 1959 and *Shoot the Piano Player* in 1960). Although a case can be made for Godard's *Breathless* (based on a story by Truffaut), *Jules and Jim* was perhaps the most influential and arguably the best of those first astonishing films that broke with the past. There is a joy in the filmmaking that feels fresh today and felt audacious at the time. In the energy pulsing from the screen you can see the style and sensibility that inspired *Bonnie and Clyde* (1967), a film

Truffaut was once going to direct, and which jolted American films out of their torpor. And you can see the sixties being born; Jules and Jim and their great love, Catherine, were flower children—for a time. The 1960s ended sadly, as did *Bonnie and Clyde*, as did *Jules and Jim*, as did *Thelma & Louise*, a film they influenced; the movement from comedy to tragedy was all the more powerful for audiences who expected one or the other.

Legend has it that Truffaut found the original novel, by Henri-Pierre Roché (1879–1959), in a discount bin outside a used-book store in 1955; he was to adapt another Roche novel into his 1971 film *Two English Girls*. Roche wrote *Jules and Jim* in old age, but the story feels written by a young man—and in a way it was, because it describes a love triangle he actually experienced. The model for Catherine was still alive when the film was released. Her real name was Helen Hessel, she became a poet, and (Daria Galateria writes in the *Bright Lights Film Journal*) she attended the premiere incognito and then confessed, "I am the girl who leaped into the Seine out of spite, who married his dear, generous Jules, and who, yes, shot Jim."

Jim (Henri Serre) is not shot in Truffaut's *Jules and Jim*, although Catherine (Jeanne Moreau) does wave a pistol at him; Truffaut has a sadder ending in mind, and there is such poignancy in Catherine's final words, "Watch us, Jim!" But that is at the end of the film, which begins in lighthearted gaiety, which continues with romance and passion, and then resumes after the First World War as if the war, having broken the spirit of Europe, broke theirs, too.

Jules (Oskar Werner) and Jim were born to be friends, and as young men in Paris they lead lives of charm and freedom. After giving up on professionals, Jules believes he has found his ideal girl in Thérèse (Marie Dubois), first seen painting an anarchist slogan on a wall and then being slapped by her boyfriend "because people will think anarchists can't spell." Thérèse is the girl who creates the famous moment of the "steam engine," popping the lighted end of a cigarette into her mouth and blowing smoke out the other end. When Jules discovers she is not, after all, his perfect mate, his explanation to Jim is a masterpiece: "She was both mother and daughter to me."

The friends attend a slide show of sculptures and are both struck by

the same image, a bust of a girl who is beautiful and yet opaque. Then and there they decide to travel to the Adriatic to see the original statue, and do; and soon after they return they meet Catherine, whose face looks exactly like the statue's. Jules senses everything has changed. The friends have traded and shared their girlfriends, "but not this one, Jim. OK?" Jules says. Jim agrees. The three of them go everywhere together. A famous shot shows them in a rented cottage at the beach, talking as they lean out of their separate windows. There is a night when they come from a play by Strindberg, which the men disliked; Catherine admires the heroine's freedom and illustrates it by suddenly jumping into the Seine. Here the narrator is indispensable, because otherwise how could we know this: "Her jump strikes Jim like lightning."

So they are both in love with her, but Jules takes her to Austria to be married, and then the war separates them. As members of enemy armies, they fear that one might shoot the other. After the war, Jim visits Jules and Catherine in their cottage on the Rhine. They have a daughter, Sabine, but their marriage is unhappy. Jules confides that Catherine has run away and had affairs, but he stays with her because he loves her and understands her nature. One night at dinner she reveals her bottled-up misery by rattling off the names of countless French wines. The friends look uneasy. Jules will do anything to make her happy—even share her with Jim. "If you love her," Jules tells him, "don't think me an obstacle." Catherine asks Jim to move into the house. "Careful, Jim—careful for both of you," Jules says. Jules wonders if perhaps it would be best to divorce Catherine so Jim can marry her; he believes their friendship would survive this.

Their tragedy is that they shared a magical youth, and adulthood will not and cannot accommodate it. No practical arrangement of their lives can duplicate the freedom of their early days in Paris. The men can try to come to terms with this, but Catherine cannot, and *Jules and Jim* is really Catherine's film. This is Jeanne Moreau's first great performance, all the greater because of the art with which she presents Catherine's discontent. A lesser actress might have made Catherine mad or hysterical, but although madness and hysteria are uncoiling beneath the surface, Catherine depends mostly on unpredictability—on a fundamental unwillingness to behave as expected. She shocks her friends as a way of testing them.

The style of the film came as a revelation in 1962. Truffaut skips lightly through the material, covering twenty-five years while never seeming to linger. In *Day for Night* (1973), his autobiographical hero steals eight-by-ten glossies of *Citizen Kane* from the front of a theater; *Kane*'s influence here can be guessed in the way Truffaut uses newsreel footage to re-create the war, and a newsreel of Nazi book burning to foreshadow World War II. (Oskar Werner would be the star of Truffaut's 1966 film *Fahrenheit 451*, about a world where books are banned.)

Truffaut's camera is nimble, its movement so fluid that we sense a challenge to the traditional Hollywood grammar of establishing shot, close-up, reaction shot, and so on; *Jules and Jim* impatiently strains toward the handheld style. The narrator also hurries things along, telling us what there is no time to show us. The use of a narrator became one of Truffaut's favorite techniques; it's a way of signaling to us that the story is over and its ending known before it even begins. His use of brief, almost unnoticeable freeze-frames treats some of the moments as snapshots, which also belong to the past.

The mystery (some would say the flaw) of the film is how it moves so quickly through these lives. Perhaps the secret is in the nature of an old man's memory, as understood by Truffaut (who was twenty-nine during the filming). Henri-Pierre Roché lived through events like the ones in the film, he was one of the characters, all the stages of the story were known to him, and he had remembered them so often and so well that in his novelist's imagination key events were highlighted while the passages in between had faded.

Would the film be better as a cumbersome traditional narrative, with all the motives laid out and all the behavior explained? Should Truffaut have dragged a psychiatrist onstage to diagnose Catherine, as his hero Hitchcock did two years earlier for Norman Bates in *Psycho*? Not at all. *Jules and Jim* is one of those rare films that knows how fast audiences can think, and how emotions contain their own explanations. It's about three people who could not concede that their moment of perfect happiness was over, and pursued it into dark and sad places. Galateria quotes Truffaut: "I begin a film believing it will be amusing—and along the way I notice that only sadness can save it."

KIESLOWSKI'S THREE COLORS TRILOGY

After he completed *Red* (1994), the final film in his Three Colors trilogy, Krzysztof Kieslowski announced that he would retire. This was not a man weary of work. It was the retirement of a magician, a Prospero who was now content to lay aside his art—"to read and smoke," he said. When he died two years later, he was only fifty-four.

Because he made most of his early work in Poland during the Cold War, and because his masterpiece, *The Decalogue*, consists of ten one-hour films that do not fit easily on the multiplex conveyor belt, he has still not received the kind of recognition given those he deserves to be named with, like Bergman, Ozu, Fellini, Keaton, and Buñuel. He is one of the filmmakers I would turn to for consolation if I learned I was dying, or to laugh with on finding I would live after all.

He often deals with illness, loss, and death, but deep pools of humor float beneath the surfaces of his films. There is a sequence in *White* (1994) where his hero, a Polish hairdresser, is so desperately homesick in Paris that he arranges to be sent back to Warsaw curled up inside a suitcase. His friend at the other end watches the airport conveyor belt with horror: The bag is not there. It has been stolen by thieves who break the lock, find only the little man, beat him savagely, and throw him on a rubbish heap. Staggering to his feet, he looks around, bloody but triumphant, and cries out, "Home at last!"

From *Blue*

From *White*

From *Red*

In *Blue* (1993), Juliette Binoche plays a young woman whose husband and child are killed in a car crash. After a period of emotional paralysis, she telephones an old friend who has always been in love with her and tells him his chance has come around at last. They have sex. She wants to see if it will help. It does not. She moves to an obscure street in an anonymous corner of Paris, determined to see no one she knows and make no new friends. But as chance would have it, she does meet someone. She meets her husband's mistress.

Red, the best film among equals, stars Irène Jacob as Valentine, a woman in Geneva whose car strikes a beautiful golden retriever. She nurses the dog back to health and returns it to its owner, a retired judge (Jean-Louis Trintignant), who tells her she can keep it. He is beyond worrying about dogs. He occupies his days intercepting the telephone calls of his neighbors, and he watches them through his windows, almost like God (actually, just like God), curious, since they have free will, about what they will do next. After a lifetime of passing verdicts, he wants to be a detached observer.

This judge was a young man who was once in love, who lost that love, and who has lived on hold ever since. He all but caresses his emotional wounds. Although at first he rudely turns Valentine away, slowly he begins to tell her his story. There is a moment in *Red* where Valentine leans forward to listen with such attention and sympathy that she seems at prayer. Only gradually do we learn that the story of the judge and his lost love reveals parallels with the story of Valentine and her lover who is always absent, and with the life of a young law student who lives across from her apartment in the city—a student she has never met.

On another time line, in a parallel universe, the judge and Valentine might have themselves fallen in love. They missed being the same age by only forty years or so. Now that Hubble has seen back to the dawn of time, that doesn't seem a great many years. There is a passage in one of Loren Eiseley's books where he climbs down a crevice in the desert and finds himself looking at the skull of one of man's early ancestors, who gazes back at him over countless centuries. He reflects that from a cosmological perspective, they lived at almost the same instant.

The Decalogue and the trilogy were written in collaboration with

Krzysztof Piesiewicz, a lawyer Kieslowski met during the Solidarity trials. "He didn't know how to write," the director remembered, "but he could talk." Shut up in a smoke-filled room, they talked through the films together. Although he always wrote with Piesiewicz, curiously Kieslowski used a different cinematographer for almost every film; he didn't want them to look as if they matched. One imagines Piesiewicz as the advocate for contrarian views, since the films so consistently resist delivering in the expected way.

In the trilogy, *Blue* is the antitragedy, *White* is the anticomedy, and *Red* is the antiromance. All three films hook us with immediate narrative interest. They are metaphysical through example, not theory: Kieslowski tells the parable but doesn't preach the lesson. It's the same with his *Decalogue,* where each film is based on one of the Ten Commandments, but it is not always possible to say which commandment, or precisely what the film is saying about it. I know this because I taught *The Decalogue* in a film class, where we discovered that the order of the commandments differs slightly in the Jewish, Catholic, and Protestant versions. "And in the Kieslowski version," a student sighed.

In the same elusive way, using symbolism that only seems to be helpful, *Blue, White,* and *Red* stand for the three colors of the French tricolor, representing liberty, equality, and fraternity. Juliette Binoche, in *Blue,* has the liberty, after her loss of husband and child, to start life again, or not at all. Zbigniew Zamachowski, in *White,* is dropped by his beautiful wife (Julie Delpy) after he goes to a great deal of trouble to move her to Paris. Back home in Poland, he wants to make millions so that he can be her equal, and have his revenge. Valentine and the old judge in *Red* have a fraternity of souls that springs across barriers of time and gender because they both have the imagination to appreciate what could have been.

There is also, lurking unsaid, the possibility that the judge, so intent on studying the lives of his neighbors without involving himself, might be the catalyst for one final act of magic involving Valentine and that young man who lives across from her. That young man who might have been him or, this being Kieslowski, might actually be him, his time lines overlapping slightly and specific details, of course, altered by circumstances.

The Columbia University professor and film critic Annette Insdorf, who knew Kieslowski well and often translated for him, says, "It's rare that you say about some film director, 'What a good man.' But he was. Very by-the-way, emotional, very nonsentimental, dry in his wit and in his bearing, but he really made an impression." Her book, *Double Lives, Second Chances: The Cinema of Krzysztof Kieslowski*, provides the key to his work in its title. Kieslowski almost never made a film about characters who lacked choices. Indeed, his films were usually about their choices, how they arrived at them, and the close connections they made or missed.

Most films make the unspoken assumption that their characters are defined by and limited to their plots. But lives are not about stories. Stories are about lives. That is the difference between films for children and films for adults. Kieslowski celebrates intersecting time lines and lifelines, choices made and unmade. All his films ask why, since God gave us free will, movie directors go to such trouble to take it away.

There is a moment in *The Double Life of Véronique* (1991) where if the heroine had only glanced out a bus window a second sooner, she might have glimpsed herself in the city square. How could that be? A moment's rent in the fabric of time? A flash from a parallel universe? Kieslowski would never have dreamed of saying and probably didn't know.

"Kieslowski truly loved his characters and invites us into a poignant awareness of both our limitations and our capacity for transcendence," Insdorf says, and you can feel that in the tenderness of every frame. The old judge in *Red* is harsh and dismissive, but with the sense that it hurts him, not entertains him, to treat Valentine so harshly. We see him like so many of Kieslowski's characters, swimming upward through a suffocating life toward the possibility that hope still floats somewhere above.

I connect strongly with Kieslowski because I sometimes seek a whiff of transcendence by revisiting places from earlier years. I am thinking now of a café in Venice, a low cliff overlooking the sea near Donegal, a bookstore in Cape Town, and Sir John Soane's breakfast room in London. I am drawn to them in the spirit of pilgrimage. No one else can see the shadows of my former and future visits there, or know how they are the touchstones of my mortality, but if someday as I approach the café I see myself just getting up to leave, I will not be surprised to have missed myself by so little.

Kieslowski would have understood. A link between all three films in the trilogy is provided by a brief shot of an old lady trying to deposit a bottle in a street recycling bin. The slot is a little too high for her to reach. In *Red*, Valentine tries to help her. The first two movies are set in Paris. What is the old lady doing in Geneva? Exactly.

Kind Hearts and Coronets

In the years after World War II, there emerged from the Ealing Studios of England a series of comedies so dry and droll, so literate and cynical that the phrase "Ealing comedy" described them and no others. Many starred Alec Guinness, then in his thirties, so anonymous in appearance that he was told by an early teacher, "You will never make an actor." It was like that until the end of his days; once, while dressed as Hitler for a costume fitting, he stepped outside and failed to raise the eyebrow of a passing policeman. While the other great actors of his generation—Olivier, Gielgud, Richardson—attracted crowds wherever they went, Guinness could, he reported, go to the cinema without ever being asked for his autograph.

If he was unremarkable in person, he played a series of remarkable characters in the movies, each one a newly minted original. He was shy, stammering Herbert Pocket in *Great Expectations* (1946) and two years later the diabolical Fagin in *Oliver Twist*. He blew up the bridge in *The Bridge on the River Kwai* (1957), was an eccentric painter in *The Horse's Mouth* (1958), a genial colonel in *Tunes of Glory* (1960) and the same year was a vacuum-cleaner salesman as *Our Man in Havana*. He was a desert prince in *Lawrence of Arabia* (1962), a Soviet official in *Dr. Zhivago* (1965), an imperturbable Indian doctor in *A Passage to India* (1984), and Cromwell, Disraeli, Father Brown, Scrooge, and, of course, Hitler. Little wonder his autobiography is titled *Blessings in Disguise*. It is an injustice that he is best remem-

bered as Obi-Wan Kenobi in the *Star Wars* movies, which he told me were boring to make because he spent most of his time standing alone in front of a back-projection screen, reciting dialogue.

Consider how unnecessary such special effects were in *Kind Hearts and Coronets* (1949), in which Guinness plays eight different members of the same family, of both genders and a six-decade age span, by doing relatively subtle things with makeup, posture, and behavior. Because he was nobody he could be anybody, and here he creates characters who are pompous, silly, inconsequential, and even actually nice. ("I was glad," says the hero of the film about his employer, Ascoyne D'Ascoyne, "after all his kindness to me, that I should not have to kill him.")

The film began a classic run of Ealing comedies, which continued with *The Lavender Hill Mob* and *The Man in the White Suit* (both 1951) and *The Ladykillers* (1955), in which a sweet little old lady buys the story that her new roomers, all crooks, are actually musicians. Their rehearsal sessions are priceless. All of these Ealings were being revived with new prints when I was in London in August 2002. The big screen underlined the quality of the black-and-white cinematography, which in the case of *Kind Hearts* seems to owe something to *Citizen Kane*—another film that begins at the end and then circles back with narration.

The opening scene of *Kind Hearts and Coronets* shows Dennis Price as Louis Mazzini, a newly minted duke who has methodically tried to murder his way to the title. In the last night before he is to be hanged, Louis writes his memoirs, and as he reads them aloud we journey back through his life. His mother, we learn, was a daughter of the aristocratic D'Ascoyne family who ran away with an Italian tenor and was disowned. After the tenor died on the day of the boy's birth, his mother's appeals to her family were coldly rejected, and mother and son were reduced to a life of genteel poverty. But Louis's mother always held out the hope that he might someday inherit the title (which in the D'Ascoyne family descended through women as well as men). After his mother dies and she is cruelly barred from the D'Ascoyne family crypt, Louis buries her in "a hideous suburban grave" and vows revenge.

He pastes the family tree onto the back of his mother's painting of the family home, where she spent her happy early days, and one by one he crosses off D'Ascoynes as they die. A "fortunate epidemic of diphtheria" carries off one, but Louis will have to personally murder some of the others, and as he takes a sixpenny tour of the family seat he wonders how he will get close enough, observing sadly, "It is so difficult to make a neat job of killing people with whom one is not on friendly terms."

Price is impeccable as the murderer: elegant, well-spoken, a student of demeanor. That is what gets him a job in the family bank, where an uncle takes pity on him. The uncle and all of the other D'Ascoynes are played by Guinness (the list includes the Duke, the Banker, the Parson, the General, the Admiral, Young Ascoyne D'Ascoyne, Young Henry, and Lady Agatha D'Ascoyne). What is intriguing is that all of these characters, while obviously members of the same family, are not obviously Guinness, unless we insist on thinking of them in that way. One tactic that helps his impersonations is the tendency of the director, Robert Hamer, to shoot mostly in long and medium shot, generally avoiding close-ups that can be too carefully scrutinized.

Guinness plays D'Ascoynes who are tall, short, or stooped, young or old, male or female, finding the characters largely in his body language and a few wigs or beards. It is helpful, probably, that the focus of most of the scenes is on young Louis; it is significant, somehow, that the actor playing eight characters is not given top billing and the movie is not about him.

The methods of Louis's murders are in the spirit of George Orwell's famous essay "Decline of the English Murder" (1946), in which he regretted the modern practice of simply shooting people and being done with it. Praising the ingenuity of an earlier generation of English murders, Orwell examines those crimes "which have given the greatest pleasure to the British public," finding that poison is the preferable means, and that an ideal murderer is a member of the middle class who hopes to improve his social position or get hold of a legacy.

Kind Hearts and Coronets, set circa 1900, admirably meets his criteria. One D'Ascoyne is dispatched by poison, another is blown up at tea, and a third is swept over a waterfall after Louis unties his boat. (The victim was spending an illicit weekend with his mistress at the time, and Louis observes, "I was sorry about the girl, but found some relief in the reflection that she had presumably during the weekend already undergone a fate worse than death.") My favorite murder involves a suffragette D'Ascoyne who is demonstrating in a hot-air balloon when Louis shoots her down, observing, "I shot an arrow into the air/She fell to earth in Berkeley Square."

In the course of his rise to the dukedom, Louis conducts parallel affairs, one with a woman he loves, the other with a woman he needs. Sibella (Joan Greenwood) is the daughter of the family where he boarded after his mother's death; she loves him but, believing he has no prospects, marries a boring man and then begins to call on Louis. Greenwood's performance is luscious, with her little lisp and air of languorous petulance. The other woman, Edith (Valerie Hobson), is the widow of one of his victims, and well placed with money and position in society. When the amoral Louis is not with the one he loves, he loves the one he's with.

Despite its murders and intrigues, its betrayals and blood feuds, *Kind Hearts and Coronets* has a dry and detached air, established by the memoirs of Louis, who maintains a studied distance from the evils he has committed. Wounded by the slights to his mother, he essentially believes the D'Ascoynes are asking for it. The movie is unusually dependent on voice-over narration, objective and understated, which is all the funnier by being so removed from the sensational events taking place. Murder, Louis demonstrates, and Orwell would agree, can be most agreeably entertaining, so long as the story lingers on the eccentricities of the villain rather than on the unpleasant details of the crimes.

Note: The title comes from Tennyson, whose advice Louis should have taken: "Kind hearts are more than coronets,/And simple faith than Norman blood."

KING KONG

On good days I consider *Citizen Kane* the seminal film of the sound era, but on bad days it is *King Kong*. That is not to say I dislike *King Kong*, which, in this age of technical perfection, uses its very naïveté to generate a kind of creepy awe. It's simply to observe that this low-rent monster movie, and not the psychological puzzle of *Kane,* pointed the way toward the current era of special effects, science fiction, cataclysmic destruction, and nonstop shocks. *King Kong* is the father of *Jurassic Park,* the *Alien* movies, and countless other stories in which heroes are terrified by skillful special effects. A movie like *The Silence of the Lambs,* which finds its evil in a man's personality, seems humanistic by contrast.

I've seen *King Kong* (1933) many times, most memorably in its rerelease in the 1950s, when it did indeed scare me. In recent years I have focused on the remarkable special effects, based by Willis O'Brien and others on his F/X work in *The Lost World* (1925) but achieving a sophistication and beauty that eclipsed anything that went before. The movie plunders every trick in the book to create its illusions, using live action, back projection, stop-motion animation, miniatures, models, matte paintings, and sleight of hand. And it is not stingy with the effects; after a half hour of lumbering dialogue and hammy acting, the movie introduces Kong and rarely cuts away from sequences requiring one kind of trickery or another.

But *King Kong* is more than a technical achievement. It is also a curiously touching fable in which the beast is seen not as a monster of destruction but as a creature that in its own way wants to do the right thing. Unlike the extraterrestrial spiders in the *Alien* pictures, which embody single-minded aggression, Kong cares for his captive human female, protects her, attacks only when provoked, and would be perfectly happy to be left alone on his Pacific island. It is the greed of a Hollywood showman that unleashes Kong's rage, and anyone who thinks to exhibit the beast on a New York stage in front of a live audience deserves what he gets—indeed, more than he gets.

The movie was directed by Merian C. Cooper and Ernest Schoedsack and produced by them with the legend David O. Selznick, then head of RKO Radio Pictures. Selznick took little credit for the film, saying his key contribution was to put O'Brien's F/X techniques together with Cooper and Schoedsack's story ideas.

Although it has the scope and feel of an expensive epic, *Kong* had a relatively moderate budget of about $600,000. Sequences that would take weeks these days—such as when Kong shakes a log to dislodge the men clinging to it—were done in two days, and the giant wall that separates the island villagers from the monster was a set originally built as the Temple of Jerusalem for Cecil B. DeMille's *The King of Kings* (1927). Although Fay Wray had been in movies since 1919 and was a B-list star, her leading man, Bruce Cabot, was appearing in his first picture after having been spotted by Cooper as the doorman in a Hollywood club.

The story is not sophisticated. A movie director (Robert Armstrong) hires a ship, recruits his leading lady from off the streets of New York at the last moment, and sails for a mysterious Pacific island he heard about in Singapore. The island contains a legendary giant ape, which he hopes to use as the star of his movie. Fay Wray plays Ann Darrow, Kong's costar, and Cabot is the sailor who falls in love with her and saves her from Kong.

Modern viewers will shift uneasily in their seats during the stereotyping of the islanders in a scene where a bride is to be sacrificed to Kong (it is rare to see a coconut brassiere in a noncomedy), but from the moment Kong appears on the screen the movie essentially never stops for breath. In an astonishing outpouring of creative energy, O'Brien and his collaborators

(including RKO's legendary visual effects artist Linwood Dunn and sound man Murray Spivack) show Kong in battle with two dinosaurs, a giant snake, a flying reptile, and a *Tyrannosaurus rex*. Later, in New York, he will climb to the top of the Empire State Building and bat down a biplane with his bare hand.

The visual techniques are explained by film historian Ron Haver, whose commentary track on the 1985 Criterion laser disc was one of the first ever recorded. He is amusing in describing how some live-action scenes were miniaturized to make the Kong model look larger; searching for the right screen to project them on, the filmmakers hit on a screen made of condoms, to the consternation of a nearby druggist, who could not understand their orders for a gross at a time. Haver also observes how Kong's fur seems to crawl during several scenes; the model was covered with rabbit fur, and the fingers of the stop-action animators disturbed it between every stop-action shot. The effect, explained by the filmmakers as "muscles rippling," is oddly effective.

From the moment of its making, *King Kong* fell under the censors' scissors. Cooper himself removed one notorious sequence after the world premiere: The men shaken from the log fell into a chasm, where they were devoured by giant spiders, but the effect "stopped the picture in its tracks," and people walked out. Another scene was taken out after the Motion Picture Association of America code came into being. It shows Kong curiously removing some of Wray's clothes, tickling her, and sniffing his fingers. Close-ups of humans being crunched between Kong's jaws were also cut for various versions, but now the movie is intact again—except for the spiders.

How terrifying was it, really? *Variety*'s original 1933 review conceded that "after the audience becomes used to the machinelike movements and other mechanical flaws in the gigantic animals on view, and becomes accustomed to the phony atmosphere, they may commence to feel the power." The showbiz bible complained, however, that "it's a film-long screaming session for [Wray], too much for any actress and any audience." Yes, but nobody has ever forgotten that performance. (At a Hollywood party in 1972, I saw Hugh Hefner introduced to Fay Wray. "I loved your movie," he told her. "Which one?" she asked.)

Variety then and now is hard to impress, but my guess, based upon my first viewing as a teenager, is that audiences found it plenty scary. In modern times the movie has aged, as critic James Berardinelli observes, and "advances in technology and acting have dated aspects of the production." True, although in the very artificiality of some of the special effects, there is a creepiness that isn't there in today's slick, flawless, computer-aided images.

In *Jurassic Park* you are looking, more or less, at a real dinosaur. In *King Kong*, you are looking at an *idea* of a dinosaur, created by hand by technicians who are working with their imaginations. When Kong battles the large flesh-eating dinosaur in his first big battle scene, there is a moment when he forces its jaws apart and the bones crack and blood drips from the gaping throat, and something immediate happens that is hard to duplicate on any computer.

There are, of course, questions we cannot help asking. Haver asks one: Why did the natives build a door in their wall, so that Kong could come through? Common sense asks another: How tall is Kong, really? (The filmmakers take poetic license: He's eighteen feet tall on the island, twenty-four feet on stage, fifty feet on the Empire State Building.) Even allowing for its slow start, wooden acting, and wall-to-wall screaming, there is something ageless and primeval about *King Kong* that still somehow works.

{ THE LAST LAUGH }

The old man is proud beyond all reason of his position as a hotel doorman, and even prouder of his uniform, with its gold braids and brass buttons, its wide shoulders, military lapels, and comic opera cuffs. Positioned in front of the busy revolving door, he greets the rich and famous and is the embodiment of the great hotel's traditions—until, in old age, he is crushed by being demoted to the humiliating position of washroom attendant.

F. W. Murnau's *The Last Laugh* (1924) tells this story in one of the most famous silent films, and one of the most truly wordless, because it does not even use printed intertitles. Silent directors were proud of their ability to tell a story through pantomime and the language of the camera, but no one before Murnau had ever entirely done away with all written words on the screen (except for one sardonic comment we'll get to later). He tells his story through shots, angles, moves, facial expressions, and easily read visual cues.

The film would be famous just for its lack of titles, and for its lead performance by Emil Jannings, which is so effective that both Jannings and Murnau were offered Hollywood contracts and moved to America at the dawn of sound. But *The Last Laugh* is remarkable also for its moving camera. It is often described as the first film to make great use of a moving point of view. It isn't, really; the silent historian Kevin Brownlow cites *The Second in Command,* made nine years earlier. But it is certainly the film that made

the most spectacular early use of movement, with shots that track down an elevator and out through a hotel lobby, or seemingly move through the plate-glass window of a hotel manager's office (influencing the famous shot in *Citizen Kane* that swoops down through the skylight of a nightclub).

Murnau's technical mastery makes all of his films exciting to see. In the vampire movie *Nosferatu,* in the fiendish visions of *Faust,* in the imaginary city of *Sunrise,* he created phantasmagoric visions that seemed to define his characters: They were who they were because of what surrounded them. This is a key to German expressionism, the influential silent style that told stories through bold and exaggerated visual elements—reality slipping over into nightmare and back again.

In the case of *The Last Laugh,* however, Murnau's story is more of a traditional narrative than usual. He follows the old doorman in almost every shot, cutting away only to show what the doorman sees. And he exaggerates the scale of the hotel and the city to emphasize how important it seems to the doorman; the opening shot, coming down in the elevator and tracking across the lobby (the camera was in a wheelchair), peers out through revolving doors into the rain, showing elegant people and glittering surroundings; the doorman is full of himself as he whistles for cabs and salutes arriving customers.

In those early scenes Murnau shoots the doorman from a low angle, so that he seems to tower over other characters. He is tall and wide, his face surrounded by a beard and whiskers, which frame its cherubic pomp. But beneath the grand display his body is failing him, and we see him struggle with an enormous steamer trunk and then take a moment's rest in the lobby—just long enough for the prissy assistant manager to see him and write up a note. And the next day when he arrives for work, his world shakes and the camera swirls as he sees another man in uniform, doing his job.

Much of the doorman's happiness in life depends on the respect paid to his uniform by his neighbors around the courtyard of his apartment building. Murnau built this enormous set (most of the film, including rainy exteriors, was shot on sound stages), and peopled it with nosy busybodies who don't miss a thing. Ashamed to be seen without his uniform, the doorman actually steals it from a locker to wear it home. Later, when his deception is revealed, there is a nightmarish montage of laughing and derisive faces.

His tragedy "could only be a German story," wrote the critic Lotte Eisner, whose 1964 book on Murnau reawakened interest in his work. "It could only happen in a country where the uniform (as it was at the time the film was made) was more than God." Perhaps the doorman's total identification with his job, his position, his uniform, and his image helps foreshadow the rise of the Nazi Party; once he puts on his uniform, the doorman is no longer an individual but a slavishly loyal instrument of a larger organization. And when he takes the uniform off, he ceases to exist, even in his own eyes.

Murnau was bold in his use of the camera, and lucky to work with Karl Freund, a great cinematographer who also immigrated to Hollywood. Freund filmed many other German silent films, notably Fritz Lang's futurist parable *Metropolis* (1926), and his first important American film was *All Quiet on the Western Front* (1930). He was one of the links between German expressionism and its American cousin, film noir (see his work with John Huston and Humphrey Bogart in *Key Largo*). Here he liberated the camera from gravity. There is a shot where the camera seems to float through the air, and it literally does; Freund had himself and the camera mounted on a swing. (Abel Gance borrowed the technique a few years later for his *Napoleon*.) There are shots where superimposed images swim through the air, the famous shot that seems to move through the glass window, and a moment when the towering Hotel Atlantic seems to lean over to crush the staggering doorman.

I mentioned the one place in the film where a title card is used. It is not necessary, and the film would make perfect sense without it. But Murnau seemed compelled to use it, almost as an apology for what follows. We see the pathetic old man wrapped in the cloak of the night watchman, who was his friend, and the movie seems over. Then comes the title card, which says, "Here the story should really end, for, in real life, the forlorn old man would have little to look forward to but death. The author took pity on him and has provided a quite improbable epilogue."

Improbable, and unsatisfying, because a happy ending is conjured out of thin air. The doorman accidentally inherits a fortune, returns to the hotel in glory, and treats all his friends to champagne and caviar, while his old enemies glower and gnash their teeth. It is this ending that inspires the English-language title. The original German is *Die Letzte Mann,* literally "the last man," which in addition to its obvious meaning may also evoke "the previous man"—the doorman who was replaced. The dim-witted practice of tacking a contrived happy ending onto a sad story was not unique with Murnau (who had the grace to apologize in advance for it), and has only grown more popular over the decades.

As for Emil Jannings (1884–1950), he made *The Last Laugh* at the top of his form; considered one of the world's greatest stars, he specialized in towering figures like Peter the Great, Henry VIII, Louis XVI, Danton, and Othello. The doorman's fall from grace was all the greater because the audience remembered the glory of his earlier roles. Jannings came to America at the same time as Murnau, won the Academy Award for *The Last Command* (1928), was rendered unemployable by the rise of the talkies, returned to Germany, and found one of his most famous roles, as Marlene Dietrich's erotically mesmerized admirer in *The Blue Angel* (1930). Jannings embraced the rise of the Nazis, made films that supported them, was appointed head of a major German production company, and fell into disgrace after the war. The coat no longer fit.

{ LAURA }

I've seen Otto Preminger's *Laura* three or four times, but the identity of the murderer doesn't spring quickly to mind. That's not because the guilty person is forgettable but because the identity is so arbitrary: It is not *necessary* that the murderer be the murderer. Three or four other characters would have done as well, and indeed if it were not for Walter Winchell we would have another ending altogether. More about that later.

Film noir is known for its convoluted plots and arbitrary twists, but even in a genre that gave us *The Maltese Falcon,* this one takes some kind of prize. *Laura* (1944) has a police detective who never goes to the station; a suspect who is invited to tag along as other suspects are interrogated; a heroine who is dead for most of the film; a man insanely jealous of a woman even though he never for a moment seems heterosexual; a romantic lead who is a dull-witted Kentucky bumpkin moving in Manhattan penthouse society; and a murder weapon that is *returned* to its hiding place by the cop, who will "come by for it in the morning." The only nude scene involves the jealous man and the cop.

That *Laura* continues to weave a spell—and it does—is a tribute to style over sanity. No doubt the famous musical theme by David Raksin has something to do with it: The music lends a haunted, nostalgic, regretful cast to everything it plays under, and it plays under a lot. There is also Clifton Webb's narration, measured, precise, a little mad: "I shall never forget the weekend Laura died. A silver sun burned through the sky like a huge magnifying glass. It was the hottest Sunday in my recollection. I felt as if I were the only human being left in New York. For Laura's horrible death, I was alone. I, Waldo Lydecker, was the only one who really knew her."

It is Clifton Webb's performance as Waldo Lydecker that stands at the heart of the film, with Vincent Price, as Laura's fiancé, Shelby Carpenter, nibbling at the edges like an eager spaniel. Both actors, and Judith Anderson as her neurotic Aunt Ann, create characters who have no reality except their own, which is good enough for them. The hero and heroine, on the other hand, are cardboard. Gene Tierney, as Laura, is gorgeous, has perfect features, looks great in the stills, but never seems emotionally involved; her work in *Leave Her to Heaven* (1945) is stronger, deeper, more convincing. Dana Andrews, as Detective Mark McPherson, stands straight, chain-smokes, speaks in a monotone, and reminded the studio head Darryl F. Zanuck of "an agreeable schoolboy." As actors, Tierney and Andrews basically play eyewitnesses to scene stealing by Webb and Price.

This was Clifton Webb's first big starring role and his first movie role of any kind since 1930. He was a stage actor who refused the studio's demand for a screen test; Otto Preminger, who began by producing the film and ended by directing it, in desperation filmed Webb on a Broadway stage and showed that to Zanuck. "He doesn't walk, he flies," an underling told Zanuck, but Webb, who had a mannered camp style, impressed Zanuck and got the role. Vincent Price creates an accent somewhere between Kentucky and Transylvania for his character, who is tall and healthy and inspires Waldo Lydecker to complain to Laura, "With you, a lean, strong body is the measure of a man."

Lydecker is lean but not strong. Webb was fifty-five when he played the role, Tierney twenty-four. A similar age difference was no problem for Bogart and Bacall, but between Webb and Tierney it must be said there is not the slightest suggestion of chemistry. He plays a bachelor critic and columnist (said to be modeled after Alexander Woollcott), and the first time we see him he is sitting in his bathtub, typing. This is after Laura's body has been murdered with shotgun blasts and the detective comes to question her closest friend.

The scene develops with more undercurrents than surface, as McPherson enters the bathroom, glances at Lydecker, seems faintly amused. Then Lydecker swings the typewriter shelf away, so that it shields his nudity from the camera but not from the detective. Lydecker stands up, off-screen, and a reaction shot shows McPherson glancing down as Lydecker asks him to pass a bathrobe. Every time I see the movie, I wonder what Preminger is trying to accomplish with this scene. There is no suggestion that Lydecker is attracted to McPherson, and yet it seems odd to greet a police detective in the nude.

Lydecker is Laura's Svengali. In flashbacks, we follow the progress of their relationship. He snubs her in the Algonquin dining room, then apologizes, becomes her friend, and takes over her life; he chooses her clothes, redoes her hair, introduces her to the right people, promotes her in his column. They spend every night together out on the town, except Tuesdays and Fridays, when Waldo cooks for her at home. Then other men enter the picture, and leave again as Waldo blasts them in his column. Big, dumb Shelby with his lean, strong body is the latest and most serious threat. Considering this Waldo-Shelby-Laura love triangle, it occurs to me that the only way to make it psychologically sound would be to change Laura into a boy.

The movie basically consists of well-dressed rich people standing in luxury apartments and talking to a cop. The passion is unevenly distributed. Shelby and Laura never seem to have much heat between them. Waldo is possessive of Laura, but never touches her. Ann Treadwell (Anderson), a society dame, lusts for Shelby but has to tell him or he'd never know. And Detective McPherson develops a crush on the dead woman. There is an extraordinary scene where he enters her apartment at night, looks through her letters, touches her dresses, sniffs her perfume, pours himself a drink from her bottle, and sits down beneath her enormous portrait, which is placed immodestly above her own fireplace. It's like a date with a ghost.

McPherson's investigation and his ultimate revelations are handled in an offhand way, for a 1940s crime picture. He is forever leading people to believe they're going to be charged, then backing off. Lydecker asks to tag along as the cop interviews suspects; murder is his "favorite crime," he says, and "I like to study their reactions." Astonishingly, McPherson lets him.

This is useful from a screenplay point of view, since otherwise McPherson would be mostly alone.

All of these absurdities and improbabilities somehow do not diminish the film's appeal. They may even add to it. Some of the lines have become unintentionally funny, James Naremore writes in *More Than Night: Film Noir in Its Contexts:* "Where *Laura* is concerned, the camp effect is at least partly intended—any movie that puts Clifton Webb, Judith Anderson, and Vincent Price in the same drawing room is inviting a mood of fey theatricality."

The story of Preminger's struggle to get the movie made has become Hollywood legend. As he tells it in his autobiography, Zanuck saw him as a producer, not a director, and assigned Rouben Mamoulian to the piece. When the early rushes were a disaster, Preminger stepped in, reshot many scenes, replaced the sets, and fought for the screenplay. Zanuck insisted that another ending be shot; the new version was screened for Zanuck and his pal Walter Winchell, a real gossip columnist, who said he didn't understand the ending. So Zanuck let Preminger have his ending back, and while the business involving the shotgun in the antique clock may be somewhat labored, the whole film is of a piece: contrived, artificial, mannered, and yet achieving a kind of perfection in its balance between low motives and high style. What makes the movie great, perhaps, is the casting. The materials of a B-grade crime potboiler are redeemed by Waldo Lydecker, walking through every scene as if afraid to step in something.

{ LEAVING LAS VEGAS }

Mike Figgis's *Leaving Las Vegas* is not a love story, although it feels like one, but a story about two desperate people using love as a form of prayer and a last resort against their pain. It is also a sad, trembling portrait of the final stages of alcoholism. Those who found it too extreme were simply lucky enough never to have arrived there themselves. Few films are more despairing and yet, curiously, so hopeful as this one, which argues that even at the very end of the road, at the final extremity, we can find some solace in the offer and acceptance of love.

The movie tells the story of Ben and Sera, played by Nicolas Cage and Elisabeth Shue. He is a Hollywood agent, she is a prostitute. Although prostitutes can be a cliché in the movies, and those with a good heart even more so, the details of their relationship leave clichés far behind, and the movie becomes the story of these specific characters and exactly who they are. There is also the truth that a man in Ben's condition would be unable to begin any relationship without paying for it.

Ben is in the final stages of an alcoholic meltdown. We watch as he asks a friend in a bar for a loan and is told bluntly, "Don't drink it in here." We sense his loneliness and need in his attempt to pick up a woman in a bar: "I really wish you'd come home with me. You smell great and you look great." We see him being fired from his job, and agreeing that he should be fired, and telling his boss the severance check is too generous. Then he

burns all of his possessions, and there is a curling photograph in the fire that seems to come from a failed marriage. He moves to Las Vegas with the intention of using his severance to drink himself to death.

Cage's performance in these early scenes is an acutely observed record of a man going to pieces. He shows Ben imploding, rigid in his attempt to maintain control, to smile when he does not feel a smile, to make banter when he wants to scream. He *needs* a drink. During the movie, Cage will take Ben into the regions of hell. There will be times when he has the DTs, times when he must pour booze into his throat like an antidote to death, times of nausea, blackouts, cuts, and bruises. There is a scene in a bank when his hands shake so badly he cannot sign a check, and we empathize with the way he tries to function, telling the bank teller whatever he can think of ("I've had brain surgery"). Yes, sometimes he feels better, and sometimes we can sense the charm he must have had (we sense his boss's affection for him even as he's being fired). But for Ben these moments are not about pleasure but about the temporary release from pain.

Sera is seen in three ways: as Ben sees her, as her pimp and her clients see her, and as she sees herself in close-up monologues during therapy sessions. Her pimp (Julian Sands) is soon off the scene; it is bold of Figgis to establish him, to show his sadomasochistic control of Sera, and then to make him disappear. We need to know where Sera is coming from, but we don't need to linger there. For Ben, who almost runs her down in a crosswalk, she is literally the last person in his life he will be able to focus on. He loves her with the purity of a love that has no components except need and gratitude. He doesn't want to have sex with her, doesn't want her for companionship, isn't looking for an "experience." He is simply touched, somewhere inside his suffering where nothing else can reach, that this woman would care for him.

Why does Sera love Ben? The movie leaves that for us to intuit, and the therapy sessions do not explain her feelings; they only show her trying to discover them. There is an early monologue where she boasts about her skill as a hooker, how she can sense exactly what a client wants, and provide it. That is how she wants to see herself. We also see that her pimp cuts her ("never on the face"), and we witness a night when she goes into a motel room with four drunken high-school athletes, and this is so unwise that we read it as deliberately self-destructive. Sera still has her looks, but she once had innocence and hope, and they are gone. When she looks at Ben, she feels sympathy and empathy, but more than that, I think, she feels admiration for the purity of his gesture: Having arrived at the end of his road, he accepts his destiny with a certain stoic courage.

Of course, he could be saved. Alcoholics Anonymous meetings are filled with healthy, functioning people who were once living Ben's life. But most drunks are not lucky enough to find sobriety. And in Ben's case, there may be another component; he is actively committing suicide. "Is drinking a way of killing yourself?" Sera asks him, and he replies, "Or, is killing myself a way of drinking?"

Sera senses she cannot save him. "You can never, ever, ask me to stop drinking," he tells her soon after they meet. "Do you understand?" She says: "I do. I really do." As a hooker in Vegas she has met a lot of sad and desperate men and no doubt a lot of drunks, but there is something about Ben, she tells her therapist, that she can't get out of her mind. Oddly enough, we sense it, too. There are not many terminal drunks we would want to spend a movie with, but we feel tender toward Ben. Of other famous movie alcoholics, Ray Milland's, in *The Lost Weekend,* was a case study, seen from outside, and Albert Finney's, in *Under the Volcano,* lacked Ben's self-knowledge.

The movie was made quickly, inexpensively, close to ground level. Mike Figgis is a British director whose career is a litany of risk taking and original concepts; his boldest experiment was *Timecode* (2000), filmed on video in four unbroken ninety-minute shots, which were simultaneously seen on a screen divided into quadrants. He shot *Leaving Las Vegas* on location, without permits or permissions, using an unobtrusive sixteen-millimeter camera and sometimes sending his actors into real situations. The cinematography, by Declan Quinn, creates a high-contrast noir look, the shadows sometimes invaded by garish neon. The music reinforces it. Figgis wrote the original score, and he also uses the kinds of songs ("Angel Eyes," "Come Rain or Come Shine") drunks punch into the jukebox at three A.M. He repeats some of the songs, which is right: A drinking session can develop its own theme song.

The film was nominated for best actor, actress, director, and screenplay. Cage won, and deserved to. Shue did not win (Susan Sarandon did, for *Dead Man Walking*). It is impossible to imagine one performance without the other, and Shue is the emotional center of the film, because the Cage character is on a set trajectory and beyond the possibility of change. Shue before and since has been in mostly mainstream commercial movies; like Halle Berry with *Monster's Ball* and Charlize Theron with *Monster*, she found a role that took her absolutely to the limit, and went all the way, fearlessly.

The screenplay is by Figgis, based on a novel by John O'Brien, who killed himself at about the time the film went into production. He was thirty-four. His father said the book was his suicide note. The character of Ben is certainly a man who has made his decision and will stay with it; why he kills himself with alcohol, instead of, say, shooting himself in the head as O'Brien did, may have two answers. The first, more pragmatic, is that it allows a story arc to develop, as Sera follows Ben on his final lonely journey. The second, which I feel when I watch the film, is that Ben's guilt, or despair, or self-loathing, are so great that he doesn't want a quick end. He wants to suffer all the way out.

That Sera brings him some comfort does not lessen his pain, and if he truly loved her he would not want to leave her. But perhaps he is too deranged to have such thoughts. "You are my angel," he tells her, not long before the unbearably sad and tender death scene. By then he is much more dead than alive.

{ LE BOUCHER }

She is a schoolmistress, he is a butcher, their everyday lives obscure great loneliness, and their ideas about sex are peculiarly skewed. They should never have met each other. When they do start to spend time together, their relationship seems ordinary and uneventful, but it sets terrible engines at work in the hiding places of their beings. It is clear by the end of the film how this friendship has set loose violent impulses in the butcher—but what many viewers miss is how the schoolmistress is also transformed, in a way no less terrible.

Claude Chabrol's *Le Boucher* (1969) takes place in the tranquil French village of Trémolat. Like almost all of his films, it begins and ends with a shot of a river and includes at least one meal. It seems a pleasant district, if it were not for the ominous stirrings and sudden hard chords on the sound track. It is a movie in which three victims are carved up off-screen, but the only violence visible to us is psychic, and deals with the characters' twists and needs.

There is no great mystery about the identity of the killer; it must be Popaul the butcher, since no other plausible suspects are brought on-screen. We know it, the butcher knows it, and at some point Miss Hélène, the school mistress, certainly knows it. Is it when she finds the cigarette lighter he dropped, or does she begin to suspect even earlier? The movie's suspense involves the haunting dance that the two characters perform around the fact of the butcher's guilt. Will he kill her, too? Does she want to be killed? No, not at all, but perhaps she wants to get teasingly close to being killed; perhaps she is fascinated by the butcher's savagery.

During a class trip to the nearby Lescaux caves and their wall paintings, she speaks approvingly of Cro-Magnon man. His instincts and intelligence were human, she says. A child asks: "What if he came back now, the Cro-Magnon? What would he do?" Miss Hélène replies: "Maybe he would adapt and live among us. Or maybe he would die." Is she thinking of the butcher?

Perhaps even at their first meeting she was fascinated by the danger she sensed in Popaul (Jean Yanne). Miss Hélène (Stéphane Audran) is seated next to him at the wedding of her fellow teacher, and the first thing she sees him do is carve a roast. Notice how avidly she follows the movement of the knife, how eagerly she takes her slice, how she begins to eat before anyone else has been served. And notice too how she seems curiously happy, as if she has found something she was looking for; she is intense and alert to the presence of the butcher.

As the wedding ends and he walks her home to her rooms above the school, Chabrol gives us a remarkable unbroken shot, three minutes and forty-six seconds in duration. They walk through the entire village, past men in cafés and boys at play. She takes out a Gauloise and lights up, and he asks, "You smoke in the street?" She not only smokes, she smokes with an attitude, holding the cigarette in her mouth, Belmondo-style, even while she talks. She is sending a message of female dominance and mystery to Popaul. Later, when he visits her, he sits on a chair that makes him lower than her, like one of her students.

She has been in Tremolat for three years. She has never married; ten years before, she had an unhappy affair and has decided to do without men. He can talk of little but his fifteen years in the French army. He served in Algiers and Indochina, and he hints of the indescribable brutality he witnessed. He brings her a joint of lamb, wrapped in tissue like a bouquet, and they spend time together. News arrives from day to day about bodies found in the woods, and the police are everywhere. On the day of the trip to the caves, Miss Hélène and her students rest on a ledge to eat their lunches, and

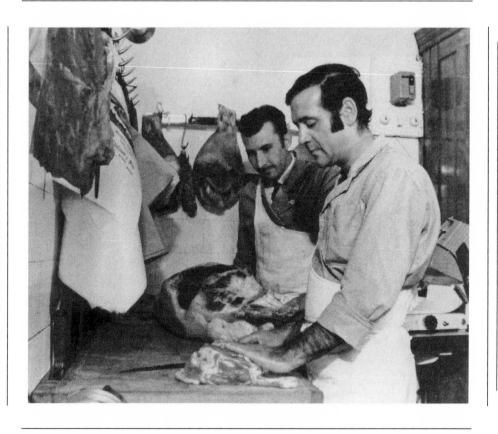

a drop of blood falls on one little girl's bread. It is the blood of the latest victim—the bride in the opening scene.

As she discovers the body, Miss Hélène also finds a distinctive lighter she has given Popaul. We follow her response closely, trying to guess what she's thinking. She puts the lighter in a drawer and tells the police she found no clues. Soon after, Popaul comes over with a jar of cherries marinated in brandy. "They're the best I ever had," she says, before she has eaten one. Our suspense is matched by our curiosity: Does she think she is sitting alone with a killer? Does he wonder if she knows? Eventually she asks for a light. He pulls out a lighter just like the one she gave him. She begins to laugh.

Smoking is a motif in the movie. We never see him smoking until she does. When and why he smokes is always important—in that scene he glances at an ashtray but deliberately doesn't smoke, for example, until she asks for a light and he can produce the lighter. Another motif, Hitchcockian, is her blond hair; we see it many times from behind, once with an ominous push-in, and then at the end of the movie there is a matching push to her face. Another match: On his first and last visits to the school, his face is framed in the same window.

Le Boucher has us always thinking. What do they know, what do they think, what do they want? The film builds to an emotional and physical climax, which I will not describe except to urge you to pay particular attention to a sequence toward the end where Chabrol cuts from her face to his. Popaul's face shows desperate devotion and need. What does her face show? Is it triumph? Pity? Fear? A kind of sexual fulfillment? Interpret that expression and you have the key to her feeling. It sure isn't concern.

Stéphane Audran, who was married to Chabrol from 1964 to 1982, has one of those faces like Deneuve's or Moreau's: The beauty is classic but can be undercut by glimpses of deep and peculiar need. Audran in that last sequence is like Deneuve in *Belle de Jour*, impassive in the face of enormous inner excitement. Audran worked with Chabrol in *The Champagne Murders* (1967), *Les Biches* (1968), and *La Femme Infidèle* (1969), and was in *Les Cousins* (1959), which was one of the founding films of the French New Wave.

Chabrol, born in 1930, was, like Godard and Truffaut, a movie critic writing for *Cahiers du Cinéma,* the voice of the auteur movement. He has outlasted many of his contemporaries and outproduced all of them, making more than fifty films; *Merci pour le Chocolat* (2000) was about a bourgeois family poisoning itself literally and figuratively, and his *La Fleur du Mal* (2003) is about another bourgeois family, rotten to the core. His good or great films make a long list, and include four collaborations with Isabelle Huppert: *Violette Nozière* (1978), *Madame Bovary* (1991), *La Cérémonie* (1995), *Merci pour le Chocolat.* Her face, like Audran's, is capable of maddening passivity—a mask for ominous and alarming thoughts. Both actresses have that rare ability to compel us to wonder what in the hell they are thinking.

Sample the reviews of *Le Boucher* and you'll find it described as a film about a savage murderer and the schoolmistress who doesn't know the danger she's in. This completely misses the point. It's not that the point is hard to find—Chabrol is very clear about his purpose—but that we've been hammered down by so many slack-witted thrillers that we've learned to assume that the killer is the villain and the woman is the victim.

Popaul is a killer, all right, but is he also a victim? Was he traumatized by the army, by blood and meat? Is he driven to kill because Miss Helene, whom he idolizes beyond all measuring, remains cool and distant—tantalizingly unavailable? Some think that Chabrol even blames Miss Hélène for the crimes; if she'd only slept with Popaul, his savage impulse would have been diverted. But it's not that simple. First, he is attracted to her *because* she is unavailable, and it's her butchy walk through the village, smoking that cigarette, that seals his fate. Second, since (as I believe) she is excited in a perverse, obscure way by the danger he represents, does he sense that? Are his killings in some measure offerings, as a cat will lay a bird at the feet of its owner?

So much goes unsaid between these two people. So much is guessed or hinted at. They're a pair, all right, and she senses it at the wedding feast. They don't fit, in any ordinary romantic or matrimonial way, but what happens in this movie happens because of them as a couple. If you bring enough empathy to her character, you can read that final scene more deeply. It is a sex scene. They don't touch, but then they never did.

THE LEOPARD

The Leopard was written by the only man who could have written it, directed by the only man who could have directed it, and stars the only man who could have played its title character. The first of these claims is irrefutable, because Giuseppe Tomasi di Lampedusa, a Sicilian aristocrat, wrote the story out of his own heart and based it on his great-grandfather. Whether another director could have done a better job than Luchino Visconti is doubtful; the director was himself a descendant of the ruling class that the story eulogizes. But that Burt Lancaster was the correct actor to play Don Fabrizio, Prince of Salina, was at the time much doubted; that a Hollywood star had been imported to grace this most European—indeed, Italian—indeed, Sicilian—masterpiece was a scandal.

It was rumored that Lancaster's presence was needed to make the epic production bankable, and when the film finally opened in America, in a version with forty minutes ruthlessly hacked out by the studio, and a sound track unconvincingly dubbed into English, it was hard to see what Visconti and Lancaster had been thinking of. "Unfortunately Mr. Lancaster does have that blunt American voice that lacks the least suggestion of being Sicilian," wrote Bosley Crowther in the New York Times. Visconti himself was savage: "It is now a work for which I acknowledge no paternity at all," he said, adding that Hollywood treated Americans "like a public of children."

"It was my best work," Lancaster himself told me sadly, more than twenty years later. "I bought eleven copies of *The Leopard* because I thought it was a great novel. I gave it to everyone. But when I was asked to play in it, I said, no, that part's for a real Italian. But, lo, the wheels of fortune turned. They wanted a Russian, but he was too old. They wanted Olivier, but he was too busy. When I was suggested, Visconti said, 'Oh, no! A cowboy!' But I had just finished *Judgment at Nuremberg*, which he saw, and he needed three million dollars, which Twentieth Century–Fox would give them if they used an American star, and so the inevitable occurred. And it turned out to be a wonderful marriage."

When we talked, the original film—uncut, undubbed—had scarcely been seen since the time of its European release. But in 1980, four years after Visconti's death, the cinematographer Giuseppe Rotunno supervised a restoration; at 185 minutes his version is still shorter than the original 205 minutes, but it is the best we are ever likely to see, and it is magnificent.

What's clear at last is that Lancaster was an inspired casting decision. An actor who always brought a certain formality to his work, who made his own way as an independent before that was fashionable, he embodies the Prince as a man who has a great love for a way of life he understands must come to an end. He is a natural patriarch, a man born to have authority. Yet as we meet him he is aware of his age and mortality, inclined to have spiritual conversations with his friend Father Pirrone, and prepared to compromise in order to preserve his family's fortunes.

We see him first leading his family at prayer. That is also the way Lampedusa's novel begins, and one of Visconti's achievements is to make that rare thing, a great film of a great book. Word comes that there is a dead soldier in the garden. This means that Garibaldi's revolution has jumped from the mainland to Sicily, and the days of the ancient order are numbered.

The Prince has a wife named Maria Stella, whom he dutifully honors more for her position than her person, three daughters of only moderate loveliness, and a feckless son. He looks to his nephew Tancredi (Alain Delon) to embody the family's noble genes. Tancredi is a hothead who leaves to join Garibaldi, but also a realist who returns as a member of the army of the victorious Victor Emmanuel.

Because of land reforms, which he can clearly see on the horizon, the Prince believes it is time for the family to make an advantageous marriage. He moves every year with his household from the city to the countryside to wait out the slow, hot summer months, and in the small town of Donnafugata, he is welcomed as usual by the mayor, a buffoon named Don Calogero (Paolo Stoppa). This mayor has suddenly become rich through lucky land investments, and he feels wealth has given him importance—an illusion the Prince is willing to indulge, if it can lead to a liaison between the mayor's money and the Prince's family.

He invites the mayor to dinner, in a scene of subdued social comedy in which Visconti observes, without making too much of a point of it, how gauche the mayor is and how pained the Prince is to have to give dinner to such a man. The mayor has brought with him not his unpresentable wife but his beautiful daughter Angelica, played by Claudia Cardinale at the height of her extraordinary beauty. Tancredi is moonstruck, and the Prince swallows his misgivings as arrangements go ahead with the marriage.

All of this would be the stuff of soap opera in other hands, but Lampedusa's novel sees the Prince so sympathetically that we share his regrets for a fading way of life. We might believe ideologically that the aristocracy exploits the working class (Visconti was a Marxist who believed just that), but the Prince himself is such a proud and good man, so aware of his mortality, so respectful of tradition and continuity, that as he compromises his family in order to save it, we share his remorse.

There is another factor at work. The Prince is an alpha male, born to conquer, aware of female beauty if also obedient to the morality of his church. He finds Angelica as attractive as his nephew does. But Lancaster doesn't communicate this with soulful speeches or whispered insinuations; he does it all with eyes, and the attitude of a head, and those subtle adjustments in body language that suggest the desired person exerts a kind of animal magnetism that must be resisted. Observe how Lancaster has the Prince almost lean away from Angelica, as if in response to her pull. He is too old at forty-five (which was old in the 1860s) and too traditional to reveal his feelings, but a woman can always tell, even though she must seem as if she cannot.

The film ends with a ballroom sequence lasting forty-five minutes.

"This is a set piece that has rarely been equaled," writes the critic Derek Malcolm, and Dave Kehr called it "one of the most moving meditations on individual mortality in the history of the cinema." Visconti, Lancaster, and Rotunno collaborate to resolve all of the themes of the movie in this long sequence in which almost none of the dialogue involves what is really happening. The ball is a last glorious celebration of the dying age; Visconti cast members of noble old Sicilian families as the guests, and in their faces we see a history that cannot be acted, only embodied. The orchestra plays Verdi. The young people dance on and on, and the older people watch carefully and gauge the futures market in romances and liaisons.

Through this gaiety the Prince moves like a shadow. The camera follows him from room to room, suggesting his thoughts, his desires, his sadness. Visconti, confident that Lancaster can suggest all of the shading of the Prince's feelings, extends the scene until we are drawn fully into it. He creates one of those sequences for which we go to the movies: We have grown to know the Prince's personality and his ideas, and now we enter, almost unaware, into his emotions. The cinema at its best can give us the illusion of living another life, and that's what happens here.

Finally the Prince dances with Angelica. Watch them as they dance, each aware of the other in a way simultaneously sexual and political. Watch how they hold their heads. How they look without seeing. How they are seen, and know they are seen. And sense that, for the Prince, his dance is an acknowledgment of mortality. He could have had this woman, would have known what to do with her, would have made her his wife and the mother of his children and heard her cries of passion, if not for the accident of twenty-five years or so that slipped in between them. But he knows that, and she knows that. And yet of course if they were the same age he would not have married her, because he is Prince Don Fabrizio and she is the mayor's daughter. That Visconti is able to convey all of that in a ballroom scene is miraculous and emotionally devastating, and it is what his movie is about.

THE LIFE AND DEATH OF COLONEL BLIMP

One of the many miracles of *The Life and Death of Colonel Blimp* is the way the movie transforms a blustering, pigheaded caricature into one of the most loved of all movie characters. Colonel Blimp began life in a series of famous British cartoons by David Low, who represented him as an overstuffed blowhard. The movie looks past the fat, bald military man with the walrus mustache and sees inside, to an idealist and a romantic. To know him is to love him.

Made in 1942 at the height of the Nazi threat to Great Britain, Michael Powell and Emeric Pressburger's work is an uncommonly civilized film about war and soldiers—and, rarer still, a film that defends the old against the young. Its hero is a blustering old windbag, Clive Wynne-Candy, a warhorse of the army since the Boer War, now twice retired from regular duty and relegated to leading the Home Guard.

As the film opens, the general has ordered military training exercises and announced, "War starts at midnight." A gung-ho young lieutenant decides that modern warfare doesn't play by the rules and jumps the gun, leading his men into the general's London club and arresting him in the steam room. When Wynne-Candy bellows, "You bloody young fool—war starts at midnight!" the lieutenant observes that the Nazis do not observe gentlemen's agreements, and insults the old man's belly and mustache.

Wynne-Candy is outraged. "You laugh at my big belly but you don't know how I got it! You laugh at my mustache but you don't know why I grew it!" He punches the young lieutenant, wrestles him into a swimming pool—and then, in a flashback of grace and wit, the camera pans along the surface of the water until, at the other end, young Clive Candy emerges. He is thin and without a mustache, and it is 1902.

The Life and Death of Colonel Blimp has four story threads. It mourns the passing of a time when professional soldiers observed a code of honor. It argues to the young that the old were young once, too, and contain within them all that the young know, and more. It marks the general's lonely romantic passage through life, in which he seeks the double of the first woman he loved. And it records a friendship between a British officer and a German officer, which spans the crucial years from 1902 to 1942.

This is an audacious enough story idea to begin with, but even more daring in 1942, when London was bombed nightly and the Nazis seemed to be winning the war. Powell at first wanted Laurence Olivier to play his title role, but the screenplay ran into fierce opposition from Winston Churchill, and the Ministry of War refused to release Olivier from military duty. Then Powell cast Roger Livesey, a young actor who had worked for him before, and as the German officer, an émigré Austrian actor named Anton Walbrook.

That led to an encounter between Churchill and Walbrook, recounted by the British film critic Derek Malcolm: "Churchill's reaction was furious. He is said to have stormed into Walbrook's dressing room when he was appearing in a West End play demanding: 'What's this film supposed to mean? I suppose you regard it as good propaganda for Britain.' Anton's reply was quite telling, he said, 'No people in the world other than the English would have had the courage, in the midst of war, to tell the people such unvarnished truth.' "

Ah, but he praised his adopted homeland too soon. Churchill continued to resist. Powell could not borrow gear and trucks from the army, "so," he says, "we stole them." The film was at first banned, then reluctantly released in a shorter version, and in the United States it lost fifty minutes of its 163-minute running time; the entire flashback structure was replaced by a chronological story line. Only in 1983 was the film finally restored, and

hailed as a masterpiece. "It stands," wrote the critic Dave Kehr, "as very possibly the finest film ever made in Britain."

The Life and Death of Colonel Blimp is a film of balance and insight—a civilized film that even in a time of war celebrates civilized values. What it regrets is the loss, in two world wars, of the sense of decency and fair play that had governed the European military classes. Near the film's end, the German refugee corrects the sentimentalism of the old general, telling him from firsthand experience that Nazism is the greatest evil the world has ever known, and saying there is no point in playing fair when the enemy plays foul if that means you lose and evil wins.

Despite this sober undercurrent, *Colonel Blimp* is above all a comedy of manners, and Powell and his writing and producing partner Pressburger conduct it with style and humor. Jolly music underlines an opening sequence in which motorcycle messengers distribute news of the war games, and there is wit in the movie's ingenious flashbacks and flashforwards. Photographed by Georges Périnal with help from Jack Cardiff, the movie is one of the best-looking Technicolor productions ever made, its palette controlled to make wise use of bright contrasts in a world of subdued harmony.

Several scenes surprise us by how they pay off. Note the early duel between the British and German officers (they do not even know each other; the German was drawn by lot to respond to an insult to the German army). A high-angle shot refuses to take sides, the Swedish referee scuttles back and forth like a crab—and then, just when we expect to see the outcome, the camera cranes up to an exterior shot of the army gymnasium (a model), with snow falling on Berlin. The message is made visually: The season of traditional values is ending, and these soldiers will not again play so fair.

In the hospital, Clive Candy and his opponent, Theo Kretschmar-Schuldorff, are visited by Candy's British friend, Edith Hunter (Deborah Kerr). The German falls in love with her and proposes marriage. Candy is at first delighted, but as he returns home he realizes he loved her, too, and begins a lifelong search for a substitute. Fifteen years later, in a World War I hospital, he sees a young nurse who is Edith's spitting image, and arranges a dance for war nurses just to meet her again. This is Barbara Wynne, again played by Deborah Kerr. Note the dinner scene when Candy explains his motive for seeking her out, and the subtle chill with which Barbara says she quite understands. The marriage fades out like the duel did, as if there is nothing else worth saying. Kerr appears a third time as a working-class girl named Angela Cannon, who is Wynne-Candy's driver during the Second World War. It is a remarkable performance by the twenty-year-old new-comer, playing three roles; Wendy Hiller was originally cast, but became pregnant, and Powell cast Kerr both because he thought "she would be a star one day" and because he was falling in love with her.

The friendship between Clive and Theo is traced for forty years. They meet again at a German prisoners' camp in England, after World War I; Theo ignores Clive and stalks away, but the next day he calls to apol-ogize, and is a guest at a dinner of British establishment types at which, gentlemen all, they assure him his homeland will be rebuilt: "Europe needs a healthy Germany!" When the two men meet again, it is after the German has fled his homeland in 1939. In a long speech all done in one take, Theo explains why he has chosen England over his birthplace. Walbrook's acting here is sublime with its mastery of tone and mood, and this speech, more than any other, explains why Churchill was wrong to oppose the film.

The most poignant passages involve the general growing older. He looks like a caricature to younger officers, with his beefy face, pink complex-ion, mustache (grown to hide the dueling scar), and raspy voice. But in his heart he is still young, still in love, still idealistic. At the end of the movie he looks at a pool of water in the basement of his bombed-out house and is reminded of a lake across which he once pledged love. He insists to himself that it is the same lake, and he is the same man. Rarely does a film give us such a nuanced view of the whole span of a man's life. It is said that the child is father to the man. *Colonel Blimp* makes poetry out of what the old know but the young do not guess: The man contains both the father and the child.

THE MANCHURIAN CANDIDATE

The phrase "the Manchurian candidate" has entered everyday speech as shorthand for a brainwashed sleeper, a subject who has been hypnotized and instructed to act when his controllers pull the psychological trigger. In the movie, an American patrol is captured by Chinese Communists during the Korean War, and one soldier is programmed to become an assassin; two years later, he's ordered to kill a presidential candidate. That such programming is impossible has not prevented it from being absorbed as fact; this movie, released in 1962, has influenced American history by forever coloring speculation about Lee Harvey Oswald. Would the speculation about Oswald's background and motive have been as fevered without the film as a template?

The film has become so strongly linked with the Kennedy assassination that a legend has grown up around it. Frank Sinatra purchased the rights and kept it out of release from 1964 until 1988, and the story goes that he was inspired by remorse after Kennedy's death. In fact, the director John Frankenheimer told me, Sinatra had a dispute with United Artists about the profits, and decided it would earn no money for the studio or anyone else. The DVD includes a conversation among Sinatra, Frankenheimer, and writer George Axelrod, taped when the movie was finally re-released. Sinatra says it was the high point of his acting career; nobody mentions why it was unseen for twenty-four years.

Seen today, *The Manchurian Candidate* (1962) feels astonishingly contemporary; its astringent political satire still bites, and its story has uncanny contemporary echoes. The villains plan to exploit a terrorist act, "rallying a nation of viewers to hysteria, to sweep us up into the White House with powers that will make martial law seem like anarchy." The plot cheerfully divides blame between right and left; it provides a right-wing demagogue named Senator Iselin, who is clearly modeled on Senator Joseph McCarthy, and makes him the puppet of his draconian wife, who is in league with foreign Communists. The plan, which the senator hardly suspects, is to use anti-Communist hysteria as a cover for a Communist takeover.

The movie was based on the 1959 novel by Richard Condon, who must have been astonished that it became a film with big stars like Sinatra, Angela Lansbury, and Laurence Harvey—and still more astonished that Frankenheimer and Axelrod did not soften its wicked satire. Frankenheimer says on the commentary track that he is proudest that the film hammered McCarthyism; there's a scene where the hard-drinking Senator Iselin can't decide how many Communists he thinks are in the State Department and settles on fifty-seven after studying a ketchup bottle.

Frankenheimer (1930–2002) was a tall man, movie-star handsome, who told hilarious stories about his adventures as a boy wonder in the days of live network television. He used his TV experience to give *The Manchurian Candidate* a quick-moving, hard-edged urgency. Filming in black and white, incorporating inside details about political campaigns and journalism, he sweeps the story along with such conviction that its implausibility is concealed.

The film trusts its viewers to follow its twisting, surrealistic plot, especially in the way fragmented memories of the Korean brainwashing leak into the nightmares of the survivors of that patrol. A flashback shows us what happened: After being hypnotized by their Chinese captors, they think they're attending a meeting of a garden club in a New Jersey hotel, while we see their Communist hypnotist lecturing a room of other party officials. To show how strong the programming is, he orders Staff Sergeant Raymond Shaw (Harvey) to strangle one of the Americans and shoot another; the film's point of view cuts freely between the different versions of reality.

Back in the United States, Raymond is given the Medal of Honor and greeted by his smothering mother (Angela Lansbury) and her second husband, the weak, alcoholic Senator Iselin (James Gregory). It's a running gag in the film that Raymond is constantly referred to as the senator's son and keeps repeating, "I am not his son." Mrs. Iselin has incestuous feelings for Raymond, which in the novel lead them to bed but in the movie are revealed through a famous full-lip kiss. Raymond hates her, hates himself, and has a bitter speech about how he is not lovable.

Sinatra plays Major Bennett Marco, another member of the Korean patrol, whose fragmented nightmares lead him to suspect the brainwashing. He leads an army investigation that determines that Raymond may have been programmed as an assassin—but Marco crucially fails to bring him in for questioning, believing that Raymond's fledgling romance with Jocelyn Jordan (Leslie Parrish), daughter of a senator, may cure him. The climax plays out inside Madison Square Garden, where Mrs. Iselin has ordered her son to shoot her party's presidential candidate during his acceptance speech; Senator Iselin, the vice presidential candidate, will catch and cradle his falling body and then, she says, deliver "the most rousing speech I've ever read. It's been worked on, here and in Russia, on and off, for over eight years."

The film moves freely between realism and surrealism. Frankenheimer shows Iselin at a press conference and Senate hearing, with details lifted directly from the Army-McCarthy hearings; as Iselin waves a list of "card-carrying Communists," TV sets in the foreground show the same scene being carried on the news. Yet other scenes are from Raymond's disturbed point of view, especially when his hypnotic trigger (the queen of diamonds) appears in a solitaire game. There's a scene where Sinatra's character holds up a deck full of queens while trying to deprogram Raymond; it's a little out of focus, and Frankenheimer confesses on the commentary track that although Sinatra supplied several other takes, they weren't as good—so he went with the flawed one, only to be praised for the unfocused shot showing Raymond's disturbed perceptions.

Angela Lansbury's Mrs. Iselin, nominated for an Academy Award, is one of the great villains of movie history. Fierce, focused, contemptuous of the husband she treats like a puppet, she has, we gather, plotted with the Russians and Chinese to use the Red scare fomented by "Iselinism" to get him into office—where she will run things from behind the scenes. But it comes as a shock to her that her own son has been programmed as the assassin. It so enrages her that, in another turn of the corkscrew plot, she tells him, "When I take power, they will be pulled down and ground into dirt for what they did to you. And what they did in so contemptuously underestimating me." So let's get this straight: She plans to have her son assassinate a presidential candidate so that her husband can become president, and she can then use his power to grind down the people who worked with her on this plan in the first place. Do not look for logic here.

Frankenheimer uses a heightened visual style to underline the Byzantine complexity of his story. There are tilt shots, odd angles, and the use of deep focus for his favorite composition, in which a face is seen in close-up in the foreground while action takes place behind it in the middle distance. This look is matched by Axelrod's dialogue, which often jumps the tracks of reality. Consider the peculiar first meeting between the Sinatra character and Rosie (Janet Leigh), who will become his wife. He's so shaky on a train that he can't light a cigarette. She follows him to the platform between cars, lights his cigarette, and then says, "Maryland's a beautiful state." "This is Delaware," Sinatra says, and she replies: "I know. I was one of the original Chinese workmen who laid the track on this stretch. But nonetheless, Maryland is a beautiful state. So is Ohio, for that matter."

Soon she has broken off an engagement and married Sinatra, leaving us to wonder what in the hell that dialogue was about. Was it in code? Was Sinatra hallucinating? It seems strange that the Chinese brainwashed the entire patrol but needed only Raymond as an assassin. Why, then, spare the others, with their nightmares and suspicions? Is Sinatra's Major Marco another Manchurian sleeper, and is Rosie his controller? If you look at their scenes carefully you find that she broke off her engagement immediately after their awkward train meeting and before their first date. Reflect on the scene where she talks about Sinatra beating up "a very large Korean gentleman," and ask yourself what she means when she calls this man, whom she has never seen, "the general." I don't know. Maybe Rosie just talks funny. It would be a nice touch, though, for this screwball story to have another layer circling beneath.

The Manchurian Candidate is inventive and frisky, takes enormous chances with the audience, and plays not like a "classic" but like a work as alive and smart as when it was first released. "It may be," Pauline Kael wrote at the time, "the most sophisticated satire ever made in Hollywood." Yes, because it satirizes no particular target—left, right, foreign, domestic—but the very notion that politics can be taken at face value.

{ THE MAN WHO LAUGHS }

Movie villains smile so compulsively because it creates a creepy disconnect between their mouth and their eyes. Imagine, however, a good man, condemned to smile widely for an entire lifetime. Such a creature would be bullied as a child and shunned as an adult. *The Man Who Laughs* (1928), one of the final treasures of German silent expressionism, is about such a man.

His name is Gwynplaine. His father was a nobleman. Orphaned as a child, he is captured by outlaws who use a knife to carve his face into a hideous grin. Disfigured, alone, he rescues a baby girl, and together they are raised by a fatherly vaudeville producer. As adults, they star in the producer's sideshow and fall in love. Because she is blind, she does not know about his grin.

This story, set in seventeenth-century England, was written by Victor Hugo and made into one of the last (almost) silent films by Paul Leni, the director of *Waxworks* (1924) and *The Cat and the Canary* (1927). He was an art director who grew up in Germany during the era of expressionism—of films dominated by twisted sets and characters, harsh angles, deep shadows, careening staircases. He and his star, the great Conrad Veidt, two early refugees from Hitler, made the film for Universal in Hollywood.

The image of Veidt's face, with its disturbing grimace, became familiar to anyone who opened a film history, but the film itself was hard to find; I saw it for the first time at the Telluride Film Festival in 1998, where

Peter Bogdanovich programmed a series entitled Hollywood's Greatest Year. That was 1928, he said, when they had gotten silent films right and had not yet started to get sound films wrong. It was filmed just at the moment when Hollywood was uneasily experimenting with sound. Like many other films from the same year, it was conceived in silence, and then a little sound was grafted on. The movie has no significant spoken dialogue but does have rudimentary sound effects, and the Kino DVD restoration includes a musical score, a song, and some indistinct shouts during a mob scene.

The Man Who Laughs is a melodrama, at times even a swashbuckler, but so steeped in expressionist gloom that it plays like a horror film. Everything centers on the extraordinary face of Gwynplaine, whose wide and mirthless grin inspired the Joker character in the original Batman comic books. Unlike the Joker and most villains who smile, however, he is a good and decent man, one so horribly aware of his disfigurement that he reveals it only on the stage, as a way to earn a living. The rest of the time he hides behind masks, scarves, handkerchiefs, or his own upturned arm. The blind girl, Dea (Mary Philbin), loves him, but he thinks that is only because she does not know his secret.

The buried story here is similar to Victor Hugo's far better known novel The Hunchback of Notre Dame, which also has a grotesque loner in love with an innocent girl. Universal had a great success with that 1923 film, and with The Phantom of the Opera (1925), which also starred Mary Philbin as the woman in the arms of a disfigured hero; no doubt the studio had those films in mind when it went ahead with this one. Another connection was through the executive producer, Paul Kohner, who at one time ran Universal's operation in Berlin (barely escaping the Nazis), and knew Leni and Veidt in Germany.

Veidt's performance is far more than a stunt. Best known to modern audiences for his portrayal of the erect, unsmiling Major Strasser in Casablanca, he appeared in more than one hundred films, including the German silent landmark The Cabinet of Dr. Caligari. He was one of a group of German refugees who might have made a great impact on Hollywood, had they lived. He died of a heart attack at fifty, a year after Casablanca was released. Leni died at forty-four, a year after The Man Who Laughs, and

F. W. Murnau, director of *Nosferatu* and *Sunrise,* was dead in 1931, at forty-three.

Veidt wore a makeup device that distended his mouth while supplying grotesque teeth. It was horribly uncomfortable, making it even harder for him to project emotions only with his eyes. And yet there are scenes where we sense love, fear, pity, and lust, and an extraordinary scene (bold for the time) in which a shameless royal woman, the Duchess Josiana, attempts to seduce him. (In a note after a sideshow performance, she writes him, "I am she who did not laugh. Was it pity, or was it love? My page will meet you at midnight.")

Her interest is genuine, if perverse, although she has no idea where it will lead. He is tempted. In a way, he wants sex, which he has never experienced, and in another way he wants to remain loyal to Dea—and yet he will never have intimacy with Dea until he reveals his secret, and he fears she could not love him after learning it. His scene with the duchess has a disturbing power because as he (no doubt) thinks of these things, Josiana attempts to kiss him, and we sense that her attraction to his mouth is cruel or fetishistic. He does not want to be kissed—or touched, or known—there.

Oh, but the plot is much more complicated. Gwynplaine is, in fact, the rightful heir to a royal title and a stately home and lands that, inevitably, are now being enjoyed by Josiana. This is known to a jealous courtier, who wants to humiliate her by forcing her to marry Gwynplaine in order to remain a duchess. In a scene both pitiful and bizarre, the sideshow performer is brought to the court of Queen Anne, inducted into the House of Lords, and then ordered to marry Josiana. She agrees out of greed and, probably, fascination; he resists because he loves Dea—and then the film grows truly melodramatic, with the intervention of a faithful wolf-dog named Homo, who grabs at Dea's dress and literally drags her into the action.

The film is more disturbing than it might have been because of Leni's mastery of visual style. In *The Haunted Screen,* her history of the German silent period, Lotte Eisner notes that the Expressionists often used unusually low ceilings and doorways in order to force their characters to walk stooped over or sideways. Their staircases rarely climbed frankly from floor to floor, but seemed to twist away into mystery. Dramatic lighting left much of the screen in darkness. Concealment and enhancement, not revelation, was the assignment of the camera. Eisner quotes Leni on the visual style of his *Waxworks,* made four years before *The Man Who Laughs*: "All it seeks to engender is an indescribable fluidity of light, moving shapes, shadows, lines, and curves. It is not extreme reality that the camera perceives, but the reality of the inner event."

A film like *The Man Who Laughs* is, of course, so alien to modern moviegoers that it may repel those who can't accept it, while at the same time creating an eerie netherworld fascination for those who can. I find that sound pictures usually inspire a certain comfort level in the way they mirror, if not life, then the way life is perceived most of the time. Silent films, like black-and-white films, add by subtracting. What they do not have enhances what is there, by focusing on it and making it do more work. When images cannot be discussed, they must explain themselves; when no colors are visible, all colors are potential.

Watching the film again last night, I fell into a reverie, sometimes moved, sometimes amused, sometimes involved in a strange dreamlike way. By not alerting us with the logic of language, silent films can more easily slip us off into the shadows of fantasy. Remarkable, how a film like *The Man Who Laughs* refuses to declare its intentions but freely moves from pathos to pity, from melodrama to true excitement, from cheerful horror elements to the dark stirrings of Josiana's desire, from easy laughter when the wolf-dog saves the day to—well, to something very moving when the blind girl realizes the nature of her lover's secret.

{ MEAN STREETS }

Martin Scorsese's *Mean Streets* is not primarily about punk gangsters at all, but about living in a state of sin. For Catholics raised before Vatican II, it has a resonance that it may lack for other audiences. The film recalls days when there was a greater emphasis on sin—and rigid ground rules, inspiring dread of eternal suffering if a sinner died without absolution.

The key words in the movie are the first ones, spoken over a black screen: "You don't make up for your sins in church. You do it in the streets. You do it at home. All the rest is bullshit and you know it." The voice belongs to Scorsese. We see Charlie (Harvey Keitel) starting up in bed, awakened by a dream, and peering at his face in a bedroom mirror. The voice is Scorsese's, but it possibly represents words said to Charlie by a priest. Later Charlie talks in a voice-over about how a priest gave him the usual "ten Hail Marys and ten Our Fathers," but he preferred a more personal penance. In the most famous shot in the film, he holds his hand in the flame of a votive candle before the altar, testing himself against the fires of hell.

"The clearest fact about Charlie," Pauline Kael wrote in her influential review launching the film, "is that whatever he does in his life, he's a sinner." The film uses lighting to suggest his slanted moral view. The real world is shot in ordinary colors, but then Charlie descends into the bar run by his friend Tony, and it is always bathed in red, the color of sex, blood, and guilt.

He enters the bar in a series of shots at varying levels of slow motion (a Scorsese trademark). He walks past his friends, exchanging ritual greetings, and eventually he gets up on the stage with the black stripper and dances with her for a few bars of rock and roll. He fantasizes about the stripper (Jeannie Bell), and later in the movie even makes a date with her (but, fearing being seen by his friends with a black woman, stands her up). He also dreams of his friend Johnny Boy's cousin, Teresa (Amy Robinson). They have sex, but when she says she loves him, he says, "Don't say that."

For him both women—and any woman he feels lust for—represent a possible occasion of sin, which invests them with such mystery and power that sex pales by comparison. (Immediately after dancing with the stripper, he goes to the bar, lights a match, and holds his finger above it—instant penance.)

Charlie walks through the movie seeking forgiveness—from his Uncle Giovanni (Cesare Danova), who is the local Mafia boss, from Teresa, from his best friend, Johnny Boy (Robert De Niro), from the local loan shark Michael (Richard Romanus), and even from God. He wants redemption. Scorsese, whose screenplay has autobiographical origins, understands why Charlie feels this way: He knows in his bones that the Church is right and he is wrong and weak. Although he is an apprentice gangster involved with men who steal, kill, and sell drugs, Charlie's guilt centers on sex. Impurity is the real sin; the other stuff is business.

The film watches Charlie as he uneasily tries to reconcile his various worlds. He works as a collector for Giovanni, hearing the sad story of a restaurant owner who has no money. Charlie is being groomed to run the restaurant, but he must obey Giovanni, who forbids him to associate with Johnny Boy ("Honorable men go with honorable men") and with Teresa, whose epilepsy is equated in Giovanni's mind with madness.

Trouble is brewing because Johnny Boy owes money to Michael, who is growing increasingly unhappy about his inability to collect. De Niro plays Johnny almost as a holy fool: a smiling jokester with no sense of time or money, and a streak of self-destruction. The first time we see him in the film, he blows up a corner mailbox. Why? No reason. De Niro and Keitel have a scene in the bar's back room that displays the rapport these two actors would carry through many movies. Charlie is earnest, frightened,

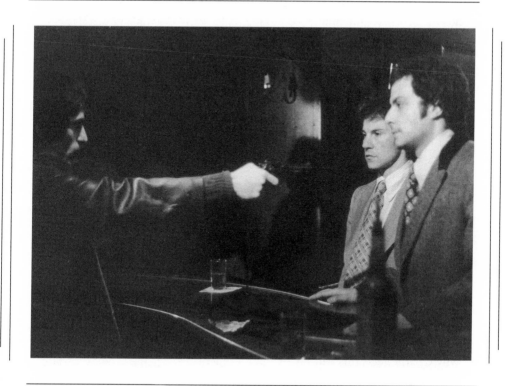

telling Johnny he has to pay the money. Johnny launches into a rambling, improvised cock-and-bull story about a poker game, a police raid, a fight—finally even losing the thread himself.

Scorsese first displayed his distinctive style in his first feature, *Who's That Knocking at My Door?* (1967), which was also set in Little Italy and also starred Keitel. In both films he uses a handheld camera for scenes of quick movement and fights, and scores everything with period rock-and-roll music (a familiar tactic now, but unheard of in 1967). The style is displayed joyously in *Mean Streets* as Charlie and friends go to collect from a pool hall owner, who is happy to pay. But then Johnny Boy is called a "mook," and although nobody seems quite sure what a mook is, that leads to a wild, disorganized fight. These are not smooth stuntmen, slamming each other in choreographed action, but uncoordinated kids in their twenties who smoke too much, drink too much, and fight as if they don't want to get their shirts torn. The camera pursues them around the room, and Johnny Boy leaps onto a pool table, awkwardly practicing the karate kicks he's learned in Forty-second Street grind houses; on the sound track is "Please Mr. Postman," by the Marvelettes. Scorsese's timing is acute: Cops barge in to break up the fight, are paid off by the pool hall owner, leave, and then another tussle breaks out.

Underlying everything is Charlie's desperation. He loves Johnny and Teresa but is forbidden to see them. Although he tries to be tough with Teresa, he lacks the heart. His tenderness toward Johnny Boy is shown in body language (hair tousling, backslapping) and in a scene where Johnny is on the roof, "shooting out the light in the Empire State Building." Charlie essentially feels bad about everything he does; his self-hatred colors every waking thought.

At one point, late in the film, he goes into the bar, orders a Scotch, and holds his fingers over the glass as the bartender pours, copying the position of the priest's fingers over the chalice. That kind of sacramental detail would also be a motif in *Taxi Driver,* where overhead shots mirror the priest's-eye view of the altar, and the hero also places his hand in a flame. Everything leads, as it must, to the violent conclusion, in which Michael, the loan shark who feels insulted, drives while a gunman (Scorsese) fires in revenge. Who can be surprised that Charlie, after the shooting, is on his knees?

Mean Streets is a little creaky at times; this is an early film by a director who was still learning, and who learned so fast that by 1976 he would be ready to make *Taxi Driver,* one of the greatest films of all time, also with De Niro and Keitel. The movie doesn't have the headlong flow, the unspoken confidence in every choice, that became a Scorsese hallmark. It was made on a tiny budget with actors still finding their way, and most of it wasn't even shot on the mean streets of the title but in disguised Los Angeles locations. But it has an elemental power, a sense of spiraling doom, that a more polished film might have lacked.

And in the way it sees and hears its characters, who are based on the people Scorsese knew and grew up with in Little Italy, it was an astonishingly influential film. If Coppola's *The Godfather* fixed an image of the Mafia as a shadow government, Scorsese's *Mean Streets* inspired the other main line in modern gangster movies, the film of everyday reality. *The Godfather* was about careers. *Mean Streets* was about jobs. In it you can find the origins of all those other films about the criminal working class, like *King of the Gypsies, Goodfellas, City of Industry, Sleepers, State of Grace, Federal Hill, Gridlock'd,* and *Donnie Brasco.* Great films leave their mark not only on their audiences but on films that follow. In countless ways, right down to the details of modern TV crime shows, *Mean Streets* is one of the source points of modern movies.

{ MON ONCLE }

Jacques Tati is the great philosophical tinkerer of comedy, taking meticulous care to arrange his films so that they unfold in a series of revelations and effortless delights. Consider a shot early in *Mon Oncle,* where the camera regards the outside of the building where Tati's character, Hulot, lives in a room on the roof. It seems at first to be two buildings, side by side, and Hulot enters the ground floor of one of them. But then, as he climbs upstairs, his body or legs or head or shoes are glimpsed through a series of windows, doors, and passageways, revealing that the two buildings are linked. When he finally arrives at the top, he disappears, only to emerge not where we expect him to but at the other side of the screen.

There is more. Opening a window, he hears a canary sing. Adjusting the window slightly, he hears it stop. Opening it again, he hears the song. It seems that the window itself is singing, until he realizes that it reflects sunshine onto the cage of his neighbor's canary. He adjusts the pane to provide the neighborhood with song. Later, another visual smile: Again watching from the outside of the building, we see a woman in a negligee start up the stairs as Hulot starts down; as they pass, he pauses, and we can see only his shoes—pointing toward us, to indicate that he has politely turned his back.

These are not the kinds of sight gags that would inspire envy in Jim Carrey. They tickle us with their quiet bemusement; they involve us in a

conspiracy with Tati to discover serendipity in a world of disappointment. That's especially the case with *Mon Oncle* (1958), which places Hulot in a gimmicky 1950s society of garish materialism. In Tati's great earlier film *Mr. Hulot's Holiday* (1953), Hulot was seen on vacation at the seaside, bumbling his way with the best of intentions through a series of social catastrophes. Now he is in a city. Two cities, actually—an old French city of bistros and street sweepers and junk carts, of ramshackle buildings and jolly stray dogs and vegetable markets, and then a modern city of automated homes, sterile factories, and hideous fashions.

Hulot is always the same. Tati's character, who also appeared in *Playtime* (1967) and *Traffic* (1971), varies as little as Chaplin's tramp, and is often seen in a brown fedora, a tan raincoat, a bow tie, pants too short, socks with stripes. He is never without his long-stemmed pipe, and at moments of urgency or confusion he nervously taps it against his heel. He hardly ever says anything, and indeed *Mon Oncle* is halfway a silent film, with the dialogue sounding like an unexpected interruption in a library. The music is repetitive, simple, cheerful, like circus music while we're waiting for the clowns.

Hulot was the hero of *Mr. Hulot's Holiday*, but in *Mon Oncle* he is a lost soul, unemployed, bemused and confused by the modern world. His sister, Madame Arpel (Adrienne Servantie) believes she can help him. She lives with her husband Monsieur Arpel (Jean-Pierre Zola) and their young son Gérard (Alain Bécourt) in a futuristic architectural monstrosity, and a great deal of the movie's time is spent exploring their cold new world.

The house they live in, a masterpiece of production design by Henri Schmitt, has automatic gates, doors, windows, and kitchen appliances, as well as a hideous aluminum fountain made from a fish that spouts water from its mouth. The fish is turned on for company, left off for family, tradesmen, and relatives. Two round upstairs windows look like eyeballs, especially when the backlit heads of Monsieur and Madame Arpel function as their pupils. The garden has a winding path to the door, allowing a wicked shot where two women effusively greet each other while the path has them walking in opposite directions. When Madame Arpel decides that her brother should meet a neighbor for possible matrimony, there is a garden party of agonizing bourgeois awkwardness, during which chairs and tables are shuffled clumsily, a climbing vine comes to a bad end, and the underground tube to the fish is punctured.

Things like that happen around Hulot. Arpel, an executive in a plastic-hose factory, gets him a job that leads to all sorts of difficulties, including mysterious footprints on the personnel director's desk and a hose that looks like a string of frankfurters. The only person who seems to understand Hulot is his nephew, Gerard, who treats life in the modernist house as a bore, and escapes to scamper about town with his prankster playmates. The family dog, a dachshund in a plaid overcoat, also sneaks out to run with the local strays.

Mon Oncle introduces us casually to a large cast of local characters, including a street sweeper who is perpetually in conversation and always means to use his broom but never does, and a produce vendor whose scale is off because a flat tire causes his truck to tilt. There is a tender, subtle subplot involving Betty (Betty Schneider), the concierge's daughter, who offers Hulot sweets and conducts a little flirtation; in a bittersweet closing scene she looks all grown up and almost inspires Hulot to make a romantic gesture—before, alas, her mother appears.

There's also a supporting cast of dogs, who are seen in the first shot and the last, and hurry on their doggy business in between. They don't have an important role in the plot; they're just there, checking things out, marking their territory. I learned from the elegant Web site Tativille.com that Tati found the dogs in the pound and didn't train them but simply observed and encouraged them. "At the end of the film we had to get rid of them," Tati wrote. Unwilling to send them back to the pound, he had an inspiration: He took an ad in the paper describing them as movie stars, and they all found good homes. There is a lot of Tati in that serendipitous story.

Jacques Tati (1909–1982) made only six features and a few shorts and TV shows, and yet he ranks with the great silent clowns among masters of visual comedy. He was a perfectionist whose precise construction of shots, sets, actions, and gags is all the more impressive because he remained within a calm emotional range; Hulot doesn't find himself starving, hanging from clock faces, besotted with romance, or in the middle of a war; he simply putters away at life, genial and courteous, doing what he can to negotiate the hurdles of civilization.

The grandson of the czar's ambassador to France, Tati sidestepped a career in his father's picture-framing shop by going into show business. A popular vaudeville performer, after World War II he switched to films, first with a short about postal carriers and then with *Jour de Fête,* also about a mailman. *Mr. Hulot's Holiday* introduced Hulot and was a huge international success, and *Mon Oncle* won the Grand Jury Prize at Cannes and the Oscar for best foreign-language film. His next three films, financed with great difficulty, kept him in debt and didn't achieve the same success, although a case can be made that he grew more daring and radical in the way his human hero confronted an inhuman society.

I love Monsieur Hulot. I love him because he wishes no harm, causes no harm, sees (whenever possible) no harm. He does not forgive his trespassers because he does not feel trespassed against; in the face of rudeness, he nods politely, tries to look interested, and stays out of the way. In an emergency he does what he can, stepping on the leak in the lawn so that the fish can continue to spout. What he would like to do, I think, is to set out each morning and walk here and there, tipping his hat, tapping his pipe, grateful for those amusements that come his way. If his heart breaks even a little when he says good-bye to the landlady's daughter, he doesn't let us know.

"What my brother needs is an objective," Madame Arpel declares, but that is precisely what Hulot does not need. He simply needs to be left alone to meander and appreciate, without going anywhere or having anywhere to go. Jean-Luc Godard once said, "The cinema is not the station. The cinema is the train." I never knew what that meant, until Monsieur Hulot showed me. The joy is in the journey, the sadness in the destination.

{ MOONSTRUCK }

When Ronny Cammareri sweeps Loretta Castorini off her feet in *Moonstruck,* he almost, in his exuberance, throws her over his shoulder. "Where are you taking me?" she cries. "To the bed!" he says. Not to bed, but to the bed. There is the slightest touch of formality in that phrasing, and it is enough to cause Loretta to let her head fall back in surrender. Such sublime abandon, by Nicolas Cage and Cher, is part of the magic of Norman Jewison's 1987 romantic comedy, but it also depends on truth spoken in plain words.

When Rose Castorini, Loretta's mother, discovers that her husband, Cosmo, is cheating on her, she asks her daughter's fiancé, Johnny Cammareri, why men cheat. Maybe it's because they fear death, he says. Later that night, when Cosmo sneaks in late, she nails him in the hallway: "I just want you to know that no matter what you do, you're still gonna die! Just like everyone else!" He looks at her with the eyes of a man who has been long married to this woman, and replies, "Thank you, Rose."

Moonstruck is a romantic comedy founded on emotional abandon and poignant truth. Not content with one romance, it involves five or six, depending on how you count, and conceding that some characters are involved in more than one. It takes place in a Brooklyn that has never existed, a Brooklyn where the full moon makes the night like day and drives people crazy with *amore,* when the moon-a hits their eye like a big-a pizza pie. The sound track is equal parts *La Bohème* and Dean Martin, and Ronny Cammareri's feelings are like those of an operatic hero, larger than life and more dramatic, as when he tells Loretta why he hates his brother Johnny. One day Johnny distracted him at the bakery, he says, and his hand got caught in the bread slicer. As a result, his girlfriend dumped him. Holding his wooden hand in the air and pointing to it dramatically, he cries, "I want my hand! I want my bride! Johnny has his hand! Johnny has his bride!"

Johnny's bride-to-be is, in fact, Loretta, who has come to the bakery to persuade Ronny to attend their wedding. But after he takes her to the bed, everything changes, and Johnny (Danny Aiello), who is in Sicily at the bedside of his dying mother, is in for a shock when he returns to Brooklyn.

In a career of playing goofballs, Nicolas Cage has never surpassed his Ronny Cammareri. Who else could bring such desperation to his speech when he declares his love? "Love don't make things nice. It ruins everything. It breaks your heart. It makes things a mess. We aren't here to make things perfect. The snowflakes are perfect. The stars are perfect. Not us. Not us! We are here to ruin ourselves and to break our hearts and love the wrong people and *die*." And then, she having gone through the motions of resistance, he concludes: "Now I want you to come upstairs with me and *get* in my bed!"

The performance is worthy of an Oscar. Cher won the Academy Award as Loretta. Oscars went also to Olympia Dukakis as Rose, and to the screenplay by John Patrick Shanley. There were nominations for best picture, best director, and for Vincent Gardenia for his performance as Cosmo. Jewison assembled a large cast, flawlessly chosen from character actors who are all given important scenes and speeches, so that at the end, the big emotional climax involves so many people it has to be held around the kitchen table.

Ronny and Loretta are the thirty-something couple who represent this film's version of young love, but there is love, too, between two older couples. Loretta's Aunt Rita (Julie Bovasso) and her husband, Raymond (Louis Guss), have a moment of heartbreaking tenderness, when he stands at the window to look in wonder at the full moon and she says, "You know, in that light, with that expression on your face, you look about twenty-five years old." And Rose and Cosmo are in love, too, despite everything—even

despite Cosmo's secret girlfriend, Mona (Anita Gillette), to whom he proudly recounts his sales pitch to a plumbing client: "There's copper, which is the only pipe I use. It costs money. It costs money because it saves money." She listens adoringly. "What did they say then?" she asks.

Jewison, working from Shanley's original and inspired screenplay, is a master at telling the parallel stories of his large cast. One of his best sequences takes place on the night when Ronny and Loretta go to the opera—and Cosmo and Mona are also there, which is another story. On that night, Rose dines alone at the corner Italian restaurant and watches as a middle-aged man gets a glass of water thrown in his face by a young girl who walks out. Rose asks the man to join her for dinner. He is a professor named Perry, played by John Mahoney in a pitch-perfect performance as a man who knows it is futile to chase his young students but doesn't know what else to do. As they talk about life, as he walks her home under the moon, there is the clear possibility that love could bloom between them, if not in this universe then in another one. But: "I can't go home with you," she says, "because I know who I am." And we know what she means. She has a home and a husband and a family and an identity, and isn't needy the way he is.

Part of Jewison's success comes through the control of tone. The movie is never slapstick, even when it threatens to be, even when Cage's character is in full display. There is a muted bittersweet quality to it, and a surprising amount of dialogue about death, which for the older characters gives a poignant quality to their lives and desires. The emotional center of the film is in the two older couples (four, if you count Rose and Perry and Cosmo and Mona), who in the right light, or even out of it, still feel the passions they felt at twenty-five.

The cinematography by David Watkin often bathes the characters in the cold light of the full moon, when they are for a second seized with sublimity; otherwise he uses warm domestic colors, and creates an unusual sense of place. The Castorini home, with its massive dark bedroom furniture and piles of comforters, its family portraits on the wall, its dining room unused, its kitchen the family stage, becomes so familiar to us that there is surprising impact in the final shot, which simply backs out through the rooms.

Norman Jewison, a Canadian born in 1926, is a master craftsman equally at home in such genres as musicals (*Fiddler on the Roof* and *Jesus Christ, Superstar*), comedies, and social-problems pictures. Three of his best-received films have African-American themes: *In the Heat of the Night,* the Oscar winner as best picture of 1967; *A Soldier's Story* (1984), nominated for best picture, and *The Hurricane* (1999), which won Denzel Washington a nomination for his performance as the unjustly imprisoned boxer "Hurricane" Carter. He began with romantic comedies, working early with Doris Day (*Send Me No Flowers,* 1964), and his *Only You* (1994) is an over-looked treasure of the genre.

Jewison's films are solidly in the Hollywood mainstream; he likes to work with stars, he has flawless production values, and yet he rarely seems inspired merely by box office considerations. His quality control is unusually high. Such titles as *Agnes of God* (1985), *Other People's Money* (1991), and *In Country* (1989), with Bruce Willis as a troubled Vietnam vet, are quirky personal projects, daring for a high-profile director; so was *The Hurricane* and, for that matter, *Moonstruck.*

Seeing it for the third or fourth time, I was struck by how subtle and gentle it is, despite all the noise and emotion. How it loves its characters, and refuses to limit their personalities to a few comic traits. What goes on between Rose and Perry is nuanced and insightful; it doesn't limit them to "dirty old man" and "lonely housewife" but shows them open to the beauty and mystery of life. The movie makes you laugh, which is very difficult, but it also makes you feel more open to your better impulses, and that is harder still.

{THE MUSIC ROOM}

Satyajit Ray's *The Music Room* (1958) has one of the most evocative opening scenes ever filmed. A middle-aged man, his face set into deep weariness, sits on the wide, flat roof of his house in an upholstered chair that has been dragged outdoors for his convenience. He stares into space. His servant, his face betraying long alarm about his master, scurries toward him with a hookah, one of those ancient water pipes smoked by the Cheshire Cat in *Alice's Adventures in Wonderland* and by the idle in Indian films. The man observes the preparations. "What month is it?" he finally asks.

This man is named Biswambhar Roy. He lives in a crumbling palace on the banks of a wide river, in the midst of an empty plain. It is the late 1920s. He is the last in a line of landlords who flourished in Bengal in the nineteenth century; the time for landlords has passed, and his money is running out. For years he has had little to do and only one passion: listening to concerts in his music room.

He has been long jealous of his closest neighbor, the despised moneylender Mahim Ganguly. Mahim is low-caste and vulgar, but hardworking and ambitious. From time to time sounds carried on the air inform him of Mahim's doings: far-off music, or the distant putt-putt of a generator, revealing that he has even brought electricity into his home. Biswambhar learns that Mahim has held a party. "Was I invited?" Biswambhar asks his

servant. He was, he learns—and Mahim was much distressed that he did not attend. "Do I ever go anywhere?" "No."

After winning worldwide fame with the first two films of his Apu trilogy, Satyajit Ray paused before finishing his trilogy about abject poverty to make this film about genteel poverty. Available on video at last in a high-quality print, it is the story of a man who has been compared to King Lear because of his pride and stubbornness, and the way he loses everything that matters.

Almost every scene involves Biswambhar, played by Chhabi Biswas, an actor who was such a favorite of Ray's that when he died, in 1962, Ray said he simply stopped writing important middle-aged roles. In *The Music Room* Biswas plays a man so profoundly encased in his existence that few realities can interfere. With no income and a dwindling fortune, he is nevertheless called "lord" by the shifty Mahim, and although his enormous castle is neglected and only two servants remain, he carries on, oblivious.

His life centers on music. More precisely, on giving expensive concerts to show off his music room, or *jalsaghar*, with its shimmering chandelier, its ornamental carpet, and its portraits of Biswambhar and his ancestors. He lives to flaunt what remains of his wealth. After the opening sequence on the rooftop, much of the film is told in flashback to a time years earlier, and centers around two concerts given in the room.

The first is a coming-of-age "thread ceremony" in honor of his son, Khoka. Only the best musicians will suffice, and Biswambhar reclines on pillows, flanked by his male neighbors and relatives, as the musicians and a celebrated woman singer perform. A slow camera pans the faces of the listeners, pausing at the vulgar Mahim, who is restless, does not enjoy Indian classical music, and reaches for a drink. The evening is a triumph, even though Biswambhar's wife, waiting impatiently upstairs, berates him for mortgaging her jewels to pay for it. He is asleep before she finishes. Not long after, his wife and son leave for a river journey to the house of her father. In a touching scene she bows to him as they leave, and then reveals a modern note: "Behave yourself!"

But the despised Mahim comes to see him with an invitation for a concert of his own. Ray structures the scene as a confrontation between privilege and new wealth: Biswambhar composes himself on a sofa and appears to be so deeply engrossed in his reading that he hardly notices Mahim. Then he counters that he, himself, is planning a concert for that very same evening! In the background, the servant, who knows the condition of their finances, looks stunned.

The second concert has disturbing undercurrents. Even the singer, a bearded man with a stricken face, seems aware of approaching doom. Biswambhar has sent word that his wife and son must return for the event, but they have not yet arrived, and as the chandelier sways in the wind and lightning streaks through the sky, Biswambhar looks down and sees an insect drowning in his glass. It is an omen of great loss.

The third concert comes at the end of the long period of withdrawal. We are back in the present. The last of the jewels will be pawned. Biswambhar will go out in style. He impetuously outbids Mahim for the services of a famous, even scandalous, woman singer and dancer. At the end, when Mahim commits the folly of attempting to tip the woman, the crook of Biswambhar's walking stick comes down firmly on his hand: It is for the lord to tip in his own house. Biswambhar hands the woman the last of his gold coins. The great closing sequence shows Biswambhar in the afterglow of this reckless grand gesture. Drunk, he toasts the portraits of his ancestors, until he sees a spider crawling up the leg of his own portrait. It is dawn. The loyal retainer pulls away the draperies to admit the cold light.

Satyajit Ray (1921–1992) was an unusually tall man, handsome as a movie star, the grandson of a landlord such as Biswambhar's ancestors. In Calcutta in the late 1940s he was a commercial artist for an ad agency, and founded a cinema club that bought its own print of *Potemkin* and imported films from around the world. He rejected the mass-produced Bengali films of the time as so much sub-Hollywood tripe, and with *Pather Panchali* (1955), the first of his famous Apu trilogy, he won a top prize at Cannes and established himself as the preeminent Indian filmmaker in the eyes of the world.

At the New York Film Festival in 1970, he was asked why he was now moving his camera more than in the Apu trilogy. "Because I can afford the equipment," he said with a smile. In his book *Our Films, Their Films,* he recalled that he had never shot a foot of film before the first day of filming

Pather Panchali. When his cinematographer, Subrata Mitra, visited the Hawaii film festival in the early 1990s, he told me, "We started together. I had never exposed a single foot of film before that day."

Ray made many fine films. The Apu trilogy and *The Music Room* rank highest, I think, but he also directed *The Big City* (1963), about a woman who breaks with convention and goes to work when her husband is laid off; *Days and Nights in the Forest* (1970), about office workers who take a holiday of self-discovery; *Distant Thunder* (1973), about an Indian village hearing echoes of World War II; *The Chess Players* (1977), about British attempts to seize the land of a lord who can barely bring himself to notice them; and *The Home and the World* (1984), based on the Rabindranath Tagore novel about a landowner who prides himself on his modern ideas, until his wife falls in love with his friend.

The Music Room is his most evocative film, and he fills it with observant details. The insect in the glass, the bliss of an elephant being bathed in the river, the joy of the servants reopening the dusty music room, the way the chandelier reflects Biswambhar's states of mind, how when the servant sprinkles the guests with scent he adds an extra, contemptuous shake for Mahim.

Despite the faded luxury that surrounds Biswambhar, the film is not ornate in any way. Perhaps as a reaction to the hundreds of overwrought Indian musical melodramas churned out annually, Ray made an austere character study—also with music. His hero deserves the comparison with King Lear, because like Lear he arouses our sympathy even while indulging his vanity and stubbornly doing all the wrong things. Like Lear, he thinks himself a man more sinned against than sinning. Like Lear, he is wrong.

MY DINNER WITH ANDRE

Someone asked me the other day if I could name a movie that was entirely devoid of clichés. I thought for a moment, then answered, *My Dinner with Andre*. Now I have seen the movie again, in a restored print, and I am impressed once more by how wonderfully odd this movie is, how there is nothing else like it. It should be unwatchable, and yet those who love it return time and again, enchanted.

The title serves as a synopsis. We meet the playwright Wallace Shawn, on his way to have dinner, he says, with "a man I'd been avoiding, literally, for a matter of years." The man is Andre Gregory, a well-known New York theater director. Gregory had dropped out of sight, Shawn tells us, and there were reports that he was "traveling." Then one evening recently a friend had come across him in Manhattan, leaning against a building and weeping. Gregory had just come from an Ingmar Bergman movie, and was shattered by this line: "I could always live in my art, but not in my life."

Wally and Andre meet, sit down, talk for almost two hours. As in all conversations, the tide of energy flows back and forth, but mostly it is Andre doing the talking, and Wally the listening. Wally is a man who likes to wrap himself in cozy domesticity. He is round, earnest, squinting; the character he played in *Manhattan* was described by Woody Allen as a "homunculus"—one of those little men in bottles in the laboratory of Dr.

Pretorius. His father, William, was for many years the editor of the *New Yorker*. "When I was young and rich," he says, "all I thought about was art and music. Now I'm thirty-six, and all I think about is money." His friend Andre is tall, thin, angular. He has returned from far-off lands with strange tales, which he relates with twinkling eagerness.

We listen with Wally as Andre tells of trips to Tibet, the Sahara, and a mystical farm in England. Of being buried alive and conducting theatrical rituals by moonlight in Poland. Of being in church when suddenly "a huge creature appeared with violets growing out of its eyelids, and poppies growing out of its toenails." After this last statement, Wally, desperately trying to find a conversational segue, seizes on the violets. "Did you ever see that play *Violets Are Blue*?" he asks. "About people being strangled on submarines?"

Like many great movies, *My Dinner with Andre* is almost impossible to nail down. "Two men talk and eat (in real time) at a fancy New York restaurant," writes CineBooks. Wrong, and wrong. Not in real time but filmed with exquisite attention to the smallest details by director Louis Malle over a period of weeks. And not in a New York restaurant but on a studio set. The conversation that flows so spontaneously between Andre Gregory and Wallace Shawn was carefully scripted. "They taped their conversations two or three times a week for three months," Pauline Kael writes, "and then Shawn worked for a year shaping the material into a script, in which they play comic distillations of aspects of themselves."

Comic? Yes. Although the conversation is often despairing (Gregory speculates that the 1960s were "the last burst of the human being before he was extinguished"), the material is given a slight sly rotation toward the satirical. There is a lot to think about in the torrent of ideas, but also a saving humor. Gregory plays a man besotted by the ideas of the New Age; he almost glows when he tells Shawn about an agricultural commune in Britain where, instead of using insecticides, "they will talk to the insects, make an agreement, set aside one vegetable patch just for the insects."

Wally's response to this is exasperation. What he basically wants from his life, he says, is to write his plays, pay his bills, and enjoy that nice hot cup of coffee in the morning, and the *Times* delivered right to his door. He likes simple pleasures: Having dinner with his girlfriend, Debbie.

Sleeping under an electric blanket. Reading the autobiography of Charlton Heston. Near the end of the film he launches into an impassioned defense of the scientific method. While superstition might have seemed reasonable in ignorant centuries, he argues, he is no longer prepared to believe that a fortune cookie contains his fortune, or that "omens" have anything at all to do with whether an airplane will successfully complete its flight.

Andre doesn't really question the scientific method. He simply doesn't find it helpful. At a time when men are starving for new visions and ideas, he feels, the quest for transcendence is important even if there is, in fact, no transcendence to be found. On and on the two friends talk, while a spectral waiter with a facial tic (Jean Lenauer) serves their dinner like the ghost at Macbeth's banquet.

I saw *My Dinner with Andre* at its first public screening, at the 1981 Telluride Film Festival. During the standing ovation, I found that the two men seated directly behind me were Gregory and Shawn. Few people had known who they were when they'd entered the theater. Now they would never be forgotten where films are taken seriously.

The story of their film is one of serendipity. How as the two old friends talked they began to see how their conversation might be shaped into a play—or perhaps a film. How Louis Malle (1932–1995), the eclectic French director (*Lacombe, Lucien; Pretty Baby; Atlantic City; Au Revoir les Enfants*), signed on and devised the understated but sophisticated shooting style, in which the distance from the camera to the actors at key moments is calculated to the millimeter, while half-seen reflections in mirrors create the illusion of a real restaurant, and the rhythm of the reaction shots subtly reflects the buried tension between the two men. How the film opened in New York, faltered, almost closed, and then gathered helpful reviews and went on to run for more than a year in that theater and—despite its challenging style—in nine hundred others.

Gene Siskel and I did an onstage question-and-answer session with Gregory and Shawn after the first-anniversary screening of the film's New York run. What I remember best from that night is that the two men, asked what they might do differently a second time around, said they would switch roles—"so that no one would think we were playing ourselves." *Are* they playing themselves? Perhaps not, but I think they're playing their own *personalities.* The people they seem to be on the screen are the same people they seem to be in life. ("Whatever that means," Andre might say.)

In another sense, they are simply carriers for a thrilling drama—a film with more action than *Raiders of the Lost Ark*. What *My Dinner with Andre* exploits is the well-known ability of the mind to picture a story as it is being told. Both Shawn and Gregory are born storytellers, and as they talk we see their faces but we picture much more: Andre being buried alive, and a monk lifting himself by his fingertips, and fauns cavorting in a forest. And Wally trudging around to agents with his plays, and happily having dinner with Debbie, and, yes, enjoying Heston's autobiography. We see all of these things so vividly that *My Dinner with Andre* never, ever, becomes a static series of two-shots and close-ups but seems only precariously an-chored to that restaurant, and in imminent danger of hurtling itself to the top of Everest (where, Wally stubbornly argues, it is simply not necessary to go to find the truth).

What they actually say is not really the point of the film. I made a lot of notes about Andre's theories and Wally's doubts, but this is not a log-ical process; it is a conversation, in which the real subject is the tone, the mood, the energy. Here are two friends who have each found a way to live successfully. Each is urging the other to wake up and smell the coffee. The difference is that in Wally's case, it's real coffee.

{ My Neighbor Totoro }

Here is a children's film made for the world we should live in, rather than the one we occupy. A film with no villains. No fight scenes. No evil adults. No fighting between the two kids. No scary monsters. No darkness before the dawn. A world that is benign. A world where if you meet a strange, towering creature in the forest, you curl up on its tummy and have a nap.

My Neighbor Totoro has become one of the most beloved of all family films without ever having been much promoted or advertised. It's a perennial best-seller on video. On the Internet Movie Database, it's been voted the fifth-best family film of all time, right behind *Toy Story 2* and ahead of *Shrek*. The new *Anime Encyclopedia* calls it the best Japanese animated film ever made. Whenever I watch it, I smile, and smile, and smile.

This is one of the lovingly handcrafted works of Hayao Miyazaki, often called the greatest of the Japanese animators, although Isao Takahata, his colleague at the Studio Ghibli, may be his equal. Remarkable that *Totoro* and Takahata's *Grave of the Fireflies,* both included in this book, were released on the same double bill in 1988. Miyazaki has not until very recently used computers to help animate his films; they are drawn a frame at a time, the classic way, with the master himself contributing tens of thousands of the frames.

Animation is big business in Japan, commanding up to a quarter of the box office some years. Miyazaki is the "Japanese Disney," it's said, al-

though that is a little unfair, since Walt Disney was more producer and visionary than animator, and Miyazaki rolls up his sleeves and draws his films himself. He is wildly popular in Japan; *Titanic* took the all-time Japanese box office crown away from *Princess Mononoke* (1999), but then his *Spirited Away* (2001) outgrossed *Titanic*. Of his nine other major films, those best known in the States are *Kiki's Delivery Service* (1989), *Castle in the Sky* (1986), *Nausicaa of the Valley of the Wind* (1984), and *The Castle of Cagliostro* (1979).

Miyazaki's films are, above all, visually enchanting, using a watercolor look for the backgrounds and working within the distinctive Japanese anime tradition of characters with big round eyes and mouths that can be as small as a dot or as big as a cavern. They also have an unforced realism in the way they notice details; early in *Totoro,* for example, the children look at a little waterfall near their home, and there on the bottom, unremarked, is a bottle someone threw into the stream.

The movie tells the story of two young sisters, Satsuki and Mei Kusakabe. As the story opens, their father is driving them to their new house, near a vast forest. Their mother, who is sick, has been moved to a hospital in this district. Now, think about that. The film is about two girls, not two boys or a boy and a girl, as all American animated films would be. It has a strong and loving father, in contrast to the recent Hollywood fondness for bad or absent fathers. Their mother is ill; does illness exist in American animation?

When they ask a neighbor boy how to find their new house, we see—but they don't—that he makes a face. Later he tells them it is haunted. But not haunted in the American sense, with ghosts or fearsome creatures. When Mei and Satsuki let light into the gloom, they get just a glimpse of little black fuzzy dots scurrying to safety. "Probably just dust bunnies," says their father, but there is an old nanny who has been hired to look after them, and she confides that they are "soot sprites," which like abandoned houses, and will pack up and leave when they hear the sound of laughter.

Consider the way the children first approach the house. It has a pillar on its porch that is almost rotted through, and they gingerly push it a little, back and forth, showing how precariously it holds up the roof. But it *does* hold up the roof, and we avoid the American cliché of a loud and sensational collapse, with everyone scurrying to safety. When they peek into the house and explore the attic, it's with a certain scariness—but they disperse their fear by throwing open windows and waving to their father from the upper floor.

And consider that the father calmly accepts their report of mysterious creatures. Do sprites and totoros exist? They certainly do in the minds of the girls. So do other wonderful creatures, such as the Cat Bus, which scurries through the forest on eight quick paws, its big eyes working as headlights. "While it's a little hard to tell whether the adults *really* believe in them," writes the critic Robert Plamondon, "not once does Miyazaki trot out the hoary children's literature chestnut of 'the adults think I'm a liar, so I'm going to have to save the world by myself.' This accepting attitude towards traditional Japanese spirit-creatures may well represent an interesting difference between our two cultures."

My Neighbor Totoro is based on experience, situation, and exploration—not on conflict and threat. This becomes clear in the lovely extended sequences involving totoros—which are not mythological Japanese forest creatures but were actually invented by Miyazaki just for this movie. Little Mei finds the first baby totoro, which looks like a bunny, scurrying around their yard, and she follows it into the forest. Her father, home alone and absorbed in his work, doesn't notice her absence. The baby leads her down a leafy green tunnel, and then there's a soft landing on the stomach of a vast, slumbering creature. Miyazaki doesn't exploit clichés about the dark and fearsome forest; when Setsuki and her father go looking for Mei, they find her without much trouble—sleeping on the ground, for the totoro has disappeared.

Later, the girls go to meet their father's bus. But the hour grows late and the woods grow dark. Silently, casually, the giant totoro joins them at the bus stop, standing protectively to one side like an imaginary friend. It begins to rain. The girls have umbrellas, and they give one to the totoro, who is delighted by the raindrops on the umbrella, and jumps up and down to shake loose a cascade of drops from the trees. Then the bus arrives. Notice how calmly and positively the scene has been handled, with the night and the forest treated as a situation, not a threat. The movie requires no villains. I am reminded that *Winnie-the-Pooh* also originally had no evil characters—but that in its new American movie version evil weasels have been written into A. A. Milne's benign world.

There are two family emergencies: a visit to the hospital to visit their mother, who wants to hear all about their new house, and another occasion when Setsuki gets a call from the doctor and needs to contact her father in the city. In both scenes, the mother's illness is treated as a fact of life, not as a tragedy sure to lead to doom.

There is none of the kids-against-adults plotting of American films. The family is seen as a safe, comforting haven. The father is reasonable, insightful, and tactful; he accepts stories of strange creatures, trusts his girls, listens to explanations with an open mind. The movie lacks those dreary scenes where a parent misinterprets a well-meaning action and punishes it unfairly.

I'm afraid that in praising the virtues of *My Neighbor Totoro* I have made it sound merely good for you, but it would never have won its worldwide audience just because of its warm heart. It is also rich with human comedy in the way it observes the two remarkably convincing, lifelike little girls (I speak of their personalities, not their appearance). It is awe-inspiring in the scenes involving the totoro, and enchanting in the scenes with the Cat Bus. It is a little sad, a little scary, a little surprising, and a little informative, just like life itself. It depends on a situation instead of a plot, and suggests that the wonder of life and the resources of imagination can supply all the adventure we need.

{ NIGHTS OF CABIRIA }

Cabiria's eyebrows are straight black horizontal lines, sketched above her eyes like a cartoon character's. Her shrug, her walk, her way of making a face all suggest a performance. Of course a prostitute is always acting in one way or another, but Cabiria seems to have a character in mind—perhaps Chaplin's Little Tramp, with a touch of Lucille Ball, who must have been on Italian TV in the 1950s. It's as if Cabiria thinks she can waltz untouched through the horrors of her world, as long as she shields herself with a comic persona. Or perhaps this actually is Cabiria, and not a performance: Perhaps she is a waiflike innocent, a saint among the sinners. It is one of the pleasures of Giuletta Masina's performance that the guard never comes down. As artificial as Cabiria's behavior sometimes seems, it always seems her own, and this little woman carries herself proudly through the gutters of Rome.

Nights of Cabiria, directed by Masina's husband, Federico Fellini, in 1957, won her the best actress award at Cannes, and the film won the Oscar for best foreign picture—his second in a row, after *La Strada* in 1954 (he also won for *8½* in 1963, and *Amarcord* in 1974). Strange, then, that it is one of Fellini's least-known works—so unfamiliar that he was able to recycle a lot of the same underlying material again in *La Dolce Vita* only three years later. Now the movie has been re-released in a restored thirty-five-millimeter print, with retranslated, bolder subtitles giving a better idea of the dialogue by Pier Paolo Pasolini. There is also a seven-and-a-half-minute scene that was suppressed in earlier versions of the film.

Seeing it in its new glory, with a score by Fellini's beloved composer Nina Rota, *Nights of Cabiria* plays like a plucky collaboration on an adult theme between Fellini and Chaplin. Masina deliberately based her Cabiria on the Little Tramp, I think—most obviously with some business with an umbrella, and a struggle with the curtains in a nightclub. But while Chaplin's character inhabited a world of stock villains and happy endings, Cabiria survives at the low end of Rome's prostitution trade. When she's picked up by a famous actor and he asks her if she works the Via Veneto, the center of Rome's glitz, she replies matter-of-factly that, no, she prefers the Archaeological Passage, because she can commute there on the subway.

Cabiria is a working girl. Not a sentimentalized one, as in *Sweet Charity*, the Broadway musical and movie based on this story, but a tough cookie who climbs into truck cabs, gets in fights, and hides in the bushes during police raids. She's proud to own her own house—a tiny shack in an industrial wasteland—and she dreams of sooner or later finding true romance, but her taste in men is dangerous, it's so trusting; the movie opens with her current lover and pimp stealing her purse and shoving her into the river to drown.

By the nature of their work prostitutes can find themselves almost anywhere in a city, in almost any circle, on a given night. She's admitted to the nightclub, for example, under the sponsorship of the movie star (Amedeo Nazzari). He picks her up after a fight with his fiancée, takes her to his palatial villa, and then hides her in the bathroom when the fiancée turns up unexpectedly (Cabiria spends the night with his dog). Later, seeking some kind of redemption, she joins another girl and a pimp on a visit to a reputed appearance by the Virgin Mary. And in the scene cut from the movie, she accompanies a Good Samaritan as he visits the homeless with food and gifts (she is shocked to see a once-beautiful hooker crawl from a hole in the ground).

All of these scenes are echoed in one way or another in *La Dolce Vita*, which sees some of the same terrain through the eyes of a gossip columnist (Marcello Mastroianni) instead of a prostitute. In both films, a hooker peeps through a door as a would-be client makes love with his mis-

tress. Both have nightclub scenes opening with exotic ethnic dancers. Both have a bogus appearance by the Virgin. Both have a musical sequence set in an outdoor nightclub. And both have, as almost all Fellini movies have, a buxom slattern, a stone house by the sea, a procession, and a scaffold seen outlined against the dawn. These must be personal touchstones of his imagination.

Fellini was a poet of words and music. He never recorded the dialogue at the time he shot his films. Like most Italian directors, he dubbed the words in later. On his sets, he played music during almost every scene, and you can sense in most Fellini movies a certain sway in the way the characters walk: Even the background extras seem to be hearing the same rhythm. Cabiria hears it, but she often walks in counterpoint, as if to her own melody. She is a stubborn sentimentalist who cannot believe that the man she loved—the man she would do anything for—would try to drown her for forty thousand lira. ("They'd do it for five thousand," her neighbor assures her.)

She is a woman seeking redemption, a woman who works as a sinner but looks for inner spirituality. One night she happens into a performance by a hypnotist, is called onstage, and in the film's most extraordinary sequence is placed in a trance (half vaudeville, half enchanted fantasy) in which she reveals her trust and sweetness. She also informs the rude audience that she has a house and a bank account.

A man named Oscar (François Périer) sees her on the stage and begins to court her with flowers and quiet sincerity. He is touched by her innocence and goodness, he says, and she believes him. At last she has found a man she can trust, one with whom to spend her whole life. She is filled with joy, even as her friends (and we in the audience) despair of her naïveté.

Fellini's roots as a filmmaker are in the postwar Italian neorealist movement (he worked for Rossellini on *Open City* in 1945), and his early films have a grittiness that is gradually replaced by the dazzling phantasms of the later ones. *Nights of Cabiria* is transitional; it points toward the visual freedom of *La Dolce Vita* while still remaining attentive to the real world of postwar Rome. The scene involving the Good Samaritan provides a framework to show people living in city caves and under bridges, but even more touching is the scene where Cabiria turns over the keys of her house to the large and desperately poor family that has purchased it.

These scenes provide an anchor, an undertow, that lends a context to the lighter scenes, like the one where she is mocked by two Via Veneto prostitutes who are more elegant (and much taller) than she is. Or the scene where she drives away in the actor's big American car while flaunting her new client to her rival prostitutes (again, a scene Fellini would recycle in *La Dolce Vita*). In all of those scenes she remains in defiant character, and then we sense a certain softening toward the end. As she allows herself to believe that her future lies with Oscar, her eyebrows subtly soften their bold horizontal slashes, and begin to curve above eyes and a face that seem more vulnerable. It's all in preparation for the film's unforgettable last shot, in which we see Cabiria's face in all its indomitable resolve.

Of all his characters, Fellini once said, Cabiria was the only one he was still worried about. In 1993, when Fellini was given an honorary career Oscar, he looked down from the podium to Masina sitting in the front row, and told her not to cry. The camera cut to her face, showing her smiling bravely through her tears, and there was Cabiria.

ONE FLEW OVER THE CUCKOO'S NEST

There is a curiously extended close-up of Jack Nicholson about four-fifths of the way through *One Flew over the Cuckoo's Nest*. We notice it because it lingers noticeably. It shows his character, R. P. McMurphy, lost in thought. It comes at the balancing point between the pranks and laughter of the earlier parts of the film and the final descent into tragedy. What is he thinking? Is he planning new defiance, or realizing that all is lost? The mystery of what McMurphy is thinking is the mystery of the movie. Everything leads up to a late scene where he is found asleep on the floor next to an open window. By deciding not to escape, he has more or less chosen his own fate. Has his life force run out at last? After his uprising against the mental institution, after the inmates' rebellion he led, after his life-affirming transformations of Billy and the Chief, after his comeback from an initial dose of shock therapy, has he at last reached the end of his hope?

One Flew over the Cuckoo's Nest (1975) is on every list of favorite films. It was the first film since *It Happened One Night* (1934) to win all five of the top Academy Awards, for best picture, actor (Nicholson), actress (Louise Fletcher), director (Miloš Forman), and screenplay (Lawrence Hauben and Bo Goldman). It could, for that matter, have also won for cinematography (Haskell Wexler) and editing (Richard Chew). I was present at its world premiere, at the 1975 Chicago Film Festival, in the two-thousand-seat Riviera Theater, and have never heard a more tumultuous re-

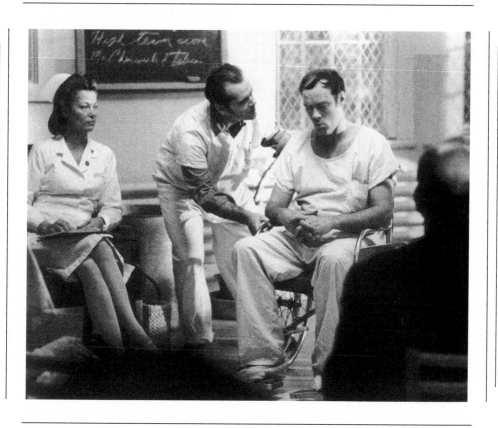

ception for a film (no, not even during *E.T.* at Cannes). After the screening, the young first-time coproducer, Michael Douglas, wandered the lobby in a daze.

But what did the audience, which loved the film so intensely, think it was about? The film is remembered as a comedy about the inmate revolt led by McMurphy, and the fishing trip, the all-night orgy, and his defiance of Nurse Ratched (Fletcher)—but in fact it is about McMurphy's defeat. One can call it a moral victory and rejoice in the Chief's escape, but that is small consolation for McMurphy.

The film is based on Ken Kesey's 1962 best-selling novel, which Pauline Kael observed "contained the prophetic essence of the whole Vietnam period of revolutionary politics going psychedelic." Toned down for the 1970s into a parable about society's enforcement of conformism, it almost willfully overlooked the realities of mental illness in order to turn the patients into a group of cuddly characters ripe for McMurphy's cheerleading. We discover that the Chief is not really mute, Billy need not stutter, and others need not be paralyzed by shyness or fear. They will be cured not by Nurse Ratched's pills, Muzak, and discussion groups, but by McMurphy liberating them to be guys—to watch the World Series on TV, go fishing, play pickup basketball, get drunk, get laid. The message for these wretched inmates is: Be like Jack.

The movie's simplistic approach to mental illness is not really a fault of the movie, because it has no interest in being about insanity. It is about a free spirit in a closed system. Nurse Ratched, who is so inflexible, so unseeing, so blandly sure she is right, represents momism at its radical extreme, and McMurphy is the Huck Finn who wants to break loose from her version of civilization. The movie is, among other things, profoundly fearful of women; the only two portrayed positively are McMurphy's hooker friends Candy and Rose. I mean this as an observation, not a criticism.

McMurphy's past is hinted at early in the film; he was sentenced to a prison farm for criminal assault against an underage girl ("She told me she was eighteen"), and has been sent to the mental institution for "evaluation." He is thirty-eight years old, obviously a hell-raiser, and yet deeply democratic: He takes the patients at face value, treats their illnesses as choices that can be reversed, and tries by sheer force of will to bust them loose into a taste of freedom. The movie sees the patients in the same way. The photography and editing supply reaction shots that almost always have the same message: A given patient's fixed expression is misinterpreted because of the new context supplied by McMurphy. Consider the scene where McMurphy has stolen the boat and has his friends on board. When he is questioned, he introduces them all as doctors, and there are quick cuts to close-ups of each one looking doctorly on cue. This has nothing to do with mental illness but everything to do with comedy.

Nicholson's performance is one of the high points in a long career of enviable rebels. Jack is a beloved American presence, a superb actor who even more crucially is a superb male sprite. The joke lurking beneath the surface of most of his performances is that he gets away with things because he knows how to, wants to, and has the nerve to. His characters stand for freedom, anarchy, self-gratification, and bucking the system, and often they also stand for generous friendship and a kind of careworn nobility. The key to the success of his work in *About Schmidt* is that he conceals these qualities—he becomes one of the patients, instead of the liberating McMurphy.

If his performance is justly celebrated, Louise Fletcher's, despite the Oscar, is not appreciated enough. This may be because her Nurse Ratched is so thoroughly contemptible, and because she embodies so completely the qualities we all (men and women) have been taught to fear in a certain kind of female authority figure—a woman who has subsumed sexuality and humanity into duty and righteousness. Dressed in her quasi-military nurse's costume, with its little hat and its Civil War–style cape, she is dominatrix and warden, followed everywhere by the small, unspeaking nurse who is her acolyte.

Because we respond so strongly to her we hardly see Fletcher's performance. But watch her preternatural calm, her impassive "fairness," her inflexible adherence to the rules, as in the scene where she demands that McMurphy get a majority vote in order to turn on the World Series on TV—this despite the fact that a majority of the patients don't understand what they are voting on. At the end, when McMurphy's final fate is decided upon, note how the male administrator tentatively suggests he be sent back to the prison farm, but Ratched firmly contradicts him: "We must not pass our responsibilities on to someone else."

Is *One Flew over the Cuckoo's Nest* not a great film because it is manipulative, or is it great because it is so superbly manipulative? I can see it through either filter. It remains enduringly popular as an antiestablishment parable but achieves its success by deliberately choosing to use the mental patients as comic caricatures. This decision leads to the fishing trip, which is at once the most popular and the most false scene in the movie. It is McMurphy's great joyous thumb in the eye to Ratched and her kind, but the energy of the sequence cannot disguise the unease and confusion of men who, in many cases, have no idea where they are, or why.

Consider, by comparison, the quiet, late-night speech by the Chief (Will Sampson), who speaks of his father. This is a window into a real character with real problems, who has chosen to be considered deaf and mute rather than talk about them. McMurphy's treatment works for him and leads up to the sad perfection of the very final scenes—during which, if he could see them, McMurphy would be proud of his star pupil.

Miloš Forman, born in Czechoslovakia in 1932, has become one of the great interpreters of American manners and mores. A leader of the Czech New Wave, he made early films like *Loves of a Blonde* (1965) and *The Firemen's Ball* (1968) that won worldwide audiences with their use of paradoxical humor. (In what was seen as a parable of life under communism, the firemen arrive too late to save a barn, but when the farmer complains of the cold, they helpfully move him closer to the flames.)

After the "Prague spring" came the Soviet crackdown, and Forman fled to America, where he has had extraordinary success. (His *Amadeus* in 1984, produced by *Cuckoo* coproducer Saul Zaentz, won seven Oscars, including best picture and director.) Look at the quintessentially American topics of his films: the runaway young people and conventional parents of *Taking Off* (1971), the antiwar musical *Hair* (1979), the New York historical romance *Ragtime* (1981), the defense of a rabble-rouser in *The People vs. Larry Flynt* (1996), the portrait of the McMurphy-like prankster Andy Kaufman in *Man on the Moon* (1999). He sees his adopted land in terms of its best nonconformist and outsider traditions, at a time when conformity is the new creed. His McMurphy succeeds and prevails as a character, despite the imperfections of the film, because he represents that cleansing spirit that comes along now and again to renew us.

{ ORPHEUS }

In the Greek myth about Orpheus, a musician descends into the underworld to reclaim his dead wife, and so enchants the gods with the music of his lyre that they permit her to return to the land of the living—on the condition that he never look at her. Jean Cocteau set his 1949 film of the story in modern-day Paris and added twists that would have startled the Greeks, especially a romantic triangle with Death as the third partner.

Orpheus showcases Cocteau's taste for magic and enchantment; he uses simple but dramatic special effects and trick shots to show his characters passing into the world of death by stepping through mirrors, and when he wants a character to spring back to life, he simply runs the film backward. He weaves his effects so lightly into the story that after a time they aren't tricks at all, but simply the conditions of his mythical world.

His story begins in the Poet's Café in Paris, where a famous middle-aged poet named Orpheus (Jean Marais) is scorned by younger poets who want to displace him. A brawl breaks out, and a young rival named Cegeste (Édouard Dermithe) is struck down. A Rolls-Royce materializes, and its owner, a striking Princess (Maria Casarès) orders her chauffeur to put the young man in the back seat. Then she orders Orpheus to come along "as a witness," although their route takes them not to the hospital but into a cloudy shadowland that eventually becomes the underworld.

"Do you know who I am?" the Princess asks Cegeste. "I am your death." And so she is, looking like a dominatrix in her slinky black gown and severe makeup. Her chauffeur, named Heurtebise (François Périer) is a sort of guardian spirit who watches as she schemes. Orpheus returns with Heurtebise to the living world, orders the chauffeur to hide the Rolls in his garage, and becomes obsessed with the cryptic messages that come from the car's radio—messages that might be inspiration for his art. His wife, Eurydice (Marie Déa), is impatient with his obsession, and Heurtebise tries to comfort her. But eventually (to leap ahead) Eurydice is dead, all the principals are back in the underworld, and there are complications: Orpheus is in love with both his wife and the Princess, the Princess is in love with him, and the chauffeur is in love with Eurydice. This is, of course, against all of the rules, and indeed the Princess may have caused Eurydice's death out of jealousy. Soon the principals find themselves testifying before a fact-finding tribunal of old and severe men.

This sounds, perhaps, like an angel-and-reincarnation movie from modern Hollywood, and I foresee a remake with a rock star descending to hell, reclaiming his girlfriend, and growing obsessed with MP3 files he downloads from the Internet. But Cocteau's version has mystery and beauty. He was not a prolific filmmaker (he was also busy writing poems, novels, and plays, producing paintings and sculptures, and being addicted to opium). But when he made films, they proceeded not from commercial formulas but from the wellsprings of his unconscious, and as a fellow traveler of the surrealists he was not shy about bizarre imagery.

Orpheus became famous for its use of two leather-clad motorcyclists as the errand boys of death; their costumes, especially the high boots and leather corsets, edged into fetishism, and the Princess, arrogantly asking death's tribunal if she may smoke, is from the same image pool. Orpheus was played by the handsome Jean Marais (in real life, Cocteau's lover). Moviegoers in 1949 could find parallels between his career and the poet he was playing; both were famous at an early age, both were associated with important work (Marais as the Beast in Cocteau's 1946 masterpiece *Beauty and the Beast*), and both were keenly aware of a new generation snapping at their heels.

Cocteau himself would have been called a dilettante if he had not been so accomplished at the many arts he moved between. The joke was

that if he had stayed with one thing—poems, painting, films, whatever—he would have been hailed as a master, but the public distrusted his versatility. He directed his first film, *Blood of a Poet*, in 1930. It was produced by the Viscount de Noailles, who financed Dalí and Buñuel's *L'Age d'Or* the same year; when their film was condemned by the Vatican, the viscount shelved it and timidly delayed the release of *Blood of a Poet* for two years. (It went on to become a famous surrealist work that played daily for fifteen years in one New York theater.)

Cocteau claimed to think little of his first film, although modesty did not prevent him from mentioning its fifteen-year run in his memoirs. He didn't direct another until *Beauty and the Beast* in 1946. Then there was the 1948 masterpiece *The Storm Within*. *Orpheus*, in 1949, has been linked in a trilogy with *Blood of a Poet* and the minor *Testament of Orpheus* (1959), but it stands alone.

Seeing *Orpheus* today is like glimpsing a cinematic realm that has now passed completely from the scene. Films are rarely made for purely artistic reasons, experiments are discouraged, and stars as big as Marais are not cast in eccentric remakes of Greek myths. In Cocteau's hands the story becomes unexpectedly complex; we see that it is not simply about love, death, and jealousy, but also about how art can seduce the artist away from ordinary human concerns, so that after Orpheus astonishingly returns from the land of death, he is more concerned with the nonsensical radio transmissions than with his wife, who loves him. (A cynic might whisper in his ear that a trip to the underworld is more inspiration than most poets ever receive.)

Marais, tall and with a great shock of hair, cuts a fine figure as the famous man. François Périer, as the chauffeur, plays the second most important character in the play, although we realize that only belatedly. Marie Déa uses some nice, almost comic timing after returning from the dead, in a series of scenes where Orpheus almost but not quite looks at her.

The film is not perfect. A subplot involving Eurydice's involvement with Aglaonice (Juliette Gréco) and her League of Women is left hanging. The weakness in the cast is Maria Casarès, as the Princess, death's embodiment. She lacks the presence for the role. Despite all the tricks of costuming and makeup, she is slight and inconsequential. Cocteau wanted either

Garbo or Dietrich, and to imagine either one as the Princess is to see the film with its final piece in place. (There is a moment that would have become famous if performed by either one; after the tribunal abruptly disappears, the Princess turns to the chauffeur and observes, "If this were our former world, I'd say, let's have a drink.")

One of the pleasures of the film is to see how audacious the tricks are in their simplicity. Rubber gloves leap onto hands in reverse photography. Glass jumps back into its frame. Mirrors are sometimes mirrors and sometimes sets on the other sides of mirrors. As characters emerge from mirrors, Cocteau simply cuts to their hands being lifted from a still pool of water that reflects their faces. Just once he uses a technique he also used in *Beauty and the Beast*, where a character is pulled on a wheeled platform we cannot see, so that he appears to be gliding.

The characters themselves are never overplayed, never too dramatic, never reaching for classical effects as if they knew they were in a Greek myth. The humor, when it comes, is dry. Certain lines—not too many—employ Cocteau's own poetic language. The best is: "Mirrors are the doors through which death comes and goes. Look at yourself in a mirror all your life and you'll see death do its work."

{ PARIS, TEXAS }

The man comes walking out of the desert like a biblical figure, a penitent who has renounced the world. He wears jeans and a baseball cap, the universal costume of America, but the scraggly beard, the deep eye sockets, and the tireless lope of his walk tell a story of wandering in the wilderness. What is he looking for? Does he remember?

Wim Wenders's *Paris, Texas* (1984) is the story of loss upon loss. This man, whose name is Travis, was once married and had a little boy. Then that all went wrong, and he lost his wife and child, and for years he wandered. Now he will find his family and lose it again, this time not through madness but through sacrifice. He will give them up out of his love for them.

The movie lacks any of the gimmicks used to pump up emotion and add story interest, because it doesn't need them: It is fascinated by the sadness of its own truth. The screenplay was written by Sam Shepard, that playwright of alienation and rage, and it reflects themes that repeat all through Wenders's career. He is attracted to the road movie, to American myth, to those who stand outside and witness suffering. Travis in *Paris, Texas* is like Damiel, the guardian angel in *Wings of Desire*. He loves and cares, he empathizes, but he cannot touch. He does not have that gift.

The movie's story is simply told. Travis (Harry Dean Stanton) asks

for water at a backroads gas station, collapses, is cared for at the local hospital. His brother Walt Henderson (Dean Stockwell) comes to fetch him, but when they stop on the road he starts walking away again, down the railroad tracks. He will not speak. And when he finally does start speaking, it's as if he is haltingly reassembling a self that he lost track of. Walt and his wife, Anne (Aurore Clement), live in Los Angeles with Hunter (Hunter Carson), who is Travis's son. We gradually learn pieces of the story: Hunter was left with the Hendersons by Travis's wife, Jane (Nastassja Kinski), who could no longer care for him, but who sends a check every month from a bank in Houston.

Travis is not insane, not acting out his alienation. He is simply lost in grief, despairing at the way his marriage was joyous for a brief time and then was destroyed by his own drinking and jealousy. He stays for a time with the Hendersons, slowly wins Hunter's trust, walks home with him from school in a sweet little scene where they copy each other's gaits. Then he has a serious conversation with Hunter that leads to them getting into Travis's old Ford pickup and driving to Houston to find Jane.

The movie is always compared to John Ford's *The Searchers,* a film in which a man wanders in the desert to look for a young woman lost to the Indians. Another film said to be inspired by *The Searchers* is Scorsese's *Taxi Driver,* where the hero (also named Travis) tries to rescue a young woman from the clutches of a pimp. In the Wenders and Shepard telling, Jane is discovered working in a sex club, where her specialty is sitting behind one-way glass and talking with her customers over a telephone. The buried theme in each case is the need to save the woman from what is perceived as sexual bondage. All three heroes—those played by John Wayne, Robert De Niro, and Stanton—are somewhat misguided in their quest, not quite understanding the role of the woman.

The journey from Los Angeles to Houston includes many long talks between Travis and Hunter, and I was reminded of Wenders's *Kings of the Road* (1976), where two men share a long journey and talk especially about women, how they need them and do not understand them. Travis and Hunter talk obliquely about the missing wife and mother, but they also cover the big bang and the theory of relativity. Although they are sharing the front seat of the truck, they sometimes speak over walkie-talkies. This mechanical intervention in their conversation is reflected later, when Travis talks with his wife on the telephones in the booths at the sex club.

Paris, Texas is as linear as an arrow. Travis is hauled back from despair and reunited with his brother's family and Hunter. The more he sees the family, the more he feels that Hunter belongs with his biological mother. The journey takes them to Houston, and then everything narrows down to the heartbreaking scenes in which Travis and Jane try to explain themselves to each other. Their first conversation is halting and painful, as Travis tries to determine if Jane goes home with her customers for money. She does not. We understand that Travis asks not out of jealousy but because he is forming a plan. In the second conversation, even though Jane cannot see him and his voice is distanced by the tinny sound of the phone, Travis turns his back to the window. He cannot even look at Jane while telling her a story.

"I knew these people," Travis begins, in one of the great monologues of movie history. "These two people. They were in love with each other. The girl was very young, about seventeen or eighteen, I guess. And the guy was quite a bit older. He was kind of raggedy and wild. And she was very beautiful, you know?"

He tells of a time when even a trip to the grocery store was an adventure. When he would quit jobs just so he could be at home with her. And then how the jealousy began to eat at him: "Then he'd yell at her and start smashing things in the trailer." When Jane repeats, "The trailer?" it is clear she knows this is Travis (I think she knows sooner, and gives it away with a sideways flicker of her eye). He continues with his story, ending when the marriage is in wreckage and he awakens with the trailer on fire: "Then he ran. He never looked back at the fire. He just ran. He ran until the sun came up and he couldn't run any further. And when the sun went down, he ran again. For five days he ran like this until every sign of man had disappeared."

This confession inspires Jane to turn her back to the window and tell her own story. At one point she turns off the light in her cubicle and he turns a light to his face and she can even see him. He tells her that Hunter is waiting for her in the Meridian Hotel, Room 1520. "He needs you now, Jane. And he wants to see you."

The film ends with the mother and child reunited. In a decision that is both dramatically and cinematically inspired, Travis watches their meeting from the rooftop of a nearby garage, and then drives away. There is the same feeling as when John Wayne, in *The Searchers*, restores the missing girl to her family and then looks on, alone again and forgotten, before turning to walk back into the wilderness.

Practical and logical objections can be raised about this story. Was Travis right to take Hunter away from Walt and Anne? Can Jane care for him? Could Jane work in the club and not be a prostitute? But never mind. Wenders uses the materials of realism, but this is a fable, as much as his great *Wings of Desire*. It's about archetypal longings, set in American myth. The name Travis reminds us of John D. MacDonald's Travis McGee, the private investigator who rescued lost souls and sometimes fell in love with them but always ended up alone on his boat. The Texas setting evokes thoughts of the Western, but this movie is not for the desert and against the city; it is about a journey that leads from one to the other and ends in a form of happiness.

Wenders is part of that circa-1970 flowering of talent known as the German New Wave (it includes also Herzog, Fassbinder, Schlondorff, and von Trotta). He has always been fascinated by American movies and music; many of his films are set at least partly in the United States. The music in *Paris, Texas* is by Ry Cooder, and it's lonely and filled with distance (they collaborated again on the Cuban music documentary *The Buena Vista Social Club*). The photography by Robby Müller contains the sense of a far horizon beyond every close shot. The Shepard dialogue lacks all flourish and fanciness, and is about hard truth, long rehearsed in the mind.

Then there are the miracles of the performances by Harry Dean Stanton, Nastassja Kinski, and Hunter Carson (the son of Karen Black and L. M. "Kit" Carson). Stanton has long inhabited the darker corners of American noir, with his lean face and hungry eyes, and here he creates a sad poetry. Kinski, a German, perfects the flat, half-educated accent of a Texas girl who married a "raggedy" older man for reasons no doubt involving a hard childhood. Young Carson, debating relativity and the origin of the universe, then asking even more difficult questions, such as "Why did she leave us?," has that ability some child actors have of presenting truth without decoration. We care so much for their family, framed lonely and unsure, within a great emptiness.

{ PATTON }

I love it, God help me, I do love it. I love it more than my life.

So says General George S. Patton about war, in *Patton*. In his words we hear a premonition of the most memorable of all war movie speeches, Colonel Kilgore's "I love the smell of napalm in the morning," from *Apocalypse Now*. It is surely no coincidence that both screenplays were cowritten by Francis Ford Coppola. The Kilgore character seems like a screwball spin-off of Patton, a man who observes to his staff at the end of the war, "All good things must come to an end."

In his own eyes, Patton was larger than life and stood outside time. Surveying a North African battlefield where Carthage was attacked by Rome, he says "I was here," and he means it. He believes in reincarnation and destiny, and when he is benched on the eve of the invasion of Europe, he rants, "The last great opportunity of a lifetime and I'm left out of it? God will not allow it to happen." That obsession and swagger was his strength and weakness. He could inspire men to heroic feats, he was a brilliant strategist, but he was a genius at getting himself into trouble. In a war where millions died horribly, he slapped a shell-shocked soldier and his career was derailed.

Franklin J. Schaffner's *Patton* (1970), released at the height of the unpopular war in Vietnam, was described by many reviewers at the time as

"really" an antiwar film. It was nothing of the kind. It was a hard-line glorification of the military ethic, personified by a man whose flaws and eccentricities marginalized him in peacetime but found the ideal theater in battle. In this he was not unlike Churchill; both men used flamboyance, eccentricity, and a gift for self-publicity as a way of inspiring their followers and perplexing the enemy. That Patton was in some ways mad is not in doubt—at least to the makers of this film—but his accomplishments overshadowed, even humiliated, his cautious and sane British rival, Montgomery.

The film is nearly three hours long and George C. Scott is on-screen for most of that time, when we are not seeing battle scenes or Nazi planners (always speculating about Patton). It is one of those sublime performances in which the personalities of the actor and the character are fulfilled in each other. Although the role was offered to other actors who were bigger stars (critic Tim Dirks lists Burt Lancaster, Rod Steiger, Lee Marvin, Robert Mitchum, and John Wayne), it is unimaginable without Scott. His comic-opera General Buck Turgidson in *Dr. Strangelove* (1964) informs more than a little of Patton's nuttiness and his hatred of the Russians. Scott (1927–1999) was big, powerful, lonely, brilliant, a drinker, a perfectionist who stood so far outside Hollywood circles it was a foregone conclusion he would not turn up at the Academy Awards. In his career he sought out challenges like the plays of Shakespeare, O'Neill, and Miller, in the same way Patton hungered for battle. Like Patton, he was a man without a purpose when he was offstage.

Consider the scene where Patton is dressed by his aide, who adjusts his helmet reverently on his head as if placing a crown. Patton regards himself in the mirror and muses to himself, "All my life I've wanted to lead a lot of men in a desperate battle." He could be an actor preparing to walk onto a stage. "General, the men don't always know when you're acting or not," a subordinate tells him after one flamboyant speech. "They don't need to know," Patton says. "Only I need to know."

Headlines and newsreels personified armies by referring to their generals: Rommel was defeated in Africa, Patton swept north through France. Patton saw it the same way, and when he promises he will liberate Messina before Montgomery gets there, he is thinking in the first person. General Omar Bradley (Karl Malden), who has the film's only other significant leading role, quails at the risk of lives and equipment that Patton is willing to contemplate, because he does not quite see that for Patton his men and equipment are the limbs of his ego. Vanity and courage found their intersection in Patton. "If you were named admiral of the Turkish navy," Bradley tells him, "I believe your aides could dip into their haversacks and come up with the appropriate decoration."

Patton is not a war film so much as the story of a personality who has found the right role to play. Scott's theatricality is electrifying. As Patton he always stands up in his Jeep, loves making speeches, grandstands, plunges into the action to personally goad his men, even directs traffic. There is a touch of the manic about him. He seems to have no personal life. The film makes no mention of family, children, even close friends; his heart-to-heart talks are with himself. He seems formidably well read, lecturing his subordinates on the history of the battlefields, the lessons of Napoleon, the experiences of earlier leaders who came this way. He has a classical quotation for every occasion. "You son of a bitch," he gloats after outsmarting Rommel, "I read your book!"

Scott's performance is not one-dimensional but portrays a many-layered man who desires to appear all of a piece. Instead of adding tiresome behavioral touches, he allows us small glimpses of what may be going on inside. Having made a fetish of bravery, he obtains a dog that is terrified most of the time, and affectionately drags the cowardly beast wherever he goes. Told by the press that the American public is fascinated by his "pearl-handled revolver," he stone-faces: "Ivory. Only a pimp from a cheap New Orleans whorehouse would carry a pearl-handled revolver." That shows he's given it some thought. Early in the film, under surprise air attack by the Nazis, he stands in the middle of a street firing at them with the revolver. Crazy, yes, but it adds to the legend.

The most famous scene is the first one, Patton mounting a stage to address his troops from in front of an American flag that fills the huge, seventy-millimeter screen. Seen in a theater, he appears unsettlingly life-size. His speech is unapologetically bloodthirsty. ("We will cut out their living guts and use them to grease the treads of our tanks.") His uniform and decorations, ribbons and medals, jodhpurs and riding boots and swagger stick fall just a hair short of what Groucho Marx might have worn. Scott's great nose could be the beak of an American eagle. The closing shot is the other side of the coin, a graying and lonely old man, walking his dog. Even then, we suspect, Patton is acting. But does he know it?

Franklin Schaffner (1920–1989) was a master of bold, uncluttered canvases. After a start directing live television in the 1950s, he made dramas (including *The Best Man,* one of the finest Hollywood films about politics) before finding his natural footing with epics such as *The War Lord* (1965), *Planet of the Apes* (1968), and, after *Patton, Nicholas and Alexandra* (1971) and *Papillon* (1973). His *Patton* is one of the most uncluttered of war movies, devoid of side plots, colorful supporting characters, and "human interest." There are no individual soldiers whose adventures we follow, and the battle scenes are seen in long shot, not personalized; they have the sweep of Victorian canvases instead of the hand-to-hand intimacy of *Platoon, Saving Private Ryan,* or *We Were Soldiers.* Even the Bradley character has no purpose other than to admonish, support, and puzzle over Patton—to stand there and look at him. The movie sees the war as Patton saw it, as Patton's story. Well, that's one way of looking at it.

Note: I see the war most vividly through the eyes of an old friend, the director Russ Meyer, who enlisted at seventeen and believed, with Patton, that it was the best thing that ever happened to him. Over the years he has talked about it endlessly, and I have a glimpse of Patton from Meyer. In the closing days of the war, when Meyer was a Signal Corps cameraman near the German lines in France, he was routed from his bed in the middle of the night and ordered to join an unauthorized raid behind enemy lines to be led by Patton. The general had become convinced Hitler was making a secret visit to the front, and planned to capture him personally. "We drove off into the night," Meyer recalls. "Hitler wasn't there. We returned, and were warned to keep quiet about it. That was Patton for you."

PICNIC AT HANGING ROCK

On a drowsy St. Valentine's Day in 1900, a party of girls from a strict boarding school in Australia go on a day's outing to Hanging Rock, a geological outcropping not far from their school. Three of the girls and one of their teachers disappear into thin air. One of them is found a week or so later, but can remember almost nothing. The others are never found. On this foundation, Peter Weir's *Picnic at Hanging Rock* (1975) constructs a film of haunting mystery and buried sexual hysteria. It also employs two of the hallmarks of modern Australian films: beautiful cinematography, and stories about the chasm between settlers from Europe and the mysteries of their ancient new home.

The movie, which has been long out of release and was unavailable even on video, has been restored in a new director's cut that, unlike most revisions, takes out footage instead of adding it. Weir has pared seven minutes from an already lean and evasive film. The result is a movie that creates a specific place in your mind; free of plot, lacking any final explanation, it exists as an experience. In a sense, the viewer is like the girls who went along on the picnic and returned safely: For us, as for them, the characters who disappeared remain always frozen in time, walking out of view, never to be seen again.

The movie is based on a 1967 novel by Lady Joan Lindsay, then seventy-one, who presented it as fiction but hinted that it might be based on fact. A cottage industry grew up in Australia about the novel and the movie; old newspapers and other records were searched without success for reports of disappearing schoolgirls. Much was made of the fact that the movie is set on a Saturday and Valentine's Day did not fall on a Saturday in 1900; did the girls disappear into another time line? Were they raped by two teenage boys who were also at Hanging Rock that day? Did they simply fall into a crevice? What about the girl who was found alive a week later? She had lost her shoes, and yet her feet were not injured by the sharp rock paths. Had she levitated? There is even a book, *The Murders at Hanging Rock,* that explains that the disappearances were fiction but nevertheless offers several theories, including UFO abduction, for what happened.

Of course, the entire point is that there is no explanation. The girls walked into the wilderness and were seen no more. Aborigines might speculate that the rock was alive in some way—that it swallowed these outsiders and kept its silence. As Russell Boyd's camera examines the rock in lush and intimate detail—its snakes and lizards, its birds and flowers—certain shots seem to suggest faces in the rock, as if the visitors are being watched.

The movie has been compared to Antonioni's *L'Avventura* (1960), a film in which a man's wife wanders away on an island in the Mediterranean and is never seen again. Antonioni's *Blow-Up* (1967) involves a body that may or may not be there and a mystery that is never solved. For me, *Picnic at Hanging Rock* evokes E. M. Forster's novel *A Passage to India,* made into a film by David Lean in 1984. In that story, a party of British visitors tour the Marabar Caves, which have the peculiar property of turning all speech into a meaningless echo. One of the women has something happen to her inside the cave—the novel never explains what it is—and her sexual hysteria fuels the rest of the story. The underlying suggestion is that Victorian attitudes toward sex, coupled with the unsettling mysteries of an ancient land, lead to events the modern mind cannot process. That is exactly the message of *Picnic at Hanging Rock.*

The film opens as if it will make perfect sense. At Appleyard College in Woodend, Victoria, firm discipline and ladylike behavior are offered as a substitute for learning. The "college" is more of a finishing school for adolescents, who live in a hothouse atmosphere where schoolgirl crushes are inevitable. Mrs. Appleyard (Rachel Roberts) herself seems to contain

unexamined needs, and she punishes one girl, a passionate rebel, by making her stay home from the outing.

The other girls, nineteen of them, with two teachers, leave in a carriage for Hanging Rock. They are all dressed in Victorian clothing that emphasizes modesty and inconvenience (an early scene shows them lined up, lacing one another's corsets). On the slopes of the rock their parasols and happy laughter are a contrast to the ancient, brooding land. Close-up photography shows the rock crawling with countless forms of animal, reptile, and insect life, which hurries on its murderous business with no thought to the visitors. Music, some of it classical, played by panpipes, is an unsettling contrast.

"We worked very hard," Weir told an interviewer for *Sight &* *Sound*, "at creating an hallucinatory, mesmeric rhythm, so that you lost awareness of facts, you stopped adding things up, and got into this enclosed atmosphere. I did everything in my power to hypnotize the audience away from the possibility of solutions."

Although I don't recall my 1975 viewing of the film in enough detail to be sure, my guess is that Weir's seven minutes of trims are intended to further discourage a "solution." The other party on the rock that day— the two young men and an older couple—are there not as possible suspects, I believe, but simply to show that a picnic on the rock could be perfectly safe. The film wants us to sense that the heightened and repressed sexuality of the young students was in some way connected to their disappearance, as if their emotional states interlocked somehow with the living presence of the land.

There are other fragmentary suggestions that help us toward this idea. Of the girls who originally set out on the walk, one named Edith returns quickly, screaming the warning that the others are gone. Later she remembers that she saw the missing teacher in her underwear. Scraps of lacy underclothing are found later during a search. Back at the school, unspoken sexual feelings lie beneath many of Mrs. Appleyard's disciplinary actions, especially in connection with the rebellious Sarah—the girl who was not allowed to go on the trip.

"The film is just too damn impenetrable for its own good," writes the critic Kevin Maynard. I'm sure he speaks for a lot of viewers, but of course if you could penetrate it, there would be no film—simply a police case, or an account of an accident. My idea of Australia has been fashioned almost entirely from its films, and I picture it as a necklace of coastal cities, from which depend smaller inland towns, surrounding the vast and ancient Outback—where modern logic does not apply, and inexplicable things can happen.

Nicolas Roeg's *Walkabout* touches on some of the same feelings as *Picnic at Hanging Rock*. In it, a white girl and her brother are left abandoned in the wilderness when their father kills himself. They would quickly die, but are saved by an Aborigine boy who, in an ironic reversal, kills himself after leading them back to civilization. The suggestion in both *Walkabout* and *Picnic* is that Aboriginal life cannot be sustained in cities, nor European-based life in nature, and it is intriguing that girls on the brink of maturity are the focal point in both films.

Peter Weir, born in 1944, went on to great success after *Picnic at Hanging Rock*. His titles include *Witness, Gallipoli, The Last Wave, The Year of Living Dangerously, The Mosquito Coast, Dead Poets Society,* and *Green Card*—and his widely praised 1998 film, *The Truman Show*. It's interesting that most of these titles deal in one way or another with outsiders who find themselves in places where they are not a good fit. Somewhere at the very bottom of his imagination must lurk the conviction that you'll be all right if you stay at home, but if you wander into other lands you may find that you have disappeared.

PLANES, TRAINS AND AUTOMOBILES

Some movies are obviously great. Others gradually thrust their greatness upon us. When *Planes, Trains and Automobiles* was released in 1987, I enjoyed it immensely, gave it a favorable review, and moved on. But the movie continued to live in my memory. Like certain other popular entertainments (*It's a Wonderful Life, E.T., Casablanca*) it not only contained a universal theme but matched it with the right actors and story, so that it shrugged off the other movies of its kind and stood above them in a kind of perfection. This is the only movie our family watches as a custom, almost every Thanksgiving.

The movie is founded on the essential natures of its actors. It is perfectly cast and soundly constructed, and all else flows naturally. Steve Martin and John Candy don't play characters; they embody themselves. That's why the comedy, which begins securely planted in the twin genres of the road movie and the buddy picture, is able to reveal so much heart and truth.

The story is familiar. Martin plays Neal, a Chicago advertising man, sleek in impeccable blues and grays, smooth shaven, recently barbered, reeking of self-confidence, prosperity, and anal-retentiveness. Candy plays Del, a traveling salesman from Chicago who sells shower-curtain rings ("the best in the world"). He is very tall, very large, and covered in layers of mismatched shirts, sweaters, vests, sport coats, and parkas. His bristly little

mustache looks like it was stuck on crooked just before his entrance; his bow tie is also askew.

Both of these men are in Manhattan two days before Thanksgiving, and both want to get home for the holidays. Fate joins their destinies. Together they will endure every indignity that modern travel can inflict on its victims. What will torture them even more is being trapped in each other's company. Del wants only to please. Neal wants only to be left alone.

John Hughes, who wrote, directed, and produced the film, is one of the most prolific filmmakers of recent decades. He is not often cited for greatness, although some of his titles, like *The Breakfast Club*, *Weird Science*, and *Ferris Bueller's Day Off*, have fervent admirers. What can be said for him is that he usually produces a real story about people he has clear ideas about; his many teenage comedies, for example, are miles more inventive than the recent sex-and-prom sagas. The buried story engine of *Planes, Trains and Automobiles* is not slowly growing friendship or odd-couple hostility (devices a lesser film might have employed) but empathy. It is about understanding how the other guy feels.

Del, we feel, was born with empathy. He instinctively identifies with Neal's problems. He is genuinely sorry to learn he stole Neal's cab. He is quick to offer help when their flight is diverted to Wichita and there are no hotel rooms available. Neal, on the other hand, depends on his credit cards and self-reliance. He wants to make his own plans, book his own room, rent his own car. He spends the movie trying to peel off from Del, and failing; and Del spends the movie having his feelings hurt and then coming through for Neal anyway.

The movie could have been a shouting match, like the unfortunate *Odd Couple II* (1998). Hughes is more subtle. The key early scene takes place in the Wichita motel room they have to share, when Neal explodes, telling Del his jokes stink, his stories are not interesting, and he would rather sit through an insurance seminar than listen to any more of the fat man's pointless anecdotes. Look at Candy's face fall. He shows Del as a man hurt and saddened—and not for the first time. Later he remembers how the most important person in his life once told him he was too eager to please and shouldn't always try so hard.

At this point, Del wins our hearts, and the movie is set up as more than a comedy. But a comedy it is. Not one movie a year contributes a catch-phrase to the language. We remember Jack Nicholson ordering the toast. "If you build it, they will come." "E.T., phone home." "I'm walkin' here!" "I love the smell of napalm in the morning." "Are you talking to me?" And we remember the scene where Del and Neal wake up cuddled together in the cramped motel bed, and Neal asks Del where his hand is, and Del says it's between some pillows, and Neal says, "Those aren't pillows," and the two men bolt out of bed in terror, and Neal shouts, "You see that Bears game last week?" and Del cries, "What a game! What a game! Bears gonna go all the way!" This is not homophobia but the natural reaction of two men raised to be shy and distant around other men—to fear misunderstood intimacy.

The other great comic set piece in the movie is responsible for its R rating; nothing else in the movie would qualify for other than PG-13. This is Neal's verbal symphony for the f-word, performed by the desperate man after a rental-car bus strands him three miles from the terminal without a car. He has to walk back through the snow and mud, crossing runways, falling down embankments, until he finally faces a chirpy rental agent (Edie McClurg) who is chatting on the phone about the need for tiny marshmallows in the ambrosia. When she sweetly asks Neal if he is disturbed, he unleashes a speech in which the adjectival form of the f-word functions as the prelude to every noun, including itself, and is additionally used as punctuation. When he finishes, the clerk has a two-word answer that supplies one of the great moments in movie dialogue.

Neal is uneasy around ordinary people and in unstructured situations. His mind is organized like a Day-Timer. He's lived in a cocoon of affluence and lacks the common touch. Consider the scene on the bus where Del suggests a sing-along, and Neal, awkwardly trying to be a good sport, begins "Three Coins in a Fountain" (and doesn't know the words). His fellow passengers look at him as if he's crazy. Del saves the moment with a boisterous rendition of a song everybody except Neal knows: "We're the Flintstones!"

The last scenes of the movie carry the emotional payoff we have been half-awaiting all along. For Neal, they reflect a kind of moral rebirth such as Scrooge experiences in another great holiday tale: He has learned his lesson and will no longer judge people by their appearances, or by his own selfish standards. There is true poignancy in the scene where Neal finds Del waiting alone in the elevated station.

One night a few years after *Planes, Trains and Automobiles* was released, I came upon John Candy (1950–1994) sitting all by himself in a hotel bar in New York, smoking and drinking, and we talked for a while. We were going to be on the same TV show the next day. He was depressed. People loved him, but he didn't seem to know that, or it wasn't enough. He was a sweet guy and nobody had a word to say against him, but he was down on himself. All he wanted to do was make people laugh, but sometimes he tried too hard, and he hated himself for doing that in some of his movies. I thought of Del. There is so much truth in the role that it transforms the whole movie. Hughes knew it, writer-director Chris Columbus captured it in *Only the Lonely* (1991), and Steve Martin knew it, and played straight to it.

The movies that last, the ones we return to, don't always have lofty themes or Byzantine complexities. Sometimes they last because they are arrows straight to the heart. When Neal unleashes that tirade in the motel room and Del's face saddens, he says, "Oh. I see." It is a moment that not only defines Del's life but is a turning point in Neal's, because he also is a lonely soul, and too well organized to know it. Strange, how much poignancy creeps into this comedy, which only becomes stronger while we're laughing.

{ THE PRODUCERS }

Zero Mostel and Gene Wilder have a scene in *The Producers* where they roll on the floor so ferociously we expect them to chew on each other. Mostel is so manic and barbarian, Wilder so panicked and hysterical, you wonder why spit didn't get on the camera lens. The whole movie is pitched at that level of frenzied desperation, and one of the many joys of watching it is to see how the actors are able to control timing and nuance even while screaming.

This is one of the funniest movies ever made. To see it now is to understand that. To see it for the first time in 1968, when I did, was to witness audacity so liberating that not even *There's Something About Mary* rivals it. The movie was like a bomb going off inside the audience's sense of propriety. There is such rapacity in its heroes, such gleeful fraud, such greed, such lust, such a willingness to compromise every principle, that we cave in and go along.

The movie stars Mostel and Wilder as Max Bialystock, a failing Broadway producer, and Leo Bloom, a nebbish accountant. Bialystock raises money for his productions by seducing checks out of little old ladies, who come to his office to fool around. ("We'll play the innocent little milkmaid and the naughty stable boy!") Bloom is sent to do his books and finds that Bialystock raised $2,000 more than he lost on his last failure. You could make a lot of money by overfinancing turkeys, he muses, a glint in his eye: "The IRS isn't interested in flops."

This leads to their great inspiration: Max will venture into "little old lady–land" and raise thousands of dollars more than they need for a production that will be guaranteed to fail. The critic David Ehrenstein traces the first use of the phrase "creative accounting" to *The Producers,* and Bialystock and Bloom make it into a fine art. "Hello, boys!" says Max, plopping down next to his safe and patting the piles of money.

Their formula for failure is a musical named *Springtime for Hitler,* with a dance line of jackbooted SS girls and lyrics like "Don't be stupid, be a smarty! Come and join the Nazi party!" Their neo-Nazi playwright Franz Liebkind (Kenneth Mars) roars up to opening night on a motorcycle, wears a Nazi helmet into the lobby, and tells them, "It's magic time!" Reaction shots during the first act show the audience paralyzed in slack-jawed horror.

How did Mel Brooks, the writer and director, get away with this? I think it was by establishing the amoral desperation of both key characters at the outset, and by casting them with actors you couldn't help liking, even so. Like Falstaff, Zero Mostel's Max Bialystock is a man whose hungers are so vast they excuse his appetites. There is a scene where he scrubs his filthy office window with coffee, peers through the murk, sees a white Rolls-Royce, and screams, "That's it, baby! When you've got it, flaunt it! Flaunt it!" You can taste his envy and greed. "See this?" he says to Bloom, holding up an empty jewelry setting. "This used to hold a pearl as big as your eye. Look at me now! I'm wearing a cardboard belt!" It is typical of this movie that after he says the line, he takes off the belt and rips it to shreds.

Mostel was a serious actor, a blacklist target, an intellectual. His performance here is a masterpiece of low comedy. Despite a comb-over that starts just above his collar line, he projects optimistic vanity, spitting on his hand to slick back his hair before Miss "Hold me! Touch me!" (Estelle Winwood) enters for her weekly visit. What Mostel projects above all is utter confidence. He never has second thoughts. Perhaps he never thinks at all, but only proceeds out of Darwinian urgency.

Gene Wilder was a new face in 1968, introduced to audiences with a key supporting role in *Bonnie and Clyde* (1967), also as a character consumed by nervousness. His performance in *The Producers* is a shade shy of a panic attack. On the floor with Mostel looming over him, he screams,

341

"Don't jump! Don't jump!" Mostel starts to hop in a frenzy, and Wilder escapes to a corner, hides behind a chair, and screams, "I'm hysterical! I'm hysterical!" Mostel pours a glass of water and throws it in his face. Wilder delivers the classic line: "I'm wet! I'm hysterical, and I'm wet! I'm in pain, and I'm wet, and I'm *still* hysterical!"

The movie's supporting stars became briefly famous after the movie came out, although none found equally funny material again. Mars was a bug-eyed fanatic, up on the roof with his pigeons, singing Nazi songs, later ordering an audience member to stop laughing because "I am the author! I outrank you!" To the Nazi jokes Brooks added gay jokes, with the flamboyant couple of Broadway director Roger De Bris (Christopher Hewett) and his valet, Carmen Giya (Andréas Voutsinas). At one point Max, Leo, and Carmen crowd into a tiny elevator and are expelled breathless and flustered. Heterosexuality is represented by the pneumatic Lee Meredith, as Ulla, the buxom secretary, who types one letter at a time and then pauses for a smile of self-congratulation. The other great supporting performance is by Dick Shawn as the actor who plays Hitler; in a movie made at the height of the flower-power period, he's a hippie constructed out of spare parts, with his finger cymbals, Campbell's soup can necklace, and knee-high fringed boots.

To produce a musical named *Springtime for Hitler* was, of course, in the worst possible taste, as an escaping theater patron observes in the movie—to the delight of Bialystock and Bloom, who were counting on just that reaction. To make a movie about such a musical was also in bad taste, of course. It is obvious that Bialystock and Bloom are Jewish, but they never refer to that. As Franz Liebkind rants, they nod, because the more offensive he is, the more likely it is that his play will fail. Brooks adds just one small moment to suggest their private thoughts. As the two men walk away from the playwright's apartment, Bloom covers the red-and-black Nazi armband Franz has given him. "All right, take off the armband," says Bialystock, taking off his own. They throw both armbands into a trash can. Leo spits into it, and then Max does.

The best sight gag in the movie is the one at the end of a long day spent by Max and Leo walking around Manhattan and perfecting their scheme. Finally at night they find themselves in front of the fountain at Lincoln Center. The music swells. Leo cries, "I want everything I've ever seen in the movies!" And *then* the fountain leaps up. Everyone remembers the fountain. The music and the dialogue make it into a punch line instead of just a surprise.

Like most of Brooks's films, *The Producers* is cheerfully willing to go anywhere for a laugh. In Brooks's next film, *Blazing Saddles* (1974), he produced the famous campfire scene, long before Eddie Murphy's Klumps had their troubles with intestinal gas. Gene Wilder worked with him again in the wonderful *Young Frankenstein* (also 1974), and Brooks has remained prolific; high points are *Silent Movie* (1976), with its narcissistic Burt Reynolds shower scene; the Hitchcock spoof *High Anxiety* (1977), where the tracking shot breaks a plate-glass window; and the underrated *Life Stinks* (1991), inspired by Preston Sturges's *Sullivan's Travels*.

Mel Brooks began in big-time show business as a writer for Sid Caesar's *Your Show of Shows* in the 1950s; Carl Reiner and Neil Simon were fellow writers. That he didn't have a career as a stand-up comedian is surely only because he chose not to. I remember finding myself in an elevator with Brooks and his wife, the actress Anne Bancroft, in New York City a few months after *The Producers* was released. A woman got onto the elevator, recognized him, and said, "I have to tell you, Mr. Brooks, that your movie is vulgar." Brooks smiled benevolently. "Lady," he said, "it rises below vulgarity."

RAIDERS OF THE LOST ARK

Steven Spielberg's *Raiders of the Lost Ark* plays like an anthology of the best parts from all the Saturday matinee serials ever made. It takes place in South America, Nepal, Egypt, Greece, at sea, and in a secret submarine base. It contains trucks, bulldozers, tanks, motorcycles, ships, subs, Pan Am Clippers, and a Nazi flying wing. It has snakes, spiders, booby traps, and explosives. The hero is trapped in a snake pit, and the heroine finds herself assaulted by mummies. The weapons range from revolvers and machine guns to machetes and whips. And there is the supernatural, too, as the Ark of the Covenant triggers an eerie heavenly fire that bolts through the bodies of the Nazis.

The Saturday-serial aspects of *Raiders of the Lost Ark* have been much commented on and relished. But I haven't seen much discussion of the movie's other driving theme, Spielberg's feelings about the Nazis. "Impersonal," Pauline Kael called the film, and indeed it is primarily a technical exercise, with personalities so shallow they're like a dew that has settled on the characters. But Spielberg is not trying here for human insights and emotional complexity; he finds those in other films. In *Raiders* he wants to do two things: make a great entertainment, and stick it to the Nazis.

We know how deeply he feels about the Holocaust. We have seen *Schindler's List* and we know about his Shoah Project. Those are works of a thoughtful adult. *Raiders of the Lost Ark* is the work of Spielberg's recaptured

adolescence, I think; it contains the kind of stuff teenage boys like, and it also perhaps contains the daydreams of a young Jewish kid who imagines blowing up Nazis real good. The screenplay is by Lawrence Kasdan, based on a story by Philip Kaufman, George Lucas, and an uncredited Spielberg, whose movie is great fun on the surface—one of the classic entertainments—and then has a buried level.

Consider. The plot hinges on Hitler's desire to recapture the long-lost Ark. "Hitler's a nut on the subject," Indiana Jones (Harrison Ford) is told by a government recruiter. "Crazy. He's obsessed with the occult." But not just anything occult. The Ark, if found, would be the most precious Jewish artifact imaginable—the chest that held the Ten Commandments, which God gave Moses on the mountaintop. "An army which carries the Ark before it is invincible," says Indy's friend Marcus Brody, the museum curator; Hitler wants to steal the heritage of the Jews and use it for his own victory.

Throughout the film, there is a parade of anti-Nazi symbolism and sly religious satire, as when a desperate Indy grabs the hood ornament of a Mercedes truck and it snaps off. And when a Nazi torturer grasps a sacred relic and it burns a stigmata into his hand. When the Ark is being transported in the hold of a Nazi ship, inside a stout lumber crate, the swastika and other Nazi markings spontaneously catch fire and are obliterated. A Nazi officer, uneasy about opening the Ark, says, "I am uncomfortable with the thought of this Jewish ritual." And when the spirit of the Ark manifests itself, it's as a writhing column of fire that skewers the Nazis. ("Keep your eyes closed," Indy desperately tells his sidekick, although one assumes the holy fire would know friend from foe.) There is even a quiet in-joke in the character of Belloq (Paul Freeman), the Frenchman who tries to play both sides against the middle, just as occupied France did.

Nazis were favorite villains of the Saturday serials, prized more for their costumes and accents than for their evil beliefs. Spielberg here makes manifest their values, and then destroys them: *Raiders of the Lost Ark* has all the qualities of an exuberant serial, plus a religious and political agenda. That Spielberg places his message in the crevices of the action makes it all the more effective. *Raiders* may have an impersonal superstructure, but its foundations are personal, and passionate.

I make these points to place it more firmly in the mainstream of Spielberg's work, since *Raiders* is widely enjoyed but just as widely dismissed as something Spielberg tossed off between more important films. It comes between *Close Encounters* and *E.T.,* films Kael compared to "a boy soprano singing with joy." That voice couldn't be heard in *Raiders,* she felt. I think I can hear it: not singing but laughing, sometimes with glee, sometimes in triumph.

The movie is just plain fun. The Kasdan screenplay is a construction of one damn thing on top of another. As the movie opens, Indy brushes aside a web taller than a man, is assaulted by giant spiders, narrowly eludes one booby trap and then another, leaps across a bottomless pit, is nearly crushed by a lowering slab, is betrayed by his companion, leaps the pit again, is pursued by a gigantic boulder that rolls behind him, is surrounded by natives with spears and dart guns, leaps into a river, crawls into an airplane, and finds a giant snake in the cockpit. "I hate snakes," he says.

The movie hurtles from one crisis to another. After the struggle for control of the flying wing (after a fistfight, gunshots, gasoline explosions, and a villain who is made mincemeat by a propeller), Indy is abruptly told, "The Ark! They're taking it on a truck to Cairo!" Indy replies, "Truck? What truck?" And that's all the exposition necessary to get us from the flying-wing scene to the famous truck chase.

Harrison Ford is the embodiment of Indiana Jones—dry, fearless, and as indestructible as a cartoon coyote. The correct casting was not as obvious in 1980, when the film was being prepared, as it is now. He had starred in *Star Wars* and *The Empire Strikes Back,* both times as Han Solo, a laconic man of action, but his other credits were a mixed bag. What he proved in the *Star Wars* movies, and went on to prove again and again, is that he can supply the strong, sturdy center for action nonsense. In a scene where everything is happening at once, he knows that nothing unnecessary need be happening on his face, in his voice, or to his character. He is the fulcrum, not the lever.

Karen Allen plays Marion, his sidekick, a gutsy broad who has the duty of following the hero from one side of the globe to the other, while in constant danger. (She is nearly burned alive twice, shot at, faces down a king cobra, and is left tied to a stake by Indy because, he explains, "If I take you out of here they'll start combing the place for us.") The female lead in an Indiana Jones movie is sort of an honorary boy, no more sexual than the girls in boys' adventure magazines, although Marion can more than take care of herself and is not helpless in the face of danger.

The special effects, astonishing at the time, now look a little cheesy; accustomed to digital perfection, we can see when model planes are being used, when dark clouds are being put in the sky by an optical printer, when the deadly rays of the Ark are being superimposed on the action. Lucas went back and tidied up the effects in *Star Wars*, but I hope Spielberg never touches *Raiders*, because the effects, just as they are, help set the tone of the movie. A serial should look a little hasty. It's a Boy's Own Adventure, a whiz-bang slamarama, a Bruised-Forearm Movie (you squeeze the arm of your date every time something startles you). It's done with a kind of heedless joy. Spielberg was old enough at thirty-four to have the clout to make the film and young enough to remember why he wanted to. All of the reasons why he wanted to.

RAISE
THE RED LANTERN

The 1991 Chinese film *Raise the Red Lantern,* like the 1964 Japanese film *Woman in the Dunes,* is about sexual enslavement. In both films the protagonist enters a closed system from which there is no escape, and life is ruled by long-established "customs." In the Japanese film a woman captures a man, who spends the night in her home at the bottom of a hole in the desert and finds in the morning that the escape ladder has been removed. In the Chinese film, a nineteen-year-old college student drops out of school after her father dies; when her stepmother is unwilling to support her, she agrees to become the concubine of a rich man—his "Fourth Mistress." All four concubines live in a house they are not allowed to leave.

It's difficult to say how realistic either film is intended to be. I have always read *Woman in the Dunes* as a parable, although evidence exists that people do, or did, live in such desert shelters. Zhang Yimou's *Raise the Red Lantern* is set in China in 1920, when concubines were commonplace, but I suspect the conditions of this particular house, long the residence of the wealthy Chen family, are unique.

The film stars Gong Li, who, after attention-getting performances in Zhang Yimou's more realistic and earthy *Ju Dou* and *To Live,* became the leading Chinese star with this film. She is beautiful, and her beauty is one of the subjects of the film, which the director photographs voluptuously. The film takes place within the gray stone-and-tile walls of the Chen complex, where the master lives in the central house and each of the four mistresses has a house of her own opening onto a central courtyard. The house is the neutral backdrop, sometimes seen covered with rain or snow, but the interiors of the four apartments are seen in rich colors, bright red predominantly, so that to enter one of these domains is to be in a space visually marked out for passion.

Although there are many shots of the house's architecture, it is curiously difficult to get a good idea of its extent and layout. It seems to extend in all directions indefinitely, as if expanding in the direction of our gaze. Much of the action takes place on the rooftops, which link in a labyrinth of passageways and stairs and include an ominous little house where, it is said, women have died—but in the past, of course.

Gong Li's character, named Songlian, immediately gets off on the wrong foot with the maid Yan'er (Kong Lin), who is a favorite of the master and has ambitions to become a mistress someday herself. The household's majordomo takes Songlian to meet the other women: First Mistress (Jin Shuyuan), older and in charge; Second Mistress (Cao Cuifeng), who seems plain and pleasant and is described as having a Buddha's face; and Third Mistress (He Caifei), a onetime opera singer, still young and beautiful—and jealous.

Much is made of the family's customs. Things have always been done in such a way, and always will be, and of course the servants are more respectful of these customs than the master. The master, for that matter, is rarely seen; the household operates as such an extension of his will that he seems to be present even when absent. So elusive is he that several reviews of the film actually say he is never seen, although he is on-screen in several long shots, or from behind, or obscured behind hanging veils, and in one scene we can actually see his face, indistinctly, in medium shot. He is not made into an individual, however, and perhaps the point is that his patriarchal dominance is so complete that he functions in this household less as a person than as an officeholder.

The first three mistresses are living in uneasy balance when Songlian arrives, and she becomes a catalyst for trouble. She learns that when the master selects the mistress he will favor for the night, a red lantern is placed outside her house. (The man who has the duty of announcing the

nightly position of the lantern is puffed up with drama and importance.) The lucky mistress then receives a foot massage and is allowed to determine the menu for the next day. There is great competition to be selected, and Songlian eventually discovers intrigues within intrigues—even learning that she cannot trust those she thinks are her friends.

Strange, how these women bow so completely to their situation, the will of the master, and the "customs" of the family, and make one another their enemies. There may be a feminist message here, but it is well concealed in the surface drama of the story. Zhang Yimou begins with a deliberately limited world (based on the novel *Wives and Concubines,* by Su Tong) and enlarges it by deepening it through our increasing knowledge of the personalities of the women, and the way their situation has twisted and shaped them.

Despite the sensual use of color and female beauty, the film has no sex in any conventional sense. No nudity, no nuzzling, almost no touching. (Incredibly, this subject is handled in a movie that was rated PG!) One or two brief bed scenes are obscured behind gauzy curtains. We know that rape is a crime of violence, not sex, and *Raise the Red Lantern* illustrates that, because these women are all essentially being raped as an effect of their position in a male-dominated society that holds them as economic captives. So the movie wisely focuses not on the sex itself but on the situation that regulates and values it. There is even the sense that the master visits his concubines not so much for pleasure as to keep them all in their places and remind them of their duties. (One task, of course, is to produce male children.)

The movie is divided into a prologue and five segments, all but one ending with a close-up of Songlian. This is her experience, and we watch as she fights for her place among the mistresses, discovers plots against her, makes a wounding charge against one of the other mistresses, and rails against the system. That the movie is lush and beautiful rather than stark and barren—that its story involves luxury rather than the vile brothels of the time—suggests, I believe, that men err in excusing discrimination against women on the grounds of "how well they are treated."

I am not a radical feminist and do not believe, as I have heard it argued, that all sex is rape and all men are rapists. I mentioned *Woman in the Dunes* because it provides an intriguing counterargument, in which the man is entrapped because his work is needed to support the woman and the economic system she belongs to. In both cases, one involving a rich man and the other a poor woman, money is the inspiration for dominance.

Zhang Yimou (born in 1951) is a member of the Fifth Generation of Chinese filmmakers, those who began working after the Cultural Revolution and dealt with Chinese society in a more open and artistic way than was permitted at the height of Maoism. Not all of the Generation's films were approved by the Chinese authorities for wide domestic release, but they were a valuable source of foreign exchange and found world audiences; *Raise the Red Lantern* tied for the Silver Lion at Venice and was nominated for an Oscar. He followed it with *To Live* (1994), also starring Gong Li, in the story of an obsessive gambler who loses everything and then makes an extraordinary wartime comeback. After the success of *The Story of Qiu Ju, Ju Dou, To Live,* and this film, all with Zhang Yimou, Gong Li worked for Chen Kaige, another Fifth Generation member, in the extraordinary *Farewell My Concubine* (1993). Few actresses have achieved such an artistic accomplishment in such a short time.

If the directors and actors of that burst of creativity have never quite equaled it since, perhaps it is because they were originally inspired by the long frustration they experienced before China's arts began to open up. *Raise the Red Lantern* is told so directly and beautifully, with such confidence, with so little evidence of compromise. It is the product of a time when the new Chinese film industry could support such work but had not yet learned to meddle with it.

{ R A N }

Akira Kurosawa's *Ran* was inspired by *King Lear*, but it may be as much about Kurosawa's life as Shakespeare's play. Seeing it again in a fine new thirty-five-millimeter print, I realized that the action doesn't center on the old man; it has a fearful energy of its own, through which he wanders. Instead of the story of a great man whose sin of pride drives him mad, Kurosawa has told the story of a man who has waged war all his life, hopes to impose peace in his old age, and unleashes even greater turmoil. There are parallels here not only with kings but with filmmakers, who, like royalty, must enforce their vision in a world seething with jealousy, finance, intrigue, vanity, and greed.

Today we include Kurosawa (1910–1998) among the greatest directors, but for years he was without honor and funds in his own country. He was master of his destiny for only sixteen years of a long life, from 1950 (*Rashomon*) to 1965 (*Red Beard*), and in that span he made the masterpieces *The Seven Samurai, Throne of Blood, Ikiru, The Hidden Fortress, High and Low,* and the twin samurai films *Yojimbo* and *Sanjuro,* among others.

Then his times grew hard. Condemned as "too Western" and old-fashioned in Japan, he begged for his budgets. His *Dodes'ka-den* (1970), a Dickensian view of life among the poor in Tokyo, was rejected by Japanese audiences. Another five years passed before he found Russian financing for *Dersu Uzala,* the story of a Mongolian woodsman who guides a Russian

explorer; it won the Oscar for best foreign film but was a failure at the box office.

In 1975 he announced he wanted to make a samurai epic based on King Lear, but he could find no financing. In 1980 he made the magnificent medieval epic *Kagemusha* as a "rehearsal" for the big film; although it was a success, there was still no money for *Ran*. He filled notebooks with drawings of locations and costumes, and storyboards of scenes. Finally he found an angel in the maverick French producer Serge Silberman, who had backed outsiders such as Buñuel and now found the funds for *Ran*. Kurosawa had directed fourteen films from 1950 to 1965, but *Ran* was only his fourth in the next twenty years.

I recount this history because I think there is much of Kurosawa in *Ran*, made when he was seventy-five. He was preoccupied with mortality in his later years. His eyesight was failing, he attempted suicide, and although he announced that *Ran* would be his last film, he returned to end thoughts in *Dreams* (1990), based on an old man's reveries, and *Madadayo* (1993), about an ancient professor who is honored by his students on his birthday; the title translates as "Not Yet!" and refers to the old man's defiant annual affirmation that he is still not dead.

Now look at *Ran* (its title means "Chaos"). There is much from *King Lear* in it, including an old king who unwisely divides his kingdom into three parts (among sons, not daughters). There is a fool to keep him company, and a loyal follower to shadow and protect him; there is exile after his sons claim that their father's troops overtax their hospitality; he jumps from a cliff that turns out to be a small rise in the ground; he descends into senility but has a flash of insight and is able to apologize to one he has wronged. Certainly the image of the crazed old man, cut loose from authority and lost in the wilderness, will remind anyone of Lear.

And yet, as the critic Stanley Kauffmann has pointed out, the movie is at least as much about war as about an old man's pride and decay. Lear is driven mad because he cuts off the daughter who loves him, and sees his folly when his other daughters betray him. Hidetora, the hero of *Ran*, is driven mad, says Kauffmann, because of the wars between his sons: "The change is from the spiritual to the physical." Lear was personal, Kauffmann says, but *Ran* is "gigantically catastrophic."

King Lear has the old man at its center. In *Ran* we sometimes get the impression that life is hurtling past Hidetoro (Tatsuya Nakadai), who wanders from one tragedy to another, pushing in from the margins, bewildered. We learn from Hidetora in an early scene that he spent his life waging war, until finally he controlled all that he saw. Now he divides his three castles among his three sons, thinking this will bring peace to the land. His youngest son, who loves him most, tells him this will never work. Hidetora banishes him (he marries into the family of a powerful warlord, as Cordelia married the King of France). Then wars consume the land, as the other two sons battle for control. As Hidetora stumbles through this landscape, accompanied by his Fool, his sons and their warriors are more concerned with their battles than with his pathetic, peripheral figure.

Kurosawa combined *King Lear* with a Japanese medieval epic that supplied him with Lady Kaede, the wife of Tara Takatora, the oldest son. Kaede (Mieko Harada), with her painted eyebrows perched high on her forehead in perpetual disapproval, could herself be inspired by Lady Macbeth. After Tara Takatora is killed, she threatens the life of his brother Jiro Masatoru, before sparing him to become his mistress (she sucks the blood from a cut she has made in his throat). Her bizarre demands of revenge marginalize the old man still further: Vengeance and beheadings go on relentlessly, as a reproach to his foolish dreams of peace. Kaede's long-overdue death, unseen below the frame but producing a great splash of blood against a wall, is a masterstroke of timing and execution.

The film is visually magnificent. Kurosawa refined everything he learned about battle scenes in *Kagemusha* and the earlier samurai epics. He uses several static cameras to film the action, cutting between them; because his cameras don't dart and whirl, we are encouraged to think of ourselves not as participants but as gods, observing, taking the long view here and then a close-up look. (One shot, of a man holding his own severed arm, no doubt inspired the similar shot in Spielberg's *Saving Private Ryan*.)

Emi Wada's costumes, which won an Academy Award, carry most of the film's color. I learned from CineBooks that the fourteen hundred costumes were handmade in Kyoto, the traditional seat of Japanese tapestries: "It took three to four months to make each beautifully colored robe (the work was done simultaneously), and it was nearly three years before all were finished." Kurosawa frequently chooses drab backgrounds—barren soil, gray slab courtyards, rock steps—to show off their dazzling beauty.

Every age gets the Shakespeare it deserves. *King Lear* was written at a time when kings still ruled by divine right. It was the Renaissance belief that human destiny was influenced by one's inner humors; Lear's pride brought about his fall. *Ran* is set in medieval times, but it is a twentieth-century film, in which an old man can arrive at the end of his life having won all his battles and foolishly think he still has the power to settle things for a new generation. But life hurries ahead without any respect for historical continuity; his children have their own lusts and furies. His will is irrelevant, and they will divide his spoils like dogs tearing at a carcass.

Did this express Kurosawa's own view in his seventy-fifth year, as he looked back on one of the most remarkable achievements in the history of the movies? Did he reflect that while the West was happy to buy, gut, and remake his work, he had lost all power and respect in the country whose films he once ruled?

Note: It is a measure of Kurosawa's worldwide influence that *The Hidden Fortress* helped inspire *Star Wars*, *The Seven Samurai* was remade as *The Magnificent Seven,* and *Yojimbo* and *Sanjuro* were transformed into the Clint Eastwood Westerns *A Fistful of Dollars* and *For a Few Dollars More.* On the other hand, Kurosawa recycled, too: *Throne of Blood* is from *Macbeth, The Lower Depths* is from Gorky, *The Idiot* is from Dostoyevsky, and *High and Low* is adapted from an Ed McBain police procedural.

{ RASHOMON }

Shortly before filming was to begin on *Rashomon*, Akira Kurosawa's three assistant directors came to see him. They were unhappy; they didn't understand the story. "If you read it diligently," he told them, "you should be able to understand it, because it was written with the intention of being comprehensible." They would not leave: "We believe we have read it carefully, and we still don't understand it at all."

Recalling this day in *Something Like an Autobiography*, Kurosawa explains the movie to them. The explanation is reprinted in the booklet that comes with the new Criterion DVD of *Rashomon*. Two of the assistants are satisfied with his explanation, but the third leaves looking puzzled. What he doesn't understand is that while there is an *explanation* of the film's four eyewitness accounts of a murder, there is not a *solution*.

Kurosawa is correct that the screenplay is comprehensible as exactly what it is: Four testimonies that do not match. It is human nature to listen to witnesses and decide who is telling the truth, but the first words of the screenplay, spoken by the woodcutter, are "I just don't understand." His problem is that he has heard the same events described by all three participants in three different ways—and all three claim to be the killer.

Rashomon (1950) struck the world of film like a thunderbolt. Directed by Kurosawa in the early years of his career, before he was hailed as a grandmaster, it was made reluctantly by a minor Japanese studio, and the studio head so disliked it that he removed his name from the credits. Then it won the Golden Lion at the Venice Film Festival, effectively opening the world of Japanese cinema to the West. It won the Academy Award as best foreign film. It set box office records for a subtitled film. Its very title has entered the English language, because, like "Catch-22," it expresses something for which there is no better substitute.

In a sense, *Rashomon* is a victim of its success, as Stuart Galbraith IV writes in *The Emperor and the Wolf,* his comprehensive study of the lives and films of Kurosawa and his favorite actor, Toshiro Mifune. When it was released, he observes, nobody had ever seen anything like it. It was the first use of flashbacks that disagreed about the action being flashed back to. It supplied first-person eyewitness accounts that differed radically—one of them coming from beyond the grave. It ended with three self-confessed killers and no solution.

Since 1950 the story device of *Rashomon* has been borrowed repeatedly; Galbraith cites *Courage Under Fire,* and certainly *The Usual Suspects* was also influenced, in the way it shows us flashbacks that do not agree with any objective reality. Because we *see* the events in flashbacks, we assume they reflect truth. But all they reflect is a point of view, sometimes lied about. Smart films know this; less ambitious films do not. Many films that use flashbacks only to fill in information are lazy. The genius of *Rashomon* is that all of the flashbacks are both true and false. True, in that they present an accurate portrait of what each witness thinks happened. False, because as Kurosawa observes in his autobiography, "Human beings are unable to be honest with themselves about themselves. They cannot talk about themselves without embellishing."

The wonder of *Rashomon* is that while the shadow play of truth and memory is going on, we are absorbed by what we trust is an unfolding story. The film depends on our faith that we'll get to the bottom of things—even though the woodcutter tells us at the outset that he doesn't understand, and if an eyewitness who has heard the testimony of the other three participants doesn't understand, why should we expect to?

The film opens in torrential rain, and five shots move from long shot to close-up to reveal two men sitting in the shelter of Kyoto's Rashomon Gate. The rain will be a useful device, unmistakably setting apart

the present from the past. The two men are a priest and a woodcutter, and when a commoner runs in out of the rain and engages them in conversation, he learns that a samurai has been murdered and his wife raped, and a local bandit is suspected. In the course of telling the commoner what they know, the woodcutter and the priest will introduce flashbacks in which the bandit, the wife, and the woodcutter say what they saw, or think they saw—and then a medium turns up to channel the ghost of the dead samurai. Although the stories are in radical disagreement, it is unlikely that any of the original participants are lying for their own advantage, since each claims to be the murderer.

Kurosawa's screenplay is only the ground that the film travels, however. The real gift of *Rashomon* is in its emotions and visuals. The cinematographer Kazuo Miyagawa evokes the heat, light, and shade of a semitropical forest. (Slugs dropped from trees onto the cast and crew, Kurosawa recalled, and they slathered themselves with salt to repel them.) The woodcutter's opening journey into the woods is famous as a silent sequence suggesting that he is traveling into another realm of reality. Miyagawa shoots directly into the sun (then a taboo), and there are shots where the sharply contrasted shadows of overhead leaves cast a web upon the characters, making them half-disappear into the ground beneath.

In one long sustained struggle between the bandit (Mifune) and the samurai (Masayuki Mori), their exhaustion, fear, and shortness of breath becomes palpable. In a sequence where the woman (Machiko Kyo) taunts both men, there is a silence in which thoughts form that will decide life or death. Perhaps the emotions evolved in that forest clearing are so strong and fearful that they *cannot* be translated into rational explanation.

The first time I saw the film, I knew hardly a thing about Japanese cinema, and what struck me was the elevated emotional level of the actors. Do all Japanese shout and posture so? Having now seen a great many Japanese films, I know that in most of them the Japanese talk more or less the same way we do (Ozu's films are a model of conversational realism). But Kurosawa was not looking for realism. From his autobiography, we learn that he was struck by the honesty of emotion in silent films, where dialogue could not carry the weight and actors used their faces, eyes, and gestures to express emotion. That heightened acting style, also seen in Kurosawa's

Seven Samurai and several other period pictures, plays well here because many of the sequences are, essentially, silent.

Film cameras are admirably literal, and faithfully record everything they are pointed at. Because they are usually pointed at real things, we usually think we can believe what we see. The message of *Rashomon* is that we should suspect even what we think we have seen. This insight is central to Kurosawa's philosophy. The old clerk's family and friends think they've witnessed his decline and fall in *Ikiru* (1952), but we have seen a process of self-discovery and redemption. The seven samurai are heroes when they save the village but thugs when they demand payment after the threat has passed. The old king in *Ran* (1985) places his trust in the literal meaning of words, and talks himself out of his kingdom and life itself.

Kurosawa's last film, *Madadayo*, made in 1993 when he was eighty-three, was about an old master teacher who is visited once a year by his students. At the end of the annual party, he lifts a beer and shouts out the ritual cry "Not yet!" Death is near, but not yet—so life goes on. The film's hero is in some sense Kurosawa. He is a reliable witness to the fact that he is not yet dead, but when he dies no one will know less about it than he will.

{ REAR WINDOW }

The hero of Alfred Hitchcock's *Rear Window* is trapped in a wheelchair, and we're trapped, too—trapped inside his point of view, inside his lack of freedom and his limited options. When he passes his long days and nights by shamelessly maintaining a secret watch on his neighbors, we share his obsession. It's wrong, we know, to spy on others, but after all, aren't we always voyeurs when we go to the movies? Here's a film about a man who does on the screen what we do in the audience—look through a lens at the private lives of strangers.

The man is a famous photographer named L. B. Jeffries—"Jeff" to his fiancée. He's played by James Stewart as a man of action who has been laid up with a broken leg and a heavy cast that runs all the way up to his hip. He never leaves his apartment and has only two regular visitors: One is his visiting nurse, Stella (Thelma Ritter), who predicts trouble ("the New York State sentence for a Peeping Tom is six months in the workhouse"). The other is his fiancée, Lisa Fremont (Grace Kelly), an elegant model and dress designer who despairs of ever getting him to commit himself. He would rather look at the lives of others than live inside his own skin, and Stella lectures him: "What people ought to do is get outside their own house and look in for a change."

Jeff's apartment window shares a courtyard with many other windows (all built on a single set by Hitchcock), and as the days pass he be-

comes familiar with some of the other tenants. There is Miss Lonelyheart, who throws dinner parties for imaginary gentleman callers, and Miss Torso, who throws drinks parties for several guys at a time, and a couple who lower their beloved little dog in a basket to the garden, and a composer who fears that his career is going nowhere. And there is Thorvald (Raymond Burr), a man with a wife who spends all her days in bed and makes life miserable for him. One day the wife is no longer to be seen, and by piecing together several clues (a saw, a suitcase, a newly dug spot in Thorvald's courtyard garden) Jeff begins to suspect that a murder has taken place.

The way he determines this illustrates the method of the movie. Rarely has any film so boldly presented its methods in plain view. Jeff sits in his wheelchair, holding a camera with a telephoto lens, and looks first here and then there, the way a movie camera would. What he sees, we see. What conclusions he draws, we draw—all without words, because the pictures add up to a montage of suspicion.

In the earliest days of cinema, the Russian director Lev Kuleshov performed a famous experiment in which he juxtaposed identical shots of a man's face with other shots. When the man was matched with food, audiences said the man looked hungry, and so on. The shots were neutral; the montage gave them meaning. *Rear Window* is like a feature-length demonstration of the same principle, in which the shots assembled in Jeff's mind add up to murder.

I sometimes fancy that various archetypal situations circled tirelessly in Hitchcock's mind, like sharks in a tank at the aquarium. One of them was the fascination of voyeurism—of watching people who do not know they are being watched. Another, famously, was the notion of an innocent man wrongly accused. And many of his films illustrate male impotence or indifference in the face of cool blond beauty. Much is said of Hitchcock's blondes (Kim Novak, Eva Marie Saint, Grace Kelly, Tippi Hedren) but observe that they are not erotic playmates so much as puzzles or threats. Lisa, the Kelly character, has a hopeless love for Jeff, who keeps her at arm's length with descriptions of his lifestyle; a fashion model wouldn't hold up in the desert or jungle, he tells her.

Perhaps his real reason for keeping her away is fear of impotence, symbolized by the leg cast; we are reminded of the strikingly similar relationship between Scotty, the Stewart character in *Vertigo*, and the fashion illustrator played by Barbara Bel Geddes. She, too, loves him. He keeps his distance. She sympathizes with his vertigo, as Kelly nurses the broken leg. Both observe his voyeuristic obsessions. In *Vertigo*, Scotty falls in love with a woman he has spied upon but never spoken to. In *Rear Window*, he is in love with the occupation of photography, and becomes completely absorbed in reconstructing the images he has seen through his lens. He wants what he can spy at a distance, not what he can hold in his arms.

Stewart is an interesting choice for these characters. In the 1930s and 1940s he played in light comedy, romances, crime stories, and Westerns, almost always as a character we liked. After the war, he revealed a dark side in the fantasy scenes of Capra's *It's a Wonderful Life*, and Hitchcock exploited that side, distant and cold, in *Rope, The Man Who Knew Too Much, Vertigo*, and *Rear Window*. To understand the curious impact of these roles, consider Tom Hanks, whose everyman appeal is often compared to Jimmy Stewart's. What would it feel like to see him in a bizarre and twisted light?

In *Rear Window*, Jeff is not a moralist, a policeman, or a do-gooder but a man who likes to look. There are crucial moments in the film where he is clearly required to act and he delays, not because he doesn't care what happens but because he forgets he can be an active player; he is absorbed in a passive role. Significantly, at the end, when he is in danger in his own apartment, his weapon is his camera's flashgun; he hopes to blind or dazzle his enemy, and as the man's eyesight gradually returns, it is through a blood-red dissolve that suggests passion expressed through the eyes.

Kelly is cool and elegant here, and she has some scenes where we feel her real hurt. She likes to wear beautiful dresses, make great entrances, spoil Jeff with champagne and catered dinners. He doesn't notice or doesn't like her attention, because it presumes a relationship he wants to elude. There is one shot, partly a point-of-view close-up, in which she leans over him to kiss him, and the camera succumbs to her sexuality even if Jeff doesn't; it's as if she's begging the audience to end its obsession with what Jeff is watching and consider instead what he *should* be drinking in with his eyes—her beauty.

The remote-control suspense scenes in *Rear Window* are Hitchcock at his most diabolical, creating dangerous situations and then letting Lisa and Stella linger in them through Jeff's carelessness or inaction. He stays in his wheelchair. They venture out into danger—Kelly even entering the apartment of the suspected wife killer. He watches. We see danger approaching. We, and he, cannot move, cannot sound the alarm.

This level of danger and suspense is so far elevated above the cheap thrills of modern slasher films that *Rear Window*, intended as entertainment in 1954, is now revealed as art. Hitchcock long ago explained the difference between surprise and suspense. A bomb under a table goes off, and that's surprise. We know the bomb is under the table but not when it will go off, and that's suspense. Modern slasher films depend on danger that leaps unexpectedly out of the shadows. Surprise. And surprise that quickly dissipates, giving us a momentary rush but not satisfaction. *Rear Window* lovingly invests in suspense all through the film, banking it in our memory, so that when the final payoff arrives, the whole film has been the thriller equivalent of foreplay.

{ RIFIFI }

The modern heist movie was invented in Paris in 1954 by Jules Dassin, with *Rififi,* and in 1955 by Jean-Pierre Melville, with *Bob le Flambeur.* Dassin built his film around a twenty-eight-minute safecracking sequence that is the father of all later movies in which thieves carry out complicated robberies. Working across Paris at about the same time, Melville's film, which translates as "Bob the High Roller," perfected the plot in which a veteran criminal gathers a group of specialists to make a big score. The Melville picture was remade twice as *Ocean's Eleven,* and echoes of the Dassin can be found from Kubrick's *The Killing* to Tarantino's *Reservoir Dogs.* They both owe something to John Huston's *The Asphalt Jungle* (1950), which has the general idea but not the attention to detail.

    Rififi was called by François Truffaut the best film noir he'd ever seen (it was based, he added, on the worst noir novel he'd ever read). Dassin's inspiration was to expand the safecracking job, which is negligible in the book, into a breathless sequence that occupies a fourth of the running time and is played entirely without words or music. So meticulous is the construction and so specific the details of this scene that it's said the Paris police briefly banned the movie because they feared it was an instructional guide.

    There is something else unique about the heist scene: It is the centerpiece of the film, not the climax. In a modern heist film, like *The Score*

(2001), the execution of the robbery fills most of the third act. *Rififi* is more interested in the human element, and plays as a parabola, with the heist at the top before the characters descend to collect their wages of sin. After the heist there is still a kidnapping to go.

The film was shot on a modest $200,000 budget on Paris locations that Dassin scouted while wandering unemployed around the town; he was on the Hollywood blacklist and hadn't worked in four years. Streets are usually wet in movies because they photograph better that way, but Paris is especially damp in *Rififi*, shot in wintertime and showing a criminal milieu where the only warmth comes in a flat where one of the crooks lives with his wife and little boy.

The film centers on Tony (Jean Servais, a Belgian actor who had gone through hard times because of alcoholism). Always referred to as "the Stéphanois," he's a sad-eyed, tubercular ex-con who dotes on the little boy, his godson. Tony reveals a nasty streak of cruelty against a former mistress and is quite capable of cold-blooded murder, but by the end he seems purified by loss. His character believes in honor among thieves, and his lonely vengeance against the kidnappers provides the film with its soul.

The boy's father is Jo the Swede (Carl Möhner). Jo and his friend Mario (Robert Manuel) have their eyes on diamonds in a store window, and want to smash and grab just before the light turns green for their getaway car. Tony nixes the plan and advises them to go for the big score—the store's safe. They enlist a safecracker named Cesar, who is played by Dassin himself (credited as "Perlo Vita"). Casing the store is done with a bold brilliance. Tony ostentatiously leaves his bulging wallet neglected on a counter, to show his indifference to money. Determining the type of safe and the kind of alarm, they stage a rehearsal, test the alarm's sensitivity (it responds to vibrations), and discover they can immobilize it with foam from a fire extinguisher.

"No rods," Tony advises. "Get caught with a rod, it's the slammer for life." But the thieves are as ruthless as necessary, tying up the couple who live over the diamond store before gingerly breaking their way through the ceiling with a cushioned hammer. The composer, Georges Auric, originally wrote music for this sequence, but agreed with Dassin that it was unnecessary, and for twenty-eight minutes we hear nothing but taps, breathing,

371

some plaster falling into an umbrella positioned to catch it, some muffled coughs, and then, after the alarm is disabled, the screech of the drills used to cut into the safe. There is, of course, no reason why the men cannot talk softly, and so the silence is Dassin's inspired directorial choice, underlining the suspense. When I saw the film in a 2002 revival in London, the twenty-eight-minute sequence played as it always does, to a theater that was conspicuously hushed in sympathy.

The movie opens with a back-room poker game, and after the heist Dassin mirrors that scene with another shot of men around a table. Nice, how he uses close-ups of their eyes before showing the diamonds. They have committed a perfect crime, but Cesar gives a ring to a girlfriend, and when it's spotted by Pierre (Marcel Lupovici), the boss of a Montmartre nightclub, he guesses the identity of the thieves and sends his men after them for the jewels.

The last third of the film centers around the kidnapping of Jo's son, who will allegedly be returned if the jewels are handed over. Tony knows better: The boy is a witness. He searches for the boy, questioning bartenders, hookers, tough guys, and old pals to get a lead. In these scenes Montmartre seems to cower beneath the damp skies of dawn.

The film's violence has a crude awkwardness that makes it seem more real. Finding a cop beside the stolen getaway car, Tony leaps from a shadow and cudgels him, not with the smooth grace and sensational sound effects of a modern crime picture but with the clumsiness of a man not accustomed to hitting policemen. Much of the violence takes place just off-screen; that may be because of the production codes of the day, but it's effective because the focus falls on the face of the person committing the violence, and not on the violence itself.

There is one scene nobody ever forgets. Cesar the safecracker, whose stupidity leads to the betrayal of the perfect crime, is found by Tony tied to a pillar in the deserted nightclub. He tries to apologize for his mistake. He's sincere, and Tony knows he's sincere. "I liked you, Macaroni," Tony tells Cesar. "But you know the rules." Cesar (played by Dassin) does, and nods sadly.

Dassin was a particular master of shooting on city locations. *The Naked City* (1948) is famous for its semidocumentary use of New York. His great London noir *Night and the City* (1950), with Richard Widmark as a desperate fugitive hunted by mobsters, makes such good use of darkness and the rubble of bomb sites that it deserves comparison with *The Third Man*. In *Rififi*, Dassin finds everyday locales—nightclubs, bistros, a construction site—and invests them with a gray reality. Just before the heist begins, there is a scene all the more lovely because it is unnecessary, in which nightclub musicians warm up and gradually slide into collaboration. There's a real sense of Montmartre in the 1950s.

Dassin, born in 1911, still giving interviews in 2002, was named as a onetime Communist during the McCarthy witch hunt. He wasn't crazy about the *Rififi* project but needed work. Its worldwide success was a blow against the blacklist, which fell after the listed writer Dalton Trumbo was openly hired by Kubrick for *Spartacus* and Otto Preminger for *Exodus*, both in 1960. By then Dassin had settled in Europe; he was married to the fiery Greek actress Melina Mercouri from 1966 until her death in 1994. His last great success, *Topkapi* (1964) was a return to the heist genre, and is credited by *Mission: Impossible*. Although Dassin returned to the United States occasionally, as for the successful black militant drama *Up Tight* (1968), he was basically lost to American moviemaking, and lives in Athens on a street named for Mercouri. The restoration of *Rififi*, long available only on a shabby videotape, rescues a milestone in movie history.

{THE RIGHT STUFF}

Two men haunt Philip Kaufman's *The Right Stuff* (1983), the story of America's first steps into space. One speaks little, the other hardly at all. The laconic one is Chuck Yeager, generally acknowledged as the best test pilot of all time, who judges himself by his achievements, not his words. The other is the minister at the air force testing grounds in the California desert, who officiates at the frequent funerals and is a spectral presence at the bar where the pilots and their women drink.

A newly arrived wife asks how her husband can get his photo on the wall. The answer: He has to die. We overhear a snatch of dialogue: "Sixty-two men in the last thirty-two weeks. You know what that average is?" Every time a pilot tests a new plane, he has a one-in-four chance of dying—or, as the pilots like to say, "screwing the pooch." Seen now in the shadow of the *Challenger* and *Columbia* disasters, *The Right Stuff* is a grim reminder of the cost of sending humans into space. It is also the story of two kinds of courage, both rare, and of the way the "race for space" was transformed from a secret military program into a public relations triumph.

In the movie, reporters at one of the early flights of the Bell X-1 rocket plane are told "No press! Those are orders. National security." Before long everyone is elbowing into the spotlight. The first seven "astronauts" are introduced along with their wives and families, and Henry Luce writes a $500,000 check to buy their exclusive stories for his *Life* magazine. Vice

President Lyndon B. Johnson fumes in his car when John Glenn's wife, Annie, a shy stutterer, won't let him into her house along with the network crews. "You need more than speed records in this day and age," a program publicist explains. "You need coverage." The Mercury program has to compete for funding with other budget items, and as the astronauts tell one another, "No bucks, no Buck Rogers."

When the Kaufman film was released in 1983, it was hailed as one of the great American films, capturing the spirit and reflecting the reporting of Tom Wolfe's 1979 book about the early days of the space program—a book arguing that Yeager (Sam Shepard) was so influential that his manner of speech was unconsciously echoed for years by commercial airline pilots while making announcements from the cockpit. Yet the movie was a puzzling flop at the box office. Some blamed confusion in the public mind between the movie and John Glenn's run for public office.

More likely, even then, audiences were not ready for a movie that approached the program with skepticism, comedy, and irony. The original astronauts labored under no similar handicap; they were heroes to *Life* magazine but knew that Wernher von Braun and the German scientists behind the first launches would have preferred to have monkeys in the capsules. (Saddled with humans, government officials considered surfers as possible astronauts—or even stock-car racers, "who have their own helmets.") Yeager, who felt they were riding, not flying, the capsules, called them "Spam in a can," and in a famous scene the astronauts argue for a porthole even though the designers point out that they have no need to see anything during their brief rides into space—no reason to do anything but sit tight.

But then John Glenn (Ed Harris) used his piloting skills to find the exact angle of entry and save a Mercury capsule from incinerating—something no monkey could have done—and later the desperate improvisations of the *Apollo 13* crew saved that mission and their lives, inspiring Ron Howard's 1995 movie. There was nothing the *Challenger* and *Columbia* crews could have done to save themselves, and that restarted the controversy over manned versus unmanned flights. But in those early days when the Soviets were the first to put a man into orbit, there was no way an American would not follow. The "space race" continues to be symbolized by human astronauts, even now, when it is less a race than the loneliness of long-distance fliers.

Tom Wolfe hung out with the Mercury 7, absorbed their culture and jargon, watched as leather helmets and goggles were replaced by shiny silver suits with NASA logos. In early scenes, as Yeager and his test pilot rival Scott Crossfield try to break through Mach 1, then Mach 2, then "punch a hole in the sky" to "where the demon lives, out at about Mach 2.3," they're watched by friends on the ground who lean against Jeeps, smoking cigarettes. A few years later, launches are pre-empting all other TV programming, and newsman Eric Severeid (playing himself) informs television viewers that they're about to witness "the greatest death-defying stunt ever broadcast." By then the "capsule" had been renamed the "spacecraft"—even though it could not fly on its own and, smaller than a tepee, worked much like Evel Knievel's original vehicles by strapping a passenger into a container on top of a rocket and blasting off. (After one launch, a pilot informs Mission Control, "The altimeter is working!")

Those were the first small steps for man, giant leaps for mankind, and at the end of the road was the 1969 moon landing and other astonishing triumphs. But at first the idea was simply to get an American up there, pronto. "I for one do not intend to go to sleep by the light of a Communist moon," declared Vice President Johnson, and Glenn agrees to take a ride on an untested rocket he is warned is dangerous. That took courage, and in one of his longest speeches in the movie, Yeager says so: To sit on top of tons of explosives and be blasted into orbit was more daring than flying an untested aircraft. The astronauts, of course, were test pilots too, good and brave ones; it's just that at first their piloting skills were not needed. "We are the monkey," says Grissom.

Wolfe's best-selling book was adapted for the screen by William Goldman, who then had a series of "nightmarish" meetings with director Kaufman; Goldman walked out, and the final writing credit is Kaufman's alone. Wolfe's book began with Yeager. Goldman wanted to dump him because he had nothing to do with the central story, but "Phil's heart was with Yeager," Goldman writes in his memoir *Adventures in the Screen Trade.*

Goldman wanted to focus on the selection and training of the Mercury 7, and on three crucial flights. But Kaufman, of course, was correct, and *The Right Stuff* is a greater film because it is not a straightforward historical account but pulls back to chronicle the transition from Yeager and other test pilots to a mighty public relations enterprise.

Two other decisions by Kaufman are more problematical. The movie's portrait of Grissom (Fred Ward) includes a scene showing the astronaut freaking out with claustrophobia after his capsule lands in the Pacific. Kaufman cuts to an exterior shot to show the escape hatch being blown open with explosive bolts, and the implication is that Grissom panicked. Grissom always said the hatch blew on its own. Certainly the space program never lost confidence in him as one of their best men. And the portrait of Lyndon Johnson (Donald Moffat) is too broadly comic, taking cheap shots at a Texas hayseed. (Still, LBJ provides the occasion for a revealing scene where John Glenn firmly supports his stuttering wife's refusal to let Johnson and the TV crews into their house.)

Kaufman's love for the Yeager character pays off in the magical closing sequence of the film, when the "best pilot in the world" eyeballs a new air force jet and says, "I have a feeling this little old plane right here might be able to beat that Russian record." And it nearly does. On an unauthorized flight, he takes it to almost 120,000 feet—the stars are visible—before plane and pilot fall, exhausted, back to the earth. The aging fan dancer Sally Rand, appearing at the 1964 Democratic convention, seems at first an odd counterpoint to this moment, but Kaufman makes the montage oddly affecting by focusing not on the performer but on her feathered wings.

When Yeager had pushed the edge of the envelope as far as it could possibly be pushed by one man in one plane, the age of the individual explorer—of Marco Polo, Magellan, Columbus, Livingston, Scott, Lindbergh—ended, and Team Man stepped into the limelight. That is the real subject of *The Right Stuff*. It's not that Yeager had the right stuff and the others didn't. They all had it, but it had become a new kind of stuff.

That a man could walk on the moon is one of the great achievements of the last century. But after seeing *The Right Stuff* it is hard to argue that manned flights should be at the center of the space program. The

Hubble space telescope has been able to glimpse the dawning of the first days of the universe. Not long after it reached orbit, we lost seven brave men and women who could do absolutely nothing to save themselves. To risk lives while putting Hubble into orbit is one thing. To risk them for high school science-fair projects is another.

{ ROMEO AND JULIET }

Romeo and Juliet is always said to be the first romantic tragedy ever written, but it isn't really a tragedy at all. It's a tragic misunderstanding, scarcely fitting the ancient requirement of tragedy that the mighty fall through their own flaws. Romeo and Juliet have no flaws, and they aren't old enough to be blamed if they did. They die because of the pigheaded quarrel of their families, the Montagues and Capulets. By writing the play, Shakespeare began the shaping of modern drama, in which the fates of ordinary people are as crucial as those of the great. Most of the theatrical tragedies of his time, including his own, involved kings, emperors, generals. Here, near the dawn of his career, perhaps remembering a sweet early romance before his forced marriage to Anne Hathaway, he writes about teenagers in love.

Romeo and Juliet has been filmed many times in many ways; Norma Shearer and Leslie Howard starred in the beloved 1936 Hollywood version, and modern transformations include Robert Wise's *West Side Story* (1961), which applies the plot to Manhattan gang warfare; Abel Ferrara's *China Girl* (1987), about a forbidden romance between a girl of Chinatown and a boy of Little Italy, and Baz Luhrmann's *William Shakespeare's Romeo + Juliet* (1996), with California punk gangs on Verona Beach. But the favorite film version is likely to remain, for many years, Franco Zeffirelli's 1968 production.

His crucial decision, in a film where almost everything went well, was to cast actors who were about the right age to play the characters (as Howard and Shearer were obviously not). As the play opens, Juliet "hath not seen the change of fourteen years," and Romeo is little older. This is first love for Juliet, and Romeo's crush on the unseen Rosalind is forgotten the moment he spots Juliet at the masked ball: "I ne'er saw true beauty until this night." After a well-publicized international search, Zeffirelli cast Olivia Hussey, a sixteen-year-old from Argentina, and Leonard Whiting, a British seventeen-year-old.

They didn't merely look their parts, they embodied them in the freshness of their personalities, and although neither was a trained actor they were fully equal to Shakespeare's dialogue for them; Anthony Holden's book *William Shakespeare: The Man Behind the Genius* contrasts "the beautiful simplicity with which the lovers speak at their moments of uncomplicated happiness" with "the ornate rhetorical flourishes that fuel so much else in the play"—flourishes that Zeffirelli severely pruned, trimming about half the play. He was roundly criticized for his edits, but much that needs describing on the stage can simply be shown on-screen, as when Benvolio is shown witnessing Juliet's funeral and thus doesn't need to evoke it in a description to the exiled Romeo. Shakespeare, who took such wholesale liberties with his own sources, might have understood.

What is left is what people love the play for—the purity of the young lovers' passion, the earthiness of Juliet's nurse, the well-intentioned plans of Friar Laurence, the hot-blooded feud between the young men of the families, the cruel irony of the double deaths. And there is time, too, for many of the great speeches, including Mercutio's poetic evocation of Mab, the queen of dreams.

Hussey and Whiting were so good because they didn't know any better. Another year or two of experience, perhaps, and they would have been too intimidated to play the roles. It was my good fortune to visit the film set, in a small hill town an hour or so outside Rome, on the night when the balcony scene was filmed. I remember Hussey and Whiting upstairs in the old hillside villa, waiting for their call, unaffected, uncomplicated. And when the balcony scene was shot, I remember the heedless energy that Hussey threw into it, take after take, hurling herself almost off the balcony for hungry kisses. (Whiting, balanced in a tree, needed to watch his footing.)

Between shots, in the overgrown garden, Zeffirelli strolled with the composer Nino Rota, who had written the music for most of Fellini's films and now simply hummed the film's central theme, as the director nodded. Pasqualino De Santis, who would win an Oscar for his cinematography, directed his crew quietly, urgently, trying to be ready for the freshness of the actors instead of making them wait for technical quibbles. At dawn, drinking strong coffee as cars pulled around to take his actors back to Rome, Zeffirelli said what was obvious: that the whole movie depended on the balcony and the crypt scenes, that his casting decision had proven itself, and that the film would succeed.

It did, beyond any precedent for a film based on Shakespeare, even though Shakespeare is the most filmed writer in history. The movie opened in the tumultuous year of 1968, a time of political upheaval around the world, and somehow the story of the star-crossed lovers caught the mood of rebellious young people who had wearied of their elders' wars. "This of all works of literature eternizes the ardor of young love and youth's aggressive spirit," wrote Anthony Burgess.

Zeffirelli, born in Florence in 1923, came early to the English language through prewar experiences hinted at in the loosely autobiographical *Tea with Mussolini* (1999). His crucial early artistic influence was Laurence Olivier's *Henry V* (1945), which inspired him to go into the theater; he has had parallel careers directing plays, films, and operas. Before the great success of *Romeo and Juliet,* he first visited Shakespeare for the shaky but high-spirited *Taming of the Shrew* (1967), with Burton and Taylor. Later he directed Plácido Domingo in *Otello* (1986), Verdi's opera, and directed Mel Gibson in *Hamlet* (1990).

Romeo and Juliet remains the magical high point of his career. To see it again is to luxuriate in romance. It is intriguing that Zeffirelli in 1968 focused on love, while Baz Luhrmann's popular version of 1996 focused on violence; something fundamental has changed in films about and for young people, and recent audiences seem shy of sex and love but eager for conflict and action. I wonder if a modern Friday night audience would snicker at the heart-baring sincerity of the lovers.

Zeffirelli got some criticism from purists by daring to show Romeo and Juliet awakening in her bed, no doubt after experiencing physical love. In the play the same dialogue plays in the Capulets' orchard, where "enter Romeo and Juliet, aloft"—on her balcony, that is. I am as sure as I can be that they have just left Juliet's bedchamber—and after all, were they not wed by Friar Laurence (Milo O'Shea), and is it not right they should consummate their love before Romeo is banished into exile?

The costumes by Danilo Donati won another Oscar for the film (it was also nominated for best picture and director), and they are crucial to its success; they are the avenue for color and richness to enter the frame, which is otherwise filled with gray and ocher stones and the colors of nature. The nurse (Pat Heywood) seems enveloped in a dry goods' sale of heavy fabrics, and Mercutio (John McEnery) comes flying a handkerchief that he uses as a banner, disguise, and shroud. Hussey's dresses, with low bodices and simple patterns, set off her creamy skin and long hair; Whiting is able to inhabit his breeches, blouse, and codpiece with the conviction that it is everyday clothing, not a costume.

The costumes and everything else in the film—the photography, the music, above all Shakespeare's language—are so voluptuous, so sensuous. The stagecraft of the twinned death scenes is, of course, all contrivance; the friar's potion works with timing that is precisely wrong, and yet we forgive the manipulation because Shakespeare has been able to provide us with what is theoretically impossible, the experience of two young lovers each grieving the other's death. When the play was first staged in London, Holden writes, Shakespeare had the satisfaction "of seeing the groundlings moved to emotions far beyond anything before known in the theater." Why? Because of craft and art, yes, but also because Romeo and Juliet were not distant and august figures, not Caesars, Othellos, or Macbeths, but a couple of kids in love, as everyone in the theater had known, and everyone in the theater had been.

THE RULES
OF THE GAME

I've seen Jean Renoir's *The Rules of the Game* in a campus film society, at a repertory theater, and on laser disc, and I've even taught it in a film class—but now I realize I've never really seen it at all. This magical and elusive work, which often places second behind *Citizen Kane* in polls of great films, is so simple and so labyrinthine, so guileless and so angry, so innocent and so dangerous that you can't simply watch it; you have to absorb it.

But for many years you couldn't even watch it properly. Without going into detail about how it was butchered after its first release and then finally restored into a version that was actually longer than the original, let it be admitted that it always looked dim and murky—even on the Criterion laser disc. Prints shown on TV or sixteen-millimeter film were even worse. Now there's a Criterion DVD of the film so clear it sparkles, it dances, and the famous deep-focus photography allows us to see clearly what all those characters are doing lurking about in the background. Like Criterion's restoration of *Children of Paradise*, it is a masterpiece reborn.

The movie takes the superficial form of a country-house farce, at which wives and husbands, lovers and adulterers, masters and servants sneak down hallways, pop up in one another's bedrooms and pretend that they are all proper representatives of a well-ordered society. Robert Altman, who once said, "I learned the rules of the game from *The Rules of the Game*," was not a million miles away from this plot with his *Gosford Park*—right down to the murder.

But there is a subterranean level in Renoir's film that was risky and relevant when it was made and released in 1939. It was clear that Europe was going to war. In France, left-wing Popular Front members like Renoir were clashing with Nazi sympathizers. Renoir's portrait of the French ruling class shows them as silly adulterous twits, with the working classes emulating them within their more limited means. His film opens by tweaking a great national hero, the aviator André Jurieu, completing a heroic transatlantic solo flight (a full ten years after Lindbergh) and then whining on the radio because the woman he loves did not come to the airport to meet him. Worse, the characters in the movie who do try to play by the rules are a Jewish aristocrat, a cuckolded gamekeeper, and the embarrassing aviator.

This did not go over well with French audiences on the eve of war. The film is preceded by a little introduction by jolly, plump Renoir, looking like an elderly version of the cherub so often painted by his father, Auguste. He recalls that a man set fire to his newspaper at the movie's premiere, trying to burn the theater down. Audiences streamed out, the reviews were savage, and the film was a disaster even before it was banned by the occupying Nazis. The French like to be funny, but they do not much like to be made fun of. "We were dancing on a volcano," Renoir says.

After a prologue at the airport and an elegant establishing scene in Paris, most of the action takes place at La Colinière, the country estate of Robert de la Cheyniest (Marcel Dalio) and his wife, Christine (Nora Gregor). Among the guests are Robert's mistress, Geneviève (Mila Parély), and the aviator (Roland Toutain), who is in love with Christine. During the course of the week, Robert and his gamekeeper, Schumacher (Gaston Modot) apprehend a poacher named Marceau (Julien Carette), who is soon flirting with Christine's very willing maid, Lisette (Paulette Dubost)—who is married to Schumacher. Another ubiquitous guest is the farcical Octave, played by Renoir, who casts himself as a clown to conceal his insecurity. And there are others—a retired general, various socialites, neighbors, a full staff of servants.

On the Criterion DVD there is a fascinating conversation, filmed many years later on the steps of the château, between Renoir and the actor

Dalio (you may remember him as the croupier in *Casablanca*). Together they try to decide whether the story has a center or a hero. Renoir doubts that it has either. It is about a world, not a plot. True to his nature, he plunged into the material, improvised as he went along, trusted to instinct. He admits to one structural fact: The murder at the end is foreshadowed by the famous sequence in the middle of the film, where the guests blaze away with hunting rifles, killing countless birds and rabbits. The death of one rabbit in particular haunts the film's audiences; its final act is to fold its paws against its chest.

As for a center, well, it may come during that same hunting scene, when Christine is studying a squirrel with binoculars and lowers them to accidentally see her husband Robert kissing his mistress, Geneviève. He had promised his wife that the affair was over. And so in a way it was; whenever we see them together, they seem to be playing at the intrigue of adultery without soiling themselves with the sticky parts. This leads Christine, an innocent soul who believes in true love, to wonder if she should take mercy on the aviator. Soon after, Marceau is smooching with Lisette and Schumacher is chasing him around the corridors. It is when the upstairs and downstairs affairs accidentally mingle that the final tragedy takes place (in true farcical style, over a case of mistaken identity).

Much has been made of the deep focus in *Citizen Kane*—the use of lighting and lenses to allow the audience to observe action in both the front and the back of deep spaces. *The Rules of the Game* is no less virtuoso, and perhaps inspired Welles. Renoir allows characters to come and go in the foreground, middle distance, and background, sometimes disappearing in the distance and reappearing in close-up. Attentive viewing shows that all the actors are acting all of the time, that subplots are advancing in scarcely noticeable ways in the background while important action takes place closer to the camera.

All of this comes to a climax in the famous sequence of the house party, which includes an amateur stage performance put on for the entertainment of guests and neighbors. Only by viewing this sequence time and again can one appreciate how gracefully Renoir moves from audience to stage to backstage to rooms and corridors elsewhere in the house, effortlessly advancing half a dozen courses of action, so that at one point during a moment of foreground drama a door in the background opens and we see the latest development in another relationship. "In the years before the Steadicam," says the director Wim Wenders, "you wonder how a film camera could possibly have been so weightless."

It is interesting how little actual sexual passion is expressed in the movie. Schumacher, the gamekeeper, is eager to exercise his marital duties, but Lisette cannot stand his touch and prefers for him to stay in the country while she remains in town as Christine's maid. The aviator's love for Christine is entirely in his mind. The poacher, Marceau, would rather chase Lisette than catch her. Robert and his mistress, Genevieve, savor the act of illicit meetings more than anything they might actually do during them. It is indeed all a game, in which you may have a lover if you respect your spouse and do not make the mistake of taking romance seriously. The destinies of the gamekeeper and the aviator come together because they both labor under the illusion that they are sincere. I said they are two of the three who play by the rules of the game—but, alas, they are not playing the same game as the others.

It is Robert (Dalio) who understands the game the best, perhaps because as a Jew he stands a little outside of it. His passion is for mechanical windup mannequins and musical instruments, and there is a scene where he unveils his latest prize, an elaborate calliope, and stands by proudly as it plays a tune while little figures ring bells and chime notes. With such a device, at least, everything works exactly as expected. Dalio and Renoir discuss this scene in their conversation. Dalio says he was embarrassed, because it seemed simple to stand proudly beside his toy, yet they had to reshoot for two days. Yes, says Renoir, because the facial expression had to be exact—proud, and a little embarrassed to be so proud, and delighted, but a little shy to reveal it. The finished shot, ending with Robert's face, is a study in complexity, and Renoir says it may be the best shot he ever filmed. It captures the buried theme of the film: that on the brink of war they know what gives them joy but play at denying it, while the world around them is closing down joy, play, and denial.

{ SATURDAY NIGHT FEVER }

Saturday Night Fever was Gene Siskel's favorite movie, and he watched it at least seventeen times. We all have movies like that, titles that transcend ordinary categories of good and bad and penetrate straight to our hearts. My own short list would include La Dolce Vita, A Hard Day's Night, and The Third Man. These are movies that represent what I yearned for at one time in my life, and to see them again is like listening to a song that was popular the first summer you were in love.

Although the movie appealed to him primarily on an emotional level, Siskel spoke about the movie in terms of its themes, and there are two central ones. First, the desire of all young people to somehow escape from a life sentence of boring work and attain their version of the beckoning towers of Manhattan. Second, the difficulty that some men have in relating to women as comrades and friends and not simply sex facilitators.

There is a scene in the movie where the hero, Tony Manero, sits on a bench with Stephanie, the girl he loves, and tells her all about one of the bridges out of Brooklyn—its height, length, how many cubic yards of concrete went into its making—and you can taste his desire to cross that bridge and leave Brooklyn behind. Earlier, Stephanie has described him in a few brutal words: "You live with your parents, you hang with your buddies, and on Saturday nights you burn it all off at 2001 Odyssey. You're a cliché. You're nowhere, goin' no place." Tony senses that she is right.

The theme of escape to the big city is central to American films and literature, and *Saturday Night Fever* has an obvious predecessor. Both the lure of Manhattan and the problems with women were treated ten years earlier in Martin Scorsese's *Who's That Knocking at My Door?* (1968), which also has a hero who suffers from what Freud called the madonna-whore complex. (The complex involves this logic: I love you so much I want to sleep with you, after which I cannot love you anymore, because you are the kind of woman who has sex with men.) By the end of the film, Tony has left his worthless friends behind and made the first faltering steps to Manhattan and to a more enlightened view of women, and so the themes have been resolved.

But I suspect that *Saturday Night Fever* had another kind of appeal to Siskel, one that reflects the way the movies sometimes complete the unfinished corners of our lives. In a way, Tony Manero represented the kind of adolescence Gene didn't have, just as Marcello, the hero of *La Dolce Vita*, led the kind of life I once lusted for. The most lasting images of the movie are its joyous ones, of Tony strutting down a sidewalk, dressing for the evening, and dominating the disco floor in a solo dance that audiences often applaud. There's a lot in the movie that's sad and painful, but after a few years what you remember is Travolta on the dance floor in that classic white disco suit, and the Bee Gees on the sound track.

The Travolta performance is a great cocky affirmation, and his performance is vulnerable and mostly lovable; playing a kid of nineteen, he looks touchingly young. The opening shots set the tone, focusing on his carefully shined shoes as he struts down the street. At home, he's still treated like a kid. When he gets a four-dollar raise at the hardware store, his father says, "You know what four dollars buys today? It don't even buy three dollars." But in his bedroom, with its posters of Al Pacino and *Rocky,* he strips to his bare chest, admires himself in the mirror, lovingly combs his hair, puts on his gold chains, and steps into his disco suit with a funny little undulation as he slides the zipper up. ("The peculiar construction of disco pants is a marvel of modern engineering," observes Scott T. Anderson, on a Web page devoted to the movie. "So loose at the ankles, yet so tight in the groin.") At the dinner table, his dad slaps him, and he's offended: "Would you just watch the hair? I work a long time on my hair, and you hit it!"

The home is a trap, presided over by the photo of Tony's older brother, Father Frank Jr. (Mrs. Manero crosses herself every time she utters the name.) Freedom is represented by cruising the streets and starring on the disco floor. The movie's plot involves his choice between Annette (Donna Pescow), the girl who loves him, and Stephanie (Karen Lynn Gorney), the girl who works in Manhattan and represents his dream of class. In the Scorsese film, the girl really was class (she was a ballerina), but Stephanie is simply a dressed-up version of Annette who got a typing job in an office where famous people (Paul Anka!) sometimes visit.

I've always thought Annette was a better choice for Tony than Stephanie, because Annette has fewer delusions. ("Why do you hate me so much," she asks him, "when all I ever did was like you?") But Tony can't see that, because he can't really see women at all, and in the cruel closing scenes of the film he makes a halfhearted attempt to rape Stephanie, then sits in the front seat of a car while Annette is raped in the back by two of his buddies. Of course, at that time, in that milieu, perhaps it wasn't considered rape, but only an energetic form of courtship.

The film is far from perfect, and some of its scenes are awkward. Watching it again, I was struck by how badly the whole subplot of Father Frank Jr. is handled. Tony's older brother comes home, announces he is leaving the priesthood, has a peculiarly superficial conversation with Tony, accompanies him to the disco, smiles gamely, and then disappears from the disco and the movie. It's as if we're glimpsing a character passing through this movie on his way to another one. It's also interesting to see how little screen time the final disco competition really has, considering how large it looms in our memories.

It's odd, too, how the rape of Annette is misplaced as the movie gets sidetracked by the death of Bobby C. (Barry Miller), who falls, halfway on purpose, off the bridge. The happy ending, as Tony and Stephanie sit on the window ledge and smile, evokes a hopeful future without finding closure for the problems of the immediate past. Tony, who has not gone to college and doesn't share Stephanie's typing skills, may indeed be able to get a job in Manhattan, but it's likely his new job won't be as interesting as the hardware clerking he's leaving behind.

So why, I wonder, did this movie mean so much to Gene Siskel?

Because he saw it at a certain time, I imagine. Because Tony Manero's dreams touched him. Because while Tony was on the dance floor his problems were forgotten, and his limitations were transcended. The first time I saw *La Dolce Vita*, it represented everything I hoped to attain. Ten years later, it represented a version of what I was trapped in. Ten years after that, it represented what I had escaped from. And yet for me its appeal only grew. I had changed but the movie hadn't; some movies are like time machines, returning us to the past.

We all have a powerful memory of the person we were at that moment when we formed a vision for our lives. Tony Manero stands poised precisely at that moment. He makes mistakes, he fumbles, he says the wrong things, but when he does what he loves he feels a special grace. How he feels and what he does transcend the weaknesses of the movie he is in; we are right to remember his strut, and the beauty of his dancing. "Devote your life to something you love—not like, but love," Siskel liked to say. *Saturday Night Fever* is about how Tony Manero does that.

Gene bought the movie's famous white suit at a charity auction. I got to inspect it once. It came with a shirt that buttoned under the crotch, so it would still look neat after a night on the dance floor. I asked Gene if he'd ever tried it on. It was too small, he said. But it wasn't the size that mattered. It was the idea.

{ SAY ANYTHING }

The first time Lloyd Dobler calls Diane Court to ask her out on a date, he dials all but one digit of her phone number, then looks in the mirror and brushes his hair with his hand before dialing the final digit. He wants to look his best. He gets her father on the phone. Her father has received a lot of phone calls from guys wanting to talk to his daughter. Lloyd stumbles through his message, carefully repeats his number twice, and then says, "She's pretty great, isn't she?" "What?" asks the father. "I said, she's pretty great." "Yes," says her dad, "she is."

This scene, early in Cameron Crowe's *Say Anything*, reflects many of the virtues of the movie. In a lesser film Lloyd would have gotten Diane on the phone with the first try. But it is important to establish her father, James (John Mahoney), as a major player, a man whose daughter chose to live with him after a divorce and who tells her she can say anything to him. The movie is about honesty, which is why Mr. Court has to grin at Lloyd's earnest closing line, and it is also about dishonesty.

Lloyd (John Cusack) is tall, loyal, and true, tells the truth, and seems especially frank about the fact that he seems to have absolutely no future. His career plans do not include college. He talks vaguely about a future as a professional kickboxer, but the only time we see him engaged in the sport professionally is when he's teaching a class of preschoolers. Diane

(Ione Skye), on the other hand, is a golden girl, the class valedictorian, winner of a scholarship to England.

She is also beautiful, which Lloyd appreciates with every atom of his being, but she doesn't date much, because she intimidates the other students. When Lloyd confides his love to his best friend, Corey (Lili Taylor), she says simply, "She's too smart for you." When Lloyd takes Diane to the all-night party on high-school graduation night, someone asks her, "Why'd you come with Lloyd Dobler?" and she says, "He made me laugh."

Diane perceives that she does not laugh enough. She tells her dad how much she enjoyed the party and says she missed that kind of fun in high school: "It's like I held everyone away from me." Lloyd and Diane begin to date, tentatively, and she notices that he is instinctively a gentleman. The moment he wins her heart is when he warns her not to step near some glass in a parking lot.

Lloyd's biggest problem, in the eyes of Mr. Court, is his complete lack of a reasonable career plan. Even Lloyd hardly seems to think kickboxing is a workable profession. But he's clear about what he doesn't want to do: "I don't want to buy anything, sell anything, or process anything as a career."

Most people go to love stories in order to identify, in one way or another, with the lovers. Usually they are unworthy of our trust, especially in the modern breed of teenage movies that celebrate cynicism, vulgarity, and ignorance. *Say Anything* is kind of ennobling. I would like to show it to the makers of a film like *Slackers* and ask them if they do not feel shamed. *Say Anything* exists entirely in a real world, is not a fantasy or a pious parable, has characters whom we sort of recognize, and is directed with care for the human feelings involved. When *Entertainment Weekly* chose it as the best modern movie romance, I was not surprised.

Cameron Crowe, who wrote as well as directed this first film, seems able to tap directly into his feelings and memories as a teenager. His autobiographical *Almost Famous* (2000) was set backstage at rock concerts, a much different world than the Seattle of *Say Anything,* but the characters played by Patrick Fugit and John Cusack could be twins in the way they earnestly try to be true to themselves. Both characters have career ambitions that are not respectable (to become a rock critic is not much better than be-

coming a kickboxer, in the eyes of parents). Both are so consumed by their dreams that they ignore conventional ambitions. Both fall in love with apparently inaccessible girls, although Lloyd Dobler has the good luck that Diane loves him, too.

The film follows them gently and tactfully through the stages of romance at eighteen. When it finally finds them in the back seat of a car and perhaps about to have sex, it doesn't descend into the sweaty, snickering dirty-mindedness of many modern teen movies but listens carefully. "Are you shaking?" she asks him. "No," he says. "You're shaking," she says. "I don't think so," he says. When she comes in late the next morning—the first time she has not called home to let her father know where she was—he is angry, but he loves her enough to cool down and listen to what she has to say. The way she describes what happened is one of the movie's flawless moments.

The two lovers both have confidants. For Diane, it is her father, played by John Mahoney as a reminder that this actor can be as convincingly nice as anyone in the movies. He exudes decency. That quality is right for this role, in which we learn that there is a great deal Diane doesn't know about her father. When the IRS looks into the financial records at the nursing home he runs, Diane goes to a local agent to argue her father's case. And the agent (Philip Baker Hall) in a small but indispensable role, tells her flatly but not unkindly, "But he's guilty."

Lloyd's confidant is Corey. This was Lili Taylor's first film after the landmark *Mystic Pizza* (1988), which also introduced Julia Roberts and Annabeth Gish. Here she plays a husky-voiced folksinger who has been dumped by the one love of her life, Joe. "I have written sixty-three songs this year, all about Joe," she tells Lloyd at the party. She sings some of them ("Joe lies when he cries . . ."). She provides advice, but because her specialty is unrequited love she can't quite understand Lloyd and Diane, who share true love. Then Diane devastates Lloyd with the opinion that they should stop seeing each other. She won't say why. ("This girl is different," Lloyd says during his period of mourning. "When we go out, we don't even have to go out, you know?")

Lloyd's exile in the wilderness away from Diane works because Cusack makes us feel the pain. He turns to his other confidant, the sister he lives with (played by his own sister Joan). He plays with his nephew, a little would-be kickboxer. He stands across the street from Diane's house, playing love laments on his boom box. He doesn't understand this sudden rejection, and because we do, we feel all the more for him. When they finally get back together, Crowe's dialogue reflects his need. She tells him she needs him. "Because you need *someone,* or because you need *me?*" Lloyd asks. And immediately answers his own question: "Forget it. I don't care."

Say Anything depends above all on the human qualities of its actors. Cusack and Skye must have been cast for their clear-eyed frankness, for their ability to embody the burning intensity of young idealism. A movie like this is possible because its maker believes in the young characters, and in doing the right thing, and in staying true to oneself. The sad teenage comedies of recent years are apparently made by filmmakers who have little respect for themselves or their characters, and sneer because they dare not dream.

{ SCARFACE }

Tony: Me, I want what's coming to me.
Manolo: What's coming to you?
Tony: The world, Chico, and everything in it.

Brian De Palma's *Scarface* rises or falls with Al Pacino's performance, which is aggressive, over the top, teeth gnashing, arm waving, cocaine snorting, scenery chewing—and brilliant, some say, while others find it unforgivably flamboyant. What were Pacino's detractors hoping for, something internal and realistic? Or low-key? The Tony Montana character is above all a performance artist, a man who exists in order to gloriously be himself. From the film's opening shots, in which he is one more disposable Cuban ex-con in a Florida detention center, his whole drive is to impress his personality and will on others. He begins with no resources or weapons except for his bravado, and fakes out more powerful men simply by *seeming* dangerous and resourceful. His act is a bluff, so there is no sense in underplaying it.

Montana is one of the seminal characters in modern American movies, a character who has inspired countless others. If the crime expert Jay Robert Nash is correct and American gangsters learned how to talk and behave by studying early Hollywood crime movies, then *Scarface* may also have shaped personal styles. There is even a documentary on the new

Scarface DVD about the movie's influence on hip-hop performers. The movie has been borrowed from so often that it's difficult to understand how original it seemed in 1983, when Latino characters were rare, when cocaine was not a cliché, when sequences at the pitch of the final gun battle were not commonplace. Just as a generation raised on *The Sopranos* may never understand how original *The Godfather* was, so *Scarface* has been absorbed into its imitators.

It takes the name and some of the story structure from Howard Hawks's famous *Scarface* (1932), starring Paul Muni and inspired by the life of Al Capone. Both movies were assailed for their violence, both are about the rise and fall of a criminal entrepreneur, both characters are obsessed with their sisters, and both die because they used their own product—in Montana's case, cocaine; in the case of the syphilitic Capone, prostitutes. But the De Palma movie is not a remake in any conventional sense; it takes a familiar story arc, which may even contain echoes of *Macbeth,* and uses it to look at a new character in a new terrain—the Florida of the early 1980s, after Fidel Castro briefly allowed large-scale immigration from his island, sending us boatloads of his tired and weary masses and seizing the opportunity to empty his jails at the same time.

Some of the early footage is documentary, showing news coverage of the arriving refugees and speeches by Castro explaining how he was happy to be rid of counterrevolutionary elements. Tony Montana, broke and a criminal, will do anything to get started in the new land, and he quickly hustles a commission to kill a fellow prisoner who is disliked by a wealthy Cuban American. The payoff will be citizenship. "I kill a Communist for fun," he says, "but for a green card, I gonna carve him up real nice." Soon he has become a lieutenant for Frank Lopez, a south Florida druglord (Robert Loggia), and from there his rise to power is inexorable.

The movie was written by Oliver Stone—interestingly, the same man who directed the largely laudatory documentary *Comandante* (2003), about his three days in conversation with Castro. Stone has always been at home with stories involving men, drugs, sex, and violence, and his work here has a fierce energy; it is possible to see Montana reflecting Stone's own drive to success. His screenplay, like Ben Hecht's work for the earlier *Scarface,* is filled with quotable lines ("All I got in my life is my balls and my word, and I don't break them for nobody"). Stone shows a certain toughness in not trying to soften Montana, who remains a snake from beginning to end; when he gives his mother $1,000, she asks him, "Who did you kill for this?"

For Al Pacino, the role was an opportunity to explore a crime boss who is the polar opposite of his Michael Corleone in Coppola's *The Godfather*. Corleone is slick and smooth, intelligent and strategic; Montana is instinctive, impulsive, and reckless. *The Godfather* was made in 1972, *Scarface* in 1983, and ten years later Pacino and De Palma worked together again on *Carlito's Way*, where Pacino plays a Puerto Rican criminal who for a time tries to go straight. His sadder and wiser Carlito, seen with psychological realism, helps us understand how many deliberate acting choices went into the creation of Tony Montana. "Though a busy performance, it's not a mannered one, meaning that it's completely controlled," Vincent Canby wrote in the *New York Times* on the film's first release.

Scarface shows a man who wants the world, and at one point even sees THE WORLD IS YOURS blinking at him from the Goodyear blimp. The world for him includes the possession of a desirable woman, and from the moment he sees the blond, slender Elvira (Michelle Pfeiffer), he determines that he must have her. She is Frank's mistress, but soon Frank is dead and his mistress and his business belong to Tony. That he must have her is clear, but what he intends to do with her is not; there is no romance between them, no joy, and they have two scenes—one with Tony in a swimming pool and the other in a vast bathtub—where her boredom is palpable. She's along for the drugs. Tony is much more interested in his sister Gina (Mary Elizabeth Mastrantonio), although his incestuous desires are deflected into a determination to keep all other men away from her. This leads him eventually to the murder of Manolo (Steven Bauer), his closest friend. Gina's response to his jealousy is so horrifyingly direct ("Is this what you want, Tony?") that it shows she knows exactly who he is and what buttons she can push.

Scarface is an example of Brian De Palma in overdrive mode. Like Tony Montana, he isn't interested in small gestures and subtle emotions. His best films are expansive, passionate, stylized, and cheerfully excessive, and yet he has never caved in to the demand for routine action thrillers. Even his failures (*Snake Eyes*) are at least ambitious. There is a mind at work in a De Palma picture, an idea behind the style, never a feeling of indifferent vulgarity. His most recent film, *Femme Fatale* (2002), was one of his best, an elegant and deceptive story based on the theft of a dress made of diamonds, which is stolen from the woman wearing it during the opening night at the Cannes Film Festival. That the movie was not more successful is an indictment of the impatience of today's audiences, who want to be assaulted, not seduced.

A film like *Scarface* is more to their liking, which accounts for the film's enduring popularity, even in an edited-for-TV version that emasculates it. The movie has a headlong energy, hurtling toward its Grand Guignol climax. The cinematography, by the great John A. Alonzo, gloriously magnifies the icons in Tony's life—the mansion, the toys, the lifestyle—and then closes in on small, tight compositions as Tony's world shrinks. One of the movie's best scenes shows Tony at a nightclub, drunk, drugged, and exhausted—and heartbroken, we sense, because he has gained the whole world but knows he has not merely lost his soul but perhaps never had one. The music is by Giorgio Moroder, whose impersonal synthesized techno-pop provides the correct tone for a lifestyle that has the surface of luxury but not the comfort.

And then it all comes around to Pacino. What a complete actor this man is. He can play big or small, loud or soft, tireless or exhausted, always as if it's the only note he has. Consider him as the sad, doped publicist in *People I Know* (2002), doggedly trying to focus on an idealistic cause through the fog of his own excesses, and see how different that drug-addicted character is from Tony Montana. Or look back at his early performance as a street hustler in *Panic in Needle Park* (1971).

Pacino has an extraordinary range of styles, and a pitch-perfect ability to evoke them. There is no such thing as "the Al Pacino performance," because there are too many different kinds of them. Here he plays Tony Montana on an operatic scale, as a man who wants more and more and is finally killed by his own excess. In the final sequence he has a pile of cocaine on his desk and plunges his nose into it as if trying to inhale life itself. Pacino plays part of that scene with white powder stuck to his nose. The detail is often parodied, but it is a correct acting choice, showing a man who has become heedless of everything except his need. If Pacino goes over the top in *Scarface,* and he does, that's because the character leads him there; over the top is where Tony Montana lives.

{ THE SEARCHERS }

John Ford's *The Searchers* contains scenes of magnificence, and one of John Wayne's best performances. There are shots that are astonishingly beautiful. A cover story in *New York* magazine called it the most influential movie in American history. And yet at its center is a difficult question, because the Wayne character is racist without apology—and so, in a less outspoken way, are the other white characters. Is the film intended to endorse their attitudes, or to dramatize and regret them? Today we see it through enlightened eyes, but in 1956 many audiences accepted its harsh view of Indians.

The film is about an obsessive quest. The niece of Ethan Edwards (Wayne) is kidnapped by Comanches who murder her family and burn their ranch house. Ethan spends five years on a lonely quest to hunt down the tribe that holds the girl, Debbie (Natalie Wood)—not to rescue her, but to shoot her dead, because she has become "the leavin's of a Comanche buck." Ford knew that his hero's hatred of Indians was wrong, but his glorification of Ethan's search invites admiration for a twisted man. Defenders of the film point to the famous scene where Ethan embraces his niece instead of killing her. Can one shot redeem a film?

Ethan's quest inspired a plot line in George Lucas's *Star Wars*. It's at the center of Martin Scorsese's *Taxi Driver*, written by Paul Schrader, who used it again in his own *Hardcore*. The hero in the Schrader screenplays is a loner driven to violence and madness by the mission to rescue a young

white woman who has become the sexual prey of those seen as subhuman. Harry Dean Stanton's search for Nastassja Kinski in Wim Wenders's *Paris, Texas* is a reworking of the Ford story. Even Ethan's famous line "That'll be the day" inspired a song by Buddy Holly.

The Searchers was made in the dying days of the classic Western, which faltered when Indians ceased to be typecast as savages. Revisionist Westerns, including Ford's own *Cheyenne Autumn* in 1964, took a more enlightened view of Native Americans, but the Western audience didn't want moral complexity; like the audience for today's violent thrillers and urban-warfare pictures, it wanted action with clear-cut bad guys.

The movie was based on a novel by Alan LeMay and a script by Ford's son-in-law Frank Nugent, the onetime film critic who wrote ten Ford films, including *She Wore a Yellow Ribbon* and *Wagon Master*. It starred John Wayne, who worked with "Pappy" Ford in fourteen major films, as a Confederate soldier who boasts that he never surrendered, who in postwar years becomes a wanderer, who arrives at the ranch of his brother Aaron (Walter Coy) and Aaron's wife, Martha (Dorothy Jordan), under a cloud: He carries golden coins that may be stolen, and Sheriff Sam Clayton (Ward Bond) says he "fits a lot of descriptions."

It is clear from the way Ethan's eyes follow Martha around the room that he secretly loves her. His hatred of Indians flares the moment he meets Martin Pawley (Jeffrey Hunter): "Hell, I could mistake you for a half-breed." Martin says he's "one-eighth Comanche." Ethan rescued young Martin when his family was killed by Indians and left him with Martha and Aaron to be raised, but it's clear he thinks one-eighth is too much.

When Martin insists on joining Ethan's search for the captured Debbie, Ethan says, "I give the orders" and treats the younger man with contempt. In a saloon, Ethan pours out drinks but snatches away Martin's glass, snarling, "Wait'll you grow up." Martin at this point has been a ranch hand, is engaged to be married, has been on the trail with Ethan for years. Does Ethan privately think it's dangerous for a "half-breed" to drink? One of the mysteries of *The Searchers* involves the relationship between Ethan and Martin on the trail. Living alone with each other for months at a time, sleeping under the stars, what did they talk about? How could they share a mission and not find common cause as men?

Martin's function on the trail is to argue for Debbie's life, since Ethan intends to find her and kill her. The younger man also figures in a romantic subplot awkwardly cobbled onto the main story. He is engaged to marry Laurie (Vera Miles), the daughter of friendly Swedish neighbors. Ford goes for cornball humor in scenes where Martin writes to Laurie only once in five years, and in that letter makes light of having mistakenly purchased a "squaw bride." Martin returns on the very day when Laurie, who never expected to see him again, is scheduled to marry Charlie (Ken Curtis), a hayseed, and the men fight for the woman in a sequence that would be more at home in *Seven Brides for Seven Brothers* than in an epic Western.

The Searchers indeed seems to be two films. The Ethan Edwards story is stark and lonely, a portrait of obsession, and in it we can see Schrader's inspiration for Travis Bickle of *Taxi Driver;* the Comanche chief named Scar (Henry Brandon) is paralleled by Harvey Keitel's pimp named Sport, whose western hat and long hair cause Travis to call him "Chief." Ethan doesn't like Indians, and says so plainly. When he reveals his intention to kill Debbie, Martin says, "She's alive and she's gonna stay alive!" and Ethan growls, "Livin' with Comanches ain't being alive." He slaughters buffalo in a shooting frenzy, saying, "At least they won't feed any Comanche this winter." The film within this film involves the silly romantic subplot and characters hauled in for comic relief, including the Swedish neighbor Lars Jorgensen (John Qualen), who uses a vaudeville accent, and Mose Harper (Hank Worden), a half-wit treated like a mascot. There are even musical interludes. This second strand is without interest, and those who value *The Searchers* filter it out, patiently waiting for a return to the main story line.

Ethan Edwards, fierce, alone, a defeated soldier with no role in peacetime, is one of the most compelling characters Ford and Wayne ever created. Did they know how vile Ethan's attitudes were? I would argue that they did, because Wayne in his personal life was notably free of racial prejudice, and because Ford made films with more sympathetic views of Indians. This is not the instinctive, oblivious racism of Griffith's *The Birth of a Nation.* Countless Westerns have had racism as the unspoken premise; this one consciously focuses on it. I think it took a certain amount of courage to cast Wayne as a character whose heroism was tainted. Ethan's redemption is intended to be shown in that dramatic shot of reunion with Debbie, where he takes her in his broad hands, lifts her up to the sky, drops her down into his arms, and says, "Let's go home, Debbie." The shot is famous and beloved, but small counterbalance to his views throughout the film—and indeed, there is no indication he has come to think any differently about Indians.

John Ford (1895–1973) was Hollywood's greatest chronicler of American history, and there was a period when his *The Grapes of Wrath* (1940) and not *Citizen Kane* was cited as the best American film. He worked on his first film in 1914, and was directing by 1917. He had an unrivaled eye for landscape, and famously used Monument Valley as the location for his Westerns, camping out with cast and crew, the company eating from a chuck wagon and sleeping in tents. Wayne told me that making a Ford Western was like living in a Western.

Ford's eye for composition was bold and sure. Consider the funeral early in the film, with a wagon at low right, a cluster of mourners in the middle left, then a diagonal up the hill to the grave, as they all sing Ford's favorite hymn, "Shall We Gather at the River." (He used it again in the wedding scene.) Consider one of the most famous of all Ford shots, the search party in a valley as Indians ominously ride parallel to them, silhouetted against the sky. And the dramatic first sight of the adult Debbie, running down the side of a sand dune behind Ethan, who doesn't see her. The opening and closing shots, of Ethan arriving and leaving, framed in a doorway. The poignancy with which he stands alone at the door, one hand on the opposite elbow, forgotten for a moment after delivering Debbie home. These shots are among the treasures of the cinema.

In *The Searchers* I think Ford was trying, imperfectly, even nervously, to depict racism that led to genocide. The comic relief may be an unconscious attempt to soften the message. Many members of the original audience probably missed his purpose; Ethan's racism was invisible to them, because they bought into his view of Indians. Eight years later, in *Cheyenne Autumn,* his last Western, Ford was more clear. But in the flawed vision of *The Searchers* we can see Ford, Wayne, and the Western itself, awkwardly learning that a man who hates Indians can no longer be an uncomplicated hero.

SHANE

Looked at a certain way, the entire story of *Shane* is simply a backdrop against which the hero can play out his own personal repression and remorse. The movie is conventionally seen as the story of farmers standing up to the brutal law of the gun in the old West, with a lone rider helping a settler hold on to his land in the face of hired thugs. Look a little more carefully, and you find that the rider and the farmer's wife feel an attraction for each other. And that Shane is touched by the admiration of young Joey, the son of the farm couple. Bring Freud into the picture and you uncover all sorts of possibilities, as the newcomer dresses in sissy clothes and absorbs insults and punishment from the goons at the saloon, before strapping on his six-gun and proving himself the better man.

It's not that a greater truth lurks in the depths of George Stevens's *Shane* (1953). It's that all of these levels coexist, making the movie more complex than a simple morality play. Yes, on the surface, Shane is the gunfighter who wants to leave his past behind him, who yearns for the sort of domesticity he finds on Joe Starrett's place in the Grand Tetons. Yes, someone has to stand up to the brutal Rufus Ryker (Emile Meyer), who wants to tear down the fences and allow his cattle to roam free. Yes, Shane is the man—even though he knows that if he succeeds he'll have to leave the valley. "There's no living with a killing," Shane tells Joey, after shooting three men dead in the saloon. "There's no going back from it. Right or wrong, it's a brand, a brand that sticks."

Yes, the picture works on that level, and on that level it was nominated as one of the best films of 1953. But if it worked only on that level, it would have grown dated, like *High Noon* and certain other classic Westerns. There are intriguing mysteries in *Shane*, puzzles and challenges, not least in the title character and the way he is played by Alan Ladd.

Ladd was a movie star of below-average stature and strikingly good looks, and for much of his career he worked around both of those attributes in roles where he was photographed to look tough and taller. In *Shane*, he is frankly seen as a neat, compact man, no physical match for the hired guns like Wilson (Jack Palance) and Calloway (Ben Johnson) who tower over him. He rides into town with a buckskin fringe on his jacket, looking a tad precious to my eyes, and goes to the store to buy a new kit—dress slacks and a blue shirt with an open collar that makes him look almost effeminate in contrast to the burly, whiskered gunmen who work for Ryker and live, apparently, in the saloon.

His first visit to the saloon sets up the undercurrent for the whole story. Dressed like a slicker, he orders a soda pop. The cowboys snicker. Calloway ambles over, calling him a "sodbuster" who smells like a pig—a reference to his plowing duties on the farm of Starrett (Van Heflin). Shane asks, "You speaking to me?" Calloway replies, "I don't see nobody else standing there." The confrontation ends with Calloway throwing a drink on Shane's new shirt, while we're wondering if Travis Bickle was a fan of this film.

On the farm, Jean Arthur plays Marion, Joe's wife and Joey's mother, and there's obvious chemistry between her and the handsome visitor who is now sleeping in the barn. She never acts on it, nor does Shane. They have too much respect for Joe, we sense. Little Joey is meanwhile so starry-eyed in admiration that Shane becomes a father figure, significantly teaching him how to fire a gun; during a fight scene, Joey watches happily, while eating a candy cane. On the Fourth of July, Shane and Marion dance while Joe watches, his face showing not so much concern as recognition of the situation.

As in many Westerns before and since, in *Shane* everything comes

down to a shootout in a barroom, although first there is an unusual amount of conversation. The people in the valley are not simple action figures, as they might be today, but struggle with ideas about their actions. Ryker twice tries to convince Joe to go to work for him, and once tries to hire Shane. Ryker and Wilson have a quiet and thoughtful conversation about the potential for violence of Torrey (Elisha Cook Jr.), another local farmer. Joe engages the settlers in debates about how to respond to Ryker's threats. The only character without much to say is Wilson, the famous hired gun from out of town. He has a dozen lines of dialogue and exists primarily as a foreboding presence. (He arrives in town on foot, leading his horse—an effective entrance, even if Hollywood lore says that Palance at the time was so awkward on horseback that Stevens put him on foot in desperation.)

Wilson embodies the older western principle of might over right. There is a chilling sequence in which Torrey rides into town for a showdown with Wilson and is shot dead. Stevens orchestrates it with hard-edged reserve, staying almost entirely in long shot, showing Torrey picking his way gingerly across the muddy wagon ruts in the road, then walking in the mud parallel to the saloon's wooden porch—a high ground where Wilson's strides match him. Torrey never even gets up onto the porch; he dies, outdrawn, in the mud. It is one of the saddest shooting deaths in any Western, comparable to Keith Carradine's death in Robert Altman's *McCabe & Mrs. Miller.*

The whole movie builds to the inescapable fact that Shane must eventually face Wilson and the other gunmen. If Shane is still alive afterward, he will have to leave town. He can't stay, not simply because he has been "branded" by a killing, but because there is no acceptable resolution for his feelings for Marion.

Now, why isn't there? Well, he could let Joe go into town and get killed, which is what Joe wants to do. That would leave Marion and Joey in need of a man. But Shane knocks Joe out to prevent that. He likes Joe too much, perhaps. Or does he? Shane is so quiet, so inward, so narcissistic in his silent withdrawing from ordinary exchanges that he always seems to be playing a role. A role in which he withholds his violent abilities as long as he can, and then places himself in a situation where he is condemned to use them, after which he will ride on, lonely, to the next town. He has . . . issues.

A story depends on who is telling it. *Shane* is told from the point of view of the town and of the boy, who famously cries, "Shane! Shane! Come back!" in the closing scene. If we were to follow Shane from town to town, I suspect we would find ritual reenactments of the pattern he's trapped in. Notice that after stopping for a drink of water at Joe's place, he's all set to leave when Ryker's men ride up. It's then that he interests himself in another man's quarrel, introduces himself as "a friend," displays his six-gun, and essentially chooses to get involved in a scenario that's none of his business and will lead to an ending we suspect he's seen many times before.

Why does he do this? There is a little of the samurai in him, and the medieval knight. He has a code. And yet—there's *something else* suggested by his behavior, his personality, his whole tone. Here is a man tough enough to handle any threat and handsome enough to win the heart of almost any woman. Why does he present himself as a weakling? Why is he without a woman? There must be a deep current of fear, enlivened by masochism. He is afraid of women? Maybe. Does he deliberately lead men to think they can manhandle him, and then kill them? Manifestly. Does he do this out of bravery and courage and because he believes in doing the right thing? That is the conventional answer. Does he also do it because it expresses some deep need or yearning? A real possibility. *Shane* never says, and maybe never knows. Shane wears a white hat and Palance wears a black hat, but the buried psychology of this movie is a mottled, uneasy, fascinating gray.

SNOW WHITE AND THE SEVEN DWARFS

If Walt Disney's *Snow White and the Seven Dwarfs* had been primarily about Snow White, it might have been forgotten soon after its 1937 premiere, and treasured today only for historical reasons, as the first full-length animated feature in color. Snow White is, truth to tell, a bit of a bore, not a character who acts but one whose existence inspires others to act. The mistake of most of Disney's countless imitators over the years has been to confuse the titles of his movies with their subjects. *Snow White and the Seven Dwarfs* is not so much about Snow White or Prince Charming as about the Seven Dwarfs and the evil Queen—and the countless creatures of the forest and the skies, from a bluebird that blushes to a turtle that takes forever to climb up a flight of stairs.

Walt Disney's shorter cartoons all centered on one or a few central characters with strongly defined personalities, starting with Mickey Mouse himself. They lived in simplified landscapes and occupied stories in which clear objectives were boldly outlined. But when Disney decided in 1934 to make a full-length feature, he instinctively knew that the film would have to grow not only in length but in depth. The story of Snow White as told in his source, the Brothers Grimm, would scarcely occupy his running time, even at a brisk eighty-three minutes.

Disney's inspiration was not in creating Snow White but in creating her world. At a time when animation was a painstaking frame-by-frame

417

activity and every additional moving detail took an artist days or weeks to draw, Disney imagined a film in which every corner and dimension would contain something that was alive and moving. From the top to the bottom, from the front to the back, he filled the frame (which is why the studio's decision in the 1980s to release a cropped "wide-screen" version was so wrong-headed, and quickly retracted).

So complex were his frames, indeed, that Disney and his team of animators found that the cels they used for their short cartoons were not large enough to contain all the details he wanted, and larger cels were needed. The film's earliest audiences may not have known the technical reasons for the film's impact, but in the early scene where Snow White runs through the forest, they were thrilled by the way the branches reached out to snatch at her, and how the sinister eyes in the darkness were revealed to belong to friendly woodland animals. The trees didn't just sit there within the frame.

Disney's other innovation was the "multiplane camera," which gave the illusion of three dimensions by placing several levels of drawings one behind another and moving them separately—the ones in front faster than the ones behind, so that the background seemed to actually move instead of simply unscrolling. Multiplane cameras were standard in animation until the recent use of computers, which achieve a similar but more detailed effect—too detailed, purists argue, because too lifelike.

Nothing like the techniques in *Snow White* had been seen before. Animation itself was considered a child's entertainment, six minutes of gags involving mice and ducks, before the newsreel and the main feature. *Snow White* demonstrated how animation could release a movie from its trap of space and time; how gravity, dimension, physical limitations, and the rules of movement itself could be transcended by the imaginations of the animators.

Consider, for example, when Snow White is singing "I'm Wishing" while looking down into the well. Disney gives her an audience—a dove that flutters away in momentary fright, then returns to hear the rest of the song. Then the point of view shifts dramatically, and we are looking straight up at Snow White from beneath the shimmering surface of the water in the well. The drawing is as easy to achieve as any other, but where did the imagination come from, to supply that point of view?

Walt Disney often receives credit for everything done in his name (even sometimes after his death). He was a leader of a large group of dedicated and hardworking collaborators, who are thanked in the first frames of *Snow White,* before the full credits. But he was the visionary who guided them, and it is a little stunning to realize that modern Disney animated features like *Beauty and the Beast, The Lion King,* and *Aladdin,* as well as the hits made outside the Disney shop, like DreamWorks's *Shrek* and Pixar's *Toy Story,* to this day still use the basic approach that you can see full-blown in *Snow White.* So do the best Japanese animators.

The most important continuing element is the use of satellite and sidekick characters, minor and major, serious and comic. A frame is not allowed to contain only a single character for long, lengthy speeches are rare, musical and dance numbers are frequent, and the central action is underlined by the bit characters, who mirror it or react to it.

Disney's other insight was to make the characters physically express their personalities. He did that not by giving them funny faces or distinctive clothes (although that was part of it) but by studying styles of body language and then exaggerating them. When Snow White first comes across the cottage of the dwarfs, she goes upstairs and sees their beds, each one with a nameplate: Sleepy, Grumpy, Dopey, and so on. When the dwarfs return home from work ("Heigh-ho! Heigh-ho!") they are frightened and resentful to find a stranger stretched across their little beds, but she quickly wins them over by calling each one by name. She knows them, of course, because they personify their names. But that similarity alone would soon become boring if they didn't also act out every speech and movement with exaggerated body language, and if their very clothing didn't seem to move in sympathy with their personalities.

Richard Schickel's 1968 book *The Disney Version* points out Disney's inspiration in providing his heroes and supporting characters with different centers of gravity. A heroine like Snow White will stand upright and tall. But all of the comic characters will make movements centered on and emanating from their posteriors. Rump-butting is commonplace in

Disney films, and characters often fall on their behinds and spin around. Schickel attributed this to some kind of Disney anal fixation, but I think Disney did it because it works: It makes the comic characters rounder, lower, softer, bouncier, and funnier, and the personalities of all seven dwarfs are built from the seat up.

The animals are also divided into body styles throughout Disney. "Real" animals (like Pluto) look more like dogs; comic animals (like Goofy) stand upright and are more bottom-loaded. In the same movie a mouse will be a rodent but Mickey will somehow be other than a mouse; the stars transcend their species. In both versions, nonstar animals and other supporting characters provide counterpoint and little parallel stories. Snow White doesn't simply climb up the stairs at the dwarfs' house—she's accompanied by a tumult of animals. And they don't simply follow her in one-dimensional movement. The chipmunks hurry so fast they seem to climb over one another's backs, but the turtle takes it one laborious step at a time and provides a punch line when he tumbles back down again.

What you see in *Snow White* is a canvas always shimmering, palpitating, with movement and invention. To this is linked the central story, which, like all good fairy tales, is terrifying, involving the evil Queen, the sinister Mirror on the Wall, the poisoned apple, entombment in the glass casket, the lightning storm, the rocky ledge, the Queen's fall to her death. What helps children deal with this material is that the birds and animals are as timid as they are, scurrying away and then returning for another curious look. The little creatures of *Snow White* are like a chorus that feels the way the kids in the audience do.

Snow White and the Seven Dwarfs was immediately hailed as a masterpiece (the Russian director Sergei Eisenstein called it the greatest movie ever made). It remains the jewel in Disney's crown, and although inflated modern grosses have allowed other titles to pass it in dollar totals, it is likely that more people have seen it than any other animated feature. The word "genius" is easily used and has been cheapened, but when it is used to describe Walt Disney, reflect that he conceived of this film, in all of its length, revolutionary style, and invention, when there was no other like it—and that to one degree or another, every animated feature made since owes it something.

{ S O L A R I S }

The films of the Russian master Andrei Tarkovsky are more like environments than entertainments. It's sometimes said they're too long, but that's missing the point: He uses length and depth to slow us down, to edge us out of the velocity of our lives, to bring us into a zone of reverie and meditation. When he allows a sequence to continue for what seems like an unreasonable length, we have a choice. We can be bored or we can use the interlude as an opportunity to consolidate what has gone before, and process it in terms of our own reflections.

At Telluride in 1982, when Tarkovsky (1932–1986) was honored and his *Nostalgia* had its North American premiere, there were long talks afterward under the stars. Moviegoers argued about a sequence in which the film's hero stands in an abandoned swimming pool, lights a candle, then attempts to walk back and forth without the candle going out. When he fails, he tries again. During the movie there was audible restlessness in the audience, and some found the scene merely silly. Others found themselves thinking of times in their own lives where some arbitrary action, endlessly repeated, was like a bet with fate: *If I can do this, it means I will get my wish.*

After Tarkovsky was given the Telluride Medal, he stalked to the edge of the stage, a fierce mustached figure in jeans and cowboy boots, to angrily say (in words translated by the gentle Polish director Krzysztof Zanussi): "The cinema, she is a whore. First she charge a nickel, now she charge five dollars. When she learns to give it away, she will be free." (The next night, the actor Richard Widmark, also honored, replied: "I want to name you some pimps. Hitchcock ... Fellini ... Bergman ... Orson Welles ...")

Tarkovsky's brief manifesto was nevertheless of value as an insight into his approach to filmmaking. His later films are uncompromised meditations on human nature and the purpose of existence, and they have a profound undercurrent of spirituality—enough to get him into trouble with the Soviet authorities, who cut, criticized, and embargoed his films, and eventually drove him into exile. He consciously embodied the idea of a Great Filmmaker, making works that were uncompromisingly serious and ambitious, with no regard whatever for audience tastes or box office success.

I saw his 1972 film *Solaris* at the Chicago Film Festival that year. It was my first experience of Tarkovsky, and initially I balked. It was long and slow, and the dialogue seemed deliberately dry. But then the overall shape of the film floated into view; there were images of startling beauty, then developments that questioned the fundamental being of the characters themselves, and finally an ending that teasingly suggested that everything in the film needed to be seen in a new light. There was so much to think about afterward, and so much that remained in my memory. With other Tarkovsky films—*Andrei Rublev, Nostalgia, The Sacrifice*—I had the same experience.

Solaris is routinely called Tarkovsky's reply to Kubrick's *2001*. Indeed, Tarkovsky could have seen the Kubrick film at the 1969 Moscow Film Festival, but *Solaris* is based on a 1961 novel by the Polish science fiction writer Stanislaw Lem. Both films involve human space journeys and encounters with a transforming alien intelligence, which creates places (*2001*) or people (*Solaris*) from clues apparently obtained by reading minds. But Kubrick's film is outward, charting man's next step in the universe, while Tarkovsky's is inward, asking about the nature and reality of the human personality.

Solaris begins with a long conversation between the psychologist Kelvin (Donatas Banionis) and the cosmonaut Berton (Vladislav Dvorzhetsky), at the country home of Kelvin's father. This home will be seen again at the end of the film in a transformed context. Berton tells Kelvin about a Soviet space station circling the planet Solaris, and of deaths

and mysteries on board. Eventually Kelvin arrives at the station (his journey is not shown) and finds one crew member dead and two more deeply disturbed by events on the station. The planet, we learn, is entirely covered by a sea, and when X-ray probes were used to investigate it, the planet apparently replied with probes of its own, entering the minds of the cosmonauts and making some of their memories real. Within a day, Kelvin is presented with one of the Guests that the planet can create: a duplicate of his late wife, Hari (Natalya Bondarchuk), exact in every detail but lacking her memories.

This Guest is not simply a physical manifestation, however. She has intelligence, self-consciousness, memory, and lack of memories. She does not know that the original Hari committed suicide. She questions Kelvin, wants to know more about herself, eventually grows despondent when she realizes she cannot be who she appears to be. To some extent her being is limited by how much Kelvin knows about her, since Solaris cannot know more than Kelvin does; this theme is made clearer in Steven Soderbergh and George Clooney's 2002 remake of the film.

When we love someone, who do we love? That person or our idea of that person? Some years before "virtual reality" became a byword, Tarkovsky was exploring its implications. Although other persons no doubt exist in independent physical space, our entire relationship with them exists in our minds. When we touch them, it is not the touch we experience but our consciousness of the touch. To some extent, then, the second Hari is as "real" as the first, although different.

The relationship between Kelvin and the new Hari plays out against the nature of reality on the space station. He glimpses other Guests. He views a taped message from the dead cosmonaut, filled with information and warning. Hari, it develops, cannot be killed—although that is tried—because she can simply be replaced. Physical pain is meaningless to her, as we see when she attempts to rip through a steel bulkhead door because she does not know how to open it. Gentle feelings are accessible to her, as seen in a scene that everybody agrees is the magic center of *Solaris*, when the space station enters a stage of zero gravity and Kelvin, Hari, and lighted candles float in the air.

The last sequence of the film, which I will not reveal, invites us to reconsider the opening sequence, and to toy with the notion that there may be more Guests in the film than we first thought. It is a crucial fact that this final shot is seen by us, the viewers, and not by those on the space station. "The arc of discovery is on the part of the audience, not the characters," writes the critic N. Medlicott. That they may be trapped within a box of consciousness that deceives them about reality is only appropriate, since the film argues that we all are.

The 2002 Soderbergh version was a good film, attentive to the vision and ideas of Tarkovsky, but much shorter (99 minutes to 165 minutes). Its shorter running time did not prevent audiences from rejecting it decisively; there was an enormous gap between the overwhelmingly favorable reviews and the audience members who said in exit surveys that they hated it. The problem obviously was that the film attracted the wrong audience, drawing people who were seeking a George Clooney science fiction film, not a philosophical meditation, and had no knowledge or interest in Tarkovsky. If they thought Soderbergh's smart, seductive rhythms were boring, they would have been catatonic after the Tarkovsky version.

It may be, indeed, that Tarkovsky's work could have benefited from trimming. No director makes greater demands on our patience. Yet his admirers are passionate, and they have good reason for their feelings: Tarkovsky consciously tried to create art that was great and deep. He held to a romantic view of the individual able to transform reality through his own spiritual and philosophical strength. Consider the remarkable sequence in *Andrei Rublev* (1966), set in medieval times, when a young boy claims he knows the secret of recasting a broken bell and commands a team of workers in a process about which, in fact, he knows nothing. When the bell peals, what we are hearing is the sound of Tarkovsky's faith.

STRANGERS
ON A TRAIN

The abiding terror in Alfred Hitchcock's life was that he would be accused of a crime he did not commit. This fear is at the heart of many of his best films, including *Strangers on a Train* (1951), in which a man becomes the obvious suspect in the strangulation of his wife. He makes an excellent suspect because of the genius of the actual killer's original plan: Two strangers will "exchange murders," each killing the person the other wants dead. They will both have airtight alibis for the time of the crime, and there will be no possible connection between killer and victim.

It is a plot made of ingenuity and amorality, based on the first novel by Patricia Highsmith (1921–1995), who in her Ripley novels and elsewhere was fascinated by brainy criminals who functioned not out of passion but from careful calculation, and usually got away with their crimes. The "crisscross" murder deal in *Strangers on a Train,* indeed, would have worked perfectly—except for the detail that only one of the strangers agrees to it.

Guy Haines (Farley Granger), a famous tennis player, is recognized on a train by Bruno Anthony (Robert Walker), whose conversation shows a detailed knowledge of Guy's private life. Guy wants a divorce from his cheating wife, Miriam (Kasey Rogers), in order to marry Anne Morton (Ruth Roman), the daughter of a U.S. senator. Over lunch in his private compartment, Bruno reveals that he wants his father dead, and suggests a

427

"perfect crime" in which he would murder Guy's wife, Guy would murder Bruno's father, and neither would ever be suspected.

Bruno's manner is pushy and insinuating, with homoerotic undertones. Guy is offended by the references to his private life, but inexplicably doesn't break off the conversation—which ends on an ambiguous note, with Bruno trying to get Guy to agree to the plan and Guy trying to jolly him along and get rid of him. Bruno does murder Guy's wife, then demands that Guy keep his half of the bargain. As a plot, this has a neatness that Hitchcock must have found irresistible—especially since Guy has a motive to murder his wife, was seen in a public fight with her earlier on the day of her death, and even told his fiancée he would like to "strangle" Miriam.

Hitchcock said that correct casting saved him a reel in storytelling time, since audiences would sense qualities in the actors that didn't need to be spelled out. Certainly the casting of Granger as Guy and Walker as Bruno is crucial. Hitchcock allegedly wanted William Holden for the role of Guy ("He's stronger," he told François Truffaut), but Holden would have been all wrong—too sturdy, too put off by Bruno (despite the way Holden allowed an aging actress to manipulate him in *Sunset Boulevard*). Granger is softer and more elusive, more convincing as he tries to slip out of Bruno's conversational web instead of flatly rejecting him. Walker plays Bruno as flirtatious and seductive, sitting too close during their first meeting, then reclining at full length across from Guy in the private compartment. The meeting on the train, which was probably planned by Bruno, plays more like a pickup than a chance encounter.

It is this sense of two flawed characters—one evil, one weak, with an unstated sexual tension—that makes the movie intriguing and halfway plausible, and helps explain how Bruno could come so close to carrying out his plan. Highsmith was a lesbian whose novels have uncanny psychological depth; Andrew Wilson's 2003 biography says she often fell in love with straight women, and her stories frequently use a buried subtext of unstated gay attraction—as in *The Talented Mr. Ripley*, made into a 1999 movie in which her criminal hero Tom Ripley falls in love not so much with his quarry Dickie Greenleaf as with his identity and lifestyle. Although homosexuality still dared not speak its name very loudly in 1951, Hitchcock was quite aware of Bruno's orientation, and indeed edited separate American and British versions of the film—cutting down the intensity of the "seductiveness" in the American print. It's worth noticing that Hitchcock also cast Granger in *Rope* (1948), based on the Leopold-Loeb case; it was another story about a murder pact with a homosexual subtext.

Strangers on a Train is not a psychological study, however, but a first-rate thriller with odd little kinks now and then. It proceeds, as Hitchcock's films so often do, with a sense of private scores being settled just out of sight. His obsession with being wrongly accused no doubt refers to a traumatic episode in his childhood, when his father sent naughty little Alfred to the police station with a note asking the sergeant to lock him up until called for. Interesting, in this context, is Hitchcock's casting of his own daughter, Patricia, as the outspoken young Barbara Morton, kid sister of Guy's fiancée, Anne. Patricia Hitchcock and Kasey Rogers look a little alike and wear very similar eyeglasses; Bruno is playfully demonstrating strangling techniques at a party when he sees Barbara, flashes back to the murder, and flips out. The kid sister gets the creepiest lines in *Strangers on a Train*, especially during an early meeting involving Guy and the senator's whole family; she keeps blurting out what everyone is afraid to say.

Hitchcock was, above all, the master of great visual set pieces, and there are several famous sequences in *Strangers on a Train*. Best known is the one where Guy scans the crowd at a tennis match and observes that all of the heads are swiveling back and forth to follow the game—except for one head, Bruno's, which is looking straight ahead at Guy. (The same technique was used in Hitchcock's *Foreign Correspondent*, where all the windmills rotate in the same direction—except one.) Another effective scene shows Bruno floating in a little boat through the Tunnel of Love at a carnival; Miriam and two boyfriends are in the boat ahead, and shadows on the wall make it appear that Bruno has overtaken them. In a scene where Guy goes upstairs in the dark in Bruno's house, Hitchcock told Truffaut, he hit on the inspiration of a very large dog to distract the audience from what he would probably find at the top. Then there's the famous sequence involving a runaway merry-go-round, on which Guy and Bruno struggle as a carnival worker crawls on his stomach under the revolving ride to get to the controls. (This shot was famously unfaked, and the stuntman could have been killed; Hitchcock said he would never take such a chance again.) Another great shot shows Bruno's face in the shadow of his hat brim, only the whites of his eyes showing.

Hitchcock was a classical technician in controlling his visuals, and his use of screen space underlined the tension in ways the audience is not always aware of. He always used the convention that the left side of the screen is for evil and/or weaker characters, while the right is for characters who are either good or temporarily dominant. Consider the scene where Guy is letting himself into his Georgetown house when Bruno whispers from across the street to summon him. Bruno is standing behind an iron gate, the bars casting symbolic shadows on his face, and Guy stands to his right, outside the gate. Then a police car pulls up in front of Guy's house, and he quickly moves behind the gate with Bruno; they're now both behind bars as he says, "You've got me acting like I'm a criminal."

The Robert Walker performance benefits from a subtle tense urgency that perhaps reflected events in his private life; he had a nervous breakdown shortly after filming was completed, was institutionalized for treatment, and died of an accidental overdose of tranquilizers. (Leftover close-ups from this film were used to finish his final film, *My Son John*.) Although Hitchcock said in François Truffaut's book-length interview that he didn't much like either of the actors, Walker's Bruno has been called one of Hitchcock's best villains, and Hitch agreed with Truffaut that the audience sympathy was more with him than with Granger's playboy.

The movie is usually ranked among Hitchcock's best (I would put it below only *Vertigo, Notorious, Psycho*, and perhaps *Shadow of a Doubt*) and its appeal is probably the linking of an ingenious plot with insinuating creepiness. That combination came in the first place from Highsmith, whose novels have been unfairly shelved with crime fiction when she actually writes mainstream fiction about criminals. There's an intriguing note from a user of the Internet Movie Database, claiming to have spotted Highsmith in a cameo in the film. She's behind Miriam in the early scene in the record store, writing something in a notebook. No Highsmith cameo has even been reported in the movie's lore (all the attention goes to Hitchcock's trademark cameo) but you can look for yourself, in chapter 6 of the DVD, twelve minutes and sixteen seconds into the running time. To think she may have been haunting it all of these years.

{ STROSZEK }

Who else but Werner Herzog would make a film about a retarded ex-prisoner, a little old man, and a prostitute, who leave Germany to begin a new life in a house trailer in Wisconsin? Who else would shoot the film in the home town of Ed Gein, the murderer who inspired *Psycho*? Who else would cast all the local roles with locals? Who else would end the movie with a policeman radioing, "We've got a truck on fire, can't find the switch to turn the ski lift off, and can't stop the dancing chicken. Send an electrician."

Stroszek (1977) is one of the oddest films ever made. It is impossible for the audience to anticipate a single shot or development. We watch with a kind of fascination, because Herzog cuts loose from narrative and follows his characters through the relentless logic of their adventure. Then there is the haunting impact of the performance by Bruno S., who is at every moment playing himself.

The personal history of Bruno S. forms the psychic background for the film. Bruno was the son of a prostitute, beaten so badly he was deaf for a time. He was in a mental institution from the ages of three to twenty-six—and yet was not, in Herzog's opinion, mentally ill; it was more that the blows and indifference of life had shaped him into a man of intense concentration, tunnel vision, and narrow social skills. He looks as if he has long been expecting the worst to happen.

Herzog, who with Wim Wenders and Rainer Werner Fassbinder brought forth the New German Cinema in the late 1960s and 1970s, saw Bruno in a documentary about street musicians. He cast him in the extraordinary film *Every Man for Himself and God Against All* (1975), also known as *The Enigma of Kaspar Hauser*. It told the story of an eighteenth-century man locked in a cellar until he was an adult, then set loose on the streets to make what sense he could of the world. Bruno was uncannily right for the role, and right, too, for *Stroszek,* which Herzog wrote in four days.

Ah, but there is a reason why the screenplay came quickly. Herzog had the location already in mind. He and the American documentarian Errol Morris had become fascinated by the story of Ed Gein, who dug up all of the corpses in a circle around his mother's grave. Did he also dig up his mother? They decided they had to open the grave to see for themselves. In question-and-answer sessions we had during tributes at Facets in Chicago and the Walker Art Center in Minneapolis, Herzog told me the story: Morris did not turn up as scheduled in Plainfield, Wisconsin, the grave was never opened, but Herzog's car broke down there and he met the mechanic whose shop provides a key location and character for the film.

With the destination in mind, Herzog found the story writing itself. The film opens with Bruno (Bruno S.) being released from prison, walking into a bar, and meeting Eva (Eva Mattes), a prostitute whose pimp mistreats her. He offers her refuge in his apartment, which has been looked after by the elderly, tiny Mr. Scheitz (Clemens Scheitz). Mr. Scheitz announces that his nephew in Railroad Flats, Wisconsin, has invited him to move there. It is time, Bruno announces, for all of them to begin their new lives. Eva raises money through prostitution (her clients are Turkish workers at a construction site), and the three find themselves in Wisconsin and in possession of a magnificent new forty-foot 1973 Fleetwood mobile home.

But this plot summary sounds mundane, and the tone of the movie is so strange. *Stroszek* is not a comedy, but I don't know how to describe it. Perhaps as a peculiarity. We get the sense that Herzog is adding detail on the spot: as Railroad Flats happens to the characters, it happens to the film. Mr. Scheitz's nephew is played by Clayton Szalpinski, the very mechanic who repaired Herzog's car, and he regales the newcomers with local color.

A farmer and his enormous tractor have gone missing, and Clayton believes they are to be found at the bottom of one of the many local lakes. He has a metal detector, and on days when the ice is thick enough, he searches.

Bruno is sure the idyll cannot last. He is positive that the papers they signed at the bank will sooner or later require them to make payments, and he is right. Scott McKain plays a painfully polite bank employee who tries to explain that the TV set "might/would" have to be repossessed (he often uses two words to take the edge off of both; McKain perfectly captures the tone of a man embarrassed to be bringing up money). Eventually there is the unforgettable sight of the Fleetwood being towed off the land, leaving Bruno to stare at the forbidding winter Wisconsin landscape. He knew something like this would happen.

The thing about most American movies is that the actors in them look like the kinds of people who might be hired for a movie. They don't have to be handsome, but they have to be presentable—to fall within a certain range. If they are too strange, how can they find steady work? Herzog often frees himself of this restraint by using nonactors. Clayton Szalpinski, for example, has an overbite and backwoods speech patterns, but he is right for his role, and no professional actor could play a small-town garage mechanic any better. And Bruno S. is a phenomenon. Herzog says that sometimes, to get in the mood for a scene, Bruno would scream for an hour or two. In his acting he always seems to be totally present: There is nothing held back, no part of his mind elsewhere. He projects a kind of sincerity that is almost disturbing, and you realize that there is no corner anywhere within Bruno for a lie to take hold.

Many movies end with hopeless characters turning to crime. No movie ends like *Stroszek*. Bruno and Mr. Scheitz take a rifle and go to rob the bank, which is closed, so they rob the barbershop next door of thirty-two dollars and, leaving their car running, walk directly across the street to a supermarket, where Bruno has time to pick up a frozen turkey before the cops arrest Mr. Scheitz. Bruno then drives to a nearby amusement arcade, where he feeds in quarters to make chickens dance and play the piano. Then he boards a ski lift to go around and around and around.

This last sequence is just about the best he has ever filmed, Herzog says on the commentary track of the DVD. His crew members hated the dancing chicken so much they refused to participate, and he shot the footage himself. The chicken is a "great metaphor," he says—for what, he's not sure. My theory: A force we cannot comprehend puts some money in the slot, and we dance until the money runs out.

Stroszek has been reviewed as an attack on American society, but actually German society comes out looking worse, and all of the Americans seem naive, simple, and nice, even the bank official. The film's tragedy unfolds because these three people have nothing in common and no reason to think they can live together in Wisconsin or anywhere else. For a time Eva sleeps with Bruno, but then she closes her door to him, and in a remarkable scene he shows her a twisted sculpture and says, using the third person, "This is a schematic model of how it looks inside Bruno. They're closing all the doors on him."

Earlier in the film, in Berlin, after he loses his job and his girl, Bruno goes to a doctor for help. This man (Vaclav Vojta) listens carefully, is sympathetic, has no answers, and takes Bruno into a ward where premature babies are being tended. Look, he says, how tenacious the grip reflex is, even in this little infant. A child clings to the doctor's big fingers. Bruno looks. We can never tell from his face what he is thinking. The baby cries, and the doctor tenderly cradles it, kissing its ear, and it goes to sleep. That is, perhaps, what Bruno needs.

A SUNDAY
IN THE COUNTRY

In a country house near Paris, toward autumn of 1912, an old man sings to himself as he prepares for the day. He brushes his teeth, shines his shoes, seems happy. Downstairs, his housekeeper sings a song of her own in the kitchen. When the old man comes downstairs, the two songs meet, in a harmony not of melody but of mood.

They have an argument about the distance to the train station. The old man thinks it should take him about ten minutes to walk it. The housekeeper reminds him that he doesn't walk as fast as he once did. It emerges that he is expecting a visit from his son and his son's family. He sets off toward the station, is intercepted halfway there by his two grandsons, and then there is much discussion with his son about whether the train was early or the clock behind, for it cannot be that he walked more slowly.

So begins *A Sunday in the Country*, Bertrand Tavernier's graceful and delicate story about the hidden currents in a family. The old man is Monsieur Ladmiral, played by Louis Ducreux with buried depths of disappointment with his life. He is a painter; his studio is in the garden of his house. His son is Gonzague (Michel Aumont), his daughter-in-law Marie-Therese (Geneviève Mnich), and there are three grandchildren. Ladmiral also has a daughter, Irene (Sabine Azéma). Gonzague's family visits almost every Sunday; Irene, who is single, rarely comes at all.

It is clear that the son has been a disappointment to his father, and

clear that the son accepts this because he loves the old man. There is some talk about how the grandsons are doing in school, and the son remembers that he worked hard at school. "Sure you did," says Ladmiral, "but it didn't help." The family communicates with the shorthand of barely visible signs; when Marie-Therese skips away to catch the end of the Mass, the old man asks, "Still devout?" and the son agrees, and an instant's look passes between them that suggests a long history, maybe unspoken, of their consideration of this woman. Later, in a half-heard aside, the old man observes that Marie-Therese has renamed Gonzague "Eduardo," because she didn't like his original name.

Tavernier never urges his story upon us, and has no great plot to unwind. He simply wants to observe his characters during the course of a long day during which we find that none of them are very happy with their lives. The son cannot please the father, hard as he tries, and the daughter cannot disappoint him, hard as she tries. To find comparable attention to the subtle forces within a family you would have to turn to Yasujiro Ozu, who made almost all of his films about Japanese families. The Japanese term *mono no aware*, which suggests a bittersweet awareness of the beauty of life and the inevitability of death, applies to Ozu, and here to Tavernier.

The surface of the movie is drowsy and pastel. It seems to yearn toward impressionism. *A Sunday in the Country* lulls us with the summery quiet of the day. There is lunch, a nap, tea, a walk, a visit to a bistro, dinner. We gather that the old man has had success as a painter, made money, been honored (the rosette on his lapel indicates that he is a chevalier of the Legion of Honor). But he missed the boat of impressionism. Now, in his seventies, it seems clear to him that he directed his career down the wrong road. ("I did what my teachers told me to do," he murmurs at one point.)

The day unfolds slowly. The boys torture a ladybug. The daughter climbs a tree and is afraid to come down. Settling down for a nap, Gonzague tells Marie-Therese that perhaps he should have continued with his early experiments with painting. His first works were not bad. "But I might have disappointed my father . . . or become his rival . . ." he says, only she is already asleep.

Irene arrives like a whirlwind, driving her own automobile. She sweeps up children in her arms, hurries through the house, is filled with energy. Together they all go to a nearby bistro. In public she is extroverted and almost too cheerful. In private we see her looking sadly at nothing. "She wanted to be not free, but alone," the narrator (Tavernier) tells us. "Look at your sister, Irene," Ladmiral tells his son. "She forged ahead. You didn't." Studying her car, the son says, "I had children, not a car."

By the end of the day, it is all there to be seen: Ladmiral's feeling that he took the wrong path in his painting, his son's feeling that he can never please the father he loves, his wife's silent bourgeois complacency, and his sister's secret unhappy urgency, with sudden telephone calls that send her away as quickly as she came. When everyone has gone, the old man takes the canvas he had been working on and turns it against the wall. He mounts a fresh canvas and sits and stares at it. The camera then focuses on a meadow that looks like an impressionist landscape, but not one that Ladmiral will ever paint. Perhaps it is in his mind.

A Sunday in the Country has a haunting, sweet, sad quality. It is about this family, and many families. It is told by Tavernier with great attention to detail, and the details add up to the way life is. There are three startling moments when reality is broken. In one, we see Gonzague, Marie-Therese, and the housekeeper looking down at the dead body of Ladmiral, impeccably dressed, laid as if sleeping on his bed. In another, Irene sees her dead mother, who tells her, "Will you stop asking so much of life, Irene?" In the third, Irene hugs her niece and intuits that she will die young, perhaps by fifteen. These scenes are not supernatural, but are realizations of the kinds of thoughts, memories, and fears we all have when we are around our families.

Tavernier, born in 1941, is one of the most gifted and humanist French directors, the leader of the generation after the New Wave. He worked as a critic and a publicist (for Godard and Chabrol) before making his first film, *The Clockmaker*, in 1974. The screenplay was by Jean Aurenche and Pierre Bost, one of the most famous screenwriting teams of the postwar years. They represented the school that the auteurist critics scornfully dismissed as "quality" and intended the New Wave to wash away. But Tavernier valued their work, and *A Sunday in the Country* is based on a novel, *Monsieur Ladmiral Is Going to Die Soon*, by Bost. There is another connection: Tavernier's *Safe Conduct* (2003), about the French filmmakers who continued to work during the Nazi occupation, uses Aurenche as a starring character.

Tavernier is a man who loves movies, and he is often associated with revivals and restorations of neglected classics. At the Telluride Film Festival and elsewhere he presents his discoveries with enthusiasm that contains no hint of competitiveness; one feels he would as soon introduce a film he loves as one of his own. He is enormously prolific (twenty-nine films since 1974). He does not have a signature subject or style but ranges widely; his work includes *Coup de Torchon* (1981), which improbably transplants a Jim Thompson novel to French Africa; *'Round Midnight* (1986), starring Dexter Gordon in the story of a tenor sax player based on Lester Young and Charlie Parker; *A Week's Vacation* (1980), with its great performance by Nathalie Baye as a schoolteacher who in a week away from work profoundly rediscovers her life; *Daddy Nostalgie* (1990), Dirk Bogarde's last performance, as a dying man reconciling with his daughter; and *L.627*, which records the routines and futility of French narcotics cops.

And there are many more. His work is an abundance of invention and generosity, and in a way the opposite of the auteur theory, which he once supported, since Tavernier never forces himself or a style upon us. If there is a common element in his work, it is his instant sympathy for his fellow humans, his enthusiasm for their triumphs, his sharing of their disappointments. To see the work of some directors is to feel closer to them. To see Tavernier's work is to feel closer to life.

{SUNRISE}

The camera's freedom to move is taken for granted in these days of the Steadicam, the lightweight digital camera, and even special effects that reproduce camera movement. A single unbroken shot can seem to begin with an entire city and end with a detail inside a window—consider the opening of *Moulin Rouge*. But the camera did not move so easily in the early days.

The cameras employed in the first silent films were lightweight enough to be picked up and carried, but moving them was problematical because they were attached to the cameraman, who was cranking them by hand. Camera movement was rare; the camera would pan from a fixed position. Then came tracking shots—the camera literally mounted on rails, so that it could be moved along following the action. But a camera that was apparently weightless, that could fly, that could move through physical barriers—that kind of dreamlike freedom had to wait until almost the last days of silent films. And then, when the talkies came and noisy sound cameras had to be sealed in soundproof booths, it was lost again for several years.

F. W. Murnau's *Sunrise* (1927) conquered time and gravity with a freedom that was startling to its first audiences. To see it today is to be astonished by the boldness of its visual experimentation. Murnau was one of the greatest of the German expressionists; his *Nosferatu* (1922) invented the vampire movie, and his *The Last Laugh* (1924) became famous for doing away altogether with intertitles and telling the story entirely with images.

Summoned to America by William Fox to make a film for his new studio, Murnau worked with the cinematographers Charles Rosher and Karl Strüss to achieve an extraordinary stylistic breakthrough. The Murnau admirer Todd Ludy wrote, "The motion picture camera—for so long tethered by sheer bulk and naiveté—had with *Sunrise* finally learned to fly."

The film was released at the very moment when silent films were giving way to sound; *The Jazz Singer* was already making its way into theaters. Murnau's film actually had a sound track, avoiding dialogue but using music and sound effects in sync with the action. By the next year, audiences would want to hear the actors speaking, and that led to an era of static compositions and talking heads, unforgettably lampooned in *Singin' in the Rain*.

Released in what Peter Bogdanovich calls the greatest year in Hollywood history, when silent films reached perfection and then disappeared, *Sunrise* was not a box office success, but the industry knew it was looking at a masterpiece. When the first Academy Awards were held, the top prize was shared: *Wings* won for "best production," and *Sunrise* won for "best unique and artistic picture."

Its story can be told in a few words. It is a fable, denying the characters even names; the key players are the Man (George O'Brien), the Wife (Janet Gaynor, who also won an Oscar), and the Woman from the City (Margaret Livingston). In a quaint lakeside village, the city woman came for a holiday, and lingered on to seduce and entrap the man. In a remarkable early sequence, we see her smoking in her room, prowling restlessly in lingerie, and then walking through the village to the lighted window of the man's cottage, where she whistles (there is a low and ominous musical note on the sound track). Inside the cottage, the man hears her, we see torment and temptation in his face, and finally he slips out of the cottage; when his wife returns to the table with their dinner, he is gone, and the movie juxtaposes her embracing their child and the woman from the city embracing him.

But look at the shot that shows the man and the city woman slipping off into a foggy marsh area. Although the ground is muddy and uneven, the camera seems to glide smoothly along with them, pushing through shrubbery, following their progress, finally watching them embrace beneath a full moon. I've seen *Sunrise* several times and always noted this shot without quite realizing how impossible it was. Now I have had it explained. The

commentary track on the Twentieth Century–Fox DVD is by the cinematographer John Bailey, who is a student of early camera techniques and a particular admirer of the cinematographer Karl Strüss. He explains that the marsh is a studio set, that the sky and the moon are actually quite close, and that the camera platform is suspended from overhead cables so that it glides behind them as they push through the mud and the shrubbery.

If the poetry of this scene is haunting, listen to Bailey as he analyzes some of the famous later scenes, including two boat trips across the lake and a fantastical interlude in the city on the other shore. He has the gift, rare among experts, of explaining his art with such love and clarity that everyone can understand; he uses the writings of Strüss, still photos taken on the set, and above all his own instinct and experience to explain how extraordinary shots were created.

Many of the best moments involve superimposed images. At one point we see the man being enveloped by two ghostly images of the woman from the city. We see a train passing in the foreground while extras walk in the middle distance and the city rises in the background. We see a frenzied nightclub scene, musicians on the left, dancers in the center, all seeming to float in a void.

These shots, Bailey explains, were created in the camera. It was an era before optical printers, let alone computers; the camera operators masked part of the film, exposed the rest, then masked those portions and exposed what remained. Meticulous control of the lens and the counting of individual frames was necessary. In addition, the shots were made of different kinds of reality; the train was a model that looked large in the foreground, the extras were real, the city was a form of matte drawing.

Listening to Bailey, it occurred to me that the best commentary tracks are often by experts who did not work on the film but love it and have given it a lot of thought. They're more useful than those rambling tracks where directors (notoriously shy about explaining their techniques or purposes) reminisce about the weather on the set that day.

The power of *Sunrise* comes precisely through its visual images, and Bailey makes a good case that Strüss, who got second billing after Charles Rosher, made the key contribution. He had purchased his own camera, powered by an electric motor, which set it free to glide through space and give *Sunrise* its peculiar, dreamlike quality. And he devised techniques to create some of the effects; looking at stills taken on the set, Bailey takes hints from such details as a black backcloth that was used to obscure part of an image so it could be replaced with another.

The story, as I said, is very simple, but it has power. The woman from the city persuades the man to drown his wife so they can run away together. The film has few titles, but they are dramatic: the word "drown" swims into view and then appears to run down the screen and disappear. As the man and his wife begin their boat journey across the lake, Bailey notes that the camera always regards him from a high angle, even when he is towering over his wife and the natural angle would have him looking down at the camera. This strategy keeps him subservient to the camera and emphasizes the pressure he's under; Murnau underlines his tortured psychological state by making the actor, O'Brien, wear shoes with lead weights in them, so that he steps slowly and reluctantly.

He does not, after all, drown his wife. In the city, which is constructed from fanciful sets that suggest the "city of the future" often seen in silent films, the man and wife fall back in love—and then, as they return across the lake, a tempest overturns the boat and it appears that she drowns by chance. It's very broad melodrama, and the realism of spoken dialogue would have made it impossible. But silent films were more dreamlike, and Murnau was a genius at evoking odd, disturbing images and juxtapositions that created a nightmare state. Because the characters are simple, they take on a kind of moral clarity, and their choices are magnified into fundamental decisions of life and death.

I imagine it is possible to see *Sunrise* for the first time and think it simplistic; to be amused that the Academy could have honored it. But silent films had a language of their own; they aimed for the emotions, not the mind, and the best of them wanted to be not a story but an experience. Murnau, raised in the dark shadows of expressionism, pushed his images as far as he could, forced them upon us, haunted us with them. The more you consider *Sunrise,* the deeper it becomes—not because the story grows any more subtle but because you realize the real subject is the horror beneath the surface.

{A Tale of Winter}

Eric Rohmer is the romantic philosopher of the French New Wave, the director whose characters make love with words as well as flesh. They are open to sudden flashes of passion, they become infatuated at first sight, but then they descend into doubt and analysis, talking intensely about what it all means. Because they're invariably charming, and because coincidence and serendipity play such a large role in his stories, this is more cheerful than it sounds. As he grows older Rohmer's heart grows younger, and in his eighties he is more in tune with love than the prematurely cynical authors of Hollywood teen romances.

A Rohmer film is a flavor that, once tasted, cannot be mistaken. Like the Japanese master Ozu, with whom he is sometimes compared, he is said to make the same film every time. Yet, also like Ozu, his films are individual and fresh and never seem to repeat themselves; both directors focus on people rather than plots, and know that every person is a startling original while most plots are more or less the same.

His earlier films were about men and women; the later ones are about women and men, or women and women. He is concerned with the search for love and pattern in life. He loves the way women look and move and talk, and the way they evaluate men. He admires physical beauty but never makes it the point; he chooses actresses who are smart and bright-eyed, and focuses on their personalities rather than their exteriors. Still,

their exteriors distract his male characters, like the hero of *Claire's Knee* (1970), who sets a labyrinthine plot into motion simply to supply himself with a reason to touch the knee of Claire.

Felicie, the heroine of Rohmer's *A Tale of Winter* (1992), is convinced that life will fall into line with her great romantic purpose. Having met the love of her life and lost track of him, she expects him to return. She believes in coincidence—but doesn't believe it is coincidence. As the film opens, she meets Charles at the beach and falls unreservedly in love with him. She knows this is the real thing. She gives him her address; he doesn't give his, because as a trainee chef he is always on the move. They promise to meet again. The ominous title "Five years later" reveals that they do not. She has a daughter now, Elise, from that summer romance. She is dating two men—Maxence, who runs a hair salon, and Loic, who works in a library. Courtship with both men seems to consist largely of verbal negotiations.

Felicie, played by Charlotte Véry, is absorbed by her own case. She knows she will never love anyone the way she loves the absent Charles. The film reveals that Charles never wrote because she stupidly gave him the wrong address. Rohmer tells her story in the way it might unfold in real life, and it's typical that he gives us a scene where Felicie seems to be following somebody out of a Métro station, but we never get a shot of who she is following (here he neatly skewers the cliché of the mistaken look-alike). He makes us wait for her to mention casually that she thinks she might have seen Charles in the street. Rohmer also bides his time before establishing that both Maxence and Loic know all about Charles—and about each other. This is not a love triangle because the only man she loves is the one who isn't there.

Felicie talks frankly with her mother, who is sensible and tactful, about the qualities of Maxence and Loic; when her mother hesitantly observes that Loic is smarter, she explains that he's too smart for her, and not physical enough. ("I like to be dominated physically, but not intellectually.") She compares the men unfavorably to each other; when Maxence invites her to Nevers to see the beauty salon they might operate together, she observes, "Your books will never fill those shelves." But she complains to Loic that nothing is real for him unless it is in a book.

The visit to Nevers is an important turning point, however, because Elise drags her into the cathedral, and she has a moment there of meditation or visualization about the absent Charles. Leaving Maxence, she cuddles with Loic but leaves him too, conceding that she will never see Charles again: "Charles reappearing is not what matters. He remains in my heart, so I can't give it to anyone else." Loic takes her to a performance of Shakespeare's *The Winter's Tale,* and she cries as King Leontes beholds the statue of his wife and is told that to bring her to life "it is required that you do awake your faith."

There have been several conversations about philosophy in *A Tale of Winter,* and now there is another one. Rohmer is a Catholic intellectual who wears his faith lightly but in all weathers. Loic is a churchgoer; Felicie avoids churches, although she believes—and she thinks belief can affect outcomes, which is more than Loic will concede. To our astonishment, we find that the purpose of *A Tale of Winter* is not to determine whether Felicie will find love but to discover whether trust and faith can affect our fates.

I have not seen a Rohmer film I did not admire. Born in 1920, christened Jean-Marie Maurice Scherer, he worked first as a high school literature teacher and film critic. He created his professional name by combining the name of the director Erich von Stroheim with that of the pulp writer Sax Rohmer—so his name is pronounced "roamer," not "ro-may." Older than the other New Wave icons, like Godard and Truffaut, more interested in stories than theory, he came to wide attention with *My Night at Maud's* (1969), which was literally an all-night conversation. His earlier films included the merciless *Girl at the Monceau Bakery* (1963), starring the future director (and longtime Rohmer producer) Barbet Schroeder as a man who loves one woman, substitutes another, and then drops her when the original reappears.

Rohmer's films are arranged into groups. He began with Six Moral Tales, each one about a man who falls in love and then meets another woman, who causes him to question his choice; the tales include *Maud's, Claire's Knee,* and *Chloe in the Afternoon* (1972). Next came the Parables, illustrating a truth that is revealed at the end; these include *The Aviator's Wife* (1980) and *A Perfect Marriage* (1982). These were followed by his Comedies and Proverbs, including *Pauline at the Beach* (1983) and *Boyfriends and*

Girlfriends (1987). And then he made Tales of the Four Seasons, in which *A Tale of Winter* is joined by *A Summer's Tale* (1996), *A Tale of Springtime* (1992), and the wonderful *An Autumn Tale* (1998), in which Marie Rivière plays perhaps the most lovable of all his heroines.

If you have not seen a Rohmer film and wonder where to start, the answer is: anywhere. You do not have to see them in order, not even the numbered tales. The title your video store has in stock is the place to begin. Rohmer is both prolific and consistently enchanting. He is at once a realist (his characters behave as people actually do) and a practitioner of subtle magic realism, in the way hidden patterns, coincidences, misunderstandings, happy chances, and fateful accidents befall his characters. There is a kind of comfort in his films, a gentle lulling through the rhythms of everyday life, and he finds great beauty in ordinary people and locations.

What pervades Rohmer's work is a faith in love—or, if not love, then in the right people finding each other for the right reasons. There is sadness in his work but not gloom. His characters are too smart to be surprised by disappointments, and too interested in life to indulge in depression. His films succeed not because large truths are discovered but because small truths will do. To attend his films is to be for a time in the company of people we would like to know, and then to realize that in various ways they are ourselves.

{THE THIN MAN}

William Powell is to dialogue as Fred Astaire is to dance. His delivery is so droll and insinuating, so knowing and innocent at the same time that it hardly matters what he's saying. That's certainly the case in *The Thin Man* (1934), a murder mystery in which the murder and the mystery are insignificant compared to the personal styles of the actors.

Powell and Myrna Loy costar as Nick and Nora Charles, a retired detective and his rich wife, playfully in love and both always a little drunk. Nick Charles drinks steadily throughout the movie, with the kind of capacity and wit that real drunks fondly hope to master. When we first see him, he's teaching a bartender how to mix drinks. ("Have rhythm in your shaking . . . a dry martini, you always shake to waltz time.") Nora enters, and he hands her a drink. She asks how much he's had. "This will make six martinis," he says. She orders five more, to keep up.

Powell plays the character with a lyrical alcoholic slur that waxes and wanes but never topples into either inebriation or sobriety. The drinks are the lubricant for dialogue of elegant wit and wicked timing, used by a character who is decadent on the surface but fundamentally brave and brilliant. After Nick and Nora face down an armed intruder in their apartment one night, they read about it in the morning papers. "I was shot twice in the *Tribune*," Nick observes. "I read you were shot five times in the tabloids," says Nora. "It's not true," says Nick. "He didn't come anywhere near my tabloids."

After a prologue set three months earlier, most of the movie takes place over the holiday season, including cocktail parties on Christmas Eve and Christmas Day, and the exposure of the killer at a dinner party sometime around New Years' Eve. The movie is based on a novel by Dashiell Hammett, one of the fathers of noir, and it does technically provide clues, suspects, and a solution to a series of murders, but in tone and intent it's more like an all-dialogue version of an Astaire and Rogers musical, with elegant people in luxury hotel penthouses and no hint of the Depression anywhere in sight.

The Thin Man was one of the most popular films of 1934, inspired five sequels, and was nominated for four Oscars (best picture, actor, director, and screenplay). Yet it was made as an inexpensive B picture. Powell and Loy had been successful together earlier the same year in *Manhattan Melodrama* (the last film John Dillinger ever saw), and were quickly cast by MGM in this crime comedy, which was filmed, incredibly, in only two weeks. The brisk shooting schedule was possible because there are very few sets and negligible exteriors, because there is much dialogue and little action, and because the director, W. S. Van Dyke, was known for sticking to a schedule. That *The Thin Man* cost so little and looks so good is possibly because the interiors are simple and elegant, and the black-and-white photography flatters the loungewear and formalwear worn by a great-looking cast (which, in addition to Powell and Loy, included Maureen O'Sullivan and a young Cesar Romero). And there is a kind of grace in the way the six-foot Powell hovers protectively over the five-foot-six Loy (or sometimes simply leans as if blown in her direction).

Although Dashiell Hammett was known for hard-boiled fiction, and John Huston's 1941 film of Hammett's *The Maltese Falcon* was one of the first examples of film noir, *The Thin Man* is essentially a drawing room comedy with dead bodies. The plot is so preposterous that no reasonable viewer can follow it, and the movie makes little effort to require that it be followed. Nick Charles typically stands in the midst of inexplicable events with a drink in his hand, nodding wisely as if he understands everything and is not about to share. When a reporter asks him, "Can't you tell us anything

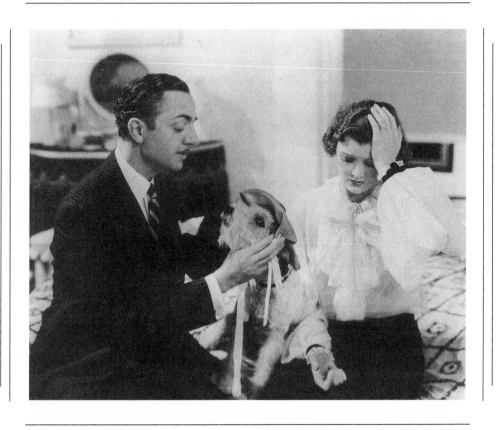

about the case?" Nick replies, "Yes. It's putting me way behind in my drinking."

Briefly, the film involves the mysterious disappearance of an inventor (Edward Ellis); the concern of his daughter (O'Sullivan), who is an old friend of Nick and Nora's; the greed of the inventor's ex-wife (Minna Gombell); the even greater greed of her gold-digging husband (Romero); the suspicious motives of the inventor's mistress (Natalie Moorhead), and various other thugs, gunsels, cops, and reporters, as well as the untiring cast of partygoers who turn up nightly at the Charleses' suite for free drinks.

One of the movie's charms is the playfulness with which Nick and Nora treat each other, and life. During one ostensibly serious scene, Nick pretends to find a piece of lint on her blouse, then flicks her on the nose when she looks down; she jabs him in the side; he pretends to be about to sock her, and then they both try to put on serious faces. On Christmas morning, Nick tests the new air rifle he got as a present by firing at the balloons on their Christmas tree. Nick throws a dinner party for all of the suspects, with plainclothes cops as waiters, and Nora tells one of them, "Waiter, will you serve the nuts? I mean, will you serve the guests the nuts?"

The movie's only real skullduggery comes when Nick goes on a midnight prowl through the inventor's laboratory, and even then the real sleuthing is done by Asta (Skippy), the couple's high-spirited terrier. Nick and Nora included him in all of their activities, and Asta became one of the most famous movie dogs of his time, in part through his ability to shield his eyes with his paws when life grew too disturbing to contemplate.

Assuming as we must that *The Thin Man* is not about a series of murders and their solution (that entire mechanism would be described by Hitchcock as the MacGuffin), what is it about? It is about personal style. About living life as a kind of artwork. Of the early lives of Nick and Nora we learn little, except that he was once a famous San Francisco detective and retired after marrying Nora. As Nick explains vaguely to a friend, her father left her a small-gauge railroad and "oh, a lot of other things," and he looks after them. As a consequence, Nick and Nora have a lot of money and spend their time traveling, seeing old friends, making new ones, and drinking pretty much all day long.

At one point in the film, when Nora wakens Nick in the middle of the night, he immediately pours himself a drink and one for her, and then as she leaves the room he greedily drinks from her glass. They are alcoholics in any realistic definition of the term, but not in the terms of the movie, because their drinking has no particular effect on themselves or the plot. It is simply a behavior, like smoking, that gives them something to do with their hands, something to talk about, and an excuse to move around the room. Even when Nora appears with an ice bag on her head, it looks more like clowning than like a hangover.

Myrna Loy was a delightful foil to Powell, but in this film she is essentially just his playmate; Powell dominates the picture with his deep, rich voice, his gliding, subtly unsteady physical movements, and his little mustache, which he hopes makes him look more grown-up than he feels. For audiences in the middle of the Depression, *The Thin Man*, like the Astaire and Rogers musicals it visually resembles, was pure escapism: Beautiful people in expensive surroundings make small talk all the day long, without a care in the world, and even murder is only an amusing diversion.

Powell's career began on the stage in 1912. He worked in silent films from 1922 and in talkies from their birth until 1955, when his last role was "Doc" in *Mister Roberts*. He was nominated for best actor for this film, the wonderful *My Man Godfrey* (1936), and *Life with Father* (1947). But he never won an Oscar. Powell lived until 1984, when he was ninety-two, and was fit and active until toward the end. All through the 1960s and 1970s his fans urged the Academy of Motion Picture Arts and Sciences to give him an Oscar for lifetime achievement, but the academy never did. To see *The Thin Man* is to watch him embodying a personal style that could have been honored but could never be imitated.

{ THIS IS SPINAL TAP }

Guitarist Nigel Tufnel explains his amplifier to documentary filmmaker Marty DiBergi:

> *Nigel:* It's very special, because, as you can see—the numbers all go to eleven. Right across the board. Eleven, eleven, eleven . . .
>
> *Marty:* And most amps go up to ten?
>
> *Nigel:* Exactly.
>
> *Marty:* Does that mean it's louder? Is it any louder?
>
> *Nigel:* Well, it's one louder, isn't it? It's not ten. You see, most blokes are going to be playing at ten—you're on ten on your guitar, where can you go from there? Where?
>
> *Marty:* I don't know.
>
> *Nigel:* Nowhere! Exactly! What we do, if we need that extra push over the cliff, you know what we do?
>
> *Marty:* You put it up to eleven.
>
> *Nigel:* Eleven. Exactly. One louder.
>
> *Marty:* Why don't you just make ten louder, and make ten be the top number, and make that a little louder?

Nigel is so baffled by this notion that he almost stops chewing his gum. "These go to eleven," he repeats finally. His faith in that extra push

over the cliff is unshakable. Marty DiBergi realizes he's dealing with a matter of guitar theology, not logic. Nigel has few ideas, but they are clearly defined and defiantly defended. DiBergi, a rational filmmaker, is helpless in the face of Nigel's rapture.

This Is Spinal Tap, one of the funniest movies ever made, is about a lot of things; one of them is the way the real story is not in the questions or in the answers but at the edge of the frame. There are two stories told in the film: the story of what the rock band Spinal Tap thinks, hopes, believes, or fears is happening, and the story of what is actually happening. We feel such affection for its members because they are so touching in their innocence and optimism. Intoxicated by the sheer fun of being rock stars, they perform long after their sell-by date, to smaller and smaller audiences, for less and less money, still seeking the roar of the crowd.

The fake documentary, released in 1984, was the directorial debut of Rob Reiner, then famous as Meathead from *All in the Family,* soon to become one of the most successful Hollywood directors (*The Sure Thing, The Princess Bride, When Harry Met Sally . . . , Misery, The American President*). He plays Marty DiBergi, the dogged documentarian who follows along on Spinal Tap's first American tour in six years. He was first attracted to the band, he says, by its "unusual loudness," so perhaps he should be more grateful for Nigel's technical secrets.

The band members are the blond rock god David St. Hubbins (Michael McKean), the bass player Derek Smalls (Harry Shearer), and Nigel Tufnel (Christopher Guest). When Nigel learns that David's girlfriend, Jeanine Pettibone (June Chadwick), is flying over from England to join the tour, his heart sinks; he sees her as an outsider who will wreak havoc with their boys' club. The two front men get most of the glory, while the drummer Mick Shrimpton (R. J. Parnell) supplies percussion on borrowed time: Previous Spinal Tap drummers have had an alarming mortality rate. One spontaneously combusted, and another choked to death on vomit ("but not his own vomit").

Support for the band on their American tour comes from a perfectly observed group of music-industry functionaries. Their manager, Ian Faith (Tony Hendra), is like a weary scoutmaster promising a troop of mama's boys that the hike is almost over. He carries a cricket bat and releases tension at crucial moments by such therapeutic activities as smashing TV sets. Bobbi Flekman (Fran Drescher) is a record company publicist trying to explain without really explaining why the band's new album, *Smell the Glove,* is not in stores. *Letterman* band leader Paul Shaffer is Artie Fufkin, the advance man who fails to provide a single fan for an autographing. Fred Willard is the upbeat Lieutenant Hookstratten, in charge of their last American concert, an officers' dance in an airplane hangar at a military base.

Guest, McKean, Shearer, and Reiner wrote the screenplay themselves, benefiting from improvisational rehearsals, and they also wrote all the songs, some of which, like "Sex Farm," became popular and were really not much worse than other heavy metal hits. (Guest liked the genre so much he directed three mockumentaries of his own, *Waiting for Guffman, Best in Show,* and *A Mighty Wind.*) For Spinal Tap, heavy metal was the band's last stop on an odyssey that began with the boys as a folk group and saw them morph into sixties flower power before emerging in their final form, as fearsome and hairy. Their tour now features props like a giant death's-head and alien pods that give birth to them one by one, or at least that is the plan.

Reiner fills the frame with background information and subtle touches (look at the way he uncertainly crosses and uncrosses his arms while delivering Marty's introductory remarks). The love triangle involving Nigel, David, and Jeanine is never overtly acknowledged. The disintegration of the tour is explained offhandedly, in asides (after the Boston concert is canceled: "It isn't a college town"). Dialogue makes its point by accurate word choices, as when Derek Smalls introduces a groupie as "my new special friend."

The biggest laugh in the second half of the film is assembled lovingly, over time, out of many small elements. It involves an assignment to set designer Polly Deutsch (Anjelica Huston) to build a replica of one of the elements of Stonehenge, which will descend onto the stage during a big production number. Bad communication causes an error in scale. To appreciate the skill of Reiner and his editors, observe the way they prepare for the payoff. Instead of simply showing the erroneous prop descending from above, they include a scene where we are told what will happen. Then, after intermediate footage to create anticipation, we see the disastrous moment. This is a rare case where it helps to know the punch line before it arrives:

We are laughing not only at what happens (which is funny enough) but at the reactions of the band members, who have *not* been prepared.

Seeing *A Hard Day's Night* recently, I was struck by how much fun the Beatles were obviously having. If there is a more joyous and orgasmic single scene in the movies than their "She Loves You" number, I have not encountered it. You can see Paul and John grinning at each other while singing—not as a performance technique but because they can't help themselves. Many musicians must go through that early stage when they want to pinch themselves because of their good luck. "We can taste how much they love embodying their roles," David Edelstein of *Slate* wrote when *This Is Spinal Tap* was re-released. "And why not? Who wouldn't want to be a rock titan, even a ludicrous and stupid and fading one? It's the supreme pipe dream of our era."

He puts his finger on the film's deepest appeal: It is funny about Spinal Tap, but not cruel. It shares their pleasure in being themselves. It has affection for these three fragile egos. Yes, they're spoiled. Yes, they make impossible demands (the scene involving the size of the bread for the dressing room sandwiches is a masterpiece of petulant behavior). Yes, their music is pretty bad.

But they're not bad men; they're holy fools, living in a dream that still somehow, barely, holds together for them. They deserve the last-minute rescue of their Japanese tour—although what have the Japanese done to deserve them? One of the loveliest ironies of *This Is Spinal Tap* is that the band took on a life of its own after the movie came out, and actually toured and released albums. Spinal Tap lives still. And they haven't gotten any better.

{ TOKYO STORY }

No story could be simpler. An old couple comes to the city to visit their children and grandchildren. Their children are busy, and the old people upset their routines. In a quiet way, without anyone admitting it, the visit goes badly. The grandparents return home. A few days later, the grandmother dies. Now it is the children's turn to make a journey.

From these few elements Yasujiro Ozu made one of the greatest films of all time. *Tokyo Story* (1953) lacks sentimental triggers and contrived emotion; it looks away from moments a lesser movie would have exploited. It wants not to force our emotions but to share its understanding. It does this so well that I am near tears in the last thirty minutes. It ennobles the cinema. It says, yes, a movie can help us make small steps against our imperfections.

It does this with characters so universal that we recognize them instantly—sometimes in the mirror. It is about our families, our natures, our flaws, and our clumsy search for love and meaning. It isn't that our lives keep us too busy for our families; it's that we have arranged them to protect us from having to deal with big questions of love, work, and death. We escape into truisms, small talk, and distractions. Given the opportunity at a family gathering to share our hopes and disappointments, we talk about the weather and watch TV.

Ozu is not only a great director but a great teacher and, after you know his films, a friend. With no other director do I feel affection for every single shot. *Tokyo Story* opens with the distant putt-putt of a ship's engine, and bittersweet music evokes a radio heard long ago and far away. There are exterior shots of a neighborhood. If we know Ozu, we know the boat will not figure in the plot, that the music will never be used to underline or comment on the emotions, that the neighborhood may be the one where the story takes place but it doesn't matter. Ozu uses "pillow shots" like the pillow words in Japanese poetry, separating his scenes with brief, evocative images from everyday life. He likes trains, clouds, smoke, clothes hanging on a line, empty streets, small architectural details, and banners blowing in the wind (he painted most of the banners in his movies himself).

His visual strategy is as simple (and therefore as profound) as possible. His camera is not always precisely three feet above the floor (the eye level of a Japanese person seated on a tatami mat), but it usually is. "The reason for the low camera position," the critic Donald Richie explains, "is that it eliminates depth and makes a two-dimensional space." So we are better able to appreciate a composition because Ozu lets us notice its lines and weights and tones—which always reflect his exact feeling about the scene.

He almost never moves his camera (it moves once in *Tokyo Story,* which is more than usual in his later work). Every single shot is intended to have a perfect composition of its own, even if that means there are continuity errors. All the shots are framed in some way. In the foreground of the interior shots, perhaps tucked in a corner, is a little teapot. Ozu loves that teapot. It's like the red signature stamp of a Japanese woodblock artist; it is his maker's mark.

When there is movement in an Ozu film, it comes from nature or people, not from the camera. He often shows a room before people enter, and lingers a second after they leave. If characters go upstairs, they are absent precisely long enough to actually do that. If a character is speaking, he shows the entire speech. No cutaways, no listening shots, no overlapping dialogue. He is comfortable with silences. Sometimes characters speak little and imply much; the old father in *Tokyo Story* often smiles and says, "Yes,"

463

and what he means is sometimes yes, sometimes no, sometimes deep regret, sometimes a decision to keep his thoughts to himself.

Does anyone go to a movie to watch the style? Well, yes. An elegantly refined style like Ozu's places people in the foreground; he focuses on the nuances of everyday life. His is the most humanistic of styles, removing the machinery of effects and editing and choosing to touch us with human feeling, not workshop storytelling technique.

Consider the Hirayama family in *Tokyo Story*. Shukichi, the grandfather, is played by Chishu Ryu, one of Ozu's favorite actors; Tomi, the grandmother, by Chieko Higashiyama. She is overweight and plain-faced; he has a tall, fallen grace. There are no extravagant displays of affection between them. We learn that he drank too much as a young man, then stopped. There are hints that their marriage was imperfect but endured.

Living at home with them is their youngest daughter, Kyoko (Kyoko Kagawa), one of the many unmarried children in Ozu's works who live with their parents. (Ozu never married, and lived with his mother until she died.) Their youngest son, Keizo (Shiro Osaka), works in Osaka, midway on their train journey. In Tokyo, their oldest son, Koichi (So Yamamura), is a doctor in a neighborhood clinic—not as distinguished as his parents imagined. He is married to Fumiko (Kuniko Miyake), and they have two sons. His sister Shige (Haruko Sugimura) is married and runs a beauty salon. A middle son was killed in World War II; their daughter-in-law Noriko (the great star Setsuko Hara) has never remarried and is an office worker living in Tokyo.

There is an extraordinary scene soon after the old parents arrive. "These are your grandparents," Fumiko tells her oldest son, Minoru. And then, to her mother: "Minoru is in middle school now." So this is the first time he has met them, yet he escapes quickly to his room. Ozu's lifelong theme is the destruction of the Japanese family through work and modernization, and in only two lines of dialogue he shows us how the generations have drifted apart.

The grown children mean well. They try to make time for their visitors. There is a moment of rich humor when we join all of them on a tour bus, everyone bouncing and leaning in unison. But old folks spend most days "resting" at home because no one is free to take them anywhere. When Shige's husband brings home cakes for her parents, Shige says they're too expensive and the old folks won't appreciate them; while discussing this, they eat the cakes. Oddly, the person who treats the parents most kindly and makes time for them is Noriko, the widow of their middle son.

The others, feeling badly that they can't spare more time for their parents, hit on a solution: They'll send them for a holiday to Atami Hot Springs. Shukichi and Tomi did not come to Tokyo to go to a spa, but they agree. At the spa we see young people dancing and playing cards, and then, in one of those perfect Ozu shots, two pairs of shoes placed neatly side by side outside the old couple's door. The next morning, as they're sitting side by side on a sea wall, he says, "Let's go home."

People spend a lot of time sitting side by side in an Ozu film. Instead of over-the-shoulder compositions, he likes two or three characters all in a row. If this causes violations of the eyeline rules (sometimes they don't seem to be looking at one another when they speak), he doesn't care. Often he views them from behind. He composes this way, I think, so we can see them all at once, the listeners as well as the speakers.

The last night in Tokyo is made of two wonderful sequences. Tomi goes to stay with Noriko, and Shukichi says he will visit an old friend from the village. Tomi and Noriko have a warm and loving conversation (the old woman tells her son's widow she should remarry), and Shukichi gets plastered with two former village friends. As they drink, they complain about their lives and children, and we see how alcohol helps them break through the resolutely positive Japanese public face.

All through the movie, Tomi and Shukichi discuss their disappointment in such guarded words, punctuated with so many nods and agreements, that their real feelings are hidden in code. Notice how they criticize their grandchildren by saying they prefer their children. Listen how they agree that their children are "better than average."

The old people go home, Tomi dies, and the family assembles for the funeral—at last all lined up together in one row for Ozu's camera. Now there are real tears, even from those who resented the visit. Chishu Ryu, that wonderful actor, is masterful in the way he buries the old man's grief in nods, agreement, pleasantries, and routine. When the old woman next door stops by to express her sympathy, he makes what for him is an outpouring of grief: "Oh, she was a headstrong woman . . . but if I knew things would come to this, I'd have been kinder to her." A pause. "Living alone like this, the days will get very long."

TOUCHEZ PAS AU GRISBI

Growing older is a balancing act between skills that have never been better and abilities that sometimes betray. At fifty, Max the Liar has never possessed more wisdom about his profession of burglary. But he no longer cares to make the effort, and his dream is to salt away ninety-six kilos in gold bars stolen at Orly Airport. Then he will retire. Max is a solid, well-groomed, impeccably dressed, flawlessly polite man whose code is so deeply embedded that he never refers to it, even indirectly. During the course of three days, he uses all of his wisdom and experience to make his dream come true, and it is almost enough.

Max is played by Jean Gabin, named "the actor of the century" in a French poll, in Jacques Becker's *Touchez Pas au Grisbi,* a 1954 French crime film that uncannily points the way toward Jean-Pierre Melville's great *Bob le Flambeur* the following year. The two films follow similar story arcs and have similar heroes: middle-aged men, well liked, able to figure the odds, familiar in their haunts of clubs and restaurants, vulnerable only because of the passions of their hotheaded pals. Gabin plays a man of few words, of warmth that is real but understated; a man who is always thinking a step ahead, using brainwork instead of footwork or gunplay to survive in the underworld.

His weakness is his friendship for Riton (René Dary), a sidekick he calls "Porcupine Head," and whom he has essentially carried for years. Does

Max love Riton? Max seems to be the current or former lover of almost every woman in the movie, and yet, yes, Riton is whom he loves. There's a lovely scene where Max outsmarts rival hoods who are trying to tail him and takes Riton with him to a safe house—an apartment Riton never knew existed. There he pours them a bottle of wine, makes a midnight meal of pâté and biscuits, and takes fresh pajamas, blankets, and toothbrushes out of a cabinet and hands them to his friend. Although Gabin's face reveals nothing, we sense that Max enjoys this domestic interlude more than anything else that happens in the movie; certainly he is bored in nightclubs and tired of crime, and although he visits his elegant mistress Betty (Marilyn Buferd) for conjugal observances, this involves more ritual than desire.

Max, like Bob and many other French gangsters, lives in Montmartre, a district seen with particular detail in the film. "I believe above all in Paris," Becker said, and his film shows an instinctive familiarity with the way the city works. The film opens and closes with Max dining in the same restaurant, and notice how quietly the point is made that ordinary civilians are not welcome, no matter how many tables are empty, when Madame Bouche's favorite gangsters are in the house. Max pays off a young friend's tab at the end of the evening, and in a later visit gives Madame some money to hold for him; the restaurant is also his bank and club.

They all leave, that first night, to escort two showgirls to the strip club where they work; they are Lola (Dora Doll), and Josy (Jeanne Moreau at twenty-five), whom Riton regards as his mistress. At the club we meet the drug dealer Angelo (Lino Ventura) and the club owner, Pierrot (Paul Frankeur), a.k.a. "Fats." Max and Angelo seem to be on good terms, but a little while later Max opens the door of a dressing room and sees Josy being embraced by Angelo.

This would come as particularly bad news to Riton, who fancies himself a ladies' man and thinks Josy belongs to him, but look how elegantly Becker resolves the situation. Instead of telling his pal that he's a cuckold, Max advises Riton to give up Josy. He points out aging playboys steering hookers around the dance floor, calls attention to the bags under Riton's eyes, and suggests that they go home early. Riton suggests that they stay for one more drink. No, says Max, with that flat, calm Gabin delivery, he knows what one more drink will lead to: a bottle of champagne with Angelo, and

then having to take the girls out for onion soup, and then having to have sex . . . it's easier just to leave now.

The plot resolves itself as a race between Max's attempts to fence the gold bars through his Uncle Oscar (another cadaverous relic with a young mistress) and Angelo's attempts to kidnap Riton and find out where the loot is hidden. Max senses that something fishy is going on and warns Riton; that leads to their midnight dinner. And as the two old friends turn out the lights, we realize that this opening sequence has occupied some forty minutes with flawless storytelling that has consisted almost entirely of small talk in the restaurant and the club, and then a subdued chase as Max is tailed to his home.

What happens the next day I will leave for you to discover, describing only an extraordinary scene where Max learns that Riton has been nabbed. Max knows that this means the gold bars will be required as ransom. But he's less concerned about the gold than about his pal, and he has a wonderful soliloquy, an interior monologue that we hear in voice-over, as Max paces around his apartment. He talks about what a dope Riton is, and what a burden he has been for twenty years: "There's not a tooth in his head that hasn't cost me a bundle." We understand that Max, who is competent above all things, almost values Riton's inability to live without his help. At the end of his soliloquy, instead of growing angry as a conventional gangster might, Max opens a bottle of champagne, plays a forlorn harmonica solo on his jukebox, sits in a comfortable chair, and lights a cigarette. He treasures his creature comforts, especially when he might be about to lose them.

Jacques Becker (1906–1960) was not the flashiest of French filmmakers; he had a way of dealing directly with his material. In this film there are no fancy shots. Almost everything is seen at eye level, point of view is respected, and the style shrinks from calling attention to itself. Becker's directness and simplicity inspired the affection of younger directors, like François Truffaut. "He invented his own tempo," Truffaut wrote after Becker died. "He loved fast cars and long meals; he shot two-hour films on subjects that really needed only fifteen minutes. . . . He was scrupulous and reflective and infinitely delicate. He loved to make detailed films about ordinary things." And in his review of *Touchez Pas au Grisbi* ("Don't Touch the

Loot"), Truffaut noticed, "He keeps only what is essential in the dialogue, even the *essential* part of the *superfluous*." Surely the monologue about Riton's teeth is an example of that; we hear all about something as inconsequential as that, but we never see the heist at Orly, nor does Max ever talk about it. "The real subjects of *Grisbi*," Truffaut concludes, "are aging and friendship."

Consider the scene where Riton looks at the bags under his eyes in the mirror, to see if they are as bad as Max said. Remember Max saying he doesn't want to go to the nightclub because he fears he will get drowsy. And when he goes to the club to enlist Fats in a probably dangerous mission, the club owner's wife asks Max to take care of her husband, observing, "At my age, there's no second chance."

Gabin himself was almost fifty when he made the film. There's not a trace of vanity in his performance. Having played the escaped prisoner in Renoir's *Grand Illusion* and the dashing criminal in *Pépé le Moko,* he grew up to play grown-ups. Becker probably met Gabin on one of Renoir's sets; he was the assistant to the great filmmaker in the 1930s, on *Grand Illusion, The Rules of the Game,* and many other films. His own work includes two titles often ranked with *Touchez Pas au Grisbi: Le Trou* (1960), about prisoners laboriously trying to escape, and *Casque d'Or* (1952), with a star-making role for Simone Signoret in a story of love and betrayal during the 1890s.

The world of French crime films is a particular place, informed by the French love for Hollywood film noir, a genre they identified and named. But the great French noirs of the 1950s are not copies of Hollywood; instead, they have a particularly French flavor. In *Touchez Pas au Grisbi,* the critic Terrence Rafferty writes, "real men eat pâté," and this is "among the very few French movies about the criminal class in which neither the characters nor the filmmakers are afflicted by the delusion that they are Americans." A few years later, in Godard's *Breathless* (1959), Belmondo would be deliberately channeling Bogart, but here Gabin is channeling only himself. He is the original, so there is no need to look for inspiration.

{ TOUCH OF EVIL }

Come on, read my future for me.
You haven't got any.
What do you mean?
Your future is all used up.

So speaks a fortune-telling madam, played by Marlene Dietrich, to the drunken sheriff of a border town, played by Orson Welles, in *Touch of Evil*. Her words have a sad resonance, because Welles was never again to direct in Hollywood after making this dark, atmospheric story of crime and corruption.

It was named best film at the 1958 Brussels World Fair (Godard and Truffaut were on the jury), but in America it opened on the bottom half of a double bill, failed, and put an end to Welles's prospects of working within the studio system. Yet the film has always been a favorite of those who enjoy visual and dramatic flamboyance. "I'd seen the film four or five times before I noticed the story," the director Peter Bogdanovich once told his friend Orson. "That speaks well for the story," Welles rumbled sarcastically, but Bogdanovich replied, "No, no—I mean I was looking at the direction."

That might be the best approach for anyone seeing the film for the first time: to set aside the labyrinthine plot and simply admire what is on the screen. The movie begins with one of the most famous shots ever made,

following a car with a bomb in its trunk for three minutes and twenty seconds. And it has other virtuoso camera movements, including an unbroken interrogation in a cramped room, and one that begins in the street and follows the characters through a lobby and into an elevator. The British critic Damian Cannon writes of its "spatial choreography," in which "every position and movement latches together into a cogent whole."

Welles and his cinematographer, Russell Metty, were not simply showing off. The destinies of all of the main characters are tangled from beginning to end, and the photography makes that point by trapping them in the same shots, or tying them together through cuts that match and resonate. The story moves not in a straight line but as a series of loops and coils.

Some of those loops were removed when Universal Studios took the film from Welles and reedited it, adding close-ups and chopping scenes, so that it existed for years in a confusing 95-minute version, and then belatedly in a 108-minute version that still reflected the studio's meddling. Now at last Welles's original intentions (explained in a fifty-eight-page memo to the studio) are reflected in a restored version that is three minutes longer and contains fifty changes, some large, some small. This version was produced by Rick Schmidlin and edited by Oscar winner Walter Murch, inspired by a crucial 1992 article in *Film Quarterly* by the critic Jonathan Rosenbaum.

The story takes place in Los Robles, a seedy Mexican-American border town ("Border towns bring out the worst in a country"). It's a place of bars, strip clubs, and brothels, where music spills onto the street from every club. In the opening shot, we see a bomb placed in the trunk of a car, and then the camera cranes up and follows the car down a strip of seamy storefronts, before gliding down to eye level to pick up a strolling couple. They are newlyweds, Mike and Susan Vargas (Charlton Heston and Janet Leigh); he's a Mexican drug-enforcement official. At a border checkpoint, they're eventually joined by the doomed car, which has been delayed by traffic and a herd of goats. Mike and Susan are completing the check when there's an off-screen explosion—and then finally a cut, to the burning car lifting in the air. (I've always felt this cut is premature; better to hear the off-screen explosion, stay on Mike and Susan as they run to the burning car, and then cut.)

Everyone awaits the arrival of Captain Hank Quinlan (Welles), a massive, sweaty, rumbling figure who looms over the camera. (Welles was not yet that big when he made the picture, and used padding and camera angles to exaggerate his bulk.) Quinlan takes charge, "intuiting" that the explosion was caused by dynamite. Vargas, a bystander, finds himself drawn into the investigation, to Quinlan's intense displeasure; the movie becomes a competition between the two men, leading to the sheriff's efforts to frame Quinlan and his bride on drug and murder charges.

Viewers familiar with the earlier version will not feel they are seeing a different film, but may be able to follow the plot more easily. The most important changes take place in these opening minutes, when the stories of the Heston and Leigh characters are now intercut (the studio positioned all of the wife's hazards with a local gang after her husband's dealings with Quinlan). Another significant change: The opening shot is now seen without superimposed credits (they've been moved to the end), and with music from car radios and clubs, instead of Henry Mancini's title theme (Welles thought source music and sound effects would better establish the atmosphere).

Welles fills his story with a meaty selection of supporting characters, including Quinlan's faithful sidekick, Menzies (Joseph Calleia); the slimy local crime boss, Grandi (Akim Tamiroff); the local madam (Dietrich); a butch gang leader (Mercedes McCambridge); an ineffectual district attorney (Ray Collins, from *Citizen Kane*); and, particularly, a sexually obsessed motel night clerk (Dennis Weaver), whose peculiar skittishness may have given ideas to Anthony Perkins for *Psycho,* two years later.

These figures move back and forth across the border, through a series of grim and grungy locations. Although the plot line can be followed, the real point is the way Quinlan veers from the investigation to follow his own agenda. He's prejudiced against Mexicans, resents Vargas for invading his turf, and supports "hunches" by planting evidence. When Vargas calls him on the fraud, he vows to destroy him.

As Vargas and Quinlan jockey for position in the investigation, Susan is endangered in scenes that work as a terrified counterpoint. Vargas unwisely checks his wife into a motel run by the local gang, and young thugs terrorize her. Her perils sometimes border on the ludicrous, especially in a scene where they shine a flashlight into her room. Later, a gang rape is implied, but the movie curiously ignores or forgets its repercussions for Susan.

Menzies, the deputy, has been faithful to Quinlan because the sheriff once stopped a bullet intended for him. The movie establishes his gradual enlightenment, as Vargas proves that Quinlan planted evidence and framed innocent people. Why does Quinlan stoop so low? Thirty years earlier his own wife was murdered, and the killer went free; now he boasts, "That was the last killer that ever got out of my hands."

The final sequence involves the disillusioned Menzies wearing a concealed microphone while prompting Quinlan into a confession. Vargas shadows them with a radio and tape recorder. This scene is visually effective, as the sheriff and deputy follow a garbage-strewn canal, but it's not logical. Vargas wades through water and climbs mountains of debris to stay within radio range of the talking men, when he could simply have hidden the tape recorder on Menzies. And he inexplicably leaves the radio turned up, so Quinlan can hear the echo of his own voice. That works as showmanship even while it fails as strategy.

The surface themes of *Touch of Evil* are easy to spot, and the clash between the national cultures gets an ironic flip: Vargas reflects gringo stereotypes while Quinlan embodies clichés about Mexican lawmen. But there may be another theme lurking beneath the surface. Much of Welles's work was autobiographical, and the characters he chose to play (Kane, Macbeth, Othello) were giants destroyed by hubris. Now consider Quinlan, who nurses old hurts and tries to orchestrate this scenario like a director, assigning dialogue and roles. There is a sense in which Quinlan wants the final cut in the plot of this movie, and doesn't get it. He's running down after years of indulgence and self-abuse, and his ego leads him into trouble.

Is there a resonance between the Welles character here and the man he became? The story of Welles's later career is of projects left uncompleted and films altered after he had left them. To some degree, his characters reflected his feelings about himself and his prospects, and *Touch of Evil* may be as much about Orson Welles as Hank Quinlan. Welles brought great style to his movies, embracing excess in his life and work as the price (and reward) of his freedom.

THE TREASURE
OF THE SIERRA MADRE

When John Huston came back from the war and Humphrey Bogart was a star big enough to choose his next project, the two of them decided to make a film about a seedy loser driven mad by greed. "Wait till you see me in my next picture," Bogart shouted to a movie critic outside a New York nightclub. "I play the worst shit you ever saw." The movie was desolate and despairing, the nicest character in it dies trying to defend men who were about to kill him, and the ending is not merely unhappy but like a cosmic joke against the hero's dreams. Jack L. Warner, the studio boss who sent the crew to Mexican locations and yanked them back when the budget ran out of control, thought it was "definitely the greatest motion picture we have ever made."

The Treasure of the Sierra Madre (1948) is a story in the Joseph Conrad tradition, using adventure not as an end in itself but as a test of its characters. It involves moral disagreements between a wise old man and a paranoid middle-aged man, with a young man forced to choose sides. It tells this story with gusto and Huston's love of male camaraderie, and it occasionally breaks into laughter—some funny, some bitterly ironic. It happens on a sun-blasted high chaparral landscape, usually desolate except for the three gold prospectors, although gangs of bandits and villages of Indians materialize when required. At the end it has Bogart in a delirious mad scene that falls somewhere between *King Lear* and *Greed*.

Bogart plays Fred C. Dobbs, one of the movie characters everybody can name. In 1925 in Tampico, he meets another drifter from America, Bob Curtin (Tim Holt). Both have been cheated out of hard-earned wages by a dishonest employer named McCormick, and when they corner him in a bar they beat him so savagely that it seems pointless to hang around town. Their next move is suggested by the old-timer Howard (Walter Huston), whom they've overheard talking about gold. They think he's good for advice and not much more, but he has the stamina of a goat and is soon filling their ears with practical advice about how to find gold, which is not too hard, and how to keep it and not get killed, which is not too easy.

The heart of the movie takes place on the slopes of mountains, which the title identifies but the characters never do; they simply address the area as "mountain." They are so exposed in this landscape that only Howard's experience and rough Spanish get them through. They start out as partners, but the moment they find real gold Dobbs grows avaricious, suggesting that they divide their gains three ways, every night. Soon they're hiding their gold separately, and there is a long night when Dobbs awakens in the tent to find Howard gone, and then Curtin awakens to find Dobbs gone, and finally old Howard observes that the turn has come back around to him and so why don't they get some sleep because they have work to do in the morning.

Howard has been here before. ("I know what gold can do to men's souls," he says.) He plays a tactful peacemaker, agreeing with Dobbs's paranoid suggestions because he knows they will make little difference at the end of the day: Either they'll get out with their gold, or they won't. The performance is a masterpiece by Walter Huston, John's father, and won an Academy Award (John Huston won two more, for direction and screenplay). Listen to the way the senior Huston talks, rapid-fire, without pause, as if he's briefing them on an old tale and doesn't have time to waste on nuance. He does a famous dance when he finally finds gold, playing the stereotype of a grizzled prospector, but see how his eyes are sometimes quiet even when he's playing the fool; he reads every situation, knows his options, tries to slow Dobbs's meltdown.

Bogart shows not a shred of star ego in the role, but then he didn't become a star by being a pretty face. His wife, Lauren Bacall, writes in her

memoirs that Bogart began to experience quick hair loss on *Dark Passage* (1947) and was completely bald when he arrived at the *Treasure* locations. Doctors blamed his drinking and a B-vitamin deficiency; B$_{12}$ shots helped his hair return, but in *Treasure* all three men wear wigs that were carefully muddied and matted every morning to reflect that day's difficulties.

Bogart's break in pictures came in John Huston's first film, *The Maltese Falcon* (1941), after the much bigger Warner Bros. star George Raft turned it down. Not tall, balding, with a scar on his lip, Bogart could play a hero but loved to be the scrappy little guy; remember his Charlie Allnut in Huston's *The African Queen* (1951). In *The Treasure of the Sierra Madre* he plays a character who diminishes steadily as the story moves along, finally disappearing into himself and his delusions. Although Howard saves Dobbs's life just by being a seasoned mountain man and Curtin pulls him unconscious from a collapsed mine, he doesn't trust them and finds that he is capable of killing either one just to get a bigger share of the gold.

He thinks he has killed Curtin, and the moment he does he tips over into madness. But the harsh logic of the situation has earlier shown that murder is always a choice in these mountains. There is a poignant episode involving the soft-spoken American Jim Cody (Bruce Bennett), who tracks them to their camp, offers his help, wants a share, and analyzes the situation for them: They can either make him a partner or kill him. The scene where the three men take a vote shows clearly how their moral weight balances out.

The movie is based on a novel by the elusive, legendary B. Traven, whose work shows men cornered by the shrinking options offered by nature and danger. Traven was famous for being unknown; the name was a pseudonym, the author was never seen, and indeed the Hollywood agent Paul Kohner, who represented both of the Hustons, acted as Traven's literary agent without ever meeting him—or did he? Both Huston and Kohner told me in the 1970s that an unprepossessing little man turned up on the Mexican locations and described himself as Traven's representative. This was, they decided, clearly Traven himself, but they went along with the fiction.

I've seen *The Treasure of the Sierra Madre* many times, but watching it again on a new DVD, I found myself gripped as always by Bogart's closing scenes. The movie has never really been about gold but about character, and Bogart fearlessly makes Fred C. Dobbs into a pathetic, frightened, selfish man—so sick we would be tempted to pity him if he were not so undeserving of pity. The other two characters get more or less what they deserve at the end of the film, but with less satisfaction for the audience. After Howard is taken in by an Indian tribe, there is a gratuitous shot where a young maiden pats his whiskers and he all but winks directly at the camera; this shot, and the idyllic village life surrounding it, belong in a lesser movie.

As the stories of Howard and Curtin evaporate into convention, however, Fred C. Dobbs somehow moves to a higher level of tragedy. Hearing things in the night, desperate for a drink of water, staggering under the desert sun with the gold he valued so much, Dobbs is the tragic hero brought down precisely by his flaws. There is a pitiless stark realism in these scenes that brings the movie to honesty and truth. Leading up to them is a down-market Shakespearean soliloquy when Dobbs thinks he is a murderer and says, "Conscience. What a thing! If you believe you got a conscience it'll pester you to death. But if you don't believe you got one, what could it do to ya?" He finds out.

Note: Bogart starred in two movies where nobody actually said their most-repeated lines. Nobody says, "Play it again, Sam" in *Casablanca,* and in *The Treasure of the Sierra Madre,* Alfonso Bedoya, as the bandit leader, never actually says, "Badges? We don't need no stinking badges!" He says, "We don't need no badges. I don't have to show you any stinking badges."

{ UGETSU }

Two brothers, one consumed by greed, the other by envy. In a time when the land is savaged by marauding armies, they risk their families and their lives to pursue their obsessions. Kenji Mizoguchi's *Ugetsu* (1953) tells their stories in one of the greatest of all films—one that, along with Kurosawa's *Rashomon*, helped introduce Japanese cinema to Western audiences. The heroes are rough-hewn and consumed by ambition, but the film style is elegant and mysterious, and somehow we know before we are told that this is a ghost story.

The opening shot is one of Mizoguchi's famous "scroll shots," so named for the way it pans across the landscape like a Japanese scroll painting. We see a village, the roofs of the rude houses weighed down by tree branches to keep them from blowing away in the wind. We meet Genjuro (Masayuki Mori), a potter, and his brother Tobei (Eitaro Ozawa), a farmer. Although gunshots on the wind suggest that an army is near, Genjuro is loading a cart with bowls, cups, and vases, packed in straw.

His wife, Miyagi (Kinuyo Tanaka), begs him not to risk a trip to the city at this time of conflict—to stay home to protect her and their son. But he insists, and Tobei, filled with goofy excitement, insists on coming along despite the protests of his wife, Ohama (Mitsuko Mito). Genjuro returns with treasure: gold coins, which he insists his wife weigh in her hand. He makes her a gift of a beautiful fabric, bought in the city, but he doesn't un-

483

derstand when she says that the cloth means less than his love for her. All he can talk about is making more pots and more money. Blinded by the gold, he returns to his work with a frenzy.

Tobei saw a great samurai on their trip and tried to enlist in his army, but was turned away as a "dirty beggar" because he had no armor. Now the two men plan their next assault on the city, although when an army sweeps through on the night they have fired the kiln, they fear that their work has been lost. Not so; the pots survive, and this time they think it will be safer to journey by boat across the lake to the city, instead of by land.

The famous lake scene is the most beautiful in the film. Shot partly on a tank with studio backdrops, it creates a world of fog and mist, out of which emerges a lone boatman, who warns them of pirates. Tobei brings along his wife; Genjuro returns to leave his wife and child on the shore, and continues with Tobei and Ohama. In the city, his work sells quickly, and he is invited to the castle of a beautiful noblewoman named Lady Wakasa, who admires his craftsmanship. She's played by Machiko Kyo, one of the greatest stars of the period, who was also the woman in *Rashomon*.

Tobei wanders off from his wife and his brother. Time passes. He clumsily kills a samurai, and steals the head of a foe that the samurai had killed. Presenting this trophy to the samurai lord, he is praised and given a horse, a house, and men to follow him. Filled with pride, he brings his men for the night to a geisha house, only to find that his wife, raped by soldiers after he abandoned her, has become a geisha.

Elsewhere in the city, Genjuro visits a fabric shop and imagines his wife's joy when he brings her more beautiful dresses, but then Lady Wakasa appears, suggesting that he may need a guide to her castle. He is mesmerized by her strange beauty; made up like a Noh heroine with smudges for eyebrows high on her forehead, her face shadowed by veils and a wide straw hat, she is like no woman he has ever seen. At the castle she drifts from behind screens and curtains and, regarding his simple pots, asks him, "How is such beauty created?" She praises and seduces him, and Pauline Kael remembers she gasped with delight when he cried, "I never dreamed such pleasures existed!" Perhaps Genjuro should have taken warning when he heard the voice of the lady's dead father echoing through the room, and when her lady-in-waiting advised him, "Don't bury your talents in a small village! You must marry her!"

Mizoguchi (1898–1956), was famous for the theory that one scene should equal one cut, although sometimes he made exceptions. The great Yasujiro Ozu had the same theory, with the difference that Ozu's camera almost never moved in his later films, while Mizoguchi's style was constructed around flowing, poetic camera movement. Consider a scene where Lady Wakasa visits Genjuro as he is bathing in an outdoor pool, and as she enters the pool to join him water splashes over the side and the camera follows the splash into a pan across rippling water that ends with the two of them having a picnic on the grass.

There is a crucial sequence when Genjuro goes back into the city and on his return to the lakeside castle is halted by a priest, who calls after him, "I see death in your face! Have you encountered a ghost?" He warns Genjuro against being "beguiled by a forbidden form of love." Back at the castle Lady Wakasa begins to embrace Genjuro but recoils, crying out, "There is something on his skin!" Indeed, the priest has covered Genjuro with symbols of exorcism, which seem to burn the noblewoman as if they are flames.

Lady Wakasa is, of course, a ghost (we never doubted it), and there is a haunting scene when Genjuro sees the castle as it really is: a burned ruin. There is a second ghost in the movie whom we do not suspect, and the revelation in that case creates a touching emotional release. It comes toward the end, after both men have returned, chastened, to their village, and are forgiven by their wives for the male weakness of blinding ambition.

I learned from an article by Gary Morris in the *Bright Lights Film Journal* that Mizoguchi may have drawn on his own life for the story of *Ugetsu.* When the director was a boy of seven, Morris writes, his father lost the family fortune in a reckless business venture. They moved to a poor district, and his fourteen-year-old sister, Suzu, "was put up for adoption and eventually sold to a geisha house." So perhaps the sins of the father were visited upon Mizoguchi's two heroes. After many earlier films (he started in 1923), Mizoguchi's career ended with a series of masterpieces, including *Life of Oharu* (1952), *Sansho the Bailiff* (1954), and *Street of Shame* (1956), which in its consideration of geishas perhaps draws on the life of his sister. To enter his world, like entering Ozu's, is to find a film language that seems to create the mood it considers; the story and its style of telling are of one piece.

The characters in *Ugetsu* are down-to-earth, and in the case of Tobei even comic, but the story feels ancient, and indeed draws on the ghost legends of Japanese theater. Unlike ghost stories in the West, Mizoguchi's film does not try to startle or shock; the discovery of the second ghost comes for us as a moment of quiet revelation, and we understand the gentle, forgiving spirit that inspired it. Nor are Lady Wakasa's seduction techniques graphic; she conquers Genjuro not by being sexy or carnal but by being distant and unfamiliar. Always completely cloaked, often hidden by veils, she enchants him not by the reality of flesh but by its tantalizing invisible nearness. I was reminded of Murnau's silent masterpiece *Sunrise* (1927), also about a country man who abandons his wife and child to follow an exotic woman across a lake to the sinful city.

The period detail is accurate and rich. The city marketplace, the headquarters of the samurai, Tobei's visit to a shop to buy armor and a spear, Genjuro's haste when he asks another merchant to watch his prized pots (for he must hurry after Lady Wakasa)—all of these create a feudal world in which life is hard and escape comes through the silly dreams of men. Women are more cautious, and there is a blunt realism in the sequence where Miyagi, left behind, tries to protect and feed their son as armies loot and rape the countryside. At the end of *Ugetsu*, aware that we have seen a fable, we also feel curiously as if we have witnessed true lives and fates.

{ UMBERTO D }

Umberto is upright, neat, exact, and the cut of his clothes shows that he was once respectable. Now he is a retired civil servant on a fixed income that is not enough to support him, not even in his simple furnished room, not even if he skips meals. He and his dog are faced with eviction by a greedy landlady who would rather rent his room by the afternoon to shamefaced couples.

Vittorio De Sica's *Umberto D* (1952) is the story of the old man's struggle to keep from falling from poverty into shame. It may be the best of the Italian neorealist films—the one that is most simply itself and does not reach for its effects or strain to make its message clear. Even the scenes involving Umberto's little dog are told without the sentimentality that pets often bring into stories. Umberto loves the dog and the dog loves him because that is the nature of the bond between dogs and men, and both try to live up to their side of the contract.

The film is told without false drama. Even when Umberto calls the ambulance and has himself taken to the hospital, there is no false crisis, no manufactured fear that he will die. Later, when Umberto considers suicide, he goes about it in such a calm and logical way that we follow his reasoning and weigh the alternatives along with him, instead of being manipulated into dread. *Umberto D* avoids all temptations to turn its hero into one of those lovable Hollywood oldsters played by Matthau or Lemmon. Umberto

Domenico Ferrari is not the life of a party but a man who wants to be left alone to get on with his business. In his shoes we might hope to behave as he does, with bravery and resourcefulness.

The movie follows its hero as he faces the possibility that he may lose his room and be turned out into the streets to beg. He has always paid his bills, and this prospect horrifies him. The opening shot shows him joining a street demonstration in Rome, as old men seek an increase in their meager state pensions. Umberto marches in the protest but is not a joiner. Indeed, when the police disperse the crowd he is angry not at the cops but at the organizers: "They didn't even get a permit!" He smuggles his dog into a dining hall where the old are given free lunches, and slips food under the table for little Flag, while tricking the stern welfare workers with some quick plate switching. He tries to sell his watch, but everyone has a watch they want to sell.

We gradually learn the outlines of his life. He lives in a room infested with ants, which the landlady will do nothing about. Adulterous couples leave his room just as he is returning to it. His friend in the rooming house is Maria the maid, who is pregnant. She isn't sure if the father is the boy from Florence or the one from Naples. He is not offended that she sleeps with more than one man; he is beyond being surprised by the trouble sex can bring. He cares about her as she cares about him, because they are both good people in a bad place.

Because his dog has needs, Umberto has needs. He must care for Flag. He is truthfully sick when he arranges to go to the hospital, but not that sick, and the trip is mostly to get a few days of clean sheets and good meals. He arranges for the maid to take care of the dog while he's gone, and even stages a pantomime with a stick and a ball to distract the dog from following him. Later he finds that the dog ran out the apartment door, maybe to look for him, and was lost. There is a scene of documentary simplicity, in which Umberto seeks Flag at the dog pound and learns how unwanted dogs are put to death. He peers helplessly into a cage so filled with barking, scrambling dogs that he cannot see for sure if Flag is even there. When he finds the dog, note how De Sica shows them greeting each other. This whole passage is all the more affecting because the movie doesn't milk it for tears but simply lets you see it happening.

Neorealism was an Italian movement, born in wartime and continuing through the 1950s, which believed that films should be made close to the surface of everyday life and played by nonprofessionals who embodied their characters. *Umberto D* is one of the most successful demonstrations of that theory. The old man is played by Carlo Battisti, then seventy, a university lecturer who had not acted before.

De Sica (1902–1974) said his method was to form a mental image of a character while working on the screenplay with his longtime collaborator Cesare Zavattini. "Until I can find the man, woman or child who fits the figure I see in my mind's eye," he wrote, "I do not begin." With *Umberto D,* he explained, "before fortune smiled on me once again, I had searched Rome, Naples, and other cities and had lingered for hours, for days even, in those places where I was most likely to find the kind of old-age pensioner who was the hero of my film . . . but I had not yet met *the* person who from the first had smiled at me with sorrowful dignity from the pages of the script."

Sorrowful dignity is exactly what Battisti embodies for Umberto. He is observant, understanding, sympathetic. He doesn't rail against the injustice of the world but is simply determined to defend the corner he occupies with his dog.

Because Umberto doesn't talk much with other characters, we have to determine his thoughts by how he looks and what he does, and there is a masterful scene in which he considers begging in the street and decides against it. Note the timing of this sequence. With a slightly different twist, it could, shot by shot, be a comic bit for Chaplin's Little Tramp, but De Sica holds it to understated pathos. Umberto watches a successful beggar. He puts out his own palm, halfway, not really committing himself. As a man is about to give him money, he turns the hand over, as if testing for rain. He cannot beg. He thinks. He gives his hat to his dog, which sits up and holds it in its mouth, while Umberto hides nearby. No, this will not work either: He will not demean his dog by making it do something he would not do.

The stages by which Umberto arrives at the idea of suicide and then is drawn away from it are among the best in the film. His dog is central to the action—both because he will not abandon it by his own death and because the dog refuses to leave his side. It is the fact of the dog's love that saves him, because he cannot ignore it. One great scene takes place when Umberto brings the dog to a couple who board unwanted dogs. It's clear they're in it only for the money, and that many of their pets don't have long to live. Umberto offers them money to take Flag, but their eyes tell him it is not enough to support the dog for long. Leaving, he hides under a bridge, but the dog finds him, and again we're reminded of a sequence that could be in a Chaplin film but has been toned down to quiet sadness.

Umberto D tells what could be a formula story, but not in a formula way: Its moments seem generated by what might really happen. A formula film would find a way to manufacture a happy ending, but good fortune will not fall from the sky for Umberto. Perhaps his best luck is simply that he has the inner strength to endure misfortune without losing self-respect. It is said that at one level or another, Chaplin's characters were always asking that we love them. Umberto doesn't care if we love him or not. That is why we love him.

{ U N F O R G I V E N }

Clint Eastwood's *Unforgiven* takes place at that moment when the old West was becoming new. Professional gunfighters have become such an endangered species that journalists follow them for stories. Men who slept under the stars are now building themselves houses. William Munny, "a known thief and a murderer," supports himself with hog farming. The violent West of legend lives on in the memories of men who are by 1880 joining the middle class. Within a few decades, Wyatt Earp would be hanging around Hollywood studios, offering advice.

Eastwood chose this period for *Unforgiven*, I suspect, because it mirrored his own stage in life. He began as a young gunslinger on TV and in the early Sergio Leone films *A Fistful of Dollars* and *For a Few Dollars More*, and he matured in *Coogan's Bluff* and *Two Mules for Sister Sara*, under the guidance of Don Siegel, the director he often cited as his mentor. By the time he made *Unforgiven*, Eastwood was in his sixties, and had long been a director himself. Leone had died in 1989 and Siegel in 1991; he dedicated *Unforgiven* to them. If the Western was not dead, it was dying; audiences preferred science fiction and special effects. It was time for an elegy.

The film reflects a passing era even in its visual style. The opening shot is of a house, a tree, and a man at a graveside. The sun is setting, on this man and the era he represents. Many of the film's exteriors are widescreen compositions showing the vastness of the land. The daytime interi-

ors, on the other hand, are always strongly backlit, the bright sun pouring in through windows so that the figures inside are dark, backlit, and sometimes hard to see. Living indoors in a civilized style has made these people indistinct.

William Munny, played by Eastwood, is not much of a hog farmer. At one point he chases a hog, lands facedown in the mud, and stays there for a moment, defeated. He has two young children to raise after the death of his beloved Claudia. There is not enough money. A rider named the Schofield Kid (Jaimz Woolvett) appears with an offer of cash money for bounty hunting. The Kid had heard that Munny was "cold as snow and don't have no weak nerve, nor fear." Munny says, "I ain't like that anymore, Kid. It was whiskey done it as much as anythin' else. I ain't had a drop in over ten years. My wife, she cured me of that, cured me of drink and wickedness."

William Munny is a chastened man, a killer and outlaw who was civilized by marriage. Thus *Unforgiven* internalizes the classic Western theme in which violent men are "civilized" by schoolmarms, preachers, and judges. When he talks about his wife, Munny sounds like a contrite little boy, determined not to be bad anymore.

The Schofield Kid has named himself, he says, after his Schofield model Smith & Wesson revolver. In an earlier day men were nicknamed by others. Now they create their own monikers, almost as marketing tools. He tells William Munny the story of two drunken cowboys who savagely attacked a prostitute in Wyoming: "They cut up her face, cut her eyes out, cut her ears off, hell, they even cut her teats. . . . A thousand dollars reward, Will. Five hundred apiece."

The hog farmer needs the money. But a running theme of the movie is the incompetence of the bounty hunters. The Kid is blind as a bat, and can't hit anything with his trademark revolver. When William Munny prepares to saddle up, he finds to his humiliation that he can hardly mount a horse anymore. ("This old horse is getting even with me for the sins of my youth," he tells his children. "Before I met your dear departed Ma, I used to be weak and given to mistreatin' animals.")

Munny initially turns down the Kid's offer, but he reflects on it, and eventually rides off to recruit an old partner, Ned Logan (Morgan Freeman). They will catch up with the Kid and share the bounty. This progression is intercut with life in Big Whiskey, Wyoming, where Sheriff Little Bill Daggett (Gene Hackman) rules with an iron fist. His law says: No guns inside the city limits. He enforces it with fearful, sadistic beatings, then returns to the riverside, where he is building himself a house.

The story works itself out in classic Western terms, with the corrupt sheriff and the righteous outlaw facing each other. It becomes less about the bounty than about their personal, mutual need for settlement, made all the sharper because they have met in the past. And eventually we see the younger William Munny emerging from his shell of age: He turns again into a fearsome man. This process takes place against a full sense of the town's life. The screenwriter, David Webb Peoples, ignores the recent tradition in which the expensive star dominates every scene, and creates a rich gallery of supporting roles. Here his models are the Western masters, like John Ford, who populated their movies with communities.

Richard Harris plays English Bob, a famous gunfighter who now lives off his publicity and is followed everywhere by W. W. Beauchamp (Saul Rubinek), a writer for pulp Western magazines; after Munny is in a gun battle, Beauchamp scribbles furious notes and wants to know, "Who'd you kill first?" Also important in the town is the madam, Strawberry Alice (Frances Fisher), who has raised the bounty and wants revenge for the mutilation of her girl Delilah (Anna Thomson). Skinny Dubois (Anthony James), the owner of the bar and brothel, has more practical concerns: He paid good money for Delilah and wants compensation; in the half-tamed West, some men now appeal to the law instead of settling things themselves.

The long final act of the movie involves William Munny's desire to avenge the death and public humiliation of his friend Ned, whose corpse has been put on display in a box outside the saloon. Here we see Eastwood as the master of the kind of sustained action sequence he learned from Leone and Siegel: not a boring montage of quick cuts and meaningless violence but a story told through deliberate strategy, in which events may not be possible but are somehow plausible. William Munny, the hapless hog farmer who couldn't even saddle his own horse, has been transformed into the efficient, omniscient figure of vengeance we know from Eastwood's earlier roles. The old pro still remembers the moves.

The title of the movie is intriguing. Does Munny still seek forgiveness from his dead wife and the others he wronged? There is a sense that he is still haunted by guilt: He has reformed but has not made amends. Munny tells Logan, "Ned, you remember that drover I shot through the mouth and his teeth came out the back of his head? I think about him now and again. He didn't do anything to deserve to get shot, at least nothin' I could remember when I sobered up." His friend says, "You ain't like that no more." Munny says, "That's right. I'm just a fella now. I ain't no different than anyone else no more." But his voice lacks conviction, and we sense unfinished business in the air. Munny says he needs the bounty money to support his kids, but the kids would be better served if the old man didn't ride off to risk his life against fresher gunfighters.

If Clint Eastwood had not been a star, he would still figure as a major director, with important work in the Western, action, and comedy genres, and unique films like *Bird* (1988), his biography of the saxophonist Charlie Parker; the love story *The Bridges of Madison County* (1995); and the wonderful *A Perfect World* (1993), which seems to be about a hunt for an escaped convict but seems oddly distanced from the chase, and more concerned with the values and histories of the characters. It has the elements of a crime picture but the freedom of an art film. *Unforgiven*, too, uses a genre as a way to study human nature. His *Mystic River* (2003), probably his best film, is Shakespearean in its portrait of guilt and revenge.

There is one exchange in *Unforgiven* that has long stayed with me. After he is fatally wounded, Little Bill says, "I don't deserve this. To die like this. I was building a house." And Munny says, "Deserve's got nothin' to do with it." Actually, deserve has everything to do with it, and although Ned Logan and Delilah do not get what they deserve, William Munny sees that the others do. That implacable moral balance, in which good eventually silences evil, is at the heart of the Western, and Eastwood is not shy about saying so.

{ VICTIM }

Recent critics find *Victim* timid in its treatment of homosexuality, but viewed in the context of Great Britain in 1961, it's a film of courage. How much courage can be gauged by the fact that it was originally banned from American screens simply because it used the word "homosexual." To be gay was a crime in the United States and the United Kingdom, and the movie used the devices of film noir and thriller to make its argument, labeling laws against homosexuality "the blackmailer's charter." Indeed, 90 percent of all British blackmail had homosexuals as its victim.

The defense of homosexuality was not a popular topic at the box office when the film was made, and director Basil Dearden tried to broaden the film's appeal by making it into a thriller and a police procedural. There is no sex on (or anywhere near) the screen, and while the hero is homosexual by nature there is doubt that he has ever experienced gay sex. The plot hinges on anonymous blackmailers who collect regular payments from wealthy and famous gays, and on the decision of a prominent barrister to stand up to them.

This man is Melville Farr, who at the young age of forty has just been offered the opportunity to become a queen's counselor. He will lose that appointment, his career, and his marriage if he's identified in the press as gay, and yet he decides that someone must stand up to the blackmailers to demonstrate the injustice of the law. As he tracks the blackmailers through a network of their victims, the movie follows him through the London of the time—its courts of law, police stations, pubs, clubs, barbershops, used-book stores, cafés, drawing rooms, car dealerships—showing how ordinary life is affected in countless ways by the fact that many of its citizens must keep their natures a secret.

Farr was played by Dirk Bogarde, as a smooth, skilled barrister who projects a surface of strength and calm. He raises his voice only two or three times in the movie, but we sense an undercurrent of anger: He finds it wrong that homosexuality is punished, wrong that gays cannot go to the police to complain of blackmail, wrong that hypocrisy flourishes. There is a moment in the movie when he unexpectedly hits someone who has just insulted him, and it comes as a revelation: Beneath his silky persona is a wound, a resentment, and a fierce determination to act at last on his convictions.

The opening sequences of the film involve him only slightly, as we follow a young man named Jack Barrett (Peter McEnery), on the run from the police. We learn fairly soon that he is gay, but only gradually do we understand that he is wanted for embezzlement. Broke, desperate for the money to get out of London, he calls Farr, is rebuffed, and is also turned away by a book dealer (Norman Bird), a car dealer, and others. His desperation is closely observed in a pub where many of the characters hang out, including an odd couple: a ratlike little man and his heftier companion, who is blind but hears all the gossip.

Barrett is arrested and found with a scrapbook of cuttings about Farr. To the almost improbably wise and civilized Detective Inspector Harris (John Barrie), it's an open-and-shut case: Barrett has no money, lived simply, had stolen thousands from his employer, seemed gay, and therefore was a blackmail victim. He calls in Farr, who offers no help, but when Harris tells him that the young man has hanged himself in his cell, Farr is deeply shaken. He has good reason: He loved Barrett.

His wife, Laura (Sylvia Syms), immediately reads his mood, and eventually learns of his friendship with Barrett. She knew when they married that he'd had a youthful infatuation with a fellow Cambridge student, but that it was "behind him." He never had sex with Barrett, he tells her, and stopped seeing the young man when he sensed their feelings were

growing too strong—but that for her is as much of a betrayal as physical contact, because he shows that what he felt for Barrett was different, more powerful, than what he feels for her.

The movie proceeds on two levels, as a crime thriller and as a character study, and it's this dual nature that makes it an entertainment at the same time it works as a message picture. There's a good deal of indirection in the clever script, which conceals motives, misdirects our suspicions, misleads our expectations, and finds truth and dignity in the scenes between Farr and his wife; what a relief that their powerful last scene together ends on a note of bleak realism rather than providing some kind of artificial release.

The movie, written by Janet Green and John McCormick, plays out primarily in a series of dialogue scenes, made rich by the gallery of British character actors who inhabit them. The best is Norman Bird, as the used-book dealer, who turns Barrett away but whose feelings about him (and Farr, as it turns out) are more complicated than it seems. The book man is one of the contacts Farr calls on in his own investigation; working with a few names supplied by one of Barrett's straight friends, he tries to get someone to say how and when he makes blackmail payments. Almost all the victims are afraid to, and one, an elderly barber named Henry (Charles Lloyd Pack), fiercely tells Farr that he has been to prison twice because of his nature, and does not intend to go again.

The photography places this action colorfully within a living, breathing London; it has a feel for the way its characters live and speak. For Pauline Kael, the British speech mannerisms of some of the characters made them seem more gay than the low-key Bogarde, and indeed we cannot always guess who is hunter and who quarry. There is a subtle subplot, for example, suggesting that one of the policemen on the case may be gay himself.

For Dirk Bogarde (1921–1999), the role in *Victim* provided a decisive break in his career. He'd been a popular leading man in the 1950s, playing conventional action and romantic roles and even making three of the *Doctor* comedies (*Doctor in the House*, *Doctor at Sea*, and *Doctor at Large*). To play a homosexual in 1961 would bring an end, his agent warned him, to those kinds of mainstream roles, and make him unemployable in

Hollywood just at the moment when American directors were interested in him.

But he went ahead anyway, just as Melville Farr did, and indeed never again appeared as a conventional male lead. That turned out, oddly, to be the key to his greatest success; at a time when his stock as a conventional leading man would probably have been falling, he was able, having broken free, to work in one challenging film after another: *The Servant, King and Country, Darling, Accident, The Fixer,* Visconti's *The Damned* and *Death in Venice,* Resnais's *Providence,* Fassbinder's *Despair.*

Bogarde himself was homosexual but never made that public; even in his touching memoirs about the life and death of his partner, Tony Forwood, he cast their relationship as actor and manager, not lovers. For that he has been criticized by some gay writers and activists, but consider: By accepting what looked like career suicide to star in *Victim,* wasn't he making much the same decision as his character Melville Farr—to do the right thing, and accept the consequences? Didn't he, in effect, come out as an actor in that and many other roles (notably as the aging homosexual in *Death in Venice*)? Was it anybody's business what he was, or did, in his private life? It is the argument of *Victim* that it was not.

I met him once, on a summer afternoon in Venice when he was making the Visconti picture. We had tea in the garden of a palazzo overlooking the Giudecca canal, and he pointed out with amusement an old lady in black who lurked behind some trees: "That's the countessa, who is renting this place to me and thinks I don't know that she didn't move out." He was quiet, crisp, introverted. Not the sort of man whom you could imagine making personal revelations for the delight of the press. Today, yes, things are different, but Bogarde was born in 1921, and homosexuality was only legalized in Britain in 1967. As an actor he risked a great deal to take a crucial role at a time when it made a difference. And didn't he anyway, through his work, tell us whatever it was about him we thought we had the right to know?

{ WALKABOUT }

Is *Walkabout* only about what it seems to be about? Is it a parable about noble savages and the crushed spirits of city dwellers? That's what the film's surface seems to suggest, but I think it's also about something deeper and more elusive: the mystery of communication. It ends with lives that are destroyed, in one way or another, because two people could not invent a way to make their needs and dreams clear.

Nicolas Roeg's film, released in 1971, was hailed as a masterpiece. Then it disappeared into oblivion, apparently because of quarrels over ownership, and was not seen for years; *Premiere* magazine put it first on a list of films that should be available on video but were not. In 1996 a new theatrical version restored five minutes of nudity that had been trimmed from the original release; that director's cut is now finally available on video.

The movie takes its title from a custom among the Aborigines of Australia: At the time of transition to young manhood, an adolescent Aborigine went on a "walkabout" of six months in the Outback, surviving (or not) depending on his skills at hunting, trapping, and finding water in the wilderness.

The film opens in the brick-and-concrete canyons of Sydney, where families live stacked one above another in condominiums. We glimpse moments in the lives of such a family—a housewife listens to a silly radio show, two children splash in a pool, and on a balcony their father drinks a cock-

tail and looks down moodily at them. There is something subtly wrong with the family, but the film doesn't articulate it, apart from a suggestive shot of a bug that does not belong here indoors. In the next scene, we see the father and children driving into the trackless Outback in a wheezy Volkswagen. They're on a picnic, the children think, until their father starts shooting at them. The fourteen-year-old girl (Jenny Agutter) pulls her six-year-old brother (Luc Roeg) behind a ridge, and when they look again their father has shot himself and the car is on fire.

Civilization, we gather, has failed him. Now the girl and boy face destruction at the hands of nature. They have the clothes they are wearing, a battery-operated radio, and whatever food and drink is in the picnic hamper. They wander the Outback for a number of days (the film is always vague about time), and stumble upon an oasis with a pool of muddy water. Here they drink and splash and sleep, and in the morning the pool is dry. At about this time they realize that a solemn young Aborigine (David Gulpilil) is regarding them.

They need saving. He saves them. He possesses secrets of survival, which the film reveals in scenes of stark, unforced beauty. We see the youth spearing wild creatures and finding water in the dry pool with the use of a hollow reed. He treats one child's sunburn with a natural salve. Some of the Outback scenes—including one where the youth spears a kangaroo—are intercut with quick flashes of a butcher shop. Man's nature remains unchanged across many platforms.

There is an unmistakable sexual undercurrent: Both teenagers are in the first years of heightened sexual awareness. The girl still wears a school uniform, which the camera regards with subtle suggestiveness. (An ambiguous earlier shot suggests that the father had an unwholesome awareness of his daughter's body.) The restored footage includes a sequence showing the girl swimming naked in a pool, and scenes of the Aborigine indicate that he is displaying his manliness for her to appreciate.

These developments are surrounded by scenes of implacable, indifferent—but beautiful—nature. Roeg was a cinematographer before he became a director (he codirected the Mick Jagger film *Performance* in 1970 before this first solo outing). His camera here shows the creatures of the

Outback: lizards, scorpions, snakes, kangaroos, birds. They are not pho-tographed sentimentally. They make a living by eating other things.

Aboriginal culture has a less linear sense of time than that of a clock-bound society, and the time line of the movie suggests that. Does everything happen exactly in the sequence it is shown? Does everything even happen at all? Are some moments imagined? Which of the characters imagines them? These questions lurk around the edges of the story, which is seemingly simple: The three young travelers survive in the Outback be-cause of the Aborigine's skills. And communication is a problem, although more for the girl than for her little brother, who seems to have a child's abil-ity to cut straight through the language to the message.

There's one tantalizing scene where the travelers actually pass close to a settlement; the Aborigine sees it but does not lead the others to the top of a rise where they could see it, too. Is he hiding it from them? Or does he not understand why they would be seeking it? (The film gives us no infor-mation about the Aborigine's background—not even whether he has ever had any contact with modern civilization.) There's a haunting scene where they explore an abandoned farmhouse; she cries while looking at some pho-tographs, and he watches her carefully as she does so. And finally a scene where the Aborigine paints himself in tribal designs and performs a dance that can be interpreted as courtship. The girl is not interested, and the gulf between the two civilizations is not bridged.

What should we have been hoping for, given the conditions of the story? That the girl and her brother learn to embrace a lifestyle that is more organically rooted in nature? That the Aborigine learn from them about a world of high-rises and radios? That the two teenagers make love as a sort of symbol of universality, before returning to their separate spheres?

I think the film is neutral about such goals. Like the lizards that sit unblinking in the sun, it has no agenda for them. It sees the life of civiliza-tion as arid and unrewarding, but only easy idealism allows us to believe that the Aborigine is any happier, or his life more rewarding (the film makes a rather unpleasant point of the flies constantly buzzing around him).

Nicolas Roeg does not subscribe to pious sentimental values; he has made that clear in the years since *Walkabout,* in a series of films that have grown curiouser and curiouser: In *Don't Look Now, The Man Who Fell to Earth, Insignificance, Track 29, Bad Timing,* and other films, many of them starring his wife, Theresa Russell, he has shown characters trapped inside their own obsessions, and fatally unable to communicate with others; all sexual connections are perverse, damaging, or based on faulty understandings.

In *Walkabout,* the crucial detail is that the two teenagers can never find a way to communicate, not even by using sign language. Partly this is because the girl feels no need to do so: Throughout the film she remains implacably middle-class and conventional, and she regards the Aborigine as more of a curiosity and convenience than a fellow spirit. Because not enough information is given, we cannot attribute her attitude to racism or cultural bias, but certainly it reveals a vast lack of curiosity. And the Aborigine, for his part, lacks the imagination to press his case—his sexual desires—in any terms other than the rituals of his people. When that fails, he is finished, and in despair.

Walkabout is not the heartwarming story of how the girl and her brother are lost in the Outback and survive because of the knowledge of the resourceful Aborigine. It is about how all three are still lost at the end of the film—more lost than before, because now they are lost inside themselves instead of merely adrift in the world. The film is deeply pessimistic. It suggests that we all develop specific skills and talents in response to our environment but cannot easily function across a broader range. It is not that the girl cannot appreciate nature or that the boy cannot function outside his training. It is that all of us are the captives of environment and programming: that there is a wide range of experiment and experience that remains forever invisible to us, because it falls in a spectrum we cannot see.

{ WEST SIDE STORY }

Although *West Side Story* was named the best picture of 1961 and won ten Academy Awards, it is not much mentioned by movie fans these days, and the old warhorse *Singin' in the Rain* is probably more seen and certainly better loved. *West Side Story* was the kind of musical people thought was good for them, a pious expression of admirable but unrealistic liberal sentiments, and certainly its street gangs at war—one Puerto Rican, one the children of European immigrants—seem touchingly innocent compared to contemporary reality.

I hadn't seen it since it was released in 1961, nor had I much wanted to, although I've seen *Singin' in the Rain, Swing Time, Top Hat, My Fair Lady,* and *An American in Paris* countless times during those years. My muted enthusiasm is shared. Although it placed No. 41 in the American Film Institute's list of the greatest films of all time, the less industry-oriented voters at the Internet Movie Database don't even have it in the top 250. Still, the new two-disc restored edition of the movie inspired me to look at it again, and I think there are great things in the movie, especially some of the songs by Leonard Bernstein and Stephen Sondheim, the powerful performances by Rita Moreno and George Chakiris, and above all Jerome Robbins's choreography. It is a great movie—in parts.

Mainstream critics loved it in 1961. Bosley Crowther in the *New York Times* thought its message "should be heard by thoughtful people—

sympathetic people—all over the land." What is the message? Doc, the little Jewish candy store owner, expresses it to warring street gangs: "You kids make this world lousy! When will you stop?" It's a strong moment, and Ned Glass's Doc is one of the most authentic characters in the film, but really: Has a racist ever walked into a movie and been converted by a line of dialogue? Isn't this movie preaching to the choir?

The scenario by Arthur Laurents was famously inspired by Shakespeare's *Romeo and Juliet,* although it shies away from the complete tragedy of the original by fudging the ending. It is not a cosmic misunderstanding but angry gunfire that kills Tony, and Maria doesn't die at all; she snatches the gun and threatens to shoot herself, but drops it—perhaps because suicide would have been too heavy a load for the movie to carry. Then as now, there is a powerful bias in Hollywood toward happy endings.

Such lapses seemed crucial to the best critics reviewing the movie. Although Stanley Kauffmann named *West Side Story* "the best film musical ever made" when it came out in 1961, the rest of his review seemed to undermine that claim; he said it lacks a towering conclusion, is useless and facile as sociology, and the hint of a reconciliation between the two gangs at the end is "utter falseness." Pauline Kael's review scorched the earth: The movie was "frenzied hokum," the dialogue was "painfully old-fashioned and mawkish," the dancing was "simpering, sickly romantic ballet," and the "machine-tooled" Natalie Wood was "so perfectly banal she destroys all thoughts of love."

Kael is guilty of overkill. Kauffmann is closer to the mark, especially when he disagrees with Kael about the dancing. Jerome Robbins, one of the most original choreographers in Broadway history, at first refused to work on the film unless he could direct it. Producer Walter Mirisch wanted a steady Hollywood hand and chose Robert Wise, the editor of *Citizen Kane* and a studio veteran. Robbins agreed to direct the dancing, and Wise would direct the drama. And then the problem became that Robbins simply could not stop directing the dancing: "He didn't know how to say 'cut,'" one of the dancers remembers in a documentary about the making of the film. Robbins ran up so much overtime he was eventually fired, but his assistants stayed, and all the choreography is his.

Certainly the dance scenes, so robust, athletic, and exhilarating,

play differently after you've seen the doc. Robbins rehearsed for three months before the shooting began, then revised everything on the locations, sometimes many times. His choreography was so demanding that no scene was ever filmed all the way through, and dancers in the "Cool" number say they never before and never again worked harder on anything. There were injuries, collapses, setbacks. Look at a brief scene where a gang runs toward a very high chain-link fence, scales it bare-handed, and drops down inside a playground. That's a job for stuntmen, not a dozen dancers, and we can only guess how many takes it took to make it look effortless and in sync with the music.

As for the music itself: Usually, says Rita Moreno, dancers work in counts of fours, sixes, or eights: "Then along comes Leonard Bernstein with his 5/4 time, his 6/8 time, his 25/6 time. It was just crazy. It's very difficult to dance to that kind of music, because it doesn't make dancer sense." And yet Robbins's perfectionism and Bernstein's unconventional rhythms created a genuinely new kind of movie dancing, and it can be said that if street gangs did dance, they would dance something like the Jets and the Sharks in this movie, and not like a Broadway chorus line.

The movie was made fresh on the heels of the enormous Broadway success of the musical, and filmed partly on location in New York and partly on sound stages (it opens on the present site of Lincoln Center). There was controversy over the casting of Natalie Wood as Maria (she was not Puerto Rican, her voice was dubbed by Marni Nixon, she was only a fair dancer) and some indifference to Richard Beymer, whose Tony played more like a leading man than a gang leader. They didn't get along in real life, we learn, but Wood does project warmth and passion in their scenes together, and a beauty and sweetness that would be with her throughout her career.

What shows up Wood and Beymer is the work of Rita Moreno and George Chakiris, as the Puerto Rican lovers Anita and Bernardo. Little wonder they won supporting Oscars and the leads did not. Moreno can sing, can dance, and exudes a passion that brings special life to her scenes. For me, the most powerful moments in the movie come when Anita visits Doc's candy store to bring a message of love from Maria to Tony—and is insulted, shoved around, and almost raped by the Jets. That leads her, in anger, to abandon her romantic message and shout out that Maria is dead—setting the engine of Shakespeare's last act into motion in a way that makes perfect dramatic sense. To study the way she plays in that scene is to understand what Wood's performance is lacking.

Kael is right about the dialogue. It's mostly pedestrian and uninspired; it gets the job done and moves the plot along but lacks not only the eloquence and poetry of Shakespeare but even the power that a twentieth-century playwright like O'Neill or Williams would have brought to it. Imagine Mamet's version. Compare the balcony scene in *West Side Story* with the one filmed seven years later by Franco Zeffirelli in *Romeo and Juliet*, and you will find that it is possible to make a box office hit while still using great language.

What I loved during *West Side Story*, and why I recommend it, is the dancing itself. The opening finger-snapping sequence is one of the best uses of dance in movie history. It came about because Robbins, reading the screenplay, asked, "What are they dancing *about?*" The writer Laurents agreed: "You couldn't have a story about murder, violence, prejudice, attempted rape, and do it in a traditional musical style." So he outlined the prologue, without dialogue, allowing Robbins to establish the street gangs, show their pecking order, celebrate their swagger in the street, demonstrate their physical grace, and establish their hostility—all in a ballet scored by Bernstein with music, finger snapping, and anger.

The prologue sets up the muscular physical impact of all of the dancing, and Robbins is gifted at moving his gangs as units while still making every dancer seem like an individual. Each gang member has his own style, his own motivation, and yet as the camera goes for high angles and very low ones, the whole seems to come together. I was reminded of the physical choreography in another 1961 movie, Kurosawa's *Yojimbo*, in which a band of samurai move quickly and swiftly through action with a snakelike coordination.

So the dancing is remarkable, several of the songs have proven themselves by becoming standards, and there are moments of startling power and truth. *West Side Story* remains a landmark of musical history. But if the drama had been as edgy as the choreography, if the lead performances had matched Moreno's fierce concentration, if the gangs had been more dangerous and less like bad-boy Archies and Jugheads, if the ending had delivered on the pathos and tragedy of the original, there's no telling what might have resulted. The movie began with a brave vision, and it is best when you sense that vision surviving the process by which it was turned into safe entertainment.

YANKEE
DOODLE DANDY

There is a story that James Cagney stood on his toes while acting, believing he would project more energy that way. That sounds like a press release, but whatever he did, Cagney came across as one of the most dynamic performers in movie history—a short man with ordinary looks whose coiled tension made him the focus of every scene.

He's best known for the gangster roles he played in the 1930s, a decade when he averaged almost four films a year for Warner Bros. From *Public Enemy* (1931, with its famous grapefruit-in-the-face scene) to *The Roaring Twenties* (1939), he was Hollywood's leading crime star—even at the studio that also had Edward G. Robinson and Humphrey Bogart under contract. But he didn't win his Oscar until 1942, when he played Broadway showman George M. Cohan in *Yankee Doodle Dandy*.

Maybe that was because Hollywood doesn't like to honor actors playing bad guys (Cagney was nominated but didn't win in 1938, as a gangster in *Angels with Dirty Faces*). Maybe it was because the nation was newly at war in 1942, and happy to honor a patriotic biopic about the composer of "It's a Grand Old Flag." Or maybe it was because Cagney threw himself into the role with such complete joy.

Audiences didn't expect to see Cagney singing and dancing. He'd been a hoofer in his stage days but danced only once in a major film (*Footlight Parade*, 1933). Now he had the lead in the life story of one of the most famous song-and-dance men of his day—a role everybody knew Fred Astaire had turned down. Cagney wasn't a dancer by Astaire's standards, or a singer by anybody's, but he was such a good actor he could fake it. "Cagney can't really dance or sing," observes the critic Edwin Jahiel, "but he acts so vigorously that it creates an illusion, and for dance-steps he substitutes a patented brand of robust, jerky walks, runs and other motions." You can sense that in an impromptu scene near the end of the movie. Cagney's Cohan is walking down a marble staircase at the White House when he suddenly starts tapping and improvises all the way to the bottom. Cagney later said he dreamed that up five minutes before the scene was shot: "I didn't consult with the director or anything, I just did it."

What's he doing at the White House? The movie is told in one of the most implausible flashbacks in the history of musical biographies—a genre famous for the tortured ways it doubles back to tell showbiz stories. As the movie opens, Cohan has been called out of retirement to star as Franklin D. Roosevelt in *I'd Rather Be Right*, a Broadway musical hailing the president as war clouds gathered. He gets a telegram summoning him to the White House and arrives on foot, drenched, late at night. He's shown into the Oval Office, where an over-the-shoulder shot of FDR identifies him by his cigarette holder. The president says he remembers seeing *The Four Cohans* in Boston forty years earlier.

"I was a pretty cocky kid in those days," Cohan muses. "Pretty cocky kid."

That sets off an entire film of flashbacks, narrated by Cohan, as he tells the president (who apparently has time on his hands) his life story. How he was born on the Fourth of July ("I was six before I realized they weren't celebrating my birthday"). How he began as a child star, touring with his parents, Jerry (Walter Huston) and Nellie (Rosemary DeCamp), and his sister, Josie (Jeanne Cagney, Cagney's own sister). How he got a swelled head after starring in *Peck's Bad Boy*, and how while still a teenager he played his own mother's father on the stage.

That memory sets up a famous sequence, as a young fan named Mary (Joan Leslie) comes backstage to get advice from the apparently bearded and ancient Cohan, who continues the deception until suddenly breaking into a frenzied dance. She shrieks as he takes off his makeup (in

515

showbiz, he tells her, "you'll have to get used to false eyebrows"), and soon he's writing a hit song for her ("Mary") and they're getting married.

These are all, of course, staples of showbiz biography—reality turned into myth, if not into press releases. Today's biopics focus on scandal and Freudian gloom, but in *Yankee Doodle Dandy* everything is upbeat, and even George's marriage proposal is couched in showbiz dialogue. No wonder that when the aging George M. Cohan himself was shown the movie, he liked it. (According to film historian Jay Robert Nash, his response was right in character: "Cohan grinned, shook his head, and paid the inimitable Cagney his highest compliment: 'My God, what an act to follow!' ") It was. Unlike Astaire, whose entire body was involved in every movement, Cagney was a dancer who seemed to call on body parts in rotation. When he struts across the stage in the "Yankee Doodle Dandy" number, his legs are rubber but his spine is steel, and his torso is slanted forward so steeply we're reminded of Groucho Marx.

There are two currents to the story: patriotism and success. Cohan sees himself as a flag-waver, and the critics attack him for writing only lightweight musical comedies. Stung, he writes a serious play, but when it flops he apologizes and returns to what his fans demand: sentiment, silliness, and rousing nationalism. (Ironically, two of his lyrics supplied the titles for antiwar films: *Born on the Fourth of July* and *Johnny Got His Gun*.)

Every scene follows the themes. He tries to enlist for World War I, is rejected for being too old, and protests, "This war is a coffee klatsch compared to what I go through in the course of a musical show." He does a tap dance in the recruiting office to demonstrate what he means, walks outside, and catches two notes from a marching band. And then, in one of those fantasies of creation so beloved in films about musicians, he sits on an empty stage with a piano and doodles with the notes until he discovers the opening for "Over There."

The movie hurries from one obligatory scene to the next: retirement of parents, off-screen deaths of mother and sister, on-screen death of father (Walter Huston goes out on a good exit line), and a montage of marquees from his hit shows. Finally comes the White House visit and, after Cohan has told the patient FDR his entire life story, a private presentation of the Medal of Honor.

There's little that's really original in *Yankee Doodle Dandy*, which was directed by Michael Curtiz, the gifted Warners workhorse whose credits included *Casablanca*, also released in 1942. The cinematography, by the legendary James Wong Howe, uses the elegant compositions of figures that were common at the time, and the staging includes two numbers where big studio treadmills are used to move groups of extras or keep them marching in place.

But the greatness of the film resides entirely in the Cagney performance. Even Walter Huston, one of the finest character actors of the era, is confined by routine material. There is a sudden chemistry in a sequence involving Fay Templeton, as a Broadway star Cohan wants to work with (the relatively unknown Irene Manning is stunning in the role). But mostly it's bio by the numbers—except for Cagney's electricity.

He doesn't dance so much as strut; he doesn't act so much as sell you his desire to entertain. In dialogue scenes, when other actors are talking, his eyes dart across their faces, silently urging them to pick up the energy; he's like Michael Jordan impatiently willing his teammates to keep up with him. And when he's in full sail, as in "Give My Regards to Broadway" or "Yankee Doodle Dandy," it's like regarding a force of nature.

Essays Appearing in
The Great Movies
(2002)

Hoop Dreams

Ikiru

It's a Wonderful Life

JFK

La Dolce Vita

The Lady Eve

Last Year at Marienbad

L'Atalante

L'Avventura

Lawrence of Arabia

Le Samourai

M

The Maltese Falcon

Manhattan

McCabe & Mrs. Miller

Metropolis

Mr. Hulot's Holiday

My Darling Clementine

My Life to Live

Nashville

Network

The Night of the Hunter

Nosferatu

Notorious

On the Waterfront

Pandora's Box

The Passion of Joan of Arc

Peeping Tom

Persona

Pickpocket

Pinocchio

Psycho

Pulp Fiction

Raging Bull

Red River

Schindler's List

The Seven Samurai

The Seventh Seal

The Shawshank Redemption

The Silence of the Lambs

Singin' in the Rain

Some Like It Hot

Star Wars

Sunset Blvd.

Sweet Smell of Success

Swing Time

Taxi Driver

The Third Man

Trouble in Paradise

Un Chien Andalou

The "Up" Documentaries

Vertigo

The Wild Bunch

Wings of Desire

The Wizard of Oz

Woman in the Dunes

A Woman Under the
    Influence

Written on the Wind

ABOUT THE AUTHOR

Roger Ebert was born in Urbana, Illinois, and attended local schools and the University of Illinois, where he was editor of *The Daily Illini*. After graduate study in English at the universities of Illinois, Cape Town, and Chicago, he became film critic for the *Chicago Sun-Times* in 1967 and won the Pulitzer Prize for criticism in 1975. The same year, he began a long association with Gene Siskel on the TV program *Siskel and Ebert*. After Siskel's death in 1999, the program continued with Richard Roeper as *Ebert and Roeper*, a show that is syndicated in more than two hundred markets. Ebert has been a lecturer on film in the University of Chicago's Fine Arts Program since 1969, is an adjunct professor of cinema and media studies at the University of Illinois, and received honorary doctorates from the School of the Art Institute of Chicago, the American Film Institute, and the University of Colorado, where he has conducted an annual shot-by-shot analysis of a film for thirty-five years at the Conference on World Affairs. In 1999 he started an Overlooked Film Festival at the University of Illinois, selecting films, genres, and formats he believes deserve more attention. He is the author of *The Great Movies* (Broadway, 2002), the bestselling annual volume *Roger Ebert's Movie Yearbook*, and *Roger Ebert's Book of Film*, in addition to a dozen other books. He lives in Chicago with his wife, Chaz Hammelsmith Ebert, an attorney.